John Milton's Roman Sojourns, 1638–1639

Neo-Latin Self-Fashioning

John Milton's Roman Sojourns, 1638–1639

Neo-Latin Self-Fashioning

Estelle Haan

American Philosophical Society Press
Philadelphia • 2020

> Transactions of the
> American Philosophical Society
> Held at Philadelphia
> for Promoting Useful Knowledge
> Volume 109, Part 4

Copyright © 2020 by the American Philosophical Society for its Transactions series.

All rights reserved.

ISBN: 978-1-60618-094-5
Ebook ISBN: 978-1-60618-099-0
U.S. ISSN: 0065-9746

Library of Congress Cataloging-in-Publication Data

Names: Haan, Estelle, author.
Title: John Milton's Roman sojourns, 1638-1639 : neo-Latin self-fashioning / Estelle Haan.
Other titles: Transactions of the American Philosophical Society ; 109.
Description: Philadelphia : American Philosophical Society Press, 2020. | Series: Transactions of the American Philosophical Society, 00659746 ; 109 | Includes bibliographical references and index. | Summary: "This study examines the impact of Rome and its vibrant culture upon Milton in the course of two two-month sojourns in the city in 1638-1639. Focusing on his neo-Latin writings pertaining to that period (*Ad Salsillum*, the three Latin epigrams in praise of the soprano Leonora Baroni, and *Epistola Familiaris* 9, addressed to Lucas Holstenius), it presents new evidence of the academic, literary, and musical contexts surrounding Milton's pro-active integration into seicento Rome. Highlighting Milton's self-fashioning as one who was hospitably embraced by Catholic Rome, it traces his networking with distinguished Italian humanists (upon whom he left no slight an impression)"-- Provided by publisher.
  Front-cover illustration credit: Title page of *Ritratto di Roma Moderna* (Portrait of Modern Rome), by Pompilio Totti, 1638, Rome. (Photo by Icas94 / De Agostini Picture Library via Getty Images.)
Identifiers: LCCN 2020030061 (print) | LCCN 2020030062 (ebook) | ISBN 9781606180945 (paperback) | ISBN 9781606180990 (kindle edition)
Subjects: LCSH: Milton, John, 1608-1674--Travel--Italy--Rome. | Humanism--Italy--Rome. | Rome (Italy)--Intellectual life.
Classification: LCC PR3584 .H33 2020 (print) | LCC PR3584 (ebook) | DDC 821/.4--dc23
LC record available at https://lccn.loc.gov/2020030061
LC ebook record available at https://lccn.loc.gov/2020030062

Also available as an ebook

For Tony

haud scio an iure dicam ullius maiora exstitisse in me benevolentiae indicia quam ea quae mihi abs te profecta sunt
(Milton, *Epistola Familiaris* 9)

CONTENTS

Acknowledgments   *ix*
Abbreviations   *xi*

Introduction   1

Chapter 1   Milton, Giovanni Salzilli, and the Academies of Rome   29

    1.1   *Ioannes Salsillus Poeta Romanus*   31
    1.2   Salzilli in the Accademia dei Fantastici   41
    1.3   Salzilli's "Written Encomium" of Milton   47
    1.4   *Ad Salsillum Poetam Romanum Aegrotantem*   54
    1.5   Salzilli as a Second Horace   59
    1.6   Milton's "Laurea Hetrusca"   69
    1.7   The Accademia degli Umoristi   74
    1.8   Academic Traditions   80
    1.9   The Topography of Rome   88

Chapter 2   Milton's Latin Epigrams to Leonora Baroni   99

    2.1   The Baroni Sisters and the Accademia degli Umoristi   101
    2.2   Contemporary Encomia of Leonora   107
    2.3   From Catholicism to Hermeticism: *Ad Leonoram* 1   113
    2.4   "Soul-swaying Song": *Ad Leonoram* 2   121
    2.5   From Naples to Rome: *Ad Leonoram* 3   130

Chapter 3   Milton, Lucas Holstenius, and the Culture of Rome   139

    3.1   Milton in the Vatican   143
    3.2   From *Katabasis* to *Anabasis*   148
    3.3   Milton at the Opera   154
    3.4   *Magnificentia Romana* and Metatheater   158
    3.5   Musical Experimentalism   164
    3.6   The Theatrical Milton   167
    3.7   An Audience with a Cardinal   169

Appendices   175
Appendix 1   Milton's Roman Sojourns, 1638–1639: The Latin Writings   177
Appendix 2   Milton's Italian Journey: *Defensio Secunda* (1654)   187

Bibliography   193
Index Nominum et Locorum   217

ACKNOWLEDGMENTS

The present monograph could not have been realized without the generous help of librarians and archivists in Belfast, Cambridge, London, and Rome. I wish to thank the Special Collections of The Queen's University of Belfast, and the Masters and Fellows of Christ's College, Cambridge, for facilitating limitless access to printed copies of Milton's Latin letters and other printed materials pertinent to this study. Thanks are also due to Trinity College Library, Cambridge; the British Library, London; and the Vatican Library, Rome. I am indebted also to the eagle eye and amazing efficiency of Pamela Lankas and the American Philosophical Society.

My preliminary thoughts on Milton and Rome were briefly articulated in part of my chapter in *Milton and Catholicism*, eds. Ronald Corthell and Thomas N. Corns (Notre Dame, IN: University of Notre Dame Press, 2017). My more recent reflections on Milton's use of neo-Latin in the context of his continental journey appeared in a chapter in *Political Turmoil: Early Modern British Literature in Transition, 1623–1660*, ed. Stephen B. Dobranski (Cambridge: Cambridge University Press, 2019). My work on Milton and Lucas Holstenius greatly develops material from my edition *Epistolarum Familiarium Liber Unus and Uncollected Letters*, Supplementa Humanistica Lovaniensia XLIV (Leuven: Leuven University Press, 2019). I am grateful to the publishers for any necessary permissions.

Particular thanks are due to friends and family, especially the late Michael McGann, for his erudite advice on points of detail, and for his friendship, support, and encouragement throughout my academic career.

I dedicate this work to my husband, Tony, whose computing, archival, and palaeographical skills are outweighed only by his gentleness, his cheer, and his love.

ABBREVIATIONS

Libraries

BAV Biblioteca Apostolica Vaticana, Rome
BNCF Biblioteca Nazionale Centrale, Florence

Reference Works

DBI *Dizionario Biografico degli Italiani* (Rome, 1960 –)
Lewis and Short *A Latin Dictionary*, eds. C. T. Lewis and Charles Short (Oxford: Clarendon Press, 1955)
Liddell and Scott *A Greek–English Lexicon*, eds. H. G. Liddell, R. Scott, and H. S. Jones (Oxford: Clarendon Press, 1940)
NDB *Neue Deutsche Biographie* (Berlin, 1953 –)
ODNB *Oxford Dictionary of National Biography*, 60 vols (Oxford, 2004)
OLD *Oxford Latin Dictionary*, ed. P. G. W. Clare (Oxford: Clarendon Press, 1968–1982)

Journals

AJP *American Journal of Philology*
BHR *Bibliothèque d'Humanisme et Renaissance*
CJ *Classical Journal*
CLS *Comparative Literature Studies*
CML *Classical and Modern Literature*
CQ *Classical Quarterly*
ELR *English Literary Review*
HL *Humanistica Lovaniensia: Journal of Neo-Latin Studies*
HLQ *Huntington Library Quarterly*
HSCP *Harvard Studies in Classical Philology*
JEGP *Journal of English and Germanic Philology*
JWCI *Journal of the Warburg and Courtauld Institutes*
MH *Medievalia et Humanistica*
MLN *Modern Language Notes*
MLR *Modern Language Review*
MP *Modern Philology*
MQ *Milton Quarterly*
MR *Music Review*
MS *Milton Studies*
N&Q *Notes and Queries*
PMLA *Publications of the Modern Language Association of America*
PQ *Philological Quarterly*
RLC *Revue de Littérature Comparée*
RS *Renaissance Studies*
SEL *Studies in English Literature*

SS	*Studi Secenteschi*
TAPhA	*Transactions of the American Philological Association*
TLS	*Times Literary Studies* (London)
UTQ	*University of Toronto Quarterly*

Introduction

> Heu quis me ignotas traxit vagus error in oras
> Ire per aereas rupes Alpemque nivosam!
> Ecquid erat tanti Romam vidisse sepultam,
> Quamvis illa foret qualem, dum viseret olim,
> Tityrus ipse suas et oves et rura reliquit?
> (*Epitaphium Damonis*, 113–117)[1]

> Alas, what erratic wandering drew me to travel to unknown shores across lofty cliffs and the snowy Alps! Was it worth so much to have seen buried Rome, even if it had been as it once was when Tityrus himself abandoned his own sheep and countryside to see it?[2]

Thus ponders the pastoral shepherd Thyrsis in *Epitaphium Damonis*, composed *c*. Autumn 1639 in the wake of Milton's Italian journey. The language is evocative of the question posed by Meliboeus to Tityrus in Virgil, *Eclogue* 1. 26: *et quae tanta fuit Romam tibi causa videndi?* ("And what motivation so great possessed you to go to see Rome?"), a question elicited by Tityrus's glowing account of his visiting Rome, then in her early ancient splendor:

> Verum haec tantum alias inter caput extulit urbes
> Quantum lenta solent inter viburna cupressi.
> (Virgil, *Eclogue* 1.24–25)[3]

> But this city has raised her head among other cities as high as cypresses are accustomed to do among pliant wayfaring trees.

As Robert Coleman remarks, "[t]he perennial reaction of the rustic on his first visit to the big city is reflected in this search for appropriate rural

---

[1] All quotations from Milton's Latin poetry are from *The Complete Works of John Milton: Volume III: The Shorter Poems*, eds. Barbara Kiefer Lewalski and Estelle Haan (Oxford: Oxford University Press, 2012; rev. 2014), hereinafter cited as Lewalski and Haan. I have modernized orthography and punctuation.

[2] Translations of all languages are mine throughout, unless otherwise indicated.

[3] Text is that of *Vergil: Eclogues*, ed. Robert Coleman (Cambridge: Cambridge University Press, 1977).

comparisons."⁴ However, Thyrsis (Milton), grief-stricken, as he is, by the premature death of his close friend Damon (Charles Diodati),⁵ uncovers rather different parallels. Milton's self-fashioning is essentially exilic by subtle fusion of Virgil's first, seventh, and tenth eclogues,⁶ whereby, as Philip Hardie observes, "Thyrsis regards the Italian journey as a journey into exile, repeating Lycoris' journey away from Gallus."⁷ And more than that. In questioning the validity of the *vagus error* (113) ("erratic wandering") that drove him to travel to unknown shores, Milton simultaneously draws upon Petrarch's explication of the allegory characterizing his own first eclogue (*Bucolicum Carmen* 1)⁸ in a letter to his brother, Gherardo: whereas his brother can enjoy the *certa sedes* ("fixed abode") of monastic seclusion, and the assured fulfillment of his *spes sepulcri* ("hope for a tomb"), Petrarch possesses only a *vagus error* ("erratic wandering") that is inextricably associated with *incerta omnia* ("every form of uncertainty").⁹ Milton's indeterminacy, moreover, is

---

⁴ *Vergil: Eclogues*, ed. Coleman, 77.

⁵ On Charles Diodati, see D. C. Dorian, *The English Diodatis* (New Brunswick, NJ: Rutgers University Press, 1950), 97–181; Gordon Campbell, "Diodati, Charles (1609/10–1638)," *ODNB* 16 (2004), 252.

⁶ Thus, for example, the pulsating refrain of *Epitaphium Damonis* (*Ite domum impasti, domino iam non vacat, agni* ["Go home unfed, lambs, your master has no time for you now"]) fuses Virgil, *Eclogue* 7.44: *Ite domum pasti, si quis pudor, ite iuvenci* ("Go home, pastured bullocks, if you have any shame, go home") and *Eclogue* 10.77: *Ite domum saturae, venit Hesperus, ite capellae* ("Go home, well-fed goats, the evening-star is rising, go home").

⁷ Philip Hardie, "Milton's *Epitaphium Damonis* and the Virgilian Career," in *Pastoral Palimpsests: Essays on the Reception of Theocritus and Virgil*, ed. Michael Paschalis (Herakleion: Crete University Press, 2007), 79–100, at 84.

⁸ Petrarch's poem appropriates and inverts the contrast in Virgil, *Eclogue* 1 between Tityrus, a wandering shepherd, and the sedentary Meliboeus secluded in pastoral *otium*, by presenting Monicus (Tityrus/Gherardo) as having found contentment in the tacit security afforded by monastic withdrawal, and inviting Silvius (Meliboeus/Petrarch), a seemingly distracted wandering scholar of sorts (*pererro* [3] ["I wander about"]; *per deserta vagari* [9] ["to roam through the wilderness"]), to enter his world. All quotations are from *Petrarch's Bucolicum Carmen*, ed. Thomas G. Bergin (New Haven, CT: Yale University Press, 1974). On wandering, on both a literal and metaphorical level, in neo-Latin pastoral, see Estelle Haan, "Pastoral," in *A Guide to Neo-Latin Literature*, ed. Victoria Moul (Cambridge: Cambridge University Press, 2017), 163–179, at 166–170.

⁹ Petrarch, *Rerum Familiarium* 10.4: *tibi enim iam certa sedes eoque certior "spes sepulcri"; mihi autem adhuc vagus error et incerta omnia* ("for you already possess a fixed abode and a 'hope for a tomb' that is all the more assured on that account; but for me there is still erratic wandering and every form of uncertainty"). All quotations

heightened by a possible pun on the twofold meaning of *error* (113) as "wandering abroad" and "error." As such, it evokes a conflict likewise expressed in early modern travel handbooks. Thus Sir John Stradling makes a clear distinction between mere "wandering"/"gazing" and careful "searching," by which alone the traveler can "attaine to true pollicie and wisdom."[10] James Howell observes that for the traveler the eye proves ineffectual "unlesse the Mind draw something from the Extreme object to enrich the Soule withall."[11] In all of this Milton proffers what Janet Knedlik aptly describes as a "qualified valuation of the Italian journey,"[12] a journey in which ancient Rome, the *urbs antiqua*, now viewed retrospectively, is both remembered and re-membered as the antithesis of Tityrus's admired city; as one buried underground rather than rearing its head above it.

Editors typically gloss *Romam ... sepultam* ("buried Rome") by reference to the fact that in Milton's time many of the remains of the ancient city had not yet been uncovered.[13] But the phrase has deeper resonances when read in the context of the "poetics of ruins," which had come to birth in consequence of "sustained meditation on the crumbled monuments of antiquity."[14] On the one hand were those for whom the city's ruins elicited a profound sense of *admiratio*, encapsulated by such works as the twelfth-century guidebook *Mirabilia Urbis Romae* or the prose fantasy *Hypnerotomachia Poliphili* (1499). One need only cite Petrarch's proclamation: *vere maior fuit Roma, maioresque sunt reliquiae quam rebar* ("in truth, Rome was greater, her remains were greater than I

---

are from Francesco Petrarch, *Le Familiari*, ed. Vittorio Rossi, 4 vols (Florence: Sansoni, 1933–1942). I have standardized orthography.

[10] John Stradling, *A Direction For Travailers. Taken Out of Iustus Lipsius, and Enlarged for the Behoofe of the Right Honorable Lord, the Yong Earle of Bedford, Being Now Ready to Travell* (London: Cuthbert Burbie, 1592), sig. A3^v.

[11] James Howell, *Instructions for Forreine Travell* (London: Humphrey Moseley, 1642), 196. For further discussion, see Estelle Haan, "England, Neo-Latin, and the Continental Journey," in *Political Turmoil: Early Modern British Literature in Transition, 1623–1660*, ed. Stephen B. Dobranski (Cambridge: Cambridge University Press, 2019), 322–338, at 327–329.

[12] J. L. Knedlik, "High Pastoral Art in *Epitaphium Damonis*," *MS* 19 (1984): 149–163, at 156.

[13] See, for example, *The Latin Poems of John Milton*, ed. Walter Mackellar (New Haven, CT: Yale University Press, 1930), 341; Douglas Bush, *A Variorum Commentary on the Poems of John Milton: Volume I: The Latin and Greek Poems* (New York: Columbia University Press, 1970), 310.

[14] Andrew Hui, *The Poetics of Ruins in Renaissance Literature* (New York: Fordham University Press, 2016), 5.

imagined")[15] or Enea Silvio Piccolomini's express delight: *Oblectat me, Roma, tuas spectare ruinas/Ex cuius lapsu gloria prisca patet* ("Rome, it gives me pleasure to behold your ruins; from your collapse your glory of old becomes evident").[16] For Piccolomini, as for many others, Rome's ruins conveyed the glory of her past.[17] Hence the popular adage: *quanta Roma fuit, ipsa ruina docet* ("Her very ruin teaches the extent of Rome's greatness").[18] On the other hand, they could also serve to evoke a sense of the loss of former grandeur. As Petrarch remarked, *nusquam minus Roma cognoscitur quam Romae* ("nowhere is Rome less recognized than in Rome").[19] Joachim Du Bellay, in *Les Antiquitez de Rome* (1558), viewed the ruined city as "poudreuse cendre" ("pulverized ashes").[20] Likewise, Michel de Montaigne confronted the typical sense of *admiratio* by proclaiming "ce n'estoit rien que son sepulchre" ("it is nothing other than its own sepulcher"),[21] thereby representing, in the words of David Sedley, "the entombment of the city's ruins."[22] And for Giovanni Battista Manso, Milton's Neapolitan host, Rome, fallen from her ancient glory ("Roma caduta dall' antica sua gloria"), retaining only her mighty name ("solo il gran nome") and her miserable ruins ("misere ruine"),

---

[15] Petrarch, *Rerum Familiarium* 2.14.

[16] See Jean Mabillon and Michel Germain, *Musaeum Italicum seu Collectio Veterum Scriptorum in Bibliothecis Italicis* (Paris: Edmund Martin, Johannes Boudot, & Stephanus Martin, 1687), I, 97.

[17] Cf. James S. Ackerman, "The Planning of Renaissance Rome, 1450–1580," in *Rome in the Renaissance: The City and the Myth*, ed. P.A. Ramsey (Binghamton, NY: Medieval and Renaissance Texts and Studies, 1982), 3–17, at 13: "[t]he crumbling, vine-sprouting ruins that encircled the city stimulated a romantic, melancholy involvement with the past."

[18] Francesco Albertini, *Opusculum de Mirabilibus Novae et Veteris Urbis Romae* (Rome: Jacobus Mazochius, 1510), f. 75^v.

[19] Petrarch, *Rerum Familiarium* 6.2.

[20] Text is that of Joachim Du Bellay, *Les Regrets et Autres Oeuvres Poëtiques*, eds. J. Joliffe and M. A. Screech (Geneva: Droz, 1974). For an excellent discussion of the motif of "ashes" in Du Bellay, see Hui, *The Poetics of Ruins*, 144–176.

[21] Michel de Montaigne, *Journal de Voyage*, ed. François Rigolot (Paris: Presses Universitaires de France, 1992), 100.

[22] David L. Sedley, *Sublimity and Skepticism in Montaigne and Milton* (Ann Arbor: University of Michigan Press, 2005), 28. Cf. Hassan Melehy, *The Poetics of Literary Transfer in Early Modern France and England* (London: Routledge, 2010), 35: "What is available to view is that, ironically, there is nothing to view; visible in the ruins are only traces of a former grandeur, at a remove from their source."

symbolized the transitory nature of earthly power.²³ In consequence, writers began to imagine the city's lost grandeur. As Andrew Hui remarks: "[i]f ancient historians had their moments of prolepsis, imagining their cities in ruins, Renaissance humanists had many moments of analepsis, imagining Rome in her complete glory."²⁴

For the grieving Thyrsis, however, that sense of *admiratio* potentially afforded by the ruins of Rome is seriously tempered by grief. Milton's presence in Italy at the moment of Diodati's death is here envisaged as the viewing of a metropolitan sepulcher, a painful substitute for the human burial (in London), which the speaker missed.²⁵ *Roma ... sepulta* (115), moreover, may draw upon an essentially humanist topos, inaugurated by the sixteenth-century Sicilian Janus Vitalis. In an epigram characterized by extreme paradox Vitalis addresses the newcomer to Rome, a newcomer in search of the city's former glory.²⁶ That search is depicted as a vain endeavor because all that can be seen are the city's cadaverous remains (*cadavera ... urbis* [5–6]). In short, *nunc victa in Roma Roma illa invicta sepulta est* (9) ("that unconquered Rome now lies buried in conquered Rome"). The topos was replicated many times, and

---

²³ Giovanni Battista Manso, Sonnet 168, in *Poesie Nomiche* (Venice: Francesco Baba, 1635), 188. This was one of two books probably gifted by the author to Milton in the course of his Neapolitan sojourn, and described allegorically in *Epitaphium Damonis* 181–197. See Michele de Filippis, "Milton and Manso: Cups or Books?" *PMLA* 51 (1936): 745–746.

²⁴ Hui, *The Poetics of Ruins*, 53.

²⁵ Charles Diodati was buried on 27 August 1638. His death may have been due to plague (in 1638 the Diodati family buried three of its members: Isabel [29 June], Philadelphia [10 August], and Charles [27 August]). For arguments as to when and where in Italy Milton received the news of his death, see John T. Shawcross, "*Epitaphium Damonis*: Lines 9–13 and the Date of Composition," *MLN* 71 (1956): 322–324, who argues that it was in April in 1639 while Milton was in Florence (since lines 9–13 refer to Italian crops [there being two wheat harvests (March/August) annually in the Arno valley], and thus two had elapsed since Diodati's death). This argument is countered by W. R. Parker, "Milton and the News of Charles Diodati's Death," *MLN* 72 (1957): 486–488, who argues that Milton heard the news when he was in Naples (i.e. December 1638 or January 1639), and that it was this that led him to cancel his journey to Sicily and Greece. Shawcross responds in Rose Clavering and John T. Shawcross, "Milton's European Itinerary and his Return Home," *SEL* 5 (1965): 49–59.

²⁶ See *Iani Vitalis Panormitani Sacrosanctae Romanae Ecclesiae Elogia* (Rome: Valerius & Aloysius Doricus, 1553), 8, reproduced in Girolamo Tumminello, "Giano Vitale, Umanista del Secolo XVI," *Archivio Storico Siciliano*, n.s. 8 (Palermo, 1883): 59–60.

in many languages:[27] by Joannes Metellus Sequanus, who proclaims: *Quis Romam in media iam quaereret, en ego Roma!/Haec vetus in nostra tota sepulta est* ("Whoever might seek Rome in the midst of Rome: behold, here I am! This ancient city is utterly buried in our city");[28] by Du Bellay, who, anthropomorphizes the whole: "Le corps de Rome en cendre est devallé" ("the corpse of Rome is entombed in ashes"),[29] and by Francisco de Quevedo in his sonnet "A Roma Sepultada en sus Ruinas" ("To Rome Buried in her Ruins").[30]

At first glance then *Roma sepulta* would seem to equate the buried Diodati with the ruins of Rome. Upon closer inspection, however, *Epitaphium Damonis* can be seen to evince what Thomas Greene has described as a "double impulse" governing Renaissance responses to the city's ruins, a duality characteristic of humanist activity more generally: the "archaeological impulse downward into the earth, into the past, the unknown and recondite, and then the upward impulse to bring forth a corpse whole and newly restored, re-illuminated, made harmonious and quick."[31] It does so by vacillating between images of its deceased subject as one borne *sub umbras* (11) ("beneath the shades"), or, in quasi-Du Bellian terms, "in cenere" ("in ashes"): *cum te cinis ater habebat* (142) ("when the black ash possessed you") and as one who can overcome that eventuality. *Sepulta* echoes the *sepulchrum* of line 28, a tomb in which, however, Diodati will *not* "be pulverized" (*non comminuere* [28]).[32] Instead, he is promised a fate antithetical to that of the ancient city. This is achievable because of his *virtus* (21) ("virtue"), later explicated in language evocative perhaps of *prisca Roma* herself: *priscamque fidem coluisse* (33) ("to have respected the faith of old"). And as the poem

---

[27] See Sante Graciotti, "La Fortuna di una Elegia di Giano Vitale, o le Rovine di Roma nella Poesia Polacca," *Aevum* 34 (1960): 122–136; Malcolm C. Smith, "Looking for Rome in Rome: Janus Vitalis and his Disciples," *RLC* 51 (1977): 510–527; G. H. Tucker, "Sur les *Elogia* (1553) de Janus Vitalis et les *Antiquitez de Rome* de Joachim Du Bellay," *BHR* 47 (1985): 103–112; Malcolm C. Smith, "Janus Vitalis Revisited," *RLC* 63 (1989): 69–75.

[28] See *Selectae Christianae Orbis Deliciae ex Urbibus, Templis, Bibliothecis, et Aliunde*, ed. Pierre François Sweerts (Cologne: Bernardus Gualterus, 1625), 15.

[29] Joachim Du Bellay, *Les Antiquitez de Rome*, 5.8. Cf. Hui, *The Poetics of Ruins*, 148.

[30] See Francisco de Quevedo, *Obra Poética*, ed. J. M. Blecua, 3 vols (Madrid: Castalia, 1969–1971), I, 418. See also Raymond Skyrme, "Quevedo, Du Bellay, and Janus Vitalis," *CLS* 19 (1982): 281–295.

[31] Thomas M. Greene, "Resurrecting Rome: The Double Task of the Humanist Imagination," in *Rome in the Renaissance*, ed. Ramsey, 41–54, at 41.

[32] See *OLD*, *comminuere*, s.v. 2: "To break up, prepare by breaking, pulverize."

progresses, the fate of the buried *Roma* (115) is literally and linguistically reversed in the palindromic *Amor* (191),[33] a Platonic Cupid, who *Semper in erectum spargit sua tela per orbes/Impiger, et pronos numquam collimat ad ictus* (195–196) ("always discharges his weapons with energy in an upward direction through the heavenly spheres, and never aims his shots downwards").[34] In the poem's ecstatic conclusion the speaker's proclamation: *nec te Lethaeo fas quaesivisse sub orco* (201) ("it was not right to search for you in the depths of Lethean Orcus") is followed by a series of resurrection motifs. Now the uncorrupted Damon (*purus* [204]) is envisaged as possessing the *purum ... aethera* (203) ("pure ether"), and feasting among heroes and gods (203–207).[35] In a celestial transformation of the Roman practice of *laureatio*, his head will be girt with a gleaming crown: *Ipse caput nitidum cinctus rutilante corona,/Laetaque frondentis gestans umbracula palmae* (215–216) ("you, yourself, your shining head girt with a glowing crown and wearing the joyful branches of the leafy palm"). Perhaps that envisaged coronation might also embrace Rome herself in the potentially punning *caput* (215) as both "head" and "capital city."[36] In essence then, Thyrsis's poignant question concerning *Roma sepulta* (115–117) is ultimately

---

[33] For punning on *Roma/Amor*, cf. Du Bellay, *Amores* III, in which *Roma*, the first word of the poem, is transformed into *Amor*, the poem's final word; George Herbert, *Lucus* XXV, which plays on no fewer than five anagrams of *Roma*: *Oram, Ramo, Armo, Mora, Amor* (George Herbert, *Poetical Works*, ed. A. B. Grosart [London: George Bell and Sons, 1876], 366). For discussion of similar puns in Virgil and Ovid, see Jay Reed, "*Mora* in the *Aeneid*," in *Wordplay and Powerplay in Latin Poetry*, eds. Phillip Mitsis and Ioannis Ziogas (Berlin: Walter de Gruyter, 2016), 87–106; Mathias Hanses, "Love's letters: an Amor-Roma Telestich at Ovid, *Ars Amatoria* 3.507-10," in *ibid.*, 199–212.

[34] The allusion is in all likelihood to Giovanni Battista Manso's *Erocallia ovvero dell'Amore e della Belleza* (Venice: Deuchino, 1628), twelve Platonic dialogues on love and beauty, celebrating heavenly, as opposed to earthly, love, a work possibly gifted by the author to Milton. See note 23; De Filippis, "Milton and Manso"; Lewalski and Haan, 498.

[35] *Epitaphium Damonis* 203–207: *purum colit aethera Damon,/Aethera purus habet, pluvium pede reppulit arcum,/Heroumque animas inter divosque perennes/Aethereos haurit latices et gaudia potat/Ore sacro* ("Damon inhabits the pure ether; pure in himself he possesses the ether and has thrust away the rainbow with his foot, and among the souls of heroes and eternal divinities he draws draughts from celestial waters, and drinks joys with his hallowed lips").

[36] See *OLD*, s.v. 14b: "the capital, chief city (of a state, province, etc." Cf. Livy 1.16.7: *ut mea Roma caput orbis terrarum sit* ("that my Rome should be the capital of the world"); Ovid, *Amores* 1.15.26: *Roma triumphati dum caput orbis erit* ("for as long as Rome is the capital of the conquered world").

answered by the positive imagery of rebirth and renewal in the poem's concluding lines.

One year prior to the composition of *Epitaphium Damonis* Rome was host to Milton (in October–November 1638) in the first of two two-month sojourns (he would revisit the city on his homeward journey in the early months of 1639). His account in *Defensio Secunda* ("after the antiquity [*antiquitas*] of that city and its renown of old [*prisca fama*] had detained me [*tenuisset*] for a period of roughly two months")[37] is tellingly complemented by parenthetical reference to humanist exemplars of modern, Catholic Rome, not least, the Vatican librarian and scholar, Lucas Holstenius: *ubi et Luca Holstenio aliisque viris cum doctis tum ingeniosis sum usus humanissime* ("where I made the very friendly acquaintance of Lucas Holstenius, and of many other men of learning and genius").[38] Milton's early biographers, while relying largely upon these words, offer somewhat differing versions. John Phillips and Anthony à Wood omit the reference to *illius urbis antiquitas et prisca fama*, mentioning only Milton's engagement with men of learning, Holstenius included.[39] Edward Phillips elaborates by qualifying Rome as "that most Glorious and Renowned City," and by presenting the motivation governing Milton's visits as a twofold desire to see her "Rarities and Antiquities" and to converse with "Lucas Holstenius, and other Learned and Ingenious men; who highly valued his Acquaintance, and treated him with all possible Respect."[40] John Toland, on the other hand, presents Rome's antiquities in essentially pejorative language, describing Milton's viewing of "the miserable Remains of that famous City, once the glorious

---

[37] *Joannis Miltoni Angli Pro Populo Anglicano Defensio Secunda. Contra Infamem Libellum Anonymum cui Titulus, Regii Sanguinis Clamor ad Coelum Adversus Parricidas Anglicanos* (London: Thomas Newcomb, 1654), 84. See Appendix 2.23–24.

[38] *Defensio Secunda*, 84–85. See Appendix 2.24–26.

[39] John Phillips, "The Life of Mr. John Milton," in *The Early Lives of Milton*, ed. Helen Darbishire, (London: Constable & Co. Ltd, 1932), 17–34, at 20: "to Rome, where, as in all places, hee spent his time in the choicest company; and amongst others there, in that of Lucas Holstein"; Anthony à Wood, *Fasti Oxonienses*, in *Early Lives*, ed. Darbishire, 35–48, at 37: "from thence he went to Sena and Rome, in both which places he spent his time among the most learned there, Lucas Holsteinius being one." In all instances I have normalized italics (used of proper names/places).

[40] Edward Phillips, "The Life of Mr. John Milton," in *Early Lives*, ed. Darbishire, 49–82, at 57: "to Rome; where he was detain'd much about the same time he had been at Florence; as well by the desire of seeing all the Rarities and Antiquities of that most Glorious and Renowned City, as by the Conversation of Lucas Holstenius, and other Learned and Ingenious men; who highly valued his Acquaintance, and treated him with all possible Respect."

Mistress of the World," and linking her ruins to her moral, religious, and political corruption. Toland concentrates upon the potential effect of modern Rome upon Milton, imagining his grief at the sight of the Catholic city, a symbol of tyranny, delusion, and superstition.[41] Only then does he mention his links with Holstenius, augmenting the whole by recourse to autobiographical details provided by Milton in *Epistola Familiaris* 9.[42] By contrast, David Masson waxes eloquently in regard to Roman ruins that Milton must surely have beheld. His gloss to Milton's aforementioned remark in *Defensio Secunda* merits full quotation:

> In other words, his chief occupation, during the month of October and part of November, was in visiting and studying "the antiquities." ... It was the usual round of the Pantheon and the Coliseum, the Capitol and the Tarpeian Rock, the Baths, the Temples, the ancient gates, the arches, the columns, the aqueducts, and the tombs. Scholar as he was, we need not doubt that the labour was gone through steadily and systematically; and that, ere he quitted the city, the seven hills were traced out by him as distinctly as change and ruin would permit, and old Rome reconstructed on them with tolerable clearness in its later imperial extent, when the space of the monuments was wholly covered, and so backward, by gradual diminution, through the less monumental era of the Republic and the Consuls, and up to the mythic reigns of the Latin-Etruscan kings. Two months by the Tiber, varied by excursions around, would enable him to carry away such a picture of ancient Latium as would illustrate his readings in Virgil, Horace, and Livy, to his life's end.[43]

---

[41] John Toland, "The Life of John Milton," in *Early Lives*, ed. Darbishire, 83–197, at 92–93: "From his beloved Florence he took his Journey next to Rome, where he stay'd two other Months to see the miserable Remains of that famous City, once the glorious Mistress of the World, and deservedly so, as being then not only the fairest thing under Heaven; but that, till the Ambition of a few Persons corrupted her equal Government, she extended Liberty and Learning as far as the Glory of her Name, or the Terror of her Arms. Here, no doubt, all the Examples he had hitherto read of the Virtue, Eloquence, Wisdom, or Valor of her antient Citizens, occur'd to his mind, and could not but oppress with grief his generous Soul, when with his own eys he saw Rome now the chief Seat of the most exquisit Tyranny exercis'd by effeminat Priests, not reigning in the World thro any conceiv'd opinion of their Justice, or dread of their Courage; for to these Qualities they are known and sworn Enemys: but deluding men with unaccountable Fables and disarming 'em by imaginary Fears, they fill their heads first with Superstition, and then their own Pockets with their Mony."

[42] Toland, *Life*, in *Early Lives*, ed. Darbishire, 93. For *Epistola Familiaris* 9, see Chapter 3 and Appendix 1.3.

[43] David Masson, *The Life of John Milton: Narrated in Connexion with the Political, Ecclesiastical, and Literary History of his Time*, 7 vols (London: Macmillan, 1881–1894; repr. Gloucester, MA: Peter Smith, 1965), I, 741–742.

Milton's early biographers certainly reveled in embellishment. Of course, it goes without saying that visitors to seicento Rome could not have failed to be impressed by its architectural splendor, as is apparent in, for example, John Evelyn's ebullient account.[44] The fact, however, remains that nowhere does Milton explicitly document the ancient Roman sites that he doubtlessly viewed. Still, perhaps something of the captivating powers of the eternal city shines through his choice of the verb *tenere*, probably in the sense of "(of physical or mental states) To hold under their sway, possess,"[45] when alluding to his detainment by her *antiquitas*. It is a detainment that was literary as well as literal for Milton, whose constant reading was, according to his Florentine friend, Carlo Dati, intrinsically linked to his deep exploration of *antiquitatum latebras* ("the hiding-places of antiquity") and *vetustatis excidia* ("the ruins of the distant past").[46]

Coinciding with Milton's first Roman sojourn (in the autumn of 1638) was the publication of the *Ritratto di Roma Moderna* by the humanist antiquary Pompilio Totti.[47] Dedicated to Cardinal Antonio Barberini, this richly illustrated and copiously annotated guide to the modern city served to complement Totti's *Ritratto di Roma Antica* published over a decade previously,[48] a point aptly signaled by its author.[49] In the course of the seven days into which the modern account

---

[44] See *The Diary of John Evelyn*, ed. E. S. De Beer, 6 vols (Oxford: Clarendon Press, 1955), II, 212–317.

[45] *OLD*, s.v. 10.

[46] Carlo Dati, Latin prose encomium of Milton, prefixed to *Poemata* in *Poems of Mr. John Milton, Both English and Latin* (London: Humphrey Moseley, 1645), 10: *Antiquitatum latebras, vetustatis excidia, eruditionis ambages comite assidua auctorum lectione exquirenti, restauranti, percurrenti* ("To one who with constant reading of authors as his companion explores, restores, traverses the hiding-places of antiquity, the ruins of the distant past, the intricacies of learning"). See Lewalski and Haan, 114–115, 419–420.

[47] Pompilio Totti, *Ritratto di Roma Moderna* (Rome: Mascardi, 1638). The dedicatory letter (from Lodovico Totti to Antonio Barberini) is dated 18 November 1638. On Totti, see Dennis E. Rhodes, "Pompilio Totti: Publisher, Engraver, Roman Antiquary," *Papers of the British School at Rome* 37 (1969): 161–172.

[48] Pompilio Totti, *Ritratto di Roma Antica* (Rome: Andrea Fei, 1627).

[49] Totti, *Ritratto di Roma Moderna*, sig. 2ᵛ: "Al Benigno Lettore: Havendo gli anni passati dato alla publica luce il ritratto di Roma Antica, che pure da molti è stata in diverse maniere stampata. Hora non hò voluto mancare d'andar' anche raccogliendo da più luoghi de' Scrittori, e mandar fuora la presente Roma Moderna, che pur da altri è stata in varie guise scritta: ma pare à me, che non sia così copiosa, per sodisfare il curioso Lettore" ("To the Kind Reader: Having spent years in seeing to publication

is divided, the reader is conducted on a series of tours of the different regions of Rome, and of the magnificent architecture afforded by each: the splendors of the Vatican, of individual churches, palaces, theaters, and monuments—all indicative of the resurgence of the capital from the ruins of its past. For Totti, seicento Rome is a tale of two cities: the ancient and the modern; the pagan and the Christian. Crucially, these are not mutually exclusive. On the volume's title page the papal triple crown is borne aloft against a backdrop depicting (on the left) symbols of the papacy: the crosier, miter, the Vatican itself; (on the right) symbols of the ancient pagan city: a wolf, suckling Romulus and Remus, behind whom can be seen the *fasces*, the bundle of rods, with an axe in the middle. Significantly, the wolf looks back respectfully at the Pope, who bears spiritual and temporal power. Beneath the work's title is a large impression of the Barberini bee emblem. And at the bottom are two seated figures: the one holding a cross and a chalice, the other bearing an amphora and a sea anchor. The interconnectedness of the two Romes is mirrored by Totti's literary methodology. His account of the modern city frequently itemizes the material aspects of antiquity, which brought it to birth. Totti's work is capable testimony to the emergence of an industry of Roman antiquarianism, itself seen as a means of closing the distance between *Roma antica* and *Roma moderna*.[50] This endeavor operated in a Janus-like way in its twofold aim of restoring the modern city to her ancient grandeur, and of transferring to *Roma moderna* something of that *prisca virtus* possessed by its past. This is nowhere more evident than in the titles gracing much of the literary output of Flavio Biondo: *De Roma Instaurata* (1444–1448), *Italia Illustrata* (1448, 1458, 1474), and *De Roma Triumphata* (1479). After all, parts of the modern city were built from stones literally pilfered from its ancient ruins.

Milton himself was forever motivated by a quasi-Petrarchan sense of discovering and rediscovering Rome, her writers, both ancient and modern, and her language, Latin. Prior to his Italian journey he had avidly studied Rome's exemplary authors, experimenting with *Latinitas* in verse that was imaginatively new. In the course of his education, both

---

the portrait of Ancient Rome, which has also been printed in many forms, I did not wish to overlook the opportunity of gathering together the foremost passages from writers, and to entrust to you the present Modern Rome, which has been written in various ways by others, but, as it seems so me, not so copiously, in order to satisfy the curious Reader").

[50] See Sedley, *Sublimity and Skepticism*, 23–24.

at St Paul's School, London,[51] and under private tutelage, he had derived great pleasure from imitating:

> the smooth Elegiack Poets, whereof the Schooles are not scarce. Whom both for the pleasing sound of their numerous writing, which in imitation I found most easie; and most agreeable to natures part in me, and for their matter which what it is, there be few who know not, I was so allur'd to read, that no recreation came to me better welcome.[52]

Subsequently, and most notably, in his Latin verse composed during his Cambridge years he had drawn upon the poetry and Latin prosody of Virgil and Ovid, among others.[53] In so doing, however, he had exemplified his ability to reinterpret, indeed to reinvent the poetry of the *urbs antiqua* by adapting it to suit his contemporary world. Thus Cambridge University is Romanized as a place occupied by "toga-clad" inhabitants;[54] his own so-called rustication is evoked by a "cross-comparison"[55] with Ovid whereby Milton, rejoicing in his "exile," transports barren Tomis to the Cambridge from which he has escaped, while enjoying in London those Roman pleasures, whose loss Ovid had

---

[51] See D. L. Clark, *John Milton at St. Paul's School: A Study of Ancient Rhetoric in English Renaissance Education* (New York: Columbia University Press, 1948).

[52] *An Apology Against a Pamphlet Call'd A Modest Confutation of the Animadversions Upon the Remonstrant against Smectymnuus* (London: John Rothwell, 1642), 15. See, in general, David Hopkins, "Milton and the Classics," in *John Milton: Life, Writing, Reputation*, eds. Paul Hammond and Blair Worden (Oxford: Oxford University Press, 2010), 23–41.

[53] See, among others, E. H. Riley, *The Virgilian Element in the Works of Milton* (PhD thesis: Cornell University, 1925), I, 15–43; Mary Campbell Brill, *Milton and Ovid* (PhD thesis: Cornell University, 1935); Davis P. Harding, *Milton and the Renaissance Ovid* (Urbana: University of Illinois Press, 1946); P. E. Kimmich, *John Milton's Technical Handling of the Latin Elegy* (PhD thesis: University of Illinois, 1958); K. J. Aylward, *Milton's Latin Versification: The Hexameter* (PhD thesis: Columbia University, 1966); G. E. Duckworth, "Milton's Hexameter Patterns—Vergilian or Ovidian?" *AJP* 93 (1972): 52–60; Estelle Haan, "*Mansueti ... Chironis*: Milton, Manso, and Ovid's Chiron," *CML* 17 (1997): 251–264; Estelle Haan, "Milton's *Elegia Quarta* and Ovid: Another Cross-comparison," *N&Q* 54 (2007): 400–405; Maggie Kilgour, *Milton and the Metamorphosis of Ovid* (Oxford: Oxford University Press, 2012).

[54] Milton, *Elegia Secunda* 11: *acies ... togatas* ("the toga-clad ranks"); *In Obitum Procancellarii Medici* 30: *gentis togatae* ("of the toga-clad race").

[55] Milton, *Elegia Prima*, passim. See Ralph W. Condee, "Ovid's Exile and Milton's Rustication," *PQ* 37 (1958): 498–502, reworked in his *Structure in Milton's Poetry: From the Foundation to the Pinnacles* (University Park: Pennsylvania State University Press, 1974), 22–27.

continually lamented.⁵⁶ A deceased bishop is presented in a celestial vision only to evoke, somewhat irreverently, Ovid's lurid description of his girlfriend's naked beauty after a torrid love-making session.⁵⁷ Methodologically too, Milton had fused the ancient and the modern by drawing upon not only classical writers, but also such Renaissance Latin poets as Mantuan,⁵⁸ Sannazaro,⁵⁹ and Vida,⁶⁰ and he would turn to Latin pastorals by Castiglione, and Zanchi in the *Epitaphium Damonis* itself.⁶¹ In advance of his Italian journey he had completely immersed himself in *evolvendis Graecis Latinisque scriptoribus*⁶² ("pouring over the Greek and Latin writers") during his Hammersmith period, funded by his father.

As for Milton's sometimes vacillating opinions of the ancient city, the people that she produced, and the values that she encapsulated, one need only turn to his later esteem for "Roman docility and courage," as conveyed in *Areopagitica*,⁶³ or to his description of Rome in *The History*

---

⁵⁶ As if to heighten these contrasts the poem echoes a broad range of Ovidian verse, including the *Tristia*, the *Ars Amatoria*, the *Heroides*, and the *Ibis*.

⁵⁷ *Talia contingant somnia saepe mihi* (*Elegia Tertia* 68 ["May dreams such as this often befall me"]). Cf. Ovid, *Amores* 1.5.26. See John K. Hale, "Milton Playing with Ovid," *MS* 25 (1989): 3–19, and his *Milton's Languages: The Impact of Multilingualism on Style* (Cambridge: Cambridge University Press, 1997), 33–37.

⁵⁸ See Harris F. Fletcher, "Milton's *Apologus* and its Mantuan Model," *JEGP* 55 (1956): 230–233; Estelle Haan, "Mantuan, Milton and 'The Fruit of that Forbidden Tree'," *MH* 25 (1998): 75–92.

⁵⁹ See James Goode, "Milton and Sannazaro," *TLS* (13 August 1931): 621.

⁶⁰ See Estelle Haan, "Milton's Latin Poetry and Vida," *HL* 44 (1995): 282–304. For later instances of Milton's echoing of Vida, see Estelle Haan, "Milton's *Paradise Regained* and Vida's *Christiad*," in *From Erudition to Inspiration: A Booklet for Michael*, ed. Estelle Haan (Belfast: Belfast Byzantine Texts and Translations, 1992), 53–77; Estelle Haan, "From Helicon to Heaven: Milton's Urania and Vida," *RS* 7 (1993): 115–136; Estelle Haan, "'Heaven's Purest Light': Milton's *Paradise Lost* 3 and Vida," *CLS* 30 (1993): 115–136.

⁶¹ See Thomas P. Harrison, "The Latin Pastorals of Milton and Castiglione," *PMLA* 50 (1935): 480–493; Lawrence V. Ryan, "Milton's *Epitaphium Damonis* and B. Zanchi's Elegy on Baldassare Castiglione," *HL* 30 (1981): 108–123.

⁶² See *Defensio Secunda* 82–83: *Paterno rure, quo is transigendae senectutis causa concesserat, evolvendis Graecis Latinisque scriptoribus summum per otium totus vacavi* ("In my father's country-house, to which he had retired to spend his old age, I completely devoted a time of the utmost scholarly leisure to pouring over the Greek and Latin writers").

⁶³ *Areopagitica: A Speech of Mr. John Milton For the Liberty of Unlicenc'd Printing To the Parlament of England* (London: s.n., 1644), 32. See, in general, Stella P. Revard, "Milton and Classical Rome: The Political Context of *Paradise Regained*," in *Rome in the Renaissance*, ed. Ramsey, 409–419.

of Britain as "that Puissant Citty,"⁶⁴ whose ancient history is presented as more secure than that of Britain. The reason for this, as John Curran suggests, is "probably because of superior Roman writers, whose excellence was commensurate with that of the Romans themselves."⁶⁵ Miltonic praise of those writers resonates throughout his work: in, for example, his encomium of Roman historiography in general and of Sallust in particular in *Epistola Familiaris* 23,⁶⁶ or in his confident salutation of Latin literature as the product of the "choycest wits of ... Rome," a paragon to be followed by the future epic poet.⁶⁷ At the same time Milton was far from blind to Rome's negative points.⁶⁸ Indeed his vibrant criticism of the modern Catholic city had already reared its head most strikingly in his five Latin epigrams on the Gunpowder Plot, and his miniature Latin epic *In Quintum Novembris* (c. 1626). The epigrams had denigrated *Roma* as a *Belua* (2.2) ("beast") dwelling upon seven hills;⁶⁹ they had described her as *profana* (2.8) ("profane"), and had openly attacked her religious fraternity, symbolized by *foedos ... cucullos* (2.7) ("filthy [Franciscan] cowls"), meriting an explosion up to the heavens,⁷⁰ her ownership of *brutos ... deos* (2.8) ("brute gods"), and her misguided doctrine of purgatory (*Purgatorem animae ... ignem* [3.1] ["the fire that purges the soul"]).⁷¹ *In Quintum Novembris* had traced the origins of a

---

⁶⁴ John Milton, *The History of Britain* (London: James Allestry, 1670), 31.

⁶⁵ John E. Curran, *Roman Invasions: The British History, Protestant Anti-Romanism, and the Historical Imagination in England, 1530–1600* (Newark: University of Delaware Press/London: Associated University Presses, 2002), 118.

⁶⁶ See *Epistola Familiaris* 23 (to Henri de Brass), dated 15 July 1657, in *Ioannis Miltonii Angli Epistolarum Familiarium Liber Unus: Quibus Accesserunt, Eiusdem, Iam Olim in Collegio Adolescentis, Prolusiones* (London: Brabazon Aylmer, 1674), 53–55, and, for further discussion, *John Milton: Epistolarum Familiarium Liber Unus and Uncollected Letters*, ed. Estelle Haan, Supplementa Humanistica Lovaniensia XLIV (Leuven: Leuven University Press, 2019), 313–325.

⁶⁷ Milton, *The Reason of Church-Government Urg'd Against Prelaty. In Two Books* (London: John Rothwell, 1641), 38: "That what the greatest and choycest wits of Athens, Rome, or modern Italy, and those Hebrews of old did for their country, I, in my proportion, with this over and above, of being a Christian, might doe for mine."

⁶⁸ For Milton's use of the image of Rome as a symbol of degeneration and corruption, see Andrew Hadfield, "The English and Other Peoples," in *A Companion to Milton*, ed. Thomas N. Corns (Oxford: Blackwell, 2001, 2003), 174–190, at 181–182.

⁶⁹ The language is evocative of Rev. 13:1.

⁷⁰ Cf. *Paradise Lost* 3.489–490 (of the Paradise of Fools): "then might ye see/Cowls, hoods and habits with their wearers tossed." All quotations are from *Milton: Paradise Lost*, ed. Alastair Fowler (London: Longman, 1998).

Catholic conspiracy back to Satan himself, satirizing the Franciscan order, the Pope, described as *Tricoronifer* (55) ("triple-crowned"), a *secretus adulter* (75) ("secret adulterer"), and an *antistes Babylonius* (156) ("Babylonian priest"), and ridiculing Catholic ritual in the Vatican, significantly located *in arce Quirini* (53) ("upon the citadel of Quirinus"). In short, the establishment of the papacy in modern Rome was glaringly presented as the antithesis of Romulus's founding of the ancient city, as the seat of deceit, treachery, and Satanic machination. It should be emphasized, however, that in these instances the Cambridge Milton was self-consciously drawing upon the well-established, essentially anti-Catholic, nature of the neo-Latin gunpowder epic tradition.[72] He had not yet set eyes on Rome. When he eventually did so, an altogether different picture seems to have emerged.[73]

---

[71] On possible links between this epigram and King James' ridicule of purgatory in *A Premonition*, prefixed to the second edition (1609) of his *Apology for the Oath of Allegiance*, see Walter MacKellar, "Milton, James I and Purgatory," *MLR* 18 (1923): 472–473; Phineas Fletcher, *Locustae vel Pietas Iesuitica*, ed. Estelle Haan, Supplementa Humanistica Lovaniensia IX (Leuven: Leuven University Press, 1996), xxv–xxix.

[72] See Estelle Haan, "Milton's *In Quintum Novembris* and the Anglo-Latin Gunpowder Epic," *HL* 41 (1992): 221–250; Francis Herring, *Pietas Pontificia*, ed. Estelle Haan, *HL* 41 (1992): 251–295; Michael Wallace, *In Serenissimi Regis Iacobi ... Liberationem*, ed. Estelle Haan, *HL* 42 (1993): 368–401; Phineas Fletcher, *Locustae*, ed. Haan, xvi–lx. See also David Quint, "Milton, Fletcher and the Gunpowder Plot," *JWCI* 54 (1991): 261–268; R. F. Hardin, "The Early Poetry of the Gunpowder Plot: Myth in the Making," *ELR* 22 (1992): 62–79; Dana F. Sutton, "Milton's *In Quintum Novembris, Anno Aetatis 17* (1626): Choices and Intentions," in *Qui Miscuit Utile Dulci: Festschrift Essays for Paul Lachlan MacKendrick*, eds. Gareth Schmeling and Jon D. Mikalson (Wauconda: Bolchazy-Carducci, 1998), 349–375; John K. Hale, "Milton and the Gunpowder Plot: *In Quintum Novembris* Reconsidered," *HL* 50 (2001): 351–366. Among useful general studies of Milton's anti-Catholicism are Raymond D. Tumbleson, "Of True Religion and False Politics: Milton and the Uses of Anti-Catholicism," *Prose Studies* 15 (1992): 253–270; Andrew Hadfield, "Milton and Catholicism," in *Milton and Toleration*, ed. Sharon Achinstein and Elizabeth Sauer (Oxford: Oxford University Press, 2007), 186–202.

[73] Indeed in a Latin letter, dated 20 April 1647, and thus postdating by almost two decades the composition of *In Quintum Novembris* and the gunpowder epigrams, and by almost one decade his Italian journey, Milton, promising to send the Latin part of the 1645 volume to his addressee, the Florentine academician, Carlo Dati (and to Dati's fellow academicians), makes the insightful remark that he would have done so already had he not feared that its antipapal content (evidently a reference to the gunpowder poems included therein) might not be too pleasing to their ears. He proceeds to convey the express hope that they will forgive his freedom of expression as, he says, they were accustomed to do. See *Epistola Familiaris* 10, in *Epistolarum Familiarium Liber Unus*, 28–32, at 31, and, for further discussion, *Epistolarum Familiarium Liber Unus and Uncollected Letters*, ed. Haan, 166–167, 182–184.

Any attempt to map Milton's Roman sojourns with specificity is a difficult task largely on account of two factors: (1) Milton's careful self-editing in *Defensio Secunda* (1654), and (2) the dearth of independent evidence relating to his Roman experiences. *Defensio Secunda* presents a retrospective account that is essentially selective, frequently abridged, less frequently augmented, as interesting for its omissions as for its inclusions.[74] It should be read *a priori* as a succinct, yet carefully worded, rebuttal of charges made in print some two years previously by Peter Du Moulin. Du Moulin claimed that Milton had been expelled from Cambridge because of his shameful behavior, had migrated to Italy in disgrace, returning to England only as rebellion was brewing and in the hope of stirring up a revolution.[75] It is hardly surprising then that Milton, in what Michael Lieb has astutely termed "an attempt at repristination,"[76] should emphasize the meritorious motives underlying his continental journey. Thus he takes pains to point out that foreign regions and Italy in particular were not places of refuge for him, but countries that he was eager to see.[77] In early modern England, the idea of continental travel had met with a somewhat ambivalent reception.[78] Italy, as denounced by Roger Ascham, was a second Circe, an evil temptress, whose pernicious "inchantmentes" were to be avoided at all costs. Otherwise, the traveler abroad would return "worse transformed," an "Englishman Italianated," so to speak, who, having utterly lost any sense of religious and national identity, would transport to his homeland a host of evils, including

---

[74] *Defensio Secunda*, 84–86. See Appendix 2.23–26; 38–46.

[75] Pierre du Moulin, *Regii Sanguinis Clamor ad Coelum Adversus Parricidas Anglicanos* (The Hague: Adrian Vlacq, 1652), 9: *Aiunt hominem Cantabrigiensi Academia ob flagitia pulsum dedecus et patriam fugisse, et in Italiam commigrasse. Inde hac rebellione ingruente spe rerum novarum in Angliam revocatum* ("They say that the fellow had been expelled from Cambridge University on account of his shameful behavior and had fled his native land in disgrace, and had migrated to Italy; and that as this rebellion was brewing, he was called back from there to England in the hope of stirring up a revolution").

[76] Michael Lieb, *Milton and the Culture of Violence* (Ithaca, NY: Cornell University Press, 1994), 182. Cf. Paul Slade, *Italia Conquistata: The Role of Italy in Milton's Early Poetic Development* (PhD thesis: University of Exeter, 2017), 203: "His account of Italy is about *him*, not about Italy, necessarily, because it was written as an exercise in self-validation."

[77] *Defensio Secunda*, 83. See Appendix 2.1–2.

[78] See, among others, Sara Warneke, *Images of the Educational Traveller in Early Modern England* (Leiden: Brill, 1995); Edward Chaney, *The Grand Tour and the Great Rebellion: Richard Lassels and "The Voyage of Italy" in the Seventeenth Century* (Geneva: Slatkine, 1985); Edward Chaney, *The Evolution of the Grand Tour: Anglo-Italian Cultural Relations Since the Renaissance* (London: Frank Cass, 1998).

"Papistrie or worse."⁷⁹ Ascham, as Sara Warneke puts it, "opened a Pandora's box" in regard to the perceived dangers of foreign travel.⁸⁰ It is certainly true that for any English Protestant, travel in Italy was not without danger. Among more serious, albeit frequently exaggerated, perils were imprisonment by the Inquisition or even conversion to Catholicism at the hands of cunning Jesuits.⁸¹ Milton's self-fashioning throughout is as the heroic defender of the Protestant faith while upon Italian soil. Thus he announces that he had decided not to introduce spontaneously the subject of religion, but that when interrogated about faith, he would dissimulate nothing, irrespective of the consequences.⁸² But this element of hyperbolic pride is to be expected in a self-defense. Certainly, when we read of Milton's claim of a so-called Jesuit plot against him in Rome,⁸³ we realize that this is probably no more than authorial recourse to the well-established "escape from Rome" genre.⁸⁴

---

⁷⁹ Roger Ascham, *The Scholemaster* (London: John Daye, 1570), sig. 24ᵛ–26ᵛ.

⁸⁰ Warneke, *Educational Traveller*, 57.

⁸¹ See Warneke, *Educational Traveller*, 167–190.

⁸² *Defensio Secunda*, 86. See Appendix 2.41–43. In Naples, however, when in the company of Giovanni Battista Manso, Milton seems to have refused to preserve his guard when discussion turned to religion (*quod nolebam in religione esse tectior* ["because I refused to be more guarded on the subject of religion"]). And it was on this account that Manso allegedly offered him an apology for his inability to show him greater hospitality in the city, even though it was his wish to do so (*Defensio Secunda*, 85. See Appendix 2.32–34). But that any tension between the English Protestant and his Neapolitan host was ultimately resolved is suggested by Manso's good-humored Latin distich composed in Milton's honor, and prefixed to *Poemata* (1645), at 4. Echoing the words of Gregory the Great, Manso states that if Milton's *pietas* ("piety"/"religion") were as his other attributes, he would be an "Angel," not an "Angle." See *Bede's Ecclesiastical History*, ed. Bertram Colgrave and R.A.B. Mynors (Oxford: Oxford University Press, 1969), 132–134. See also Anthony Low, "*Mansus*: In its Context," *MS* 19 (1984): 105–126, at 106–107; Estelle Haan, *From Academia to Amicitia: Milton's Latin Writings and the Italian Academies* (Philadelphia: American Philosophical Society, 1998), 130–136. Milton seems to turn the whole upon its head in the concluding lines of *Mansus*, where, as an implicit angel, he radiantly blushes and smiles from heaven, as he applauds himself (*Mansus* 98–100).

⁸³ *Defensio Secunda*, 85–86. See Appendix 2. 38–40.

⁸⁴ See Diana Treviño Benet, "The Escape From Rome: Milton's Second Defense and a Renaissance Genre," in *Milton in Italy: Contexts, Images, Contradictions*, ed. Mario A. Di Cesare (Binghamton, NY: Medieval and Renaissance Texts and Studies, 1991), 29–49. Benet convincingly shows that Milton's claim draws upon the "Escape from Rome" narrative, exemplified by Anthony Munday, Edward Webbe, George Sandys, Fynes Moryson, and William Lithgow. See Antony Munday, *The English Romayne Lyfe, 1582*, ed. G.B. Harrison (Edinburgh: Edinburgh University Press, 1966); *Edward Webbe, Chief Master Gunner, His Travailes. 1590*, ed. Edward Arber

Indeed, as Diana Benet observes, "[i]t is likely that Milton found a hospitable Rome when he traveled there."[85] Similarly, Milton's emphasis upon the essentially patriotic motivation (*tristis ex Anglia belli civilis nuntius* ["the grim news from England of the civil war"]) governing his decision to return to England[86] should be read as a hyperbolic countering of Du Moulin's charge, noted previously. When it comes to highlighting religious difference Milton possesses a self-awareness that is both crafted and matched by his literary self-consciousness.

As Susanne Woods remarks, "Milton in Italy was an oxymoron in search of the higher resolutions of a paradox: a Protestant in the center of Catholicism."[87] *Defensio Secunda* maintains a crucial silence about several personal links that Milton forged with certain Italian Catholics in both Florence and Rome: Antonio Malatesti, composer of a sequence of fifty erotic sonnets, which he subsequently dedicated to Milton,[88] and, most notably, Cardinal Francesco Barberini, by whom Milton was received, and with whom he was even granted a private audience.[89] We hear nothing of his dining at the Jesuit-run English College in Rome, whose Pilgrim Book provides us with a definite date: 30 October 1638. Here we discover that he was accompanied by an unnamed servant, and we even know the identity of his fellow-diners: Patrick Carey (the 14-year-old son of Viscount Falkland), the secular priest Henry Holden, and a titled member of the Fontescue family (either Sir John or, more likely,

---

(London: Alex Murray & Son, 1869); George Sandys, *Travels, Containing an History of the ... Turkish Empire* (London: W[illiam] Barrett, 1615); Fynes Moryson, *An Itinerary ... Containing His Ten Yeeres Travell through the Twelve Dominions of Germany, Bohmerland, Sweitzerland, Netherland, Denmarke, Poland, Italy, Turky, France, England, Scotland & Ireland* (London: John Beale, 1617); William Lithgow, *The Totall Discourse of the Rare Adventures and Painefull Peregrinations of Long Nineteene Yeares Travayles from Scotland to the Most Famous Kingdomes in Europe, Asia and Affrica* (London: Nicholas Okes, 1632). For a later example, see Sir Edward Herbert, *Autobiography* (composed in the 1640s), published in Strawberry Hill in 1764.

[85] Benet, "The Escape From Rome," 46.

[86] *Defensio Secunda*, 85. See Appendix 2. 35–37.

[87] Susanne Woods, "'That Freedom of Discussion Which I Loved': Italy and Milton's Cultural Self Definition," in *Milton in Italy*, ed. Di Cesare, 9–18, at 9. For further discussion of the paradoxical elements of Milton's Italian journey, see Haan, "England, Neo-Latin and the Continental Journey."

[88] See Antonio Malatesti, *La Tina: Equivoci Rusticali*, ed. Davide Messina (London: Modern Humanities Research Association, 2014); Davide Messina, "*La Tina* Regained," *MQ* 45 (2011): 118–122.

[89] See 154–157, 169–173.

his brother Sir Nicholas).⁹⁰ Leo Miller offers some interesting speculations in regard to possible topics for discussion,⁹¹ but it would be unwise to presume that over dinner Milton had somehow provoked the Catholics in his company. Likewise, we hear nothing of Milton's evident integration into Catholic Rome: his awe at the splendors of the Vatican Library;⁹² his attendance at a comedic pastoral opera in the recently completed theater of the Palazzo Barberini.⁹³ Nor is there any mention of his rapturous enthrallment upon hearing the celebrated soprano Leonora Baroni. For these details we must turn to his Latin letter to Lucas Holstenius (*Epistola Familiaris* 9) dated 29 March 1639, but published only toward the end of his life (1674),⁹⁴ and his three Latin epigrams addressed to Leonora.⁹⁵ Among Milton's other known contacts in Rome were the talented poet and academician Giovanni Salzilli, who presented him with a "written Encomium"⁹⁶ in Latin,⁹⁷ in response to which Milton composed *Ad Salsillum*;⁹⁸ the English Benedictine David Codner (he passed himself off as a native Italian under the alias Matteo Selvaggio),⁹⁹

---

⁹⁰ *A die 30. pransi s[un]t in Coll[egio] nostro D[ominus] Ill[ustrissi]m[u]s N[oster] Cary, frater Baronis de Faukeland. Doctor Holdingus Lancastrensis, D[ominus] N[oster] Fortescuto, et D[omi]n[u]s Miltonus cum famulo nobiles Angli. et excepti s[un]t Laute* (English College, Rome: Pilgrim Book: Entry for 20/30 October 1638) ("On the 30 (October) there dined in our College the most illustrious Lord Carey, brother of Baron Falkland, Dr Holding of Lancaster, Lord Fontescue, and Mr Milton with his servant, distinguished Englishmen, and they were sumptuously received"). See Leo Miller, "Milton Dines at the Jesuit College: Reconstructing the Evening of October 30, 1638," *MQ* 13 (1979): 142–146, at 142. Cf. Chaney, *The Grand Tour*, 245, 282–284.

⁹¹ Miller, "Milton Dines at the Jesuit College," 143–144.

⁹² See 143–146, 150–153.

⁹³ See 154–166.

⁹⁴ *Epistolarum Familiarium Liber Unus*, 25–28. See Appendix 1.3, *Epistolarum Familiarum Liber Unus*, ed. Haan, 140–163. For further discussion of this key letter, see Chapter 3.

⁹⁵ *Ioannis Miltoni Londinensis Poemata*, in *Poems of Mr. John Milton, Both English and Latin* (1645), 42–43. See Appendix 1.1(a)–1(c), and, for further discussion, Chapter 2.

⁹⁶ The phrase is Milton's. See *The Reason of Church-Government*, 37: "But much latelier in the privat Academies of Italy ... other things which I had shifted in scarsity of books and conveniences to patch up amongst them, were receiv'd with written Encomiums, which the Italian is not forward to bestow on men of this side the Alps."

⁹⁷ Milton, *Poemata*, 4. For further discussion, see Chapter 1.

⁹⁸ Milton, *Poemata*, 70–72. See Appendix 1.2, and, for further discussion, Chapter 1.

who likewise composed a Latin tribute in Milton's honor;[100] Alessandro Cherubini, a young literary protégé;[101] and two further possibilities: the acclaimed musicologist Giovanni Battista Doni,[102] who was in Rome during the period of Milton's second sojourn in the city,[103] and of whom Milton made mention while in Italy;[104] and Thomas Gawen, who, when in Rome, according to Anthony à Wood, "accidentally sometimes fell into the company of John Milton the Antimonarchist."[105] But there are other very significant silences. Whereas there is independent evidence of Milton's active (indeed proactive) participation in at least two Florentine academies: the Accademia degli Svogliati[106] and the Accademia degli

---

[99] The identification was made by Edward Chaney in *The Grand Tour*, 244–251. See also David Lunn, *The English Benedictines, 1540–1688* (London: Barnes & Noble, 1980), 123–124, 152–153, 157–158. It would seem to be the case that Codner's fluency in Italian enabled him to achieve the deception. Whether or not Milton was aware of Selvaggio's English nationality is uncertain, but Codner had close links with the family of Jane Savage, Marchioness of Winchester, whose death was the subject of Milton's "An Epitaph on the Marchioness of Winchester" (1631).

[100] Codner's encomium sees Milton as equaling both Homer and Virgil. See *Poemata*, 4: *Graecia Maeonidem, iactet sibi Roma Maronem,/Anglia Miltonum iactat utrique parem* ("Let Greece boast of Homer, let Rome boast of Virgil; England boasts of Milton equal to both"), and Lewalski and Haan, 108–109, 416.

[101] See 140–141.

[102] On Doni, see Louise Schleiner, "Milton, G. B. Doni, and the dating of Doni's works," *MQ* 16 (1982): 36–42; Gianfranco Formichetti, "Doni, Giovanni Battista," *DBI* 41 (1992): 167–170.

[103] See Schleiner, "Milton, G. B. Doni," 38, 42.

[104] See *Epistola Familiaris* 9 at Appendix 1.3.40–42, and *Epistolarum Familiarium Liber Unus*, ed. Haan, 148–149, 162. See also 125–129.

[105] Anthony à Wood, *Athenae Oxonienses*, ed. Philip Bliss, 4 vols (London: Rivington *et al*, 1813–1820), IV, 130. For further discussion, see Allan Pritchard, "Milton in Rome: According to Wood," *MQ* 14 (1980): 92–97.

[106] The evidence is provided by the academy's minute book, which records Milton's performance of his Latin verse in the Svogliati on at least three occasions. Most notable perhaps is the minute of 6/16 September 1638, which is of interest on a number of counts: first, it singles out "particolarmente" ("in particular") "il Giovanni Miltone Inglese" ("John Milton Englishman"); second, it makes a qualitative judgment about his performance: his reading of "una poesia Latina di versi esametri multo erudita" ("a very erudite Latin poem of hexameter verses") (Biblioteca Nazionale Centrale, Florence, MSS Magliabecchiana, MSS. Cl. IX, cod. 60, f. 48ʳ). Close scrutiny of the academy's minute book indicates that this highlighting of uniqueness, nationality, and erudition in an individual performance is quite unparalleled. See Estelle Haan, *Both English and Latin: Bilingualism and Biculturalism in Milton's Neo-Latin Writings* (Philadelphia: American Philosophical Society, 2012), 97–98. Likewise, the minutes of 7/17 March and 14/24 March 1639

Apatisti,[107] his involvement in the Roman Accademia dei Fantastici and/or the Accademia degli Umoristi remains unattested, despite the incontrovertible fact that he had clear links with members of these academies, and the likelihood that he participated in both institutions.[108]

Certainly the magnetism of Rome in the late 1630s shines through Totti's *Ritratto*. The modern city had much to offer the foreign visitor in terms of architectural and artistic splendor, religious ceremony, carnival festivities, musical concerts, and academic culture. And Catholic Rome was visible everywhere. During the months of Milton's first sojourn (October/November 1638) the city's many churches afforded the opportunity to hear exceptional liturgical music, especially for the Eve of All Saints (31 October) and All Souls Day (1 November).[109] And it was surely impossible not to be impressed by the magnificent Basilica of St Peter's, recently consecrated by Urban VIII in 1636. Totti's contemporary account is insightful in its unabashed showcasing of the building as a superlative modern achievement in terms of its majesty and grandeur, its structure pertaining either to Angels on account of its beauty or to Giants on account of its vastness.[110] Not even the Greeks, the Egyptians, the

---

(*ibid.*, ff. 52^r–52^v) include Milton among those who read "alcuni nobili versi Latini" ("some noble Latin verses") and "diverse poesie Latine" ("various Latin poems"), respectively. Both the performance and the performer left an impression. Or as the speaker of *Epitaphium Damonis* would later put it: *Ipse etiam tentare ausus sum, nec puto multum/Displicui* (133–134) ("I even dared to offer my own attempts, and I don't think I greatly displeased"). In the course of his first Florentine sojourn Milton corresponded with the Svogliati academician Benedetto Buonmattei. See *Epistola Familiaris* 8, dated 10 September 1638, in *Epistolarum Familiarium Liber Unus*, ed. Haan, 116–139. On Buonmattei, see A. M. Cinquemani, *Glad To Go For A Feast: Milton, Buonmattei, and the Florentine Accademici* (New York: Peter Lang, 1998); Haan, *Bilingualism and Biculturalism*, 104–118.

[107] As first noted by Haan, *From Academia to Amicitia*, 36. Evidence is provided by a manuscript of Anton Francesco Gori (1692-1757). See Florence: Biblioteca Marucelliana MS A.36, ff. 11^r–142^v, transcribed by Allessandro Lazzeri, *Intellettuali e Consenso nella Toscana del Seicento: L'Accademia degli Apatisti* (Milan: A. Giuffrè, 1983), 57–121. At f. 53^r, under a list of the academy's membership in 1638, there occurs "Giovanni Milton inglese" ("John Milton, Englishman").

[108] See Chapters 1 and 2.

[109] See Margaret Byard, "'Adventrous Song': Milton and the Music of Rome," in *Milton in Italy*, ed. Di Cesare, 305–328, at 305.

[110] Totti, *Ritratto di Roma Moderna*, 7: "Quanto alla Maesta, e grandezza, non può chiunque riguarda il nuovo Tempio non confessare ... che o fattura degli Angeli, lo chiamarono per la bellezza; o veramente opera lo credettero de' Giganti, per la vastità" ("As for its majesty and grandeur, no one who beholds the new Church cannot but confess ... that they should call the workmanship that of Angels on account of its

Jews, or the most powerful Romans themselves, he claims, were able to approximate this edifice's excellence and vastness.[111] In Totti's view, even the great Pantheon pales into insignificance by comparison.[112] Such superlative language likewise characterizes the account provided by John Evelyn, who "went to visite St. Pietro, that most stupendious and incomparable Basilicam, far surpassing any now extant in the World, and perhapps (Solomons Temple excepted) any that was ever built."[113] By contrast, Milton, when mentioning his visit to the Vatican (probably in February 1639),[114] maintains a frustrating silence about its impressive architecture. Despite, or perhaps because of, this, scholars have not hesitated to see echoes of St Peter's in his later writings. Thus Rebecca Smith, in a seminal article, presented the case for St Peter's as the "source" of the vividly described Pandaemonium (*Paradise Lost* 1.670–798), drawing attention to such shared features as the pilasters, the carved roof, gilding, the brazen doors, and adjacent council chamber, and viewing the bee simile (1.768–776) as evocative of the *impresa* ("emblem") of Urban VIII.[115] Although Smith's argument initially met with something of a mixed critical reception,[116] it has generally won favor

---

beauty; or that they should truly believe it the work of Giants on account of its vastness").

[111] Totti, *Ritratto di Roma Moderna*, 7: "non havendo mai, non dico i Greci, gli Egittii, o gli Hebrei; ma gli stessi potentissimi Romani arrivato in alcuna lor fabrica all' eccellenza, e vastità di questa" ("Never has any race, I mean not only the Greeks, the Egyptians or the Jews, but the most powerful Romans themselves, approximated in any of their building-work the excellence and the vastness of this").

[112] Totti, *Ritratto di Roma Moderna*, 7: "Argomento ne sia, che il gran Panteone, uno de' maggiori sforzi dell'arte, e potenza Romana, non sarebbe ad una picciola sua parte comparabile" ("It is arguable that the mighty Pantheon, one of the greatest efforts of Roman art and power, would not be in the least degree comparable").

[113] John Evelyn, *Diary*, ed. De Beer, II, 255. Evelyn visited the Vatican in November 1644.

[114] See *Epistola Familiaris* 9, at Appendix 1.3.5–16. See also 143–146,

[115] Rebecca W. Smith, "The Source of Milton's Pandaemonium," *MP* 29 (1931): 187–198.

[116] See Margaret Byard, "Note on the Illustration: St. Peter's and Pandaemonium?" *MQ* 9 (1975): 65–66, at 65. Byard drew attention to an engraving of a painting by Giuseppe Tiburzio Vergelli (commemorating the canonization of five saints in 1690), arguing for similarities between the essentially diminutive depiction of the thousands present and Milton's "smallest dwarfs," and observing the presence of the Barberini bee *impresa* "on the 'hangings' of the baldacchino and on the bases of its Solomonic columns." The engraving discussed and reproduced by Byard is that published by Matteo Gregorio Rossi from the print collection of the Metropolitan Museum of Art, New York (Harris Brisbane Dick Fund, 1953). Likewise Marjorie Nicolson described

with Milton scholars,[117] with Maarten Delbeke recently taking the case even further in his argument that some of the key features of Pandaemonium (its metal work, its implied association with warfare,[118] novelty, compositeness, and problematic proportionality, especially vis-à-vis the vast surrounding space) can be traced back more precisely to the Baldacchino (the large, sculpted bronze canopy) over the Basilica's high altar.[119] In all of this, however, the literary critic and art historian must tread a careful path in an attempt to avoid the charge of presenting an argument from silence. On the one hand, it seems difficult to imagine Milton replicating such precise details some three decades after seeing them. On the other, Alastair Fowler's comment that "M[ilton] would hardly satirize those who had received him kindly"[120] seems all too

---

the parallels between the two edifices as "striking," especially the existence of an adjacent building, confidently declaring that the council chamber entered by Satan, Beelzebub, and the other more important angels "is obviously the Vatican." See M. H. Nicolson, *John Milton: A Reader's Guide to his Poetry* (London: Thames and Hudson, 1964), 196–198, at 198. On the other hand, Roland Frye pointed out a number of architectural discrepancies between Pandaemonium and St Peter's: (i) its "roof" and that of St Peter's, which, he observes, was "not even bronzed"; (ii) its Doric order, as opposed to the Corinthian order of St Peter's; (iii) its golden architrave, which is missing from St. Peter's; (iv) its "wide porches" in contrast to St Peter's, which, as seen by Milton, had "only one conceivable porch." See Roland Mushat Frye, *Milton's Imagery and the Visual Arts: Iconographic Tradition in the Epic Poems* (Princeton, NJ: Princeton University Press, 1978), 134–135. Frye's argument that Pandaemonium was more of an amalgam of differing styles and discordant architecture, "a promiscuous architectural monstrosity" (135), was likewise assumed by Amy Lee Turner in "Arts and Design: Milton and the," in *A Milton Encyclopedia*, ed. William B. Hunter et al. (Lewisburg, PA: Bucknell University Press, 1978), I, 90–102. William A. McClung, on the other hand, while offering a careful overview of the arguments to date, and presenting a convincing rebuttal of Frye's critical stance, could only admit that "neither the case against St. Peter's, nor the architectural model that is suggested, will stand up to close examination." See William A. McClung, "The Architecture of Pandaemonium," *MQ* 15 (1981): 109–112, at 109.

[117] See, for example, John N. King, *Milton and Religious Controversy: Satire and Polemic in Paradise Lost* (Cambridge: Cambridge University Press, 2000), 58: "The baroque architecture of Pandaemonium refers in some sense to the reconstruction of St. Peter's Basilica, which incorporated 'pilasters,' 'pillars,' 'architrave,' and 'frieze' (1.713–16) even in the incomplete state witnessed by Milton when he visited Rome."

[118] For an insightful discussion of the militaristic language, see James A. Freeman, *Milton and the Martial Muse: Paradise Lost and European Traditions of War* (Princeton, NJ: Princeton University Press, 1980), 86–89.

[119] See Maarten Delbeke, "An Unstable Sublime: Milton's Pandemonium and the Baldacchino at St. Peter's in Rome," *Lias* 43 (2016): 281–296.

[120] *Paradise Lost*, ed. Fowler, 104.

simplistic. Indeed it could be argued that the Pandaemonium as St Peter's analogy assumes a quite comfortable place when read in the context, and perhaps as the culmination, of the parodic Italian journey undertaken by the Satan of *Paradise Lost* 1. In many respects Satan is a misguided foreign traveler, whose convoluted and essentially confused itinerary can be mapped, at least implicitly, from the Neapolitan Phlegraean Fields,[121] to Valdarno and Fiesole on the outskirts of Florence,[122] to the Tuscan Vallombrosa,[123] and then to Rome itself, and an infernal council whose constitution and method of debate seem to offer a grim parody of Italian academic practice in general.[124] Perhaps Milton's literary construction of Pandaemonium is best regarded as the product of memory and a wealth of literary sources garnered in the course of, and subsequent to, his Italian journey. And even here it is not the case of one single identifiable architectural "source." After all, the etymology of his newly coined word "Pandaemonium" (from the Greek παν ["all"] and δαιμόνιον ["evil"]), now Latinized as *daemonium*,[125] surely suggests a linguistic perversion of "Pantheon" (from the Greek παν ["all"] and θεός ["god"]), its demonic occupants a bathetic parody of the statues of Roman deities that once

---

[121] For the argument that the "burning lake" of Hell (*Paradise Lost* 1. 210) and its fiery shores are evocative of the sulphuric landscape of the Phlegraean Fields, see M. H. Nicolson, "Milton's Hell and the Phlegraean Fields," *UTQ* 7 (1938): 500–513.

[122] Satan's shield is compared to the moon, as viewed through Galileo's telescope from the hills of Fiesole, at *Paradise Lost* 1. 284–291: "his ponderous shield/Ethereal temper, massy, large and round,/Behind him cast; the broad circumference/Hung on his shoulders like the moon, whose orb/Through optic glass the Tuscan artist views/At evening from the top of Fesole,/Or in Valdarno, to descry new lands,/Rivers or mountains in her spotty globe." See Neil Harris, "Galileo as Symbol: The 'Tuscan Artist' in *Paradise Lost*," *Annali dell' Istituto e Museo di Storio della Scienza di Firenze* 10 (1985): 3–29.

[123] As Satan stands alongside the burning lake, he issues a summons to a crew that is equated with fallen autumn leaves strewing the brooks in Vallombrosa. See *Paradise Lost* 1.299-304: "till on the Beach/Of that inflamèd sea, he stood and called/His legions, angel forms, who lay entranced/Thick as autumnal leaves that strew the brooks/In Vallombrosa, where the Etrurian shades/High overarched embower." For various interpretations of the simile and its Tuscan context, see John R. Mulder, "Shades and Substance," in *Milton in Italy*, ed. Di Cesare, 61–69; Neil Harris, "The Vallombrosa Simile and the Image of the Poet in *Paradise Lost*," in *ibid.*, 71–94; Charles A. Huttar, "Vallombrosa Revisited," in *ibid.*, 95–111; Edward Chaney, "The Visit to Vallombrosa: A Literary Tradition," in *ibid.*, 113–146.

[124] See A. K. Nardo, "Academic Interludes in *Paradise Lost*," *MS* 27 (1991): 209–241.

[125] Cf. *OLD*, s.v. "*daemonium* ... Also *ion* [Gk δαιμόνιον] The indwelling spirit or genius claimed by Socrates; a familiar." Cf. Apuleius, *Apol.* 27, and 63.

graced the ancient building.¹²⁶ In essence then, Milton's Pandaemonium is more accurately describable as an unnatural synthesis of *Roma antica* and *Roma moderna*. Something similar may be at play in *Paradise Regained*. Thus when the magnificence of the "Imperial City" (4. 33), namely, "great and glorious Rome" (4.45), with all its architectural splendor, is ironically conveyed by none other than Satan himself,¹²⁷ the satire may also be targeted at aspects of the modern city: St Peter's, the Mass, and Catholic prelates and bishops.¹²⁸ Christ can only denounce the luxury characteristic of Romans, who, in sharp contrast to their "Frugal, and mild, and temperate" (4.134) ancestors are now depicted as "degenerate, by themselves enslav'd" (4.144). Nonetheless, the artistic and cultural attractiveness of *Roma moderna* was undeniable. The Vatican had some breathtaking treasures: the Sistine Chapel, the Creation cycle in the Loggia, and the Raphael fresco cycles in the papal suite, not least those in the Stanza della Segnatura, which, as Mindele Treip has eloquently argued, may well have played their part in the formulation of Urania in *Paradise Lost*.¹²⁹ Once again, however, a cautionary note must be struck in that the Miltonic Urania, as scholars have debated at length, may owe no small debt to interpretations of the Holy Spirit that range from the Bible to the Church Fathers and to the neo-Latin poetry of Marco Girolamo Vida.¹³⁰

---

¹²⁶ See Dio Cassius, *History of Rome*, 58.27.2-3: "He [Agrippa] also completed the building which is called the Pantheon. It is perhaps given this name because, among the statues which are set up in it are images of many gods, including one of Ares and one of Aphrodite, or, as I believe, it may be so called because, being round and domed, it resembles the heavens." Translation is that of J.J. Pollitt, in *The Art of Rome c. 753 B.C–A.D. 337: Sources and Documents* (Cambridge: Cambridge University Press, 1983), 106. For further discussion, see William L. MacDonald, *The Pantheon: Design, Meaning, and Progeny* (London: Penguin Books, 1976), especially 76–77.

¹²⁷ *Paradise Regained* 4.25–89. Quotations are from *The Complete Works of John Milton: Volume II: The 1671 Poems: Paradise Regain'd and Samson Agonistes*, ed. Laura Lunger Knoppers (Oxford: Oxford University Press, 2008). See Revard, "Milton and Classical Rome."

¹²⁸ See Barbara K. Lewalski, *Milton's Brief Epic: The Genre, Meaning, and Art of Paradise Regained* (Providence, RI: Brown University Press/Methuen, 1966), 274–280; Laura Lunger Knoppers, "Satan and the Papacy in *Paradise Regained*," *MS* 42 (2002): 68–85.

¹²⁹ See Mindele Anne Treip, *"Descend from Heav'n Urania": Milton's Paradise Lost and Raphael's Cycle in the Stanza della Segnatura* (Victoria: University of Victoria, 1985).

¹³⁰ See, among others, William B. Hunter, "Milton's Urania," *SEL* 4 (1964): 35–42; Margaret Byard, "Divine Wisdom—Urania," *MQ* 12 (1978): 134–137; Stevie Davies and William B. Hunter, "Milton's Urania: 'The Meaning Not the Name I Call,'" *SEL* 28 (1988): 95–111, reprinted in William B. Hunter, *The Descent of Urania: Studies in*

What is beyond doubt is the fact that Rome came to life during the Carnival Season (January/February). This offered the newcomer to the city the opportunity to observe ceremonial processions and dramatic productions, all marked by their sheer spectacle. Here opera played an important role.[131] The Carnival of February 1639, which coincided with Milton's second sojourn, proved no exception. And there was a fresh sense of excitement in the air. Urban VIII had at last begun to recover from an illness contracted some two years previously.[132] As Margaret Murata remarks, "[t]he 1638-9 winter season was extraordinarily rich for musical drama."[133] These included a sacred opera (*San Bonifatio*), a Quarantore (Forty-Hours' devotion),[134] and, not least, a comedic opera, *Chi Soffre Speri*, which was lavishly put on by Cardinal Antonio Barberini on 17/27 February 1639 to inaugurate the recently completed theater contiguous to the Palazzo Barberini at the Quattro Fontane.[135] This performance lasted no fewer than five hours, and included splendid special effects such as the recreation of a spectacular thunder-storm, and a

---

Milton, 1946–1988 (Lewisburg PA: Bucknell University Press, 1989), 31–45; Estelle Haan, "From Helicon to Heaven"; Matthew K. Dolloff, *Mediating the Muse: Milton and the Metamorphoses of Urania* (University of Texas, 2006).

[131] See George J. Buelow, *A History of Baroque Music* (Bloomington: Indiana University Press, 2004), 38: "It was especially during the reign of Cardinal Matteo Barberini as Pope ... (1622–1644) ... that eight operas were composed for Barberini performances up to 1644, all to librettos by the Roman prelate Giulio Rospigliosi (later Pope Clement IX)."

[132] On 12 February 1639 the seventy-one year old Urban VIII told Cardinal Federico Corner that, despite the weight of his years, he was on the whole quite well, a fact attested by the new Venetian envoy. See Cardinal Corner to the Senate, 12 February 1639 (Rome), quoted in Ludwig Pastor, *The History of the Popes*, trans. Dom Ernest Graf, 40 vols (London: Kegan Paul, 1923–1953), XXIX, 401–402. See also Susan Gail Lewis, *"Chi Soffre Speri" and the Influence of the "Commedia dell' Arte" on the Development of Roman Opera* (M. Mus. Thesis: University of Arizona, 1995), 78.

[133] Margaret Murata, "Why the First Opera Given in Paris Wasn't Roman," *Cambridge Opera Journal* 7 (1995): 87–105, at 93.

[134] See Margaret Murata, *Operas For The Papal Court 1631–1668* (Ann Arbor, MI: UMI Research Press, 1981), 32–35, 204–207, 258–262; Frederick Hammond, "Girolamo Frescobaldi and a Decade of Music in Casa Barberini: 1634–1643," *Analecta Musicologica* 19 (1980): 94–124; M. A. Lavin, *Seventeenth-Century Barberini Documents and Inventories of Art* (New York: New York University Press, 1975), 58–60.

[135] For a description of the theater, its construction, and likely dimensions, see Patricia Waddy, *Seventeenth-Century Roman Palaces: Use and the Art of the Plan* (New York: The Architectural History Foundation: Cambridge MA and London: The Mit Press, 1990), 246–248; Frederick Hammond, *Music and Spectacle in Baroque Rome* (New Haven: Yale University Press, 1994), 14.

magnificent "Fair of Farfa" composed especially for the production.¹³⁶ That this was ἀκρόαμα illud musicum ("that musical entertainment") attended by Milton and briefly alluded to in *Epistola Familiaris* 9¹³⁷ is highly likely.¹³⁸ What is clearly apparent is the fact that Milton was moving in culturally erudite circles, and perhaps more. As if temporarily sloughing any sense of religious alterity, he seemed to rejoice in his physical presence in *Roma moderna*.

Coelum non animum muto, dum trans mare curro ("I change the climate, not my mind, while I race across the sea") wrote the homeward-bound Milton in the autograph book of Camillo Cardoini at Geneva on 10 June 1639.¹³⁹ The inscription, preceded by the closing lines of *A Mask*, adapts a verse by Horace.¹⁴⁰ The phrase, Campbell and Corns believe, may affirm Milton's "unwavering Protestantism,"¹⁴¹ now inscribed in a Calvinist hub. Likewise, Catherine Martin reads this "Horatian signature" as one to which Milton "while abroad ... remained basically true."¹⁴² But that this was an *animus* that could, and did, acclimatize to religious and cultural difference is suggested by, *inter alia*, the depiction of Rome in Milton's Latin writings composed in the course of his Italian journey. These amount to the aforementioned *Ad Salsillum*, the three Latin epigrams in praise of the soprano Leonora Baroni singing in Rome, and the Latin letter to Lucas Holstenius.

The present study, through close examination of what constitutes in effect a miniature neo-Latin corpus in its own right, aims to shed new light on Milton's relationship with Rome and her inhabitants in the late 1630s in an attempt to assess the impact of the modern city and its vibrant culture upon the then-sighted poet. That impact, it argues, manifests itself

---

[136] For further discussion, see 162–164.

[137] See Appendix 1.3.19–20.

[138] See 146–147, 154–166.

[139] The autograph book is now held in the Houghton Library in Harvard (MS Sumner 84).

[140] "if Vertue feeble were,/Heav'n it self would stoop to her" (*A Mask* 1022–1023). Unless otherwise stated, quotations from Milton's shorter poems are from Lewalski and Haan. Cf. Horace, *Epistles* 1.11.27: *caelum non animum mutant qui trans mare currunt* ("Those who race across the sea change their climate, not their mind"). Text is that of *Q[uinti] Horati Flacci Opera*, ed. E. C. Wickham (Oxford: Clarendon Press, 1957).

[141] Gordon Campbell and Thomas N. Corns, *John Milton: Life, Work, and Thought*, (Oxford: Oxford University Press, 2008), 126.

[142] Catherine Gimelli Martin, *Milton's Italy: Anglo-Italian Literature, Travel, and Religion in Seventeenth-Century England* (New York: Routledge, 2017), 52.

in Milton's self-fashioning, while upon Italian soil, as one who was hospitably embraced by Rome's academic, literary, and musical communities. It is here that we can trace his networking with distinguished humanists (upon whom he left no slight an impression), and ascertain something of his seemingly perennial interest in their literary pursuits, whether in printed or in manuscript form. We learn, too, of his captivation by the singing of the city's foremost soprano, of his participation in a literary vogue in her honor, and of his attendance at an opera, put on, as he describes it, *magnificentia vere Romana*[143] ("with truly Roman magnificence"), where English Protestant and Catholic Cardinal warmly shake hands. Not least, we read of Milton's attested presence in the hub of Catholicism, the Vatican, and his language is fulsome, even excited. Perhaps continental travel and the physical encounter with the symbols, personages, and institutions of the other engendered in the Milton of the Italian journey a tolerance,[144] or, more accurately, the manipulation of a seeming tolerance to serve poetic and cultural ends.[145]

---

[143] See *Epistola Familiaris* 9, at Appendix 1.3.19–20, and, for further discussion, *Epistolarum Familiarium Liber Unus and Uncollected Letters*, ed. Haan, 158–159.

[144] See, among others, John Coffey, *Persecution and Toleration in Protestant England, 1558–1689* (Harlow: Longman, 2000); Alexandra Walsham, *Charitable Hatred: Tolerance and Intolerance in England, 1500–1700* (Manchester: Manchester University Press, 2006); *Milton and Toleration*, ed. Achinstein and Sauer, passim.

[145] See Estelle Haan, "'Coelum Non Animum Muto'? Milton's Neo-Latin Poetry and Catholic Italy," in *Milton and Catholicism*, eds. Ronald Corthell and Thomas N. Corns (Notre Dame, IN: University of Notre Dame Press, 2017), 131–167.

Chapter 1

Milton, Giovanni Salzilli, and the Academies of Rome

It was probably in the course of Milton's first visit to Rome that he composed *Ad Salsillum Poetam Romanum Aegrotantem*.[1] This is suggested by its positioning in the 1645 *Poemata* (where it precedes *Mansus*, which pertains to his Neapolitan sojourn), and by its description of Milton's arrival in Italy in language suggesting that it was a relatively recent event: *diebus hisce* (10) ("in these days"). In regard to the poem's addressee, Giovanni Salzilli, biographical information has hitherto proved difficult to unearth. Although Parker's description of him as a "person, who has long since been forgotten"[2] has been offset, at least to some degree, by the investigations of James Freeman in 1984,[3] and by my own chapter in 1998,[4] now, over two decades later, time seems ripe for a reappraisal of Salzilli's academic standing in seicento Rome, of his talents as an Italian poet, and of the possible contexts in which Milton made his acquaintance.

What we know for certain is that just one year prior to Milton's visit no fewer than fifteen Italian poems by Salzilli (11 sonnets, 3 canzoni, and 1 ottavo) had seen publication in the *Poesie de' Signori Accademici Fantastici di Roma*,[5] thereby attesting to his membership of that academy, further discussed in the text that follows.[6] Freeman, following Masson, is undoubtedly correct in his supposition that since Salzilli's contribution amounts to some eleven percent of the volume as a

---

[1] See *Poemata*, 70–72; Lewalski and Haan, 202–205, 478–481. For Latin text and English translation, see Appendix 1.2.

[2] W. R., Parker, *Milton: A Biography* (Oxford: Oxford University Press, 1968; revised ed., Gordon Campbell, 1996), I, 173.

[3] James A. Freeman, "Milton's Roman Connection: Giovanni Salzilli," *MS* 19 (1984): 87–104.

[4] Haan, *From Academia to Amicitia*, 81–98.

[5] *Poesie de' Signori Accademici Fantastici di Roma* (Rome: Grignano, 1637), 148–169.

[6] See 41–46.

whole, he was a highly regarded poet.[7] In fact, his total input to the *Poesie*, the Fantastici's first public showcasing in print, far exceeds the average number of poems (typically four) per contributor, and is surpassed in terms of quantity by only three of the other fifty authors.[8] Masson conjectured that, given his absence from the *Apes Romanae* (1631–1632), a list of some 450 writers, whose work was published in Rome in those years, Salzilli was probably a young man at the time of Milton's visit.[9] This, one might add, is implied perhaps by *Ad Salsillum* itself, in which Milton informs his addressee that the motivating factor behind his Italian journey was his wish to behold the talented youth of that country: *Visum …/Virosque doctaeque indolem <u>iuventutis</u>* (15–16)[10] ("to see … the men and excellence of [Italy's] learned *youth*"). Irrespective of his age, this academician, it emerges, was suffering from an illness at the time of the poem's composition. This is denoted by *aegrotantem* in the title, and lines 19–20 of the poem proper. Although the precise nature of that illness remains unknown, the terms in which Milton describes the affliction, albeit couched in rhetorical hyperbole, suggest that it was far from a minor ailment. According to Milton, Salzilli's infection, if such it is, is deep-rooted and has spread to his kidneys.[11] And when Phoebus is invoked as the *morborum terror* (24) ("terror of diseases"), one senses that the *morbus* in question should not be underestimated. Not entirely surprising, therefore, were Masson's speculations that Salzilli was "habitually an invalid,"[12] and that perhaps "the reason why we hear so little of him afterwards was that he died early."[13] These, however, can now be countered in a number of ways.

---

[7] See Freeman, "Milton's Roman Connection," 97. Cf. Masson, *Life*, I, 754: "it is reasonable to suppose that he was an important personage among the Fantastics."

[8] Giovan Martino Longo (30 poems), Martino Lunghi (17 poems), and Tiberio Ceuli (23 poems).

[9] Masson, *Life*, I, 754.

[10] Emphasis is mine. *Iuventus* (16) ("youth") may even punningly embrace "Giovanni" (the "young") Salzilli himself. Cf. also the reference to Hebe, goddess of youth (23).

[11] *Cui nunc profunda bilis infestat renes,/Praecordiisque fixa damnosum spirat* (*Ad Salsillum* 19–20) ("An overflow of bile is presently assailing your kidneys, and, implanted in the depths of your stomach, is breathing its deadly breath").

[12] *The Poetical Works of John Milton*, ed. David Masson, 3 vols (London: Macmillan, 1874), II, 367.

[13] Masson, *Life*, I, 754.

1.1 *Ioannes Salsillus Poeta Romanus*

Hitherto scholars have cited as proof of Salzilli's survival of his illness just one documentary source, a letter, dated 4 April 1644, by Tommaso Stigliani (1573–1651).[14] Thus Freeman, without discussing the letter in question, states that this is the only information we have in addition to that provided by *Ad Salsillum* and by Salzilli's fifteen Italian poems.[15] Close examination of the actual epistle affords a number of insights into Salzilli's literary activities and whereabouts—at least for that month and year. We learn that he is in Trevico, a town in the province of Avellino, Campania, southern Italy, and hence some 155 miles from Rome. We also discover his links with nobility in that he has been endeavoring to commission on behalf of an unnamed Duchess ("Signora Duchessa") a composition by Stigliani himself. Salzilli, however, is unsuccessful in his attempt, for the whole constitutes a forthright letter of refusal, its author citing several (rather too many) excuses for his disinclination to comply: "Ma le composizioni ... non sono opera della volontà, ma dell' intelletto" ("But compositions ... are the work not of the will, but of the intellect").[16] To this he adds the rejoinder that he is an old man (which may imply that Salzilli, even in 1644, is comparatively young), tired and weary of composing, and more inclined to hurl an iron javelin than to handle a pen.[17] One detects here a sense of eventual embitterment on the part of a septuagenarian poet and academician, writing with atypical candor from his home town of Modena, and reflecting perhaps upon a life that was not uncontroversial, at least in terms of his intellectual pursuits and their repercussions. Although he had seen the publication of several works, including his pastoral poem *Polifemo* (1600), his *Canzoniere* (1605), and, not least, his masterful *Il Mondo Nuovo* (1628), on Christopher Columbus,[18] Stigliani seems to have been dogged by

---

[14] *Lettere del Cavaliere Fra Tomaso Stigliani* (Rome: Angelo Bernabo, 1664), 248–250. See Freeman, "Milton's Roman Connection," 97; Haan, *From Academia to Amicitia*, 83, 91–92; Luigi Fassò, "Stigliani, Tommaso," in *Enciclopedia Italiana di Scienze, Lettere ed Arti* 32 (Rome: Istituto dell' Enciclopedia Italiana, 1936).

[15] Freeman, "Milton's Roman Connection," 97.

[16] Stigliani, *Lettere*, 249.

[17] Stigliani, *Lettere*, 249: "Io son vecchio, ed in tal guisa stracco oramai, ed istufo di comporre, che quasi più volentieri m'indurrei à lanciare il pal di ferro, ch'a maneggiar la penna da scrivere" ("I am old, and to such a degree am I exhausted and tired of composing that I would almost more willingly throw the iron javelin than handle the quill for writing").

[18] See, among others, Mary Alexandra Watt, *Dante, Columbus and the Prophetic Tradition: Spiritual Imperialism in the Italian Imagination* (Oxford: Routledge, 2017), 11, who regards Stigliani's *Il Mondo Nuovo* as both "embrac[ing] the

misfortune wherever he went.[19] Most notable, perhaps, his vitriolic criticism of Giambattista Marino (in *Il Mondo Nuovo*) had not only provoked ill feeling between the two poets (with Marino attempting to prevent the poem's publication and thereafter to suppress copies), but had resulted in the collective anger of Marinists, which had forced Stigliani into a literary exile of sorts.[20] Indeed, even Salzilli does not seem to have escaped his censure, albeit not in print. This is attested by an autographed copy of *Il Mondo Nuovo* extant in the Biblioteca Nazionale Vittorio Emanuele, Rome, which contains marginalia attacking both Salzilli and a certain Falcidio, the latter most likely a pseudonym.[21] Nonetheless, the present letter indicates that they had previously enjoyed some form of epistolary correspondence: Stigliani is careful to apologize for his long silence ("il lungo silenzio")[22] in writing, excusing his leisure by quoting a verse from Horace's *Ars Poetica* with a colloquial ease that intimates a shared understanding that his addressee will readily pick up the reference.[23]

To this scant information can now be added some further and hitherto unnoticed biographical material. This is provided by a range of documentary sources, which serve to shed fresh light on Salzilli's age, his

---

Dantesque Columbus," and depicting him "as a new Aeneas expanding Roman dominion, and a new Paul, bringing Christianity to the gentiles."

[19] For example, as early as 1606, Stigliani, while a member of the Accademia degli Innominati in Parma, had become involved in a literary dispute with Enrico Caterino Davila, which led to a violent altercation, during which Davila struck him with his sword. See Girolamo Tiraboschi, *Storia della Letteratura Italiana*, 13 vols (Modena: Società Tipografica, 1772–1782), VIII, 270.

[20] Regarded as the archetypical anti-Marinist, Sigliani was forced to seek refuge in Rome, where he gained the protection of Virginio Cesarini, Scipio Borghese and, in his final years, Pompeo Colonna.

[21] Biblioteca Nazionale Vittorio Emanuele, MS 71.2.A.13. See Mario Menghini, *Tommaso Stigliani: Contributo all Storia Letteraria del Secolo XVII* (Modena: Sarasino, 1890), 128.

[22] Stigliani, *Lettere*, 248.

[23] Stigliani, *Lettere*, 249: "Così faccio io coi meie, e così ho caro che quegli facciano con me, dicendo con Orazio. *Hanc veniam petimusque, damusque vicissim*" ("Thus do I behave with my own companions, and thus do I hold dear the fact that they behave in accordance with me, saying, with Horace, 'This license do we both claim and grant in turn'"). Cf. Horace, *Ars Poetica* 11. It is interesting to note that the Horatian verse quoted by Stigliani is that which immediately follows the lines (*pictoribus atque poetis,/quidlibet audendi semper fuit aequa potestas* [*Ars Poetica* 9–10] ["painters and poets have always possessed the equal license to venture anything"]), which provided the motto (*quidlibet audendi*) for the Roman Accademia dei Fantastici, of which Salzilli was a member. See 61.

poetic output and, especially, his many and varied roles in a Roman academic community that stretched, in fact, far beyond that of the Fantastici. For example, his participation in the Roman Accademia degli Intrecciati[24] is attested by records indicating his recitation there of two sonnets in 1649 and 1652, respectively, neither of which, however, seems to have survived. Nonetheless, the named performances interestingly attest to Salzilli's links with an academy described by Maylender as "un' adunanza religiosa-letteraria" ("a religious-literary assembly"), and, more specific, indicate his involvement in several of its sessions marking religious feasts.[25] Thus on 29 March 1649, at a gathering commemorating Christ's Passion, "Giovanni Salzilli" recited a "Sonetto per la Passione" ("Sonnet for the Passion").[26] On 28 May 1652, at a meeting honoring the Feast of Pentecost, "Giovanni Salzilli" recited a "Sonetto in lode del Chiabrera per le sue Ode Pindariche" ("Sonnet in Praise of Chiabrera for his Pindaric Odes").[27] Noteworthy here is Salzilli's evident celebration of Chiabrera as the Pindar of his day, a viewpoint very much in accordance with his reception in humanist Italy. Giovanni Vittorio Rossi, for example, had praised him as one into whom *Pindari animus, Pythagoraeo veluti commento, ... immigrasse ... videatur* ("the soul of Pindar seems to have transmigrated, as if in accordance with the argument of Pythagoras") or else as one in whom *Pindarus ipse Hetrusca lingua loquens, revixisse videatur* ("Pindar himself appears to have come to life again, speaking in the Tuscan tongue").[28] The attribution of the

---

[24] On the Accademia degli Intrecciati, founded in 1641 by Giuseppe Carpani, see Michele Maylender, *Storia delle Accademie d'Italia*, 5 vols (Bologna: Capelli, 1926–1930), III, 336–338, which, however, does not include Salzilli among its listed members.

[25] Maylender, *Storia*, III, 337. The Intrecciati held four meetings per year to mark The Epiphany, The Passion, Pentecost, and The Ascension.

[26] See *Fasti dell' Accademia degl' Intrecciati* (Rome: Reverenda Camera Apostolica, 1673), 32. Under the heading "ACCAD[EMIA] XXVII. PER LA PASSIONE. *Discorse Lunedì 29. Marzo 1649.* VALERIO INGHIRAMI DI PRATO," and among the twelve contributors who "Recitarono diverse Compositioni" ("recited various compositions") occurs "Giovanni Salzilli. Sonetto per la Passione" ("Giovanni Salzilli. A Sonnet for the Passion").

[27] *Fasti dell' Accademia degl' Intrecciati*, 45. Under the heading "ACCAD[EMIA] XL. PER LA PENTICOSTE. *Discorse Martedì 28. Maggio 1652.* FABRITIO ONDEDEI PESARESE," and among the thirteen contributors who "Recitarono diverse Compositioni" ("recited various compositions") occurs "Giovanni Salzilli. Sonetto in lode del Chiabrera per le sue Ode Pindariche" ("Giovanni Salzilli. A Sonnet in praise of Chiabrera for his Pindaric Odes").

[28] Giovanni Vittorio Rossi [pseud. Janus Nicius Erythraeus], *Pinacotheca Imaginum Illustrium, Doctrinae vel Ingenii Laude, Virorum* (Cologne: Iodocus Kalcovius, 1645), 63.

adjective "Pindaric" to describe the Chiabreran Odes praised by Salzilli probably reflects its occurrence in the actual title of the sonnet in question, as opposed to a paraphrastic reference in the Intrecciati records. This may suggest that the sonnet celebrated aspects of Chiabrera's formally Pindaric Odes (eighteen in number, based upon the triadic structure of strophe/antistrophe/epode).[29] Alternatively, it may have lauded more generally the Pindaric nature of Chiabrera's lyric poetry.[30]

Two further Italian poems by Salzilli do, however, survive independently. Although he did not contribute to a later Fantastici volume of poetry celebrating the election of Fabio Chigi as Pope Alessandro VII in 1655,[31] a canzone by him marking this same event, and possibly connected to a special Fantastici meeting held on 12 May 1655 in honor of the occasion, is extant in the Vatican Library.[32] Here, for once, we catch an interesting glimpse of Salzilli as a poet of Catholic Rome, participating in a literary trend inspired by a momentous religious occasion, and doing so with effusive enthusiasm. His poem establishes a mock-heroic contrast between the Vatican and Hell, and between the stability guaranteed by Alessandro's papacy and the chaos of its infernal antithesis. Altogether different, however, is Salzilli's sonnet extant in the Biblioteca Nazionale Centrale of Florence. This undated piece sings the

---

[29] Twelve formally Pindaric Odes occur among the "Canzoni Eroiche," in *Rime di Gabriello Chiabrera* (Milan: Società Tipografica de' Classici Italiani, 1807), I, 188–225, and a further six among his "Canzoni Sacre," in *ibid.*, 271–280, 283–285, 295–302. For discussion of their rhyme scheme, see Robert Shafer, *The English Ode to 1660: An Essay in Literary History* (New York: Haskell House, 1966), 67–68.

[30] See, among others, Luigi Castagna, "Pindaro, Le Origini del Pindarismo e Gabriello Chiabrera," *Aevum* 65 (1991): 523–542; Luigi Castagna, "Il Pindarismo Mediato di Orazio," *Aevum Antiquum* 2 (1989): 183–214; Stella P. Revard, *Pindar and the Renaissance Hymn-Ode 1450–1700* (Tempe: Arizona Center for Medieval and Renaissance Studies, 2001).

[31] *Academia Tenuta da Fantastici a 12 di Maggio 1655. In Applauso della S[anti]tà di N[ostro] S[ignore] Alesandro VII* (Rome: Vitale Mascardi, 1655). Chigi was elected to the Papacy on 7 April and formally crowned Pope on 18 April 1655. For an account of that occasion and of contemporary literary works that it inspired, see Francesco Cancellieri, *Storia de' Solenni Possessi de' Sommi Pontefici Detti Anticamente Processi o Processioni dopo la loro Coronazione dalla Basilica Vaticana alla Lateranense* (Rome: Luigi Lazzarini, 1802), 256–275.

[32] BAV Vat. lat. 6910, ff. 322^r–325^v. The manuscript poem, most probably in Salzilli's hand, is entitled "Per l'Assuntione di N[ost]ro Sig[nore] Alessandro 7[im]o al Sommo Pontificato" ("For the Assumption of Our Lord Alessandro VII to the Supreme Pontificate") with "Del S[ignore] Gio[vanni] Salzilli" ("by Mr Gio[vanni] Salzilli") added in another hand, most likely that of Stefano Gradi, owner of the collection. In 1661 Gradi succeeded to Lucas Holstenius's post as Vatican Librarian.

praises of Count Giulio da Montevecchio for his *La Scorneide*,[33] a manuscript collection of over one hundred sonnets, presenting a relentlessly sustained attack against the Pisan canon Giovan Battista Scornio for his literary ambition and overarching pride.[34] Salzilli's poem is of interest on a number of counts, not least in its possible reflection of his connections with the leading academy of Rome, the Accademia degli Umoristi, of which Montevecchio was a member.[35] Although most of the sonnets in *La Scorneide* are by Montevecchio himself, the collection also includes contributions from Giuseppe de Totis, and Cardinal Benedetto Pamphili, who had clear links with the Umoristi. De Totis was the Academy's Secretary, and had participated therein under the pseudonym Filedo Nonacrio. Likewise, the young Cardinal Pamphili was closely affiliated to the Umoristi, even sponsoring under its auspices several dramatic performances in his palace.[36] Salzilli's sonnet also demonstrates its author's critical alertness and linguistic ingenuity. Rather atypical of his known poetic output, this self-consciously mannered composition employs the extravagant language and pungent satire of the sonnets included in *La Scorneide* itself, thereby both praising and linguistically mirroring the collection as a whole. In consequence of this act of imitation, Salzilli, in a mock-modest self-alignment with the poets whom *he* is now satirizing, can candidly proclaim: "Anc' io sovente con le Muse gracchio" ("And I too frequently croak with the Muses").[37]

Salzilli's role in the Umoristi is in fact irrefutable. Not only was he a member,[38] but also (along with Giovanni Lotti [1604–1686]),[39] one of its two Censors. This is evinced by Giacinta Gimma's *Elogi*

---

[33] BNCF II. IV. 22 (formerly Magl. Cl. XXV 524), f. 80^v: "Sonetto del Sig[nore] Giovanni Salsilli in Lode delle Autore" ("A Sonnet by Mr Giovanni Salzilli in Praise of the Author"). See *Inventari dei Manoscritti delle Biblioteche d'Italia*, eds. Giuseppe Mazzatinti, Albano Sorbelli, and Luigi Ferrari, 113 vols (Forlì: Luigi Bordandini, 1890–), IX, 96.

[34] See Lina Montalti, *Un Mecenate in Roma Barocca: Il Cardinale Benedetto Pamphili (1653–1730)* (Florence: Sansoni, 1955), 135.

[35] See Maylender, *Storia*, V, 380.

[36] See Norbert Dubowy, "'Al Tavolino Medesimo del Compositor della Musica': Notes on Text and Context in Alessandro Scarlatti's *Cantate da Camera*," in *Aspects of the Secular Cantata in Late Baroque Italy*, ed. Michael Talbot (London: Routledge, 2016), 111–134, at 117.

[37] BNCF II. IV. 22, f. 80^v.

[38] See Maylender, *Storia*, V, 379.

[39] Lotti was also a member of the Fantastici, and contributed an Italian poem, three Latin poems, and a further Latin distich to the 1655 *Academia Tenuta da Fantastici*, at 69–70, 77–79, and 80.

Accademici della Società degli Spensierati di Rossano, published in Naples in 1703, which also provides fresh evidence of Salzilli's surprising longevity. Offering a brief biography of Carlo Andrea Sinibaldi (1633–1717), President of the Filoponi Academy in Faenza, Gimma recounts that after correspondence with "Giovanni Salzilli, e … Giovan Lotti," whom he describes as the "perpetui Censori" ("perpetual Censors") of the Umoristi, and as "Letterati di maggior fama" ("most famous men of letters"), it was proposed that Sinibaldi be included among the academy's membership. It was in consequence of this, Ginna continues, that Sinibaldi was received by them on 5 March 1673.[40] The lateness of this date is revelatory. Salzilli's role as a "perpetual Censor," even if it probably postdated Milton's visit,[41] is worth emphasizing, given the key function of the Censor in seventeenth-century Italian academies. Here Eric Cochrane's summary of regular practice merits full quotation:

> From two to six censors in each academy met secretly every fortnight or so to examine the contributions deposited, usually anonymously, in

---

[40] *Elogi Accademici della Società degli Spensierati di Rossano, Descritti del Dottor Signor D[on] Giacinto Gimma* (Naples: Carlo Troise, 1703), 77–88, at 83 (under D[on] *Carlo-Andrea Sinibaldi*): "Fioriva in quella Città l'Accademia instituita fin dall' anno 1600 da Paolo Mancini col primiero titolo de *Begli-Umori*, poi detti *Umoristi*, e coll' impresa d'una Nube gravida di acque col motto: *Redit agmine dulci*: tolto da Lucrezio: e continuando egli la corrispondenza de' Letterati di maggior fama, da Giovanni Salzilli, e da Giovan Lotti, perpetui Censori di quella, fu proposto ad essere annoverato tra quei Valentuomini, e seguì l'accettazione alli 5. di Marzo del 1673" ("There flourished in this city the Academy established in the year 1600 by Paolo Mancini with the initial title 'Begli-Umori', later called 'Umoristi', and with the emblem of a cloud pregnant with water, with the motto *Redit agmine dulci*, taken from Lucretius. And continuing his correspondence with the most famous Men of Letters, with Giovanni Salzilli, and with Giovanni Lotti, perpetual Censors of that institution, he [Sinibaldi] was proposed to be numbered among those Men of Worth, and there followed the acceptance of him as a member on the 5 March 1673"). Unfortunately, the correspondence between Sinibaldi and Salzilli/Lotti alluded to here does not seem to have survived. On Gimma's *Elogia Accademici*, see Simone Testa, *Italian Academies and their Networks, 1525–1700: From Local to Global* (Basingstoke: Palgrave Macmillan, 2015), 150–154. Testa aptly observes how the biography of Sinibaldi "gives Gimma the opportunity to praise the Italian academic movement" (153).

[41] Salzilli's appointment as Censor would seem to postdate 1638 as his name does not occur among the Censors listed in the *Monumentum Romanum Nicolao Claudio Fabricio Perescio* (Rome: Typis Vaticanis, 1638). Here the Censors of the Umoristi (and authors of the dedicatory letter [33–34] to the Umoristi's Principal, Camillo Colonna [dated 16 March 1638, and prefacing the ensuing *Carmina Academicorum Romanorum*]) are named as Fabio Leonida, Domenico Benigni, Gasparo de Simeonibus, Leone Allacci, Girolamo Rocco, and Bartolomeo Tortoletti (33–34, at 34). Lotti contributed a Latin *Elogium* to the *Monumentum*, at 70.

a locked box known as the *tramoggia* or the *zucca*. The best were then selected for a formal line-by-line criticism (*critica*) and then an equally detailed defense (*difesa*) in which the speakers dwelt at length over ... particulars. ... Finally, a vote of the assembly decided either to return them to their authors for appropriate correction or to transcribe them into one of the permanent books ... depending on their relative merits.[42]

In regard to the role of Censors in the Umoristi, we are fortunate to have more specific information, provided by the academy's surviving statutes. These explicitly state that there should be two, and specify their duties: to see and assess all readings in advance, to have recourse to the President in the case of disagreement between them, to consider the academicians' individual emblems (*imprese*), which they should refer to the President and to the Academy, and to scrutinize academic materials prior to their publication:

De' Censori

Seranno due come i Consiglieri, et in assenza del Principe, e de Consiglieri sosteranno in Accademia la prima persona secondo la loro precedenza.

Vedranno le Lettioni prima che si recitino, avvertiranno e prohibiranno secondo il lor giuditio e le sottoscriverà uno di loro. Se fussero discordanti fra di loro si ricorrà al Principe. Considereranno l'imprese, e riferirano al Principe, et all' Accademia. Non si darà alle stampe cosa alcuna che prima non sia passata per le mani de' Censori, e l'istesso si farà nell' attioni che si rappresentassero mai in Accademia.[43]

In regard to Censors

There will be two, as in the case of the Councilors, and in the absence of the President and of the Councilors they will support the foremost person in the Academy in accordance with their precedence.

They will see the Readings in advance of their recitation, they will offer advice and issue prohibition in accordance with their judgment, and they will sign one of these verdicts. If there is dissension between them there will be recourse to the President. They will consider the emblems, and refer them to the President, and to the Academy. Nothing will be given to the press that has not passed in advance through the hands of the Censors, and the same practice will be observed in regard to activities that have never been performed in the Academy.

---

[42] Eric W. Cochrane, *Tradition and Enlightenment in the Tuscan Academies 1690–1800* (Chicago: University of Chicago Press, 1961), 19.

[43] Text is that of Piera Russo, "L'Accademia degli Umoristi. Fondazione, Strutte e Leggi: Il Primo Decennio di Attività," *Esperienze Letterarie* 4 (1979): 47–61, at 61.

The pairing of Salzilli and Lotti reappears in a sonnet by Angelo Rodolfini (1605–1688)[44] addressed to them both, and published in Rome in 1688.[45] Appropriating a military metaphor, the speaker sings the praises of their lyric poetry, asserting: "C'habbia i Pindari suoi la nostra etate" ("That our age has Pindars of its own"),[46] and comparing their poetic victories to that of another Giovanni (Jan Sobieski, King of Poland), who helped to save Vienna when it was besieged by the Turks in 1683.[47] In consequence:

> ... ammiri il Mondo i tre Giovanni,
> I due s'armaron d'arco, e l'un di spada,
> Trionfa l'un de' Traci, e i due degli anni.[48]

> ... The world marvels at three Giovannis, two of whom arm themselves with the bow; one with the sword. The one triumphs over the Thracians, and the two triumph over the years.

Another sonnet by Rodolfini, addressed to Salzilli alone,[49] depicts the goddesses Astraea, Minerva, and Clio in rival competition, like the deities Hera, Athena, and Aphrodite, who contended by the river Xanthus for the judgment of Paris, with Aphrodite emerging victorious.[50] The speaker concludes by proclaiming his own verdict:

> In tè Salzilli è bello il senno, e 'l canto,
> Ma bella è più l'irreprensibil vita".[51]

---

[44] On Rodolfini, see Egerton Brydges, *Res Literariae: For May 1821 to February 1822* (Geneva: W[illiam] Fick, 1822), 177. Rodolfini translated parts of Ovid's *Heroides* into Italian verse. See *L'Epistole d'Ovidio in Terza Rima del Signor Angelo Rodolfini con gli Argomenti del Signor Ippolito Aurispa* (Macerata: Giuseppe Piccini, 1682).

[45] "Alli Signori Giovanni Lotti, e Salzilli," in *Sonetti del Signor Angelo Rodolfini* (Rome: Tinassi, 1688), 53.

[46] Rodolfini, *Sonetti*, 53, line 8.

[47] Sobieski's heroism on this occasion was widely celebrated by contemporary poets, including Lotti himself. See Nadia Amendola, *La Poesia di Giovanni Pietro Monesio, Giovanni Lotti e Lelio Orsini nella Cantata da Camera del XVII Secolo* (PhD thesis: University of Johannes Gutenberg, Mainz, 2017), I, 370–378.

[48] Rodolfini, *Sonetti*, 53, lines 12–14.

[49] Rodolfini, *Sonetti*, 65: "Al Signor Giovanni Salzilli."

[50] See Homer, *Iliad* 24. 27–30.

[51] Rodolfini, *Sonetti*, 65, lines 13–14.

> In you, Salzilli, exists beautiful judgment and beautiful song, but even more beautiful is your irreprehensible life.

Salzilli's links with the Umoristi are further attested by letters included in a collection of writings associated with the European travels of Abbot Giovan Battista Pacichelli. Entitled *Memorie de' Viaggi Per L'Europa Christiana*, and published in Naples in 1685, this work includes two items of interest: (1) a letter, dated Rome: September 1674, by Sir John Price to Pacichelli, which mentions Salzilli in the context of the Umoristi, and promises to pass along to Salzilli greetings from Pacichelli and from René François de Sluse (1622–1685),[52] a Dutch scholar who had spent ten years in Rome (1642–1652), pursuing law, natural philosophy, languages and mathematics,[53] during which time perhaps he came into contact with Salzilli. His election to The Royal Society, London in 1674 (the year of the present letter), was proposed by Milton's friend and correspondent, Henry Oldenburg;[54] (2) a letter from Pachichelli addressed "Al Sig[nor] Gio[vanni] Salzilli, Academico Humorista. Roma" ("To Mr Gio[vanni] Salzilli, a Member of the Umoristi Academy, Rome"), and dated Prague: 18 July 1676.[55] Describing a series of curiosities pertaining to Prague and the kingdom of Bohemia, Pachichelli concludes by praising Salzilli's "virtuosi talenti" ("virtuous talents").[56]

---

[52] *Memorie de' Viaggi per L'Europa Christiana, Scritte à Diversi in Occasion de' Suoi Ministeri dall' Abate Gio[vanni] Battista Pacichelli: Parte Terza* (Naples: Giacomo Raillard, 1685), 82–84, at 82–83: "Fui costretto anch'io à dar la mancia al Bidello de gli Umoristi, che inaspettatamente venne col libro suo alla mia camera. Al Signor Salzilli con prima opportunità farò i saluti del Signor Francesco Slusio, e di V[ostro] S[ignore]" ("I was also forced to tip the porter of the Umoristi, who unexpectedly came to my room with his book. I will convey to Mr Salzilli at the first opportunity the greetings of Mr de Sluse and those of your lordship").

[53] See Anne-Catherine Bernès, "René-François de Sluse et Italie," in *Congrès de Namur (XLIX Congrès de la Fédération des Cercles d'Archéologie et d'Histoire de Belgique)* (Namur: Presses Universitaires de Namur, 1990), III, 305–317.

[54] Four letters from Milton to Henry Oldenburg survive in the 1674 *Epistolarum Familiarium Liber Unus*, and five from Oldenburg to Milton are extant in The Royal Society, London. See *Epistolarum Familiarium Liber Unus and Uncollected Letters*, ed. Haan, 17–18, 221–231, 267–272, 326–332, 363–368, 484–489.

[55] *Memorie de' Viaggi*, III, 144–157 [Lettera LX].

[56] *Memorie de' Viaggi*, III, 157: "Iddio però mi salvi la curiosità per altri oggetti, e guardi sempre i virtuosi talenti di V[ostro] S[ignore]" ("But may God preserve my curiosity for other subjects, and always regard the virtuous talents of your lordship").

That those talents seem to have persisted into old age is suggested by a final piece of evidence, provided by an inscription, dated 1691, on the wall of the Church of SS Nome Di Maria al Foro Traiano in Rome:

>D[OMINO] O[PTIMO] M[AXIMO]
>IN MANUS TUAS
>DOMINE
>COMMENDO
>SPIRITUM MEUM
>IOANNES
>SALZILLUS
>ANNO. M.D. CXCI[57]

>TO GOD, MOST GOOD, MOST GREAT
>INTO YOUR HANDS
>O LORD
>I COMMEND
>MY SPIRIT
>GIOVANNI
>SALZILLI
>IN THE YEAR 1691

In short, this new evidence reveals that Salzilli participated in at least three Roman academies, the Fantastici, the Intrecciati, and the Umoristi, in the last of which he played the key role of Censor. Networking with other academicians and scholars at home and abroad, and doing so sometimes on behalf of nobility, he emerges as a man who was forever alert to literary trends and debates of his day, and as one who earned quite a significant reputation among his contemporaries, not only for the quality of his poetry, especially his Odes (his "Pindaric" poetry), but also for his personal integrity. And if, as seems virtually certain, the *IOANNES SALZILLUS*, commemorated on the wall of that Roman church as having died in 1691, is indeed *Ioannes Salsillus Poeta Romanus*, academician and friend of Milton, this means that the then sick poet ultimately defied all expectations by enjoying a fruitful longevity.

---

[57] The inscription occurs on the wall of a small room adjacent to the sacristy as one enters the main chapel. See Vincenzo Forcella, *Iscrizioni delle Chiese e d'Altri Edificii di Roma* (Rome: Ludovico Cecchini, 1877), IX, 233. I have corrected Forcella's misprint *Salzzilli* (his index prints the name in its correct form as *Salzilli*). For a description of the church itself, see Antonio Martini and M.L. Casanova, *SS Nome di Maria*, Le Chiese di Roma Illustrate 70 (Rome: Marietti, 1962).

1.2 Salzilli in the Accademia dei Fantastici

To return to the years 1638–1639, it is thus evident that the Giovanni Salzilli with whom Milton struck up a congenial relationship was indeed a relatively young man.[58] The fact that he was afforded such ample space in the 1637 Fantastici volume is thus striking testimony to his perceived literary talents. For there he was certainly among learned peers.[59] One need only cite such fellow contributors as Claudio Achillini, an esteemed Marinist poet, and professor of law at various universities;[60] the eclectic

---

[58] In this regard he might be compared to prodigies, such as Carlo Dati in Florence and Alessandro Cherubini in Rome, whose company Milton seems to have particularly enjoyed.

[59] The full list of the fifty-one contributors as they appear in the volume (which is arranged alphabetically according to the forename of each) is as follows: Alberto Fabri, Alfonso Confidati, Andrea Barbazza, Antonio Bruni, Anton Francesco Tempestino, Bernardo Evangelista, Padre Maestro Fra Bonaventura Malvasia, Benedetto Benetti, Benedetto Rigogli, Carlo Spada, Claudio Achillini, Claudio Scoppa, Padre Clemente Tosi, Cesare Panimolle, Decio Mazzei, Francesco Balducci, Francesco Benetti, Francesco Carducci, Francesco Massucci, Fulvio Testi, Gabriel Marino, Giacomo Guglielmi, Gio[vanni] Antonio Goffredi, Gio[vanni] Battista Caroli, Gio[vanni] Battista Giobbe, Gio[vanni] Battista Piacenza, Gio[vanni] Francesco Maia Materdona, Gio[vanni] Maria de' Rossi, Giovan Martino Longo, Giovanni Salzilli, Girolamo Lamanna, Girolamo Garopoli, Giulio Ces[are] Valentini, Padre Giuseppe Ferretti, Lodovico Prosperi, Marco Picarelli, Martino Lunghi, Giovanni Montreglio, Napoleone Ricci, Nicolo Strozzi, Paolo Cittadonio, Pierfrancesco Paoli, Pietro Michiele, Pietro Pannini, Scipione Santacroce, Stefano Marini, Tiberio Ceuli, Vincenzo Maria Savarelli, Virginio Patriarchi, Vittorio Venturelli, and Viviano Vellori.

[60] Claudio Achillini (1574–1640) was a member of not only the Fantastici, but also of the Accademia Nazionale dei Lincei of Rome, the Innominati of Parma, the Intrepidi of Ferrara, the Incogniti of Venice, and the Notte of Bologna. He had composed the texts of two theatrical operas that were presented as part of the nuptial celebrations at the Farnese court in Parma in 1628 of Odoardo Farnese and Margherita de' Medici: the *Teti e Flora* (Parma: Seth and Erasmo Viotti, 1628); *Mercurio e Marte* (Parma: Seth and Erasmo Viotti, 1628), with music by Monteverdi. He had also seen the publication of his correspondence with Agostino Mascardi: *Due Lettere: L'Una del Mascardi all'Achillini, L'Altra dell' Achillini al Mascardi sopra le Presenti Calamità* (Rome: Lodovico Grignano, 1631), and, most notably, his *Poesie* (Bologna: Clemente Ferroni, 1632), which would reappear in several successive editions between 1633 and 1680. In 1638 Achillini was the recipient of a particular accolade, a stone erected by his home University of Bologna, inscribed *Claudio Achillino loci genio* ("to Claudio Achillini, the spirit of the region"), and dated December 1638, on which see Giovanni Fantuzzi, *Notizie degli Scrittori Bolognesi* (Bologna: St Thomas Aquinas Press, 1781), I, 55–62, at 59. Pertaining to that year also is his canzone "Oda nella nascita del Delfino" celebrating the birth of the dauphin of France (the future Louis XIV; see *Rime e Prose di Claudio Achillini* [Venice: Nicolò Pezzana, 1673], 217–219), which he sent to Cardinal Richelieu (see *ibid.*, 301–302), and for which he was

poet and future epicist Tiberio Ceuli,[61] and the celebrated poet and statesman Fulvio Testi.[62] Garuffi's interesting statement that Salzilli was "oltremodo caro al Testi" ("extremely dear to Testi")[63] can be corroborated to some degree by the fact that Testi is the addressee of one of Salzilli's Fantastici sonnets,[64] and by the glowing terms in which his poetical talents are extolled in Salzilli's canzone "La Poesia Trionfante" included in the same volume.[65]

The 1637 Fantastici volume, in which Salzilli appeared in print, is an essentially eclectic collection in terms of form and subject matter,

---

awarded a gold chain. For Richelieu's letter in response, in which he praises the poem, see *ibid.*, 302. See also the letter of Richelieu's successor Cardinal Mazarin to Achillini (dated 11 May 1640), at *ibid.*, 302–303, which passes along to him the gift, described therein as "una Catena d'oro, che sua Eminenza in segno dell'amor suo verso V[ostro] S[ignore] le invia" ("a golden chain, which his Eminence is sending along as a sign of his love for your lordship"). On Achillini, see *Le Glorie degli Incogniti* (Venice: Francesco Valuasense, 1647), 108–111; Angelo Colombo, *I "Riposi di Pindo": Studi di Claudio Achillini (1574–1640)* (Florence: Olschki, 1988); Angelo Colombo, "Sul Plagio: Una Rettifica della Bibliografia di Claudio Achillini (e di G.B. Marino)," *SS* 25 (1984): 101–113; Angelo Colombo, "Tra 'Incogniti' e 'Lincei': Per la Biografia di Claudio Achillini," *SS* 26 (1985): 141–176; Fortunato Rizzi, "Claudio Achillini e il Soggiorno Parmense," *Aurea Parma* 36 (1952): 3–13; Alberto Asor Rosa, "Achillini, Claudio," *DBI* 1 (1960): 145–148.

[61] Tiberio Ceuli, a member of both the Fantastici and the Umoristi, would deliver in 1641 (and before the Umoristi) an Oration on the death of Agostino Mascardi: *Per la Morte di Monsignor Agostino Mascardi Oratione di Tiberio Ceuli, da lui Recitata nell'Accademia de' Signori Humoristi di Roma* (Rome: Francesco Moneta, 1641). A contributor to the Fantastici's second volume (1655) on the election of Fabio Chigi as Pope Alexander VII (see *Academia Tenuta di Fantastici*, 53–60), Ceuli would later see the publication of *La Penna Canzone* (Rome: Paolo Moneta, 1670), and his epic poem *L'Oriente Conquistato Poema Heroico* (Rome: Filippo Maria Mancini, 1672).

[62] Fulvio Testi (1593–1646) had seen the publication in Modena of his *Rime* in 1617, and, more recently, his *Poesie Liriche et Alcina Tragedia* (Modena: Pompilio Totti, 1636). He would later prove to be a prolific author of numerous lyric poems and political works.

[63] Giuseppe Malatesta Garuffi, *Italia Accademica* (Rimini: Dandi, 1688), 18: "Gio[vanni] Salzilli oltremodo caro al Testi, col quale vicendevolmente conseriva i Parti dell' Ingegno" ("Gio[vanni] Salzilli, extremely dear to Testi, with whom he reciprocally retained the parts of genius").

[64] Salzilli, "Al Signor Conte Fulvio Testi," in *Poesie de' Signori Accademici Fantastici*, 149.

[65] Salzilli, "La Poesia Trionfante," in *Poesie*, 156–162, at 160: "E tu canoro mostro/Di Delo, e di Permesso,/Ornamento, e splendor del secol nostro,/Fulvio, a cui solo Apollo/Hoggi il plettro hà concesso" ("And you, the songful manifestation of Delos and of Permessus, the ornament and splendor of our age, Fulvio, to whom alone in modern times has Apollo granted the plectrum").

comprising sonnets, canzone, ottave, and odes on themes ranging from the religious to the political to the gnomic. Some contributors sing the praises of Cardinals,[66] or of Rome,[67] or of the Fantastici Academy itself, alluding to its *impresa*, praising its President, or expressing gratitude for admission.[68] Some assume the form of hymns addressed to Saints,[69] and several take as their subject Christ's passion[70] and resurrection.[71] Others, by contrast, turn to contemporary personages, whether to flatter Louis XIII of France[72] or Philip II of Spain,[73] or to lament the passing of such celebrated Italian poets as Battista Guarini[74] and Giambattista Marino.[75] Others hail the theological achievements of a certain Abbot Alessandro Salzilli,[76] or the geographical discoveries of Christopher Columbus.[77]

---

[66] See Andrea Barbazza, "Nella promotione dell' Em[inente] Sig[nore] Card[inale] Gessi" (*Poesie*, 16); Carlo Spada, "All' Eminentissimo Signor Card[inale] Cesarini" (*Poesie*, 42).

[67] See Giovan Martino Longo, "A Roma" (*Poesie*, 141).

[68] See Padre Maestro Fra Bonaventura Malvasia, "Invita i Signori Accademici Fantastici a celebrare la morte di Christo, alludendo all'Impresa dell' Accademia" (*Poesie*, 34); Gabriel Marino, "Alli Signori Accademici Fantastici, invitandoli a farsi scorta le Virtù dell' Eccellentiss[imo] Sig[nore] Don Pietro Colonna" (*Poesie*, 112); Giovan Martino Longo, "A' Signori Accademici Fantastici. Alludendo all'Impresa dell' Accademia" (*Poesie*, 138); Marco Picarelli, "Alli Signori Accad[emici] Fantastici. nell' essere aggregato nell' Accademia" (*Poesie*, 189).

[69] See, for example, Bernardo Evangelista, "A S[anta] Agnesa" (*Poesie*, 33); Francesco Benetti, "Sopra una Imagine di S[anta] Caterina da Siena" (*Poesie*, 66); Martino Lunghi, "A S[an] Luca" (*Poesie*, 198), "A S[an] Tomaso D'Aquino" (*Poesie*, 198), "A S[an] Lorenzo" (*Poesie*, 199).

[70] See Giovan Martino Longo, "Per Li Sudori di Sangue del Redentor nostro Giesu Cristo" (*Poesie*, 130–133), "La Pieta Lagrimosa" (*Poesie*, 134–139); Nicolo Strozzi, "Christo in Croce" (*Poesie*, 207); Pietro Pannini, "Alla Santissima Croce" (*Poesie*, 220); Vittorio Venturelli, "Sopra le piaghe di nostro Signor Giesu Christo" (*Poesie*, 261).

[71] Andrea Barbazza, "Nel giorno della Santissima Resurrettione" (*Poesie*, 18).

[72] See the poems by Alfonso Confidati (*Poesie*, 14) and Gio[vanni] Francesco Maia Materdona (*Poesie*, 131).

[73] See Benedetto Benetti, "Paralello tra Hercule, e Filippo II. Re di Spagna, nella rinuntia de gli Stati fattagli da Carlo V" (*Poesie*, 35).

[74] Gio[vanni] Francesco Maia Materdona, "Nella morte del Cavalier Battista Guarini" (*Poesie*, 133).

[75] Andrea Barbazza, "Visitando la Sepoltura del Cavalier Marino" (*Poesie*, 17).

[76] Fulvio Testi, "Al Signor Abbate Salzilli Filosofo, e Teologo celebre" (*Poesie*, 107–109).

[77] Tiberio Ceuli, "In lode di Christofaro Colombo. Canzone" (*Poesie*, 247–248).

Some poems are quasi-fabular,[78] whereas others are gnomic in essence, lamenting, for example, false hope[79] or the vicissitudes and fragility of human life.[80]

Salzilli's substantial input to the *Poesie* generally eschews religious topics.[81] His opening sonnet celebrates the validity of the poetic vocation, as opposed to the materialism associated with other pursuits.[82] Elsewhere, he lauds contemporary poets, such as Fulvio Testi (Sonnet 2),[83] or articulates a firmly held conviction "Che l'età nostra ha Scrittori sì di verso, come di prosa eguali a gli Antichi" ("That our age possesses Writers of verse, as of prose, that are a match for the Ancients" [Sonnet 3]).[84] His longest poem, a canzone, entitled "La Poesia Trionfante" ("The Triumph of Poetry"), proclaims the ability of poetry to confer immortality upon its talented practitioner, citing ancient and modern exemplars who have outlived time.[85] Several pieces concern themselves with love in its many forms.[86] These embrace the gothic ("On a lady who wrote to her lover in her own blood" [Sonnet 5]),[87] the domestic ("On a puppy sent to Lucca as a gift to a beautiful lady" [Sonnet 6]),[88] the

---

[78] See, for example, Gio[vanni] Antonio Goffredi, "Pararello [*sic*] Fra Un Cieco & un Amante" (*Poesie*, 118); Giovan Martino Longo, "I Delirii Humani. Canzone" (*Poesie*, 142–146).

[79] Francesco Carducci, "Speranza fallace" (*Poesie*, 100).

[80] Antonio Bruni, "La varietà delle cose humane" (*Poesie*, 21); Tiberio Ceuli, "Infelicità della vita Humana" (*Poesie*, 225); Vittorio Venturelli, "Fragilita della Vita Humana" (*Poesie*, 260).

[81] Contrast, however, his later canzone celebrating the creation in 1655 of Fabio Chigi as Pope Alessandro VII, on which see note 32.

[82] Giovanni Salzilli, "S'antepone la dignità della Poesia all' utile de gli altrui studi" (*Poesie*, 148).

[83] Giovanni Salzilli, "Al Signor Conte Fulvio Testi" (*Poesie*, 149).

[84] *Poesie*, 150.

[85] *Poesie*, 156–162.

[86] Some of Salzilli's verse (presumably his amatory poetry) is included in a manuscript anthology of love poetry, compiled in the late seventeenth century (and in at least five different hands), extant in Bologna: Biblioteca di San Francesco dei Frati Minori Conventuali as MS. 42. See Mazzatinti, *Inventari*, 106 (1990): 34–35. This collection also includes poetry by other Fantastici members, such as Giovan Martino Longo and Marco Picarelli, and by Giovanni Battista Manso, founder of the Neapolitan Accademia degli Oziosi, encomiast of Milton, and addressee of *Mansus*.

[87] Giovanni Salzilli, "Per bella Donna, che scrisse all' Amato col proprio sangue" (*Poesie*, 151).

[88] Giovanni Salzilli, "Per una Cagnola mandata a Lucca in dono a bellissima Dama" (*Poesie*, 152).

moralistic ("Modest Love" [Sonnet 7]),[89] and the encomiastic ("In praise of a beautiful lady" [Sonnet 9]).[90] Likewise, his tenth sonnet sings the praises of a certain "Giacomo."[91] At times Salzilli reverts to more gnomic themes, such as the fugitive nature of time (Sonnet 4)[92] or the irresolute temperament of the lover.[93] Other poems demonstrate his alertness to the beauties of nature. Such is true of his picturesque eighth sonnet "Lilla ranked above the Dawn,"[94] and his pulsating canzonetta on May.[95] Others are fabular, such as his eleventh Sonnet "A Rich merchant killed in a duel for wishing to avenge an injurious word"[96] (to which this discussion shall return), or quasi-chivalric, such as his ottavo entitled "Description of a brave and most handsome Cavalier in a Joust."[97]

Although it is true that Salzilli's contributions to the 1637 *Poesie* reveal, in the words of Freeman, "concerns" that are "typically Miltonic,"[98] there are further reasons why the volume as a whole might have appealed to Milton. Here he could read in print no fewer than three poems (two in Italian; one in French) on the soprano Leonora Baroni,[99] in whose honor he was soon to compose (or perhaps was already in the process of composing?) three Latin epigrams.[100] Here, too, he could find pieces about subjects that had attracted his own attention: sonnets on

---

[89] Giovanni Salzilli, "Amor Pudico" (*Poesie*, 153).

[90] Giovanni Salzilli, "In Lode di Bella Dama" (*Poesie*, 154).

[91] Giovanni Salzilli, "Al Signor Giacomo N[ome]" (*Poesie*, 154).

[92] Giovanni Salzilli, "Si ricorda à bella D[onna] la fugacità del Tempo" (*Poesie*, 151).

[93] Giovanni Salzilli, "L'Amante Irresoluto: Canzone" (*Poesie*, 163–165).

[94] Giovanni Salzilli, "Lilla anteposta all' Aurora" (*Poesie*, 153).

[95] Giovanni Salzilli, "Il Maggio: Canzonetta" (*Poesie*, 165–167).

[96] Giovanni Salzilli, "Ricco Mercante ucciso in duello, per volersi vendicar d'una parola ingiuriosa" (*Poesie*, 155).

[97] Giovanni Salzilli, "Discrittione di valoroso, e bellissimo Cavaliere in Giostra: Ottave" (*Poesie*, 168–169).

[98] Freeman, "Milton's Roman Connection," 97.

[99] Gabriel Marino, "Per la Sig[nora] Leonora Basile, Musica celebre" (*Poesie*, 113); Giovan Martino Longo, "Ad Amore, Per la Signora Leonora Basile, Musica celebre" (*Poesie*, 144); Gio[vanni] Montreglio, "Pour la Seignora Leonora Basile" (*Poesie*, 203–204). This poem was reprinted (with the omission of the final three stanzas) in *Applausi Poetici alle Glorie della Signora Leonora Baroni*, ed. Francesco Ronconi (Braccciano: Giovanni Battista Cavario, 1639), 180–182, a collection discussed in Chapter 2 of this volume.

[100] See Chapter 2. Predating the *Applausi* by two years, the Leonora poems in the Fantastici volume are of interest because of their undoubted availability to Milton.

Christ's nativity;[101] a diatribe attacking the inventor of gunpowder,[102] and poems celebrating the arrival of spring.[103] In short, this published work afforded him an illuminating snapshot of Fantastici Accademici in literary performance. It was a world to which he was continually drawn. Parker's remark that "after his experience in Florence, it would be surprising indeed if he [Milton] was not invited to attend meetings of the *Fantastici*,"[104] can and should be expanded to embrace both the Fantastici and the Umoristi, given Salzilli's attested membership of both. Here it is worth commenting on Milton's collective phrase "the privat Academies of Italy" when describing, in *The Reason of Church Government*, his integration into Italian academic culture.[105] The plural "Academies" and the general reference to "Italy" suggest an academic involvement that in all probability extended beyond Florence. And perhaps it was not a case of Milton being invited. More likely, upon his arrival in Rome, as would also seem to be true of his experience in Florence,[106] he proactively sought to gain admission. If so, he may well have been required to submit in advance his envisaged contributions for careful scrutiny by the academic Censors.

---

[101] Giovan Martino Longo, "Nel Natale di Giesu Cristo" (*Poesie*, 137). Cf. Milton, "On the Morning of Christ's Nativity" (1629).

[102] Tiberio Ceuli, "Contro l'inventore della Polvere" (*Poesie*, 226). Cf. Milton, *In Inventorem Bombardae* (c. 1626).

[103] Francesco Benetti, "Per la Primavera. Canzone" (*Poesie*, 71–75, misnumbered 63, 94, 97–99); Giovanni Salzilli, "Il Maggio Canzonetta" (*Poesie*, 165–167). Cf. Milton, *Elegia Quinta. In Adventum Veris* (c. 1629).

[104] Parker, *Biography*, II, 826. Cf. Barbara K. Lewalski, *The Life of John Milton: A Critical Biography* (Oxford: Blackwell, 2000), 95: "[i]t is quite likely that he attended meetings of the Fantastici."

[105] *The Reason of Church Government*, 37. See 19.

[106] For possible evidence of the newly arrived Milton seeking admission to the Florentine Accademia degli Svogliati (at four of whose meetings his attendance and participation are minuted), see Harris, "Galileo as Symbol," 6; Haan, *From Academia to Amicitia*, 13.

1.3 Salzilli's "Written Encomium" of Milton

Salzilli was certainly impressed by Milton's literary and linguistic talents. This is attested by his "written Encomium" of Milton (an interesting and sole instance of Salzilli's extant Latin verse), which would be prefixed, along with another four such accolades, to the *Ioannis Miltoni Londiniensis Poemata* (1645).[107] William Poole has recently posited the intriguing speculation that Milton, like other seventeenth-century travelers abroad, may have possessed a now lost *album amicorum*, in which his Italian acquaintances were invited to write their tributes.[108] Perhaps so, but it is also possible that Salzilli inscribed his encomium on a copy of the 1637 *Poesie* itself, perhaps gifted by him to Milton, which is either lost or has not yet come to light. Irrespective of where it was actually recorded, the tribute is fulsome in its terms of praise:

> *Ad Ioannem Miltonem Anglum*
> *triplici poeseos laurea coronandum*
> *Graeca nimirum, Latina, atque Hetrusca,*
> *Epigramma Ioannis Salsilli Romani.*
>
> Cede Meles, cedat depressa Mincius urna;
> Sebetus Tassum desinat usque loqui;
> At Thamesis victor cunctis ferat altior undas
> Nam per te, Milto, par tribus unus erit.[109]
>
> *An Epigram of Giovanni Salzilli of Rome*
> *to John Milton of England,*
> *who merits coronation with a threefold laurel-wreath of poetry:*
> *Greek of course, Latin and Tuscan.*
>
> Yield Meles; let Mincius yield with lowered urn;
> let Sebeto cease to talk continuously of Tasso;
> but let Thames in his victory carry his waves higher than all,
> for through you, Milton, he alone will be equal to three.

Like Milton's Florentine encomiasts, Salzilli celebrates him as a polyglot.[110] As its headnote pointedly indicates, the epigram is a tribute

---

[107] *Poemata*, 3–10. See Lewalski and Haan, 106–115; 415–420.

[108] William Poole, *Milton and the Making of Paradise Lost* (Cambridge MA: Harvard University Press, 2017), 46.

[109] *Poemata*, 4. See Lewalski and Haan, 106–107, 415–416.

[110] Cf. Antonio Francini to Milton, at *Poemata*, 9–10: "Nell' altera Babelle/Per te il parlar confuse Giove in vano,/Che per varie favelle/Di se stessa trofeo cadde su'l piano:/Ch' Ode oltr' all Anglia il suo più Idioma/Spagna, Francia, Toscana, e Grecia e Roma" (55–60) ("In vain for you did Jupiter mingle speech in lofty Babel, which,

paid by one John to another, and by a Roman to an Englishman. Then the two nationalities are brought together by invocation of the practice of *laureatio* ("crowning with laurel"), a Roman public act now envisaged as being conferred upon an Englishman (*Anglus*). Described by John Flood as "essentially humanistic in inspiration and character,"[111] the *laureatio* found its most famous model in Petrarch, the eponymous poet laureate, who had received the honor on the Campidoglio on 8 April 1341 in a carefully self-manufactured ceremony. Dressed in the purple robe of King Robert himself, Petrarch was presented with a scroll, declared a *civis Romanus* ("citizen of Rome"), and given the title *magister, poeta et historicus* ("teacher, poet, and historian").[112] Then, after the recitation of some of his Latin verse, there followed his coronation speech (*Collatio Laureationis*), delivered, he tells us, to "a large multitude and with great joy,"[113] in which he proclaimed the enduring fame and glory achievable by literary works.[114] The whole experience, in the words of Harald Weinrich, "gave his literary creativity a strong impetus,"[115] inspiring him to return to his long-neglected epic, the *Africa*. Other laureations, however, had occurred posthumously, most notably perhaps that of Tasso. Due to be crowned poet laureate on the Campidoglio in Rome in 1595, Tasso died in a monastery in April of that year, and, crucially, before the ceremony could take place. The misfortune had been explicated in detail by Giovanni Battista Manso in his *Vita di Torquato*

---

itself a trophy to a variety of languages, fell to the plain, for besides England: Spain, France, Tuscany, Greece, and Rome hear their most worthy language"); Carlo Dati to Milton, at *Poemata*, 10: *Polyglotto, in cuius ore linguae iam deperditae sic reviviscunt, ut idiomata omnia sint in eius laudibus infacunda* ("To a polyglot upon whose lips languages already dead come to life again in such a way that all terms of expression in his praise are lacking in eloquence"). See Lewalski and Haan, 112–113, 114–115, 418–419.

[111] John Flood, *Poets Laureate in the Holy Roman Empire: A Bio-bibliographical Handbook* (Berlin: Walter de Gruyter, 2006), I, lxii.

[112] See "'La Collatio Laureationis' del Petrarca," ed. Carlo Godi, *Italia Medioevale e Umanistica* 13 (1970): 13–27.

[113] Petrarch, *Rerum Familiarium*, 4.8.

[114] See Werner Suerbaum, "Poeta Laureatus et Triumphans. Die Dichterkrönung Petrarcas und sein Ennius-Bild," *Poetica* 5 (1972): 293–328; Douglas Bow, *Doctors, Ambassadors, Secretaries: Humanism and Professions in Renaissance Italy* (Chicago: The University of Chicago Press, 2002), 27–36.

[115] Harald Weinrich, *On Borrowed Time: The Art and Economy of Living with Deadlines*, trans. Steven Rendall (Chicago: The University of Chicago Press, 2005), 20.

Tasso (1621),[116] an episode possibly echoed in Milton's Latin poem *Mansus*, composed only a matter of months after this, his first Roman visit.[117] It is in this poem, too, that Milton interestingly imagines his own laureation. But his (like Tasso's) is a posthumous event to be performed by a somewhat nebulous, and as yet unknown, friend (*amicus* [78]), an envisaged other, *nectens aut Paphia myrti aut Parnasside lauri/fronde comas* (92-93) ("binding my hair with Paphian myrtle or with the leaf of Parnassian laurel").[118]

For Salzilli, however, it is the living Milton who merits *laureatio*, and, by implication, full integration into a Roman community. As if proclaiming an academic verdict of his own, he envisages the Englishman as a triple poet laureate: in Greek, Latin, and Tuscan. In all likelihood Salzilli had read or heard in performance (in the Fantastici and/or the Umoristi academies?) some of Milton's poetry: perhaps his Greek rendering of Psalm 114, his Italian sonnets, his Latin poetry: possibly some of the Latin elegies or philosophical pieces, or *Ad Patrem*, an ideal means of showcasing Milton the polyglot, advertising, as it does, his knowledge of five languages: Greek, Latin, Italian, French, and Hebrew.[119] That triple coronation, moreover, may also, and good-humoredly, confer upon its Protestant recipient honors normally associated with the Pope of Rome, traditionally the wearer of the *triregnum*, the three-tiered crown (symbolizing his power as father of kings, ruler of the world, and Vicar of Christ). But, in Salzilli's reinvention, the papal is tellingly displaced by the poetic: Milton's crown is a *triplex poeseos laurea* ("a triple laurel *of poetry*").[120] That its envisaged wearer may well have appreciated the inference, if such it be, is strengthened perhaps by the fact that he had implemented the motif in

---

[116] Giovanni Battista Manso, *Vita di Torquato Tasso* (Venice: Deuchino, 1621), 221–233.

[117] See Haan, "'Coelum Non Animum Muto?'" 139–140.

[118] See *Mansus* 89–93.

[119] *Ad Patrem* 79–85. It should be emphasized, moreover, that Milton's express thanks therein to his father for not forcing him to follow the path of money-making or to join the legal profession with its babbling law courts, but for enabling him to further his poetic pursuits (*Ad Patrem* 68–76) would have struck a particular chord with Salzilli, whose sonnet "S'antepone la dignità della Poesia all'utile de gli altri studi" ("He places the worth of Poetry above the usefulness of other pursuits") (*Poesie*, 148) had contrasted the elevating powers of poetry with mercenary pursuits and the noisy tumult of the law courts: "e sagaci/De'volumi d'Astrea chiose loquaci/Fan di tumulti risonar' il Foro" (6–8) ("and the verbose glosses of the shrewd volumes of Astraea cause the Forum to resound tumultuously").

[120] Emphasis is mine.

his own Latin poetry.[121] Where the encomium's title celebrates Milton as a polyglot, the quatrain proper goes further by presenting him as an epic poet. Hitherto critics have tended to focus their attention on the extravagant nature of the piece, at the expense, perhaps, of analyzing its language and tropes in relation to Salzilli's extant vernacular verse, and, not least, to the likely impact that it would have had upon Milton himself. Thus Masson is unhesitant in his assertion that "[t]he flattery ... is so gross that plain prose would be ashamed of [it]."[122] Likewise, Parker describes it as both "eulogistic" and "extravagant."[123] Lewalski regards it as "astonishingly laudatory,"[124] and Campbell and Corns remark that "[e]ven by the generous conventions of encomium the praise seems extravagant."[125] In fact, the quatrain, while singing Milton's praises, also showcases several themes and motifs characteristic of Salzilli's Italian verse in the Fantastici volume. These operate on both a linguistic and a thematic level. Thus the repeated injunction *Cede ... cedat* may draw the discerning reader back to Salzilli's canzone "La Poesia Trionfante." There the speaker, invoking Apollo as god of poetry, proclaims: "Per le naufraghe vie/De l'humane procelle/Tu saraì calma a le tempeste mie" ("In the course of the shipwrecked paths of human storms, it is you who will afford calm to my tempests").[126] And it is to Apollo that Jupiter himself is enjoined to yield:

> *Ceda, ceda* pur Giove
> Al tuo summo valor ...[127]
>
> Yield, yield, even Jupiter,
> To your supreme power ...

In the Latin encomium, however, the injunction is issued not to Jupiter, but to the rivers Meles and Mincius, which function metonymically as representatives of Homer and Virgil, over which and whom the Thames

---

[121] Milton, *In Proditionem Bombardicam* 3.3: *trina ... corona* ("triple crown"); *In Quintum Novembris* 55: *Tricoronifer* ("Wearer of the triple crown"); 94: *diademaque triplex* ("triple diadem"). See also 15. Cf. Sonnet 15.12: "The triple Tyrant."

[122] Masson, *Life*, I, 753.

[123] Parker, *Biography*, I, 173.

[124] Lewalski, *Life*, 95.

[125] Campbell and Corns, *Life, Work, and Thought*, 118.

[126] *Poesie*, 157.

[127] *Poesie*, 157. Emphasis is mine. Cf. also "Ceda per dunque" ("Give in therefore") (Salzilli, "Per Una Cagnuola" [9] at *Poesie*, 152) repeated in Salzilli, "Lilla anteposta all' Aurora" (9) at *Poesie*, 153.

(and by implication Milton) can enjoy a different "poetic triumph," as it were. Elsewhere in Salzilli's poetry the river motif occurs in association with time and death, forces which, nonetheless, can be overcome by poetry, by the "fecund laurel of glory," and by the immortalizing power of fame. This is resoundingly proclaimed in his first sonnet entitled "S'antepone la dignità della Poesia all'utile de gli altri studi" ("He places the worth of Poetry above the usefulness of other pursuits"),[128] to which this discussion will return.

To these two rivers Salzilli adds the Sebeto, representative of Tasso. Now through Milton the Thames alone will be equal to all three (*par tribus unus erit*).[129] That notion of poetic equivalence and of the associated emulation between the ancients and the moderns functions as a virtual leitmotif in Salzilli's verse as a whole. Indeed the equation of Milton with Homer and Virgil assumes additional significance, given the laudatory terms in which these two ancient poets are presented in his Italian poetry. Thus in "La Poesia Trionfante" Homer is periphrastically described as "Il gran cantor d'Achille" ("The mighty singer of Achilles"),[130] and Virgil is seen as the winner of an epic victory, which both resides in, and is encapsulated by, Aeneas's triumph over Turnus.[131] That element of "parity" (denoted by *par*) between the ancients and the moderns functions as the subject matter of Salzilli's sonnet entitled "Che l'età nostra ha Scrittori sì di verso, come di prosa eguali a gli Antichi" ("That our age possesses Writers of verse, as of prose, that are a match for the Ancients"). There, as if in defiance of poetic equivalence, Tasso is depicted as actually surpassing Virgil:

> E pur' io veggio al gran Maron simile
> De la tromba di Manto il Tasso herede,
> Che'l suono accresce, e'l suo retaggio eccede,
> E la pietà d'Enea si prende a vile.[132]

> And I also see Tasso, like the great Virgil, heir to
> the trumpet of Manto, who augments the sound
> and exceeds his heritage, while the piety of
> Aeneas is regarded as worthless.

---

[128] *Poesie*, 148.

[129] For the phraseology, cf. Michael Marullus, *Ep.* 2.9.5–6: *sic modo par unus cunctis, ex omnibus unum/non potes, ut cupias, deligere ipse parem* ("you alone are equal to them all only in the sense that from them all you are unable to choose a single one as your equal, although you may wish to do so").

[130] *Poesie*, 158.

[131] *Poesie*, 158.

[132] *Poesie*, 150.

Likewise, in regard to modern prose writers, the sonnet continues, Etruria possesses a boast equal to that of the splendor of Latium in the person of Agostino Mascardi, who has armed his breast with Tuscan eloquence.[133]

Salzilli's boast about Milton, however, goes one step further. The Thames is depicted as victorious (*victor*), and enjoined to carry its waves higher than the three aforementioned rivers. Thus does the river of London rise above that of ancient Greece, Rome, or modern Italy just as *Ioannes Milto Anglus* ("John Milton Englishman") outshines both ancient and modern poets: Homer, Virgil, and Tasso. That these are epic poets makes the compliment particularly high. The terms of praise may reflect Milton's self-fashioning while upon Italian soil, where, as Poole judiciously observes, he "presented himself to the Italian academicians as an epic poet, even though he was as yet without an epic poem."[134] But he was a poet in possession of epic plans, which he was far from reticent in articulating to his hosts. Indeed, that Salzillian contrast between *Thamesis victor* ("victorious Thames") and *depressa Mincius urna* ("Mincius with lowered urn") seems to resurface in a confident boast made probably only a few months later by Milton to the Neapolitan academician Giovanni Battista Manso. Thus the speaker of *Mansus* can proudly proclaim:

> Nos etiam in nostro modulantes flumine cygnos
> Credimus obscuras noctis sensisse per umbras,
> Qua *Thamesis* late *puris* argenteus *urnis*
> Oceani glaucos perfundit gurgite crines (*Mansus* 30–33)

> We too believe that we have heard swans singing in our river amid night's dark shadows, where the silver *Thames* with *pure urns* drenches her green locks in Ocean's expansive waters.[135]

---

[133] *Poesie*, 150: "E pur' io veggio ch'a l'Etruria è dato/Con vanto equale a lo splendor latino / ... Ecco MASCARDI, ... Che di tosca eloquenza il petto armato" (9–13) ("And I also see that there has been granted to Etruria with a pride that equals the splendor of Latium ... Io, MASCARDI, who has armed his breast with Tuscan eloquence"). Agostino Mascardi (1590–1640) was a prolific author, whose published prose works include *Orazioni* (Genoa: Giuseppe Pavoni, 1622), *Prose Vulgari* (Venice: Bartolomeo Fontana, 1626), *Discorsi Morali su La Tavola di Cebete Tebano* (Venice: Antonio Pinelli, 1627), and *La Congiura del Conte Giovanni Luigi de' Fieschi* (Venice: G[iacomo] Scaglia, 1629). See, among others, Eraldo Bellini, "Mascardi, Agostino," *DBI* 71 (2008): 525–532; Eraldo Bellini, *Agostino Mascardi tra "Ars Poetica" e "Ars Historica"* (Milan: V&P Università, 2002); Stefania Tutino, *Shadows of Doubt: Language and Truth in Post-Reformation Catholic Culture* (Oxford: Oxford University Press, 2014), 40–73.

[134] Poole, *Milton and the Making of Paradise Lost*, 46.

[135] Emphasis is mine.

But now the Virgilian and Miltonic rivers are not in competition. Instead, they have become one, a unification validated perhaps by the attribution of urns to river-gods by Virgil himself.[136] In *Mansus*, too, it is as a future epic poet that Milton, as if with reaffirmed confidence, presents himself. His projected epic, an *Arthuriad*,[137] and the terms in which he envisages it therein, are describable as Tassonian in essence. One wonders too whether Salzilli's succinct clustering of classical and modern epic masters, and his associated presentation of *Ioannes Milto Anglus* as both equaling and surpassing such precursors, contributed, at least in part, to Milton's later self-fashioning as an epic poet. Here it is worth highlighting his deliberations as articulated in *The Reason of Church Government* regarding "that Epick form whereof the two poems of Homer, and those other two of Virgil and Tasso are a diffuse ... model,"[138] a work in which he presents his decision to write his epic in the vernacular as one governed by Italian precedent.[139] Likewise, something of that Salzillian sense of parity as the act of a modern poet emulating only to surpass "Il gran cantor d'Achille" ("The mighty singer of Achilles") (an act conveyed in his encomium by the tellingly resonant comparative adjective *altior* ["higher"]) seems to rear its head, in a transmuted form, in Milton's professed epic

> ... argument
> Not less but more heroic than the wrath
> Of stern Achilles on his foe pursued
> Thrice fugitive about Troy wall; or rage
> Of Turnus for Lavinia disespoused,
> Or Neptune's ire or Juno's, that so long
> Perplexed the Greek and Cytherea's son.
> (*Paradise Lost* 9. 13–19)

---

[136] Virgil, *Aeneid* 7.792: *caelataque amnem fundens pater Inachus urna* ("and father Inachus pouring his stream from an embossed urn"). Cf. Statius, *Thebaid* 9.410; Silius Italicus, *Pun.* 1.407. All quotations from the *Aeneid* are from *P[ubli] Vergili Maronis Opera*, ed. F. A. Hirtzel (Oxford: Clarendon Press, 1942).

[137] *Mansus* 80–84. Cf. *Ep. Dam.* 162–171. Arthur is included in the Trinity MS among possible subjects for an epic poem.

[138] *The Reason of Church Government*, 38.

[139] *The Reason of Church Government*, 38: "I apply'd my selfe to that resolution which Ariosto follow'd against the perswasions of Bembo, to fix all the industry and art I could unite to the adorning of my native tongue."

1.4. *Ad Salsillum Poetam Romanum Aegrotantem*

Salzilli's tribute had no slight an impact upon its recipient. In the words of Campbell and Corns, "it is little wonder that Milton treasured the poem."[140] In response, he composed a Latin encomium of his own: *Ad Salsillum Poetam Romanum Aegrotantem*. While obviously exemplifying one of those pieces modestly described by him as having been "patch[ed] up"[141] in the course of his Italian journey, Milton's poem seems to rise above the injudicious censure of Walter Savage Landor, for whom it contained "not an iota of poetry,"[142] or the criticisms of Parker and Alledoni, the one viewing it as "a piece of poetical backscratching,"[143] the other regarding it as "più come una esercitazione poetica academica ben riuscite che come espressione sincera dell'animo di Milton" ("more like a well-executed academic poetic exercise than a sincere expression of Milton's soul").[144] It does so by carefully drawing upon aspects of Salzilli's encomium (and its title), only to develop them into a reciprocal tribute that, as argued later, is related to, and celebrates, the Italian poet's roles in both the Accademia dei Fantastici and the Accademia degli Umoristi. In this new reading, the poem emerges as a piece that is characterized by a skillfully attuned complexity that has hitherto escaped the notice or scrutiny of Milton scholars.

That *Ad Salsillum* was composed in response to Salzilli's encomium is indicated by its pertinent echoing of some of its features.[145] Here, and perhaps in a performance of the present piece before Roman accademici, Milton is proud to showcase the extent to which his poetry has been admired by the Italian, to whose professed judgment he seems indeed to allude: *camoena nostra cui tantum est cordi,/Quamque ille magnis praetulit immerito divis* (7–8) ("to whose heart my poetry is so dear, and which he preferred, though undeservedly, to the mighty gods"). The perfect tense *praetulit* ("preferred") would seem to point to one occasion in particular (Salzilli's writing of his tribute), while Homer, Virgil, and Tasso, said to be surpassed by Milton in the encomium itself,

---

[140] Campbell and Corns, *Life, Work, and Thought*, 118.

[141] Milton, *The Reason of Church Government*, 37, quoted at 19.

[142] Walter Savage Landor, "Imaginary Conversations," in *The Complete Works of Walter Savage Landor*, eds. T. E. Welby and Stephen Wheeler, 16 vols (London: Chapman and Hall, 1927–1936), V, 330.

[143] Parker, *Biography*, I, 173.

[144] Ettore Allodoli, *Giovanni Milton e l'Italia* (Prato: Vestri & Spighi, 1907), 22–23.

[145] As briefly noted by Parker, *Biography* I, 173, and by Low, "*Mansus*: In its Context," 105. For fuller discussion, see Haan, *From Academia to Amicitia*, 85–98.

are now transformed into *magni ... divi* ("mighty gods").[146] Milton's deification of ancient and modern poets may confer upon Salzilli a (quasi-academic?) role not dissimilar to that of Paris on Mount Ida. In this reading Milton's Muse, self-referentially described as *camoena nostra* (7),[147] functions, as it were, as a fourth contender, now surpassing, in Salzilli's judgment at least, the other three "gods."[148] Interestingly, this is the phrase used elsewhere by Milton to describe his composition of Latin elegiac verse.[149] One senses an element of contented pride on Milton's part, despite his insertion of the qualifying adverb *immerito* ("undeservedly"). Both here and in the hyperbolic Latin prose heading, subsequently prefixed to the 1645 published encomia, his qualification is not only an act of mock-modesty, but also a gesture intended to bring on board a readership (and an academic audience?) that extends beyond that of his immediate addressee.[150]

---

[146] Cf. Stella P. Revard, *Milton and the Tangles of Neaera's Hair: The Making of the 1645 Poems* (Columbia: University of Missouri Press, 1997), 225.

[147] Camena was a Roman goddess, probably originally a water-deity. On the identification of the *Camoenae* with the Muses, see Bush, *Variorum*, I, 115. Cf. Horace, *Odes* 1.12.39; 2.16.38.

[148] Cf. Angelo Rodolfini, *Sonetti*, 65: "Al Signor Giovanni Salzilli," discussed at 38–39, in which Salzilli's rivaling virtues are presented as emulating and surpassing those of the contending goddesses over whom Paris had to proclaim his judgment.

[149] Cf. Milton, *Elegia Sexta* 3: *At tua quid nostram prolectat Musa camoenam* ("But why does your Muse entice my poetry"), where the phrase may well strike a contrast between Charles Diodati's use of Greek and Milton's recourse to Latin, on which see also Bush, *Variorum*, I, 115.

[150] Cf. *Poemata*, 3: *Haec quae sequuntur de auctore testimonia, tametsi ipse intelligebat non tam de se quam supra se esse dicta, eo quod praeclaro ingenio viri nec non amici ita fere solent laudare ut omnia suis potius virtutibus quam veritati congruentia nimis cupide affingant, noluit tamen horum egregiam in se voluntatem non esse notam; cum alii praesertim ut id faceret magnopere suaderent. Dum enim nimiae laudis invidiam totis ab se viribus amolitur sibique quod plus aequo est non attributum esse mavult, iudicium interim hominum cordatorum atque illustrium quin summo sibi honori ducat negare non potest* ("The author himself realized that the following testimonials concerning him were pronounced not so much about him as over and above him for the reason that men of outstanding genius and friends as well are generally accustomed to issue praise in such a way that they embellish everything too eagerly in accordance with their own virtues rather than with the truth. Nonetheless, he was unwilling that their excellent good will towards him should not be known especially since others were giving him great encouragement to do so. For while he endeavors with all his powers to lift from himself the odious charge of excessive laudation, and prefers that nothing that is more than fair be attributed to him, in the meantime he cannot deny that he regards the judgment of intelligent and famous men as a supreme honor"). See Lewalski and Haan, 106–107, 415. Hale,

Milton's self-fashioning via the Latinized *Milto* (occurring uniquely here) picks up the precise form of his name employed by Salzilli (in contrast to *Miltonius*[151] or *Miltonus*[152] employed by other encomiasts) both in the prose heading (*Ad Ioannem Miltonem*) and in the quatrain proper (*Nam per te, Milto, par tribus unus erit* ["For through you, Milton, he alone will be equal to three"]).[153] This invites the reader to view the author of this particular tribute through Salzilli's eyes. It is a gesture that recurs as the poem progresses. Thus *alumnus ille Londini Milto* (9) ("Milton, that foster-child of London") suggests, through an emphatic *ille*, "that same *Milto* mentioned by you in the encomium," while later it is "this same" Milton who wishes Salzilli every good fortune (*Tibi optat idem hic fausta multa, Salsille* [17]).[154] Likewise, the contrast in Salzilli's heading between the *Ioannes* who is an Englishman and the *Ioannes* who is an Italian and native of Rome seems to underlie not only the title of Milton's poem (*Ad Salsillum poetam Romanum* ...), but also the very different climates of England and Italy. Thus lines 9-16 conduct Milton (and the reader) on a continental journey of sorts from the turbulent weather of England to the essential calm of Italy.[155]

But perhaps the closest parallel between Salzilli's encomium and Milton's poem is the motif of a river representative of the poet of its region. *Ad Salsillum* reciprocates the river/poet metonymy, but only to invert the whole (36-41). For whereas Salzilli had depicted the Thames, symbolizing Milton, carrying its waves higher than all the other rivers, Milton predicts that Salzilli's river, the Tiber, will curb its waves (40). In so doing, he hints at a parallel between the envisaged healing of one who had required *levamen* (30) ("alleviation"), and the calming of the Tiber, described by an adjective (*tumidus* [36]) that can also denote ill health.[156]

Milton's Languages, 92–93, briefly analyses this preface, in which he sees Milton performing a syntactical "balancing act" (92).

[151] *Miltonius* occurs in the heading to Manso's tribute: *Ad Ioannem Miltonium Anglum*. See *Poemata*, 4; Lewalski and Haan, 106–107.

[152] *Miltonus* occurs in the heading to Selvaggio's tribute: *Ad Ioannem Miltonum*. See *Poemata*, 4; Lewalski and Haan, 108–109. See also 20.

[153] As noted by Bush, *Variorum*, I, 264.

[154] Emphasis is mine.

[155] The description of Milton leaving England, his arrival in Italy, and the many learned friends whom he met in the course of his trip also occurs in the Italian encomium by Antonio Francini, who praises Milton's virtue, and outlines the reasons that led him to travel to Italy. See *Poemata*, 5–9; Lewalski and Haan, 108–113, 416–419.

[156] See, for example, Cicero, *Tusc.* 3.9: *membrum tumidum ac turgidum* ("a swollen and inflamed limb"). Cf. Hugo Grotius, *Anapaesti in Morbum Fratris*, where the

And both are disassociated with death: Salzilli, it is hoped, will recover his strength; the Tiber will not invade the tombs of kings. But Miltonic metonymy has more far reaching consequences. The effect of Salzilli's *cantus* (32) ("song") upon his native river, the Tiber, is also symbolic of the continued influence that his Italian poetry is envisaged as exerting upon the academic community (or communities) of Rome.[157]

If an esteemed Roman poet is ultimately viewed here through the eyes of his fellow academicians, it is through a Salzillian lens that *Ioannes Milto Anglus* fashions his own poetic self. This is effected by *Ad Salsillum*'s showcasing of the authorial multilingualism celebrated in the tribute itself.[158] Thus the *laurea Graeca* ("Greek laurel") is evinced by the occurrence of Greek names, such as the allusion to lyric poetry in the tradition of Alcaeus and Sappho (*Lesbium ... melos* [22] ["the song of Lesbos"]), and the reference to Hebe (23) and Paean (25). More implicitly, the description of the blustery wind (11-13) may, as Freeman suggests, echo Hesiod's account of the violently panting Typhoeus in *Theogony* 826ff., and Pindar's elaboration of the same in *Pythian* 1.[159] It is possible too that the *decentes ... suras* attributed to Deiopea (4) look back to the "comely ankles" of Hebe in Homer, *Odyssey* 11. 603.

The *laurea Latina* ("Latin laurel") of Salzilli's tribute is vindicated and showcased by the range of Latin intertexts with which Milton's poem engages. The opening line, describing the scazontic meter[160]— particularly apt for the subject, in that the lameness of the Muse parallels

---

adjective is used to describe mental ill health: *pellat [requies] tumidos/pectoris aestus, et vesanos/animi fluctus, sopor ut reddat/mite serenum* ("may [repose] dispel the tides swelling within his chest, and the frenzied waves of his mind so that sleep may render him gently serene" (*Poemata Collecta* [Leiden: Andreas Clocquius, 1617], 262).

[157] See 95–97.

[158] Cf. Freeman, "Milton's Roman Connection," 96: "By alluding to so many Greek, Latin, and modern Italian practices, Milton thus politely justifies Salzilli's epigram as well as his own accomplishment."

[159] Freeman, "Milton's Roman Connection," 94–95. The contrast between a bellowing, obstructing wind (the act of Typhoeus) and the love of poetry (the hymn which Phoebus inspires in Aetna) may underlie Milton's poem, in which a violent wind has almost impeded his journey to Italy in his aim of enhancing his love of poetry and Italian culture. The wind finds a parallel in the *profunda bilis* (19) ("overflow of bile"), which "breathes" (*spirat* [20]) through the ailing Salzilli, and shows no respect for his poetic talents (17–22). The possible allusion is particularly apt, given Salzilli's reputation as a second Pindar, on which see 38.

[160] For a discussion of the metrics of the poem, see S. M. Oberhelman and John Mulryan, "Milton's Use of Classical Meters in the *Sylvarum Liber*," *MP* 81 (1983): 131–145, at 137–138. See also 86–88.

the sickness of the poet, Salzilli (*O Musa, gressum quae volens trahis claudum* [1] ["O Muse, who drag a lame foot willingly"])—may recall Ovid's description in *Remedia Amoris* 377–378: *liber in adversos hostes stringatur iambus,/seu celer, extremum seu trahat ille pedem* ("let the free iambic be unsheathed against opposing enemies, whether it be swift or drag its final foot"). But in contrast to the afflicted addressee, the Muse of the poem takes pleasure in her physical ailment: *Vulcanioque tarda gaudes incessu* (2) ("despite your tardy progress, you rejoice in the gait of Vulcan").[161] More striking, and as if in fulfillment of Salzilli's esteemed regard for his epic potential, Milton offers, as it were, a poem within a poem—a self-inscribed miniature *Aeneid*. He does so by re-enacting Aeneas's escape from Troy and his subsequent arrival in Italy: from *Aeneid* 1, where Juno bribes Aeolus to raise a storm by offering as a reward the nymph Deiopea,[162] now reconfigured as dancing before the goddess' couch (4–5),[163] to a Miltonic protagonist who both is and is not Aeneas. Like the Virgilian hero, he has left his native land, here described as *suum ... nidum* (10) ("his own nest"), but he has had the good fortune of evading a virtual storm (*pessimus ... ventorum* [11] ["the worst of winds"]), a hyperbolic representation of England's inclement weather. Then, as in the second half of the *Aeneid*, the traveler reaches Italy (*venit feraces Itali soli ad glebas* [14] ["he has come to the fertile clods of Italy's soil"]), its landscape somewhat idealized in terms evocative perhaps of the idyllic pastoralism of Latium as glimpsed for the first time by Aeneas and his crew in *Aeneid* 7.[164] But the Latium envisaged by Milton is essentially primitive. The combined allusions to

---

[161] Vulcan's permanent lameness was the consequence of his falling from heaven. Cf. *Elegia Septima* 81–82; *Naturam non Pati Senium*, 23–24; *Paradise Lost* 1. 740–746.

[162] Virgil, *Aeneid* 1.71–75.

[163] *Ad Salsillum* 4–5: *cum decentes flava Deiope suras/Alternat aureum ante Iunonis lectum* ("when Deiopea, golden-haired, and with seemly ankles, dances trippingly before Juno's couch"). Milton's invention may owe something to *L'Allegro* 33–34: "Com, and *trip it* as ye go/On the light *fantastick* toe." Emphasis is mine. Woodhouse and Bush aptly remark: "The epithet *fantastick*, fanciful in conception (not necessarily grotesque as in *Comus* 144), is transferred from the dance to the foot that performs it." See A. S. P. Woodhouse and Douglas Bush, *A Variorum Commentary on the Poems of John Milton: The Minor Poems* (New York: Columbia University Press, 1972), II.1, 278.

[164] *Aeneid* 7.25–36. As noted by R. D. Williams, "[t]he description of the promised land is pastoral and idyllic" (*The Aeneid of Virgil: Books 7–12*, ed. R. D. Williams [Basingstoke: St Martins Press, 1973], 168).

Faunus (27), and Evander (28),[165] and, in particular, the association of Faunus with oak groves in the invocation *Querceta Fauni* (27) recall perhaps Evander's explication of pre-Saturnian Latium to the newly arrived Aeneas. Latium's woods, he tells his guest, were once inhabited by Fauns and Nymphs (*Fauni Nymphaeque* [*Aeneid* 8. 314]),[166] and a *gens ... virum truncis et duro robore nata* (*Aeneid* 8. 315) ("a race of men sprung from tree-trunks and hardy oak"),[167] who fed on berries or acorns. It is this primitive, natural resource that may offer Salzilli a potential herbal remedy: *Siquid salubre vallibus frondet vestris* (29) ("if any health-bringing plant booms in your valleys").[168] And there is good reason to be hopeful. The attribution of the adjective *mitis* ("gentle") to describe Evander (28) may look back to his hospitable reception of Aeneas in *Aeneid* 8. 102–519. Finally, and more generally, the prediction of the calming of the Tiber in the poem's final lines (36–41) may reimagine Virgil's account in *Aeneid* 8.[169] It is a conclusion, however, that is *a fortiori* fittingly Horatian.

1.5 Salzilli as a Second Horace

Whereas Milton's self-fashioning draws upon the epic poetry of Virgil, his depiction of Salzilli looks to Virgil's contemporary, Horace. This equation operates on a variety of levels, the multifaceted nature of which affords the poem a hitherto unnoticed complexity: (1) through the presentation of Salzilli in language evocative of Horace's self-description as the first to Latinize Greek lyric poetry, (2) through Milton's possible

---

[165] *Ad Salsillum* 27–28: *Querceta Fauni, vosque rore vinoso/Colles benigni, mitis Evandri sedes* ("Oak-groves of Faunus, and you, hills abounding in the dew of grapes, the abode of gentle Evander").

[166] Fauns were male deities of the countryside, frequently associated with mysterious utterances, and hence poetic inspiration. Nymphs were female deities, who inhabited springs and woods.

[167] On the relationship between *Fauni* and *robur*, see Michael Paschalis, *Virgil's Aeneid: Semantic Relations and Proper Names* (Oxford: Clarendon Press, 1997), 281.

[168] See also 94–95.

[169] Virgil, *Aeneid* 8.86–89: *Thybris ea fluvium, quam longa est, nocte tumentem/ leniit, et tacita refluens ita substitit unda,/mitis ut in morem stagni placidaeque paludis/sterneret aequor aquis, remo ut luctamen abesset* ("for all the length of that night Tiber calmed his swollen wave, ebbing and halting with silent stream in such a manner that he smoothed the surface of his waters like a stagnant marsh or placid swamp, so that there was no need to toil at the oars").

reading of Salzilli's published output as essentially Horatian, (3) through the Horatian intertexts with which *Ad Salsillum* engages.

Although celebrated by his contemporaries as the Pindar of his age,[170] the Salzilli of Milton's poem is presented as a second Horace, more specifically, as an Italianized Horace: *tu Romano/Tam cultus ore Lesbium condis melos* (21–22) ("you so elegantly fashion the song of Lesbos upon Roman lips"). The contrast between *Lesbium ... melos* and *Romano ... ore* is evocative of Horace's frequent self-fashioning in the *Odes* as one who employs and indeed redeploys the *Lesboum ... barbiton* ("lyre of Lesbos") as his instrument,[171] which, he proclaims, is now to sound a Latin song (*Odes* 1.32.3–5).[172] This reaches its height in *Epistles* 1.19, in the speaker's confident claims to primacy:

> Parios ego primus iambos
> ostendi Latio, numeros animosque secutus
> Archilochi. (*Epist.* 1.19.23–25)
>
> I was the first to display Parian rhythms to Latium,
> having followed the meters and spirit of Archilochus.
>
> hunc ego, non alio dictum prius ore, Latinus
> vulgavi fidicen. (*Epist.* 1.19. 32–33)
>
> I was the first Latin lyricist to make known this man [Alcaeus], who had not previously been celebrated by a Roman tongue.

That *vulgavi* (33) is tellingly appropriate. In Salzilli's case *Romano ... ore*, as Masson rightly remarks, probably refers to his Italian (rather than to his Latin) verse.[173] In other words, just as Horace nationalized the Greek poetry of Archilochus, Alcaeus, and Sappho by a linguistic reinvention in his native Latin, so has Salzilli nationalized the Latin lyric poetry of Horace in his vernacular Italian.[174]

---

[170] See, for example, Angelo Rodolfini, "Alli Signori Giovanni Lotti, e Salzilli," discussed at 38.

[171] Horace, *Odes* 1.1.34.

[172] Horace, *Odes* 1.32.3–5: *age dic Latinum,/barbite, carmen,/Lesbio primum modulate civi* ("come then lyre, first tuned by the citizen of Lebos, proclaim a Latin song").

[173] Masson, ed., *Poetical Works*, III, 530, adding: "it seems to have been by his Italian poetry that Salzilli was best known in Rome." The only example of Salzilli's Latin verse that has hitherto come to light is, in fact, his encomium of Milton.

[174] For the notion of "vernacularizing" classical verse, cf. Milton, *The Reason of Church Government*, 38, quoted at 53.

The equation is particularly pertinent, given the Horatian context in which the Accademia dei Fantastici[175] presented its literary endeavors, not least in its adoption of the Horatian motto QUIDLIBET AUDENDI[176] ("venturing anything") to accompany its chosen *impresa*: an artist's canvas (*tela*). In essence this iconographical act of self-promotion, signaled that the Fantastici, true to their name, enjoyed the ability to give rein to their creative powers, and possessed a liberating poetic audacity. That daring license afforded by Horace to both painters and poets is encapsulated by the frontispiece to the 1637 Fantastici volume itself, in which the Horatian motto is neatly wrapped around the top of the artist's easel, supported by two wingless putti. Significantly, the canvas is left blank, as if inviting and challenging Salzilli and his fellow contributors to venture any poetic composition in fulfillment of that Horatian dictum.[177] This is reinforced by Ottavio Tronsarelli's punning description of the academicians as "la cui Impresa è l'haver ardire di tentar' ogn' impresa" ("those whose emblem [*impresa*] is to have the audacity to attempt every undertaking [*impresa*]"),[178] and by Giovan Martino Longo, one of whose contributions presents the *impresa* as "Pinger sù questa TELA eterni essempi/Di FANTASTICHE Idee" ("a CANVAS upon which they paint eternal examples of FANTASTIC ideas").[179] After all, in the words of the fifteenth-century Italian artist Cennino Cennini, the poet, like the painter, is afforded the "libertà" ("freedom") to compose "una figura ... secondo sua fantasia" ("a picture ... in accordance with his own fantasy").[180] Or, as Tennyson would later proclaim:

---

[175] On the Accademia dei Fantastici, which traced its origins back to *c.* 1625 and to the initiative of a certain Alberto Fabri, who organized meetings of intellectuals in the Convent of the Apostles, Rome, see Garuffi, *Italia Accademica*, 11–20; Bartolomeo Piazza, *Eusevologio Romano* (Rome: Giovanni Andreoli, 1690), Tractate XII; Maylender, *Storia*, II, 346–348; Haan, *From Academia to Amicitia*, 81–82.

[176] Horace, *Ars Poetica* 9–10: *pictoribus atque poetis/quidlibet audendi semper fuit aequa potestas* ("painters and poets have always possessed the equal license to venture anything").

[177] On the copy of the *Poesie* in the British Library (shelfmark 1062.b.1) the owner has interestingly inscribed his own name ("Charles Lescuier") upon the blank canvas.

[178] *Poesie*, 5.

[179] "A' Signori Accademici Fantastici. Alludendo all' Impresa dell' Accademia" (*Poesie*, 138). See Martin Kemp, "From 'Mimesis' to 'Fantasia': The Quattrocento Vocabulary of Creation, Inspiration and Genius in the Visual Arts," *Viator* 8 (1977): 347–398; Charles Tomlinson, "The Poet as Painter," in *Essays by Divers Hands: Innovation in Contemporary Literature*, ed. Vincent Cronin, Transactions of the Royal Society of Literature 40 (Woodbridge: Boydell Press, 1979), 147–162.

[180] See *Il Libro delle' Arte o Trattato Della Pittura di Cennino Cennini*, eds. Gaetano and Carlo Milanesi (Florence: Felice Le Monnier, 1859), 2.

> Launch your vessel,
> And crowd your canvas,
> And, ere it vanishes
> Over the margin,
> After it, follow it,
> Follow The Gleam.
> (*Merlin and the Gleam*, 126–131).[181]

Certainly the artist of *Ad Salsillum* paints imaginatively on his poetic canvas by inventing a series of mythological and topographical fantasies: Deiopea dancing before Juno's couch; Numa gazing upon Egeria in entranced enthrallment, and, for all eternity, the personified hills of the Italian countryside vying in competition to deliver to the sick poet their homegrown medicinal herbs. For Milton, moreover, that Horatian challenge to venture anything (*quidlibet audendi*) would come to characterize his poetic recreation of his Italian experiences: in his identification with his *Musa*, who *Imprudens Italas ausa est volitare per urbes* (*Mansus* 29) ("has *ventured* in her rashness to fly through the cities of Italy") or, later, in his fond reminiscence of his own performance in Italian academies: *Ipse etiam tentare ausus sum* (*Epitaphium Damonis* 133) ("I even *ventured* to offer my own attempts").[182]

But *Ad Salsillum*'s implicit presentation of its addressee as a second Horace is of particular interest in that it suggests a Miltonic acknowledgment of the Horatian nature of several of Salzilli's poems in the published Fantastici volume.[183] It is thus worth pausing to consider more closely this aspect of his work. Salzilli's sequence of twelve sonnets is introduced by one entitled "S'antepone la dignità della Poesia all' utile de gli altri studi") ("He places the worth of Poetry above the

---

[181] Text is that of *The Poems of Tennyson*, ed. Christopher Ricks, 3 vols (London: Longman, 1987). Here, as Catherine Maxwell observes, "[t]he artist frantically fills out the blank space with his pictorial design, knowing that design's critical relation to a sublime which is always on [the] point of vanishing, of quitting the borders of his page." See Catherine Maxwell, *The Female Sublime From Milton to Swinburne: Bearing Blindness* (Manchester: Manchester University Press, 2001), 131.

[182] Emphasis is mine.

[183] An interesting precedent can be found in Milton's alertness to the Virgilianism of Alexander Gil's *In Sylvam-Ducis*, described by him in *Epistola Familiaris* 2 as *carmina sane grandia et maiestatem vere poeticam Virgilianumque ubique ingenium redolentia* ("your poetry, truly exalted and everywhere redolent of a real poetic majesty and Virgilian talent"). Gil's poem, to which were appended four lines from Virgil's account of the fall of Troy (*Aeneid* 2. 491–494), engages verbally with the *Aeneid* on several occasions. See *Epistolarum Familiarium Liber Unus and Uncollected Letters*, ed. Haan, 53, 55. It saw publication in Gil's *Parerga: sive Poetici Conatus* (London: Robert Milborne, 1632), 36–40.

usefulness of other pursuits").[184] Listing a series of pursuits, each of which is presented as inferior to that favored by the poet, the speaker draws upon the conventions of the classical priamel, a tradition exemplified by Sappho, Solon, Pindar, Bacchylides, Euripides, and Horace.[185] Indeed it is with Horace, *Odes* 1.1, likewise the first in a series, that the sonnet seems to engage. But where Horace delineates the vain obsessions of those who pursue chariot-racing, politics, business, farming, overseas trade, leisure, war, and hunting,[186] Salzilli censures the "alma vil" ("vile soul") that is "serva de l'oro" (1) ("enslaved to gold") in its materialistic pursuit of medicine, described here as "D'Esculapio, e Peon l'orme fallaci" (2) ("the deceptive tracks of Asclepius and Paean"). This he follows with an attack on the legal profession, where "De' volumi d'Astrae chiose loquaci/Fan si tumulti risonar' il Foro" (7–8) ("the verbose glosses of the shrewd volumes of Astraea cause the Forum to resound tumultuously").[187] The professions may differ, but the Horatian images of chariot-racing, victory, and the elevating powers of poetry recur on a metaphorical level. Just as Horace contrasts the pursuits of "others" (*sunt quos .../... iuvat* [3–4] ["there are those whom it pleases"]) with his own more sublime vocation, the latter denoted by the emphatic *me* (29, 30, 35), so Salzilli strikes a contrast between "altri" (5) ("others") and the assertive "io" (9) ("I"). In Horace, the *palma ... nobilis* (5) ("noble palm"), which can elevate such competitors to the gods (6), is transmuted in the Ode's soaring conclusion into the ivy-leaf, the reward for learned brows, that enables the poet to enter a partnership with the gods (29–30),[188] if only Polyhymnia deigns to play the *Lesboum ...*

---

[184] *Poesie*, 148.

[185] On the priamel, see, among others, W. H. Race, *The Classical Priamel from Homer to Boethius*, Mnemosyne Supplement 74 (Leiden: Brill, 1982). On its appropriation by Horace, see Karl Vretska, "Horatius, *Carm*. I.1," *Hermes* 99 (1971): 323–335; Aldo Setaiolo, "Il Proemio dei Carmina Oraziani," *Atti e Memorie dell' Accademia Toscana di Scienze e Lettere "La Columbaria,"* 38 (1973): 1–59, at 50–59, and, especially, Barbara K. Gold, "Openings in Horace's Satires and Odes: Poet, Patron, and Audience," in *Beginnings in Classical Literature*, eds. Francis M. Dunn and Thomas Cole, Yale Classical Studies 29 (Cambridge: Cambridge University Press, 1992), 161–186.

[186] Horace, *Odes* 1.1.3-28. For similar catalogues, cf. Horace, *Epode* 2.5–16, *Odes* 1.7.1–14, and *Ep*. 1.1.77–82.

[187] *Poesie*, 148.

[188] *me doctarum hederae praemia frontium/dis miscent superis* (1.1.29–30) ("Ivy, the reward for learned brows, enables me to join the company of the gods"). See, among others, Herbert Musurillo, "The Poet's Apotheosis: Horace, *Odes* 1.1," *TAPhA* 93 (1962): 230–239; H. J. Shey, "The Poet's Progress: Horace *Ode* 1.1," *Arethusa* 4

barbiton (34) ("lyre of Lesbos"). In short, if he is afforded a place among lyric poets (*quodsi me lyricis vatibus inseres* [35]), he will strike the stars with his upreared head (*sublimi feriam sidera vertice* [26]). Here Horace both aligns himself with his Greek lyric predecessors, and sets himself apart from them by virtue of his *Romanitas*. The juxtaposition of the Greek adjective (*lyricus-a-um*) and the Latin noun (*vates* as opposed to the Greek *poeta*) characterizes the poet as priest and prophet, thereby "point[ing]," in the words of Matthew Santirocco, "to the distinctly Roman side of the Odes."[189] Moreover, that express wish to be "inserted" (*inseres*) among the lyric poets may imply an associated desire "to be woven into a garland (*serta*) or anthology."[190]

If the concluding lines of *Odes* 1.1 confidently articulate a goal that "is itself a bold one,"[191] the grandiloquent sestet of Salzilli's poem seems to transform the Horatian *meta* (4), the turning-post cleared by the chariot's frantic wheels, into "le più eccelse mete" (10) ("the more lofty goals") to which his "sublime/Nobil desire" (9–10) ("sublime, noble desires") conduct him, itself a fusion of the *palma ... nobilis* ("noble palm") awarded to the victorious charioteer, and the *sublimi ... vertice* ("lofty ... head") with which the poet shall strike the stars. For Salzilli, the ultimate goal is Mount Pindus itself. The whole is likewise envisaged as a metaphorical victory, expressed this time in a gnomic conclusion that combines the imagery of coronation ("fecondo di gloria Allor" [12] ["the fertile Laurel of glory"]) with that of winning the most prestigious war trophy obtainable by a Roman: the *spolia opima* ("spolie opime" [13] ["rich spoils"]). As in Horace, that victory is only achievable by the speaker's inclusion among "de' nomi altrui" (13) ("the names of others"), an act that will ensure his escape from "il Tempo tributario a Lete" (14) ("Time, the tributary to Lethe"), and will thereby guarantee poetic immortality.[192]

(1971): 185–196; Francis Dunn, "Horace's Sacred Spring (*Odes* I,1)," *Latomus* 48 (1989): 97–109.

[189] Matthew S. Santirocco, *Unity and Design in Horace's Odes* (Chapel Hill: University of North Carolina Press, 1986), 22.

[190] As suggested by William Fitzgerald, *Variety: The Life of a Roman Concept* (Chicago: The University of Chicago Press, 2016), 180. See also Matthew Leigh, "The Garland of Maecenas (Horace, *Odes* 1.1.35)," *CQ* 60 (2010): 268–271, at 271.

[191] Santirocco, *Unity and Design*, 22.

[192] Freeman, "Milton's Roman Connection," 99, misinterprets lines 13–14 as "Time, that tributary to Lethe which sweeps away other men's rich spoils." This erroneously regards "spolie opime" (13) as the object of "porta" (14), and seems to reflect a misreading of "nomi" (13) (names) as "uomo" (man).

The poetic victory envisaged in Salzilli's first sonnet is presented as having been fulfilled in his canzone "La Poesia Trionfante" ("The Triumph of Poetry"), which immediately follows the sonnet sequence.[193] Now the Roman chariot has become the chariot of Phoebus, in which the speaker can experience an immortal flight. This metaphorical elevation is contrasted with the money-making pursuits of "il volgo profano" (8) ("the profane rabble"), a distinction conveyed, once again, by an emphatic "io" (13) ("I"). The speaker proclaims that he follows the illuminating powers afforded by the splendor of Phoebus as sun-god, a light more precious than gold. He proceeds to enunciate: "Ne curo il suo parlar, ne i detti ascolto" (16) ("I have no regard for their [sc. the profane rabble's] talk, nor do I listen to their utterances"). And when the theme recurs later in the poem it does so with renewed confidence. Now he can proclaim his ability to journey towards immortality itself ("A l'immortalità può far tragitto" [188] ["I can make my way to immortality"]) since Phoebus has invited him to join him in his triumphal chariot:

> A me già Febo addita,
> E nel suo Carro a troinfar m'invita.
> Lungi, ah lungi da me terreno fasto,
> S'a la meta del Ciel mi fai contrasto. (189–192)

> Already has Phoebus been joined to me,
> And he invites me to celebrate a triumph in his chariot.
> Begone far, ah, begone far from me earthly pomp
> If he causes me to contest for the goal of Heaven.

With the transformation of the charioteering *meta* ("turning-post") into "la meta del Ciel" ("the goal of Heaven") comes an associated sense of priestly consecration. The poet's disdain for "il volgo profano" (8) is expressed in vatic language reminiscent of Horace's contempt for the uninitiated throng (*Odi profanum vulgus et arceo* [*Odes* 3.1.1] ["I hate the profane rabble, and I keep them away"]), itself evocative of the religious formula *"procul, o procul este, profani"* ("'Begone, Oh begone, you profane ones'") uttered by ancient priests as they warded off the uninitiated from their sacred space.[194] Horace had proclaimed himself the *Musarum sacerdos* (*Odes* 3.1.3) ("priest of the Muses"), set apart from

---

[193] *Poesie*, 156–162.

[194] See the Sibyl at Virgil, *Aeneid* 6. 258. For examples of the use of *profanum* in religious contexts of the uninitiated, cf. Catullus 64.260; Ovid, *Ars Amatoria* 2.601; Juvenal, 2.89. For further instances of the formula, and of its application to literature, see R.G.M. Nisbet and Niall Rudd, *A Commentary on Horace: Odes Book III* (Oxford: Oxford University Press, 2004), 6–7.

the crowd, and the singer of hitherto unheard songs. It is a stance likewise assumed by Salzilli in the emphatically solemn injunction "Lungi, ah lungi da me" (191)[195] ("Begone far, ah, begone far from me"). That sense of distancing the vatic self from the uninitiated proceeds hand in hand with his journey to immortality. By contrast, even royalty cannot escape the powers of Parca. Echoing perhaps the Horatian truism that Death knocks equally at the hovels of the poor and the towers of kings,[196] the speaker proclaims: "Di famelica Parca/Non toglie al morso edace/ Inesausto tesor di gran Monarca" (55–57) ("the unexhausted treasure of a mighty monarch does not remove the gnawing bite of ravenous Fate"). "Morso edaci" seems to work on another neo-Horatian level. After all, as Salzilli proclaims, the devotee of the "nobile cetra" (61) ("noble lyre") can look upon Fate and Time with scorn. In short, poetry itself ensures that his life's thread ("lo stame" [64]) remains unbroken, since it enables the construction of an "edifitio eterno" (64) ("eternal ediface") that can outlive time. The language and imagery are reminiscent of *Odes* 3.30, itself concluding the three books of Odes, and responding to that challenge articulated in Odes 1.1 (a poem which it both balances and answers).[197] Now Horace can announce his fulfillment of that challenge:

> Exegi monumentum aere perennius
> regalique situ pyramidum altius,
> quod non imber edax, non Aquilo impotens
> possit diruere aut innumerabilis
> annorum series et fuga temporum (*Odes* 3.30.1–5)
>
> I have completed a monument more lasting than bronze, and loftier than the pyramids' royal rubble, one which the eroding rain, the North Wind, raging out of control, could not tear down, or the countless succession of years and the swift passage of time.

---

[195] Cf. Callimachus, *Hymn* 2.2.

[196] See Horace, *Odes* 1.4.13–14.

[197] *Odes* 1.1 and 3.30 frame the entire collection of Odes I–III, sharing the same meter (Lesser Asclepiad, the sole instances of the occurrence of that meter in Books I–III), and the theme of immortality. See Michael C. J. Putnam, "Horace C.3.30: The Lyricist as Hero," *Ramus* 2 (1973): 1–19, at 13–17, reprinted in Michael C. J. Putnam, *Essays on Latin Lyric, Elegy, and Epic* (Princeton, NJ: Princeton University Press, 1982), 133–151; Stephen Murphy, *The Gift of Immortality: Myths of Power and Humanist Poetics* (London: Associated University Presses, 1997), 64; G. O. Hutchinson, *Talking Books: Readings in Hellenistic and Roman Books of Poetry* (Oxford: Oxford University Press, 2008), 144; *Horace: Odes Book II*, ed. Stephen Harrison (Cambridge: Cambridge University Press, 2017), 3.

As Spencer Cole remarks, "[t]he conditional hope for immortality expressed at the beginning of the *Odes* (1.1.35–6) is now mirrored by a closing claim of completion (*exegi monumentum*), and the realization of textual immortality."[198] This is presented metaphorically as the monument's resilience to the natural forces of rain and wind. As Tony Woodman observes, "it is only when we have reached this stage of the image that Horace predicates the metaphors *edax* and *impotens*."[199] These, however, are offset by Horace's confident prediction: *qua violens obstrepit Aufidus* (10) ("where the violent Aufidus roars") he will be spoken of (*dicar* [10]) as *princeps Aeolium carmen ad Italos/deduxisse modos* (13–14) ("the first to have adapted Aeolian poetry to Italian measures"). Among the possible meanings of the metaphorical *deduxisse*, as Woodman remarks, is that of "a victorious general celebrating a triumph."[200] In Salzilli's case the victory is perhaps more explicitly articulated: his is a celebratory poetic triumph, hinted at in Sonnet 1, but now fulfilled by the speaker, who rides alongside Apollo in his chariot of victory. And as he expatiates upon examples of poetic eternity (Homer, Virgil, Tasso), he turns to Horace himself, evoked metonymically by his native river, that same Aufidus of *Odes* 3.30.[201] Thus "De l'Aufido sonante/Pur s'ode ancor l'armonioso plettro" (90–91) ("the harmonious plectrum of the resounding Aufidus is still heard"). And just as Horace,

---

[198] Spencer Cole, "The Dynamics of Deification in Horace's *Odes* 1–3," in *Between Magic and Religion: Interdisciplinary Studies in Ancient Mediterranean Religion and Society*, eds. S. R. Asirvatham, C. O. Pache, and John Watrous (Oxford: Rowman & Littlefield, 2001), 67–91, at 90.

[199] Tony Woodman, "*Exegi Monumentum*: Horace, *Odes* 3.30," in *Quality and Pleasure in Latin Poetry*, eds. Tony Woodman and David West (Cambridge: Cambridge University Press, 1974), 115–128, at 128. Cf. also Ovid, *Met.* 15. 234–236: *tempus edax rerum, tuque, invidiosa vetustas,/omnia destruitis vitiataque dentibus aevi/paulatim lenta consumitis omnia morte* ("Time, the devourer of things, and you, jealous old age, you destroy all things, and gradually you consume all things, impaired by the teeth of transience, in a slow death").

[200] Woodman, "*Exegi Monumentum*," 124, who compares *Odes* 1.37.31–32, and continues: "If so, Horace would be saying: 'the first to have brought Aeolian song (that is, the lyric poetry of Sappho and Alcaeus, who both wrote in the Aeolic dialect) to Italian music in triumph'. We are thereby neatly prepared for the more explicit triumph-image in lines 15–16." Woodman also considers two further metaphorical meanings "from founding colonies … or from the spinning of fine thread," and opts for the last.

[201] Cf. also Horace, *Odes* 4.9.1–4: *Ne forte credas interitura, quae/longe sonantem natus ad Aufidum/non ante vulgatas per artis/verba loquor socianda chordis* ("in case you happen to believe that the words will perish, which I, born beside the far resounding Aufidus, utter by arts not previously made known, words to be joined to the strings of the lyre").

in Salzilli's words, "S'al Cielo esalta in dotti carmi Augusto" (95) ("exalts Augustus to the heavens in his learned poetry"), so too does he seem to take his place in eternity itself. In essence then, the canzone, like *Odes* 3.30, aptly rounds off a collection by proudly attesting to the fulfillment of a Horatian (and indeed a Salzillian) self-prediction.

Salzilli's poetic self-portraiture as a second Horace and his associated recourse to Horatian language and metaphor seem to find a fitting place in *Ad Salsillum*. As noted previously, the terms in which the poem describes its addressee's "Italianization" of Horatian lyric are closely evocative of Horace's self-fashioning in regard to his "Latinization" of the lyric poetry of Archilochus, Alcaeus, and Sappho.[202] But links go further than this. Milton presents Salzilli in essentially vatic terms: he is a *sacerdos* ("priest"), this time of Apollo himself: *hic tuus sacerdos est* (26) ("this man is your priest"), as if in acknowledgment of his self-attested devotion to the god in "La Poesia Trionfante" and elsewhere. The poem also establishes a series of mirror-images between addressee and speaker, both of whom are united by the immortalizing power of poetry. Milton's journey to Italy has enabled him to escape *pessimus ... ventorum/Insanientis impotensque pulmonum* (11–12) ("the worst of winds, losing control of its madly raging lungs"). Freeman makes the interesting suggestion that "*impotens* ... probably recalls the famous boast of Horace about his own poetry."[203] Significantly, that boast was proclaimed in the aforementioned *Ode* 3.30. By implication then the Horatian monument (*monumentum*), impervious to the devastating force of wind, has become the Miltonic self.[204] That this privilege is also enjoyed by Salzilli is suggested by the poem's closing lines. Here, by way of a return compliment not only to Salzilli's Latin quatrain, but also, I would argue, to his published poetic output, Milton combines the images of river, monument, and eternity in a subtle reworking of Horace, *Odes* 1.2.13–20.[205] He also seems to invert the

---

[202] See 60. Milton himself had in a sense "vernacularized" Horatian lyric in his metaphrastic rendering of *Odes* 1.5, pertaining, in all likelihood, to his years at St Paul's School. See Charles Martindale, "Unlocking the Word-Hoard: In Praise of Metaphrase," *Comparative Criticism* 6 (1984): 47–72, reworked in his *Redeeming the Text: Latin Poetry and the Hermeneutics of Reception* (Cambridge: Cambridge University Press, 1993), 75–100; Haan, *Bilingualism and Biculturalism*, 15–25.

[203] Freeman, "Milton's Roman Connection," 96.

[204] On links between the *exegi monumentum* tradition and Milton's sonnet "On Shakespeare" prefixed to the second folio (1632), see Poole, *Milton and the Making of Paradise Lost*, 37. See also Gordon Campbell, "Shakespeare and the Youth of Milton," *MQ* 33 (1999): 95–105.

[205] For further discussion, see 95–97. For an interesting adaptation of Horace's lines in a Cambridge context, cf. Andrew Marvell, *Ad Regem Carolum Parodia*, 13–16:

structural progression of Horace's ode from the flooding river (one of many ill-omens) to a prayer addressed to a series of deities that they come to the help of Rome. The speaker of Horace's poem asks: *quem vocet divum populus ruentis/imperi rebus?* (25–26) ("which of the gods should the people invoke when the empire is collapsing in ruins?"), a question that he tries to answer by invoking Apollo (32), Venus (33), or Mars (43). He then considers another possibility. Perhaps the god is already here, having assumed the human form of Augustus (*sive mutata iuvenem figura* [41] ["or whether by changing your form, you assume the appearance of a young man]"), and allowing himself to be invoked as the avenger of Caesar (*patiens vocari/Caesaris ultor* [43–44]), as one who should delay his return to the world of the divine, and, by his presence, assist the people of Rome: *serus in caelum redeas diuque/laetus intersis populo Quirini* (45–46) ("late may you return to heaven, and long may you linger in blessedness among the people of Quirinus"). Milton *precedes* his description of the calming of the Tiber with an invocation to a series of deities to come to the assistance of a private, rather a public, need; a physical rather than a moral illness: Salus (23), Phoebus (24), and then, as in Horace, an alternative form of a god: *sive tu magis Paean/ Libenter audis* (25–26) ("or whether you give ear more readily as Paean"). In short, the *monumenta* of Salzilli's Italian (and Milton's Latin?) verse outlast potentially destructive elements. Like the *pessimus ... ventorum* or the Horatian Aquilo, any such force proves *impotens* in face of the immortality of the Salzillian and the Miltonic poetic text.

1.6   Milton's "Laurea Hetrusca"

The Miltonic text, as if in tribute to its addressee, epitomizes the fusion of the ancient and the modern. It does so by a subtle synthesis of the Horatian and the Italian, the latter in acknowledgment perhaps of that *laurea Hetrusca* ("Tuscan laurel") honorifically conferred upon its author by Salzilli himself.[206] Parker speculates that Milton "probably met while in Rome" many of the other fifty contributors to the 1637 *Poesie* produced by the Fantastici.[207] Although this lacks independent

---

vidimus Chamum fluvium retortis/litore a dextro violenter undis/ire plorantem monumenta pestis,/templaque clausa ("We have seen the river Cam, his waves violently cast back from his right-hand shore, proceed in lamentation of the plague's memorials and the closed churches"). Text and translation are those of Estelle Haan, *Andrew Marvell's Latin Poetry: From Text to Context* (Brussels: Collection Latomus, 2003), 248–249. For further discussion see *ibid.*, 38–39.

[206] See 47–49.

[207] Parker, *Biography*, II, 826.

corroboration, Milton's familiarity with that collection, and with Salzilli's contributions in particular, is highly likely. After all, as a relatively recent publication, the volume would have been easily accessible to him during his Roman sojourns, irrespective of whether or not it was gifted to him by Salzilli. Perhaps indeed he was drawn to it because of his connections with the Roman poet.

At first glance *Ad Salsillum* seems worlds apart from Salzilli's contributions to the *Poesie*. Some general points of contact were suggested by Freeman:[208] the fact that "both men speak to Phoebus Apollo," and the observation that Milton's poem "cleverly but politely incorporates certain ideas that Milton knew were important to his Roman friend."[209] Closer inspection reveals more striking parallels. Thus the reference to Paean (25–26),[210] the sole occurrence of this proper noun in Milton, may, as Freeman suggests, show the influence of the opening lines of that first sonnet discussed earlier: "Calchi ... D'Esculapio, e Peon l'orme fallaci" (1–2) ("it [the vile soul] follows the misleading tracks of Asclepius and Paean").[211] Also, the river-motif of *Ad Salsillum* (and of Salzilli's Latin tribute) may assume further significance in view of its climactic occurrence in Salzilli's first Italian sonnet. Here the poet, by acquiring the laurel of immortality, can ultimately elude "il Tempo tributario a Lete" (14) ("Time, the tributary to Lethe").[212] To these may be added some further observations. The poem's opening invocation of the Muse in the formal salutation *O Musa* (1), coupled with the invitation that she "be present" (*Adesdum* [6]) *et haec s'is verba pauca Salsillo/ Refer* (6–7) ("and convey, if you will, these few words to Salzilli"), may owe something to Salzilli's gentle rebuking of the Muse for her contemporary silence in "La Poesia Trionfante":

> Ma dove dove, ò *Musa*,
> Lasci un pregio sovrano
> Di nostra età, che'l tuo silentio accusa? (161–163).[213]
>
> But where, where, *o Muse*,
> do you abandon the sovereign merit
> of our age, which accuses you of silence?"

---

[208] Freeman, "Milton's Roman Connection," 97–100.

[209] Freeman, "Milton's Roman Connection," 99.

[210] *Ad Salsillum* 25–26: *sive tu magis Paean/Libenter audis* ("or whether you give ear more readily as Paean").

[211] *Poesie*, 148. Cf. Freeman, "Milton's Roman Connection," 99.

[212] *Poesie*, 148.

[213] *Poesie*, 161. Emphasis is mine.

If so, the Muse's desired presence and her lamented taciturnity are now countered by her conveyance of poetic utterance. That the *verba pauca* (6) ("few words") are indeed those of a contemporary (Milton himself) seems to situate him alongside Salzilli's personal defiance of such silence in the ensuing lines of his canzone. There the vibrancy and continuity of his poetic voice, symbolized by the quenching of his thirst in the waters of Hippocrene, are sharply contrasted with the oblivion associated with the river Lethe.[214] Then there is the question of Deiopea's dancing before Juno's couch, an apparent invention on Milton's part. Douglas Bush suggests that this may have been introduced to give Deiopea a function paralleling that of Hebe as cup-bearer to Jupiter.[215] One wonders, however, whether her depiction here, and aspects of the phraseology (*decentes flava Deiope suras/Alternat* [4–5] ["Deiopea, golden-haired, and with seemly ankles, *dances trippingly*"]),[216] were inspired, at least in part, by the dancing nymphs of Salzilli's canzonetta "Il Maggio":

> Ninfe amorose,
> *Con danze*, e con carole,
> Ghirlandate di rose
> Figlie del novo Sole,
> *Alternando* facciam canoro homaggio. (7–11)[217]

> Amorous Nymphs with *dances* and
> with singing, garlanded with roses,
> daughters of the new sun,
> *alternating* their expression with
> tuneful homage.

In this reading Milton has imaginatively condensed the alternating facial expressions of dancing nymphs into actual dance-moves, in essence more attractive metrical forms, with which the lame Muse and the scazontic meter are contrasted. Milton's self-fashioning as *alumnus ille Londini* (9) ("that foster-child of London"), with the etymological link between *alumnus* and *alo-alere*, and the juxtaposition with a capital city (London) as agent of the nurturing, merit comparison with the opening of Salzilli's sonnet "Al Signor Giacomo N[ome]." Here "Roma" is described as an

---

[214] "Che'n paludi sì vil già non vogl'io/Bever d'onda letea l'impure vene;/Mentre spengo mia sete in Hippocrene" ("so that for as long as I quench my thirst in Hippocrene, I already lack the wish to drink the impure streams of Lethe amid its swamps so vile") ("La Poesia Trionfante," 174–176, at *Poesie*, 161).

[215] Bush, *Variorum*, I, 264.

[216] Emphasis is mine.

[217] *Poesie*, 166. Emphasis is mine.

"*altrice* gloriosa" ("glorious nurturer"), who "in seno/*nutrir* ... un germe altero" (1-2) ("*nourishes* another seed in her womb").[218] Moreover, Milton's description of, and implied escape from, a virtual English tempest (a hyperbolic exaggeration of the cold northern climate), and of his subsequent arrival in Italy's calm haven (10–16) may owe something to Salzilli's "La Poesia Trionfante," which affords the speaker a refuge amidst metaphorical storms: "Per le naufraghe vie/De l'humane procelle/ Tu sarai calma a le tempeste mie" (33-34) ("In the course of the shipwrecked paths of human storms, it is you [sc. Apollo] who will afford calm to my tempests"). It is poetry that grants Salzilli powers of illumination preferable to the light provided by the constellations Castor and Pollux.[219] And perhaps this is the subtext of *Ad Salsillum*. For Milton has escaped the inclement weather of England, and has followed his own guiding light, traveling to the fertile climes of Italy. In Italy, and perhaps in Salzilli himself, is epitomized that "Poesia Trionfante," which by the end of Milton's poem celebrates a twin triumph by envisaging the eternal power of a recovered poet's song and by self-consciously validating that Horatian edifice of eternity.

By far the most striking parallel between *Ad Salsillum* and Salzilli's Italian poetry, although one not fully developed by Freeman, is provided by a quasi-epitaphic sonnet, entitled "Ricco Mercante ucciso in duello, per volersi vendicar d'una parola ingiuriosa" ("A Rich Merchant killed in a duel for wishing to avenge an injurious word").[220] The *argumentum* of this piece is rather odd: The speaker, a merchant, recalls the perilous sea voyages that he had to endure as a beggar, until a tranquil wind restored him to his native land as a rich man. However, some insult that he received led him to participate in a duel, which in turn brought about his death:

> D'Humano fasto a le grandezze intento,
>   Lunga stagion per l'Oceano infido
>   Mendico errai, fin ch'al bramato lido
>   Ricco m'addusse poi tranquillo vento.
> Hor mentre qui nel cumulato Argento   5
>   D'un' eterno gioir la speme affido,
>   Ecco, ò folle pensier, nel patrio nido,
>   Di propria voglia al mio morir consento.
> D'acerbo detto un momentaneo scorno
>   Vendicar volli, e la nemica sorte   10
>   Spese del viver mio l'ultimo giorno.

---

[218] *Poesie*, 154.

[219] *Poesie*, 157.

[220] *Poesie*, 155.

> Flutti, e scogli nel Mar con petto forte
>   Sostengo, e poscia di lontan ritorno,
>   Da un falso accento a mendicar la Morte.

> Intent on the grandeur of human pomp, I wandered as a beggar for a long time across the treacherous ocean, until a tranquil wind brought me as a rich man to the shore for which I had yearned. Now, while I was trusting in the hope of eternal joy in the money I had amassed, behold, o foolish thought, in my native nest, I of my own free will agreed to my death. I wanted to avenge the temporary shame of a harsh word, but hostile Fate extinguished the last day of my life. With a strong breast I endured waves and rocks in the sea, and then I returned from far away to beg for Death in a false tone of voice.

The merchant, aspiring to grandeur beyond his reach, was assisted by a "tranquillo vento" (4) ("tranquil wind"), which brought him ashore. He describes the land as his "patrio nido" (7) ("native nest"). Milton's experience is the reverse:[221] he, too, has traveled, but he has *left* his native land, his "nest" (*qui suum linquens nidum* [10] ["who leaving his own nest"]), in order to see the cities and learned youth of Italy. He describes, moreover, a wind that, far from being "tranquil" and of assistance to the traveler, is in fact "the worst" (*pessimus* [11]), almost proving an obstruction to his journey:

> Diebus hisce qui suum linquens nidum
> Polique tractum (pessimus ubi ventorum,
> Insanientis impotensque pulmonis
> Pernix anhela sub Iove exercet flabra)   (10–13)

> [Milton], who in recent days has left his own nest
> and region of the heavens (where the worst of
> winds, losing control of its madly raging lungs,
> rapidly puffs its panting blasts beneath the sky)

The riches that Milton can receive upon arrival at *his*, as it were, "bramato lido" (itself idealized as *feraces Itali soli ... glebas* [14] ["the fertile clods of Italy's soil"]), are spiritual and intellectual, as opposed to the material wealth ("cumulato Argento" [5]) that Salzilli's misguided

---

[221] Freeman, "Milton's Roman Connection," 100, who does not quote the poem, briefly notes some parallels: "The word 'nest' (*nido*) unites this odd poem to *Ad Salsillum*: Milton speaks of leaving his 'nidum,' enduring fierce (not 'quiet') winds and imploring Paean, enemy of Death, to heal his friend."

rich man hopes to enjoy. In Salzilli, the "nido" is closely associated with death, as the speaker asserts: "nel patrio nido,/Di proprio voglia al mio morir consento" (7–8) ("in my native nest I of my own free will agreed to my death"), only to voice, with a realistic sense of inevitability, his concluding imploration that death come upon him (" ... a mendicar la Morte" [14] ["to beg for Death"]). Milton inverts this. The fact that he *has left* his "nest" brings with it the hope of avoiding and averting death as he implores *Salus* (23), and Phoebus/Paean (24–25), restorers of life and well-being. Thus instead of a merchant begging for death, Milton, in praying for the speedy recovery of Salzilli (23–30), is, as it were, "begging" for a life.

Milton's situation, moreover, is antithetical to that of Salzilli's merchant, who had received "una parola ingiuriosa" ("an injurious word"), and had, in consequence, sought vengeance. As the recipient of words of praise, the encomium (alluded to in 7–8), he is seeking to return a compliment: *haec ... verba pauca* (5) ("these few words"). Instead of bringing death upon himself by avenging "un momentaneo scorno" (9) ("a temporary shame"), Milton reaches beyond the self to extend good wishes to his addressee: *Tibi optat idem hic fausta multa, Salsille* (17) ("To you, Salzilli, this same person wishes many good fortunes").

1.7   The Accademia degli Umoristi

A further, complementary, context in which to view Milton's relations with Salzilli, and his associated composition of *Ad Salsillum*, is provided by the Roman academician's attested links with the Accademia degli Umoristi. This academy traced its origins back to gatherings of friends in "la nobile habitatione de' Signori Mancini" ("the noble dwelling of the Mancinis"),[222] that is, the house of Paolo Mancini, on the Corso.[223] There they performed their own comedies, sonnets, and discourses on a variety of subjects. As the assembly attracted a wider audience, including poets, musicians, and artists, so, too, did it increase its status, momentum, and scope by expanding its hitherto informal remit to embrace other fields of literature in a more formal setting. Initially termed "i begli umori" ("beautiful humors"), these participants had established the formal name of Umoristi by 1603, and, by the time of Milton's visit, had already

---

[222] Totti, *Ritratto di Roma Moderna*, 287.

[223] The site is now occupied by the Palazzo Salviati al Corso, opposite the Palazzo Doria Pamphili. See Luigi Càllari, *I Palazzi di Roma, e le Case d'Importanze Storica e Artistica* (Rome: Bardi, 1968), 262.

earned a high reputation as the foremost academy in Rome.[224] Among its membership, which, in the words of Thomas Mayer, constitutes "a list of everyone who was anyone,"[225] the Accademia degli Umoristi could boast of Giambattista Marino, Battista Guarini, Alessandro Tassoni, and Gabriello Chiabrera, and, at the time of Milton's visit, Salzilli himself, Giovanni Battista Doni, Cardinals Francesco and Antonio Barberini, Cassiano dal Pozzo (Francesco Barberini's secretary), Pietro della Valle, Domenico Benigni, Cardinal Giulio Rospigliosi (the future Pope Clement IX), the artist Fabio della Corgna (the portraiturist of Leonora Baroni),[226] and, as argued in the text that follows, Leonora and Caterina Baroni.[227]

The Umoristi's literary aspirations are visually encapsulated in its chosen *impresa* (a cloud raining gentle showers upon the waves of the sea) and in its associated motto RÈDIT AGMINE DULCI, borrowed from Lucretius (*De Rerum Natura* 6. 637). The motto merits consideration in its original context. Lucretius recounts the amazement of men at the fact that the sea does not become larger, even though all rivers discharge into it, as do rains falling on both land and sea (6. 608–615). In response, he addresses the age-old question of how seawater becomes fresh when passed into the earth.[228] In so doing, he explains the process of evaporation, whereby the sun draws off a great deal of the moisture by its

---

[224] On the founding of the Umoristi, its statutes, and early literary activities, see Russo, "L'Accademia degli Umoristi," passim. See also, among others, Girolamo Tiraboschi, *Storia*, VIII, 44–46; Maylender, *Storia*, V, 370–381; Giuseppe Gabriele, "Accademie Romane. Gli Umoristi," *Roma* 13 (1935): 173–184; F. W. Gravit, "The Accademia degli Umoristi and its French Relationships," *Papers of the Michigan Academy* 29 (1935): 501–521; Rodolfo De Mattei, "Dispute Filosofico-Politiche nelle Accademie Romane del Seicento," *Studi Romani* 9 (1961): 148–167, at 160–167; Luisa Avellini, "Tra Umoristi e Gelati," *SS* 23 (1982): 109–137; Marco Gallo, "Orazio Borgianni, L'Accademia di S. Luca e L'Accademia degli Humoristi: Documenti e Nuove Datazioni," *Storia dell' Arte* 76 (1992): 296–345, at 301–310; Laura Alemanno, "L'Accademia degli Umoristi," *Roma Moderna e Contemporanea* 3 (1995): 97-120.

[225] Thomas F. Mayer, *The Roman Inquisition: A Papal Bureaucracy and its Laws in the Age of Galileo* (Philadelphia: University of Pennsylvania Press, 2013), 95. The list survives as Venice: Biblioteca Nazionale Marciana MS. Ital. XI. LXI (6792), ff. 159^r-164^v. It is reproduced with several errors and omissions by Maylender, *Storia*, V, 375–381, on which see Russo, "L'Accademia degli Umoristi," 56.

[226] See 102, 136.

[227] See 101–107.

[228] This was a question that had puzzled, and had been variously interpreted by, Aristophanes, Anaximander, Aristotle, Pliny, and Seneca, on which see Cyril Bailey, *Titi Lucreti Cari De Rerum Natura Libri Sex*, 3 vols (Oxford: Clarendon Press, 1946–1949), III, 1646–1647.

heat (6. 616–622). He continues by reiterating his doctrine, first expressed at 5.269–272, that clouds too lift up much moisture absorbed from the ocean, moisture which is purified in the process, before raining down again upon the earth:

> debet, ut in mare de terris venit umor aquai,
> in terras itidem manare ex aequore salso;
> percolatur enim virus retroque remanat
> materies umoris et ad caput amnibus omnis
> confluit, inde super terras redit agmine dulci
> qua via secta semel liquido pede detulit undas.[229]
> (*De Rerum Natura* 6. 633–638)

> It must needs be that, just as the moisture of water passes into the sea from the lands, it likewise filters through into the land from the salt sea levels; for the brine is strained through, and the substance of moisture oozes back and all streams together at the fountain-head of rivers, and thence comes back over the lands with freshened current, where the channel once cleft has brought down the waters in their liquid march.[230]

In short, the Lucretian motto *redit agmine dulci* encapsulates the process of distillation, whereby the salinity of seawater is drawn up by the sun, by whose heat it is purified, before raining down again upon the earth.

That the Accademia degli Umoristi was in full flourish at the time of Milton's visit is attested in several ways, not least by the number of publications in its name that had appeared, or were in the course of preparation, in the 1630s. Perhaps one of the best indicators of the extent of its networking with local and international literati was the *Monumentum Romanum* (1638), commemorating the death of Nicolas-Claude Fabri de Peiresc.[231] This consisted of 72 contributors (including Caterina Baroni), writing in thirty languages.[232] Umoristi members Bartolomeo Tortoletti, Domenico Benigni, Fabio Leonida, Gasparo de

---

[229] Text is that of *De Rerum Natura*, ed. Bailey, I, 546. Lines 635–638 constitute a virtually verbatim reiteration of 5. 269–272, except that *confluit* (6. 637) is substituted for *convenit* (5.271), and *redit* (6.637) for *fluit* (5.271). See *De Rerum Natura*, ed. Bailey, III, 1649.

[230] Translation is that of *De Rerum Natura*, ed. Bailey, I, 547.

[231] See 36.

[232] On the volume's multilingualism, see Testa, *Italian Academies*, 170. On Caterina Baroni's contribution, see 103–104.

Simeonibus, Girolamo Rocco, and Leone Allacci would also contribute to the 1639 *Applausi* in honor of Leonora Baroni.[233] That this academy was particularly receptive to foreigners is evinced by the comments of two English travelers to Rome in 1645 and 1649–1651, respectively. Thus John Evelyn recounts his reception by the Umoristi on 17 February 1645, and gives some sense of the iconography of the room in which academic performances were delivered:

> The 17, I was invited (after dinner) to the Academie of the *Humorists*, kept in a spacious Hall, belonging to Signor Mancini, where the Witts of the Towne meete on certaine daies, to recite poems, & prevaricate on severall Subjects &c: The first that Speakes is cal'd the Lord, & stands in an eminent place, & then the rest of the virtuosi recite in order: by these ingenious Exercises besides the learn'd discourses, is the purity of the Italian Tongue daily improv'd: This roome is hung round, with enumerable devises or Emblemes all relating to something of *humidum* with Motos under them: Several other Academies there are of this nature, bearing the like fantastical titles: It is in this Academie of the Humorists where they have the Picture of Guarini the famous Author of *Pastor fido*, once of this Society ... the best part of the day we spent in hearing the Academic exercises.[234]

Evelyn's account can now be both corroborated and augmented by the more detailed records of Richard Symonds less than five years later. Extant in manuscript in the British Library is an important notebook of Symonds pertaining to his visit to Rome in 1649–1651,[235] usefully transcribed (although frequently misinterpreted) by Anne Brookes.[236] Symonds' observations serve to shed much light on not only the order of academic proceedings, but also, and especially, on the precise nature of the individual emblems that graced the room. Stating that the Umoristi met late on every Sunday afternoon, Symonds also informs us that each meeting commenced with a speech, which was delivered in either Latin or Italian. This was followed by the recitation of verse on subjects of the

---

[233] See *Applausi*, 30, 77–109, 117–120, 167–170, 184, and 195–200.

[234] John Evelyn, *Diary*, ed. De Beer, II, 364–365.

[235] BL Egerton MS 1635, ff. 47^v–49^r.

[236] See Anne Brookes, "Richard Symonds's Account of his Visit to Rome in 1649–1651," *Walpole Society* 69 (2007): 1–183. See also Anne Brookes, *Richard Symonds in Rome, 1649–1651* (PhD thesis: University of Nottingham, 2000). On the artistic significance of Symonds' notebooks in general, see Mary Beal, *A Study of Richard Symonds: His Italian Notebooks and Their Relevance to Seventeenth-Century Painting Techniques* (New York: Garland, 1984).

individual member's choosing. An oration was then delivered, to which others in turn responded "with their hats on," the latter revealing the formality of the occasion:

> Accademia dei Humoristi Tis kept in the hall of Sig[no]r M[ancini] in the Corso each Sunday. 4 or 5 afternoone. First a speech in latin or Italian is made by one appointed, Then divers Recite verses of Subjects of their owne choosing. The Card[inal] Capone & the F[rench] Emb[assador] being there. He that makes ye oration, & those that repeate w[i]th their hats on, yet regard not ye Card[inal].[237]

Evelyn's observation that hanging around the room were "enumerable devises or Emblemes all relating to something of *humidum* with Motos under them" is likewise attested by Symonds: "Round ye hall are in frames painted in Oyle very many Emblemes all alluding to ye Humor."[238] Symonds also describes what would appear to be a single iconographical representation of the academy's *impresa* and motto:

> A cloud rayning upon ye Sea w[i]th this motto
> REDIT AGMINE dulci
> over it is
> Title————Humoristi[239]

And he makes notes on eighteen of the individual emblems and mottoes. Even from his rough transcriptions and attempted interpretations, it is evident that the images did indeed represent *humor* (and *humiditas*) in a multiplicity of ways. Several portray scientific instruments with accompanying mottoes. Thus a barometer, described by Symonds as "A weather glasse," comes with the subscribed motto *monstrat eventus*,[240] an

---

[237] BL Egerton MS 1635, f. 47^v. Cf. Brookes, "Richard Symonds's Account," 97, where, however, she misinterprets the abbreviated "& the F. Emb." as "etc. f[rom] ye Emb.," suggesting (at 138n467) that it "probably means an entourage." I propose "& the F[rench] Emb[assador]." On the Umoristi's reception of French ambassadors, see Andrew Dell'Antonio, *Listening as Spiritual Practice in Early Modern Italy* (Berkeley: University of California Press, 2011), 123. See also Gravit, "The Accademia degli Umoristi and its French Relationships," passim.

[238] *Ibid.*, f. 48^v. Cf. Brookes, "Richard Symonds's Account," 98.

[239] *Ibid.*, f. 48^v. Cf. Brookes, "Richard Symonds's Account," 98. Brookes, 139n473, mistranslates the Lucretian motto, incorrectly stating: "The motto means 'the army is returned gently (or pleasantly).'"

[240] *Ibid.*, f. 48^v. Cf. Brookes, "Richard Symonds's Account," 98. Contrary to Brookes' incorrect comment that "The motto may mean 'The outcome reveals'" (139n475), *monstrat eventus* should be translated "it [i.e., the depicted barometer] reveals outcomes."

alembic, with the motto *Perficit humor*, encapsulates "l'humoroso."[241] Others constitute pictorial representations of the different properties and effects of "humor." Thus "A fountayne" derives strength from its source (*vires ab ortu*),[242] "A Spunge," although naturally light, acquires weight when saturated with water (*pondus ab undis*),[243] and a waterfall possesses a roar that imitates the sound of Olympus (*Sonitus imitatur Olympi*).[244] Among Symonds's transcribed *imprese*, with their accompanying mottoes, is one that is of particular interest:

> Il Sicuro. A Bird in her neast or hatching upon a Rock
> in the middle of ye Sea.
> Salus in salo.[245]

The inherent pun here on *Salus* ("Safety") and *salum* ("the sea"), and its occurrence in combination with the image of a bird in her nest, assume a potential significance that is tantalizingly intriguing. That Umoristi members possessed an individual *impresa* is attested by the academy's statutes, according to which, as noted previously, each had to be approved first by the Censors themselves and then by the academy as a whole.[246] Might this particular *impresa* hanging on display, and observed by Symonds in the late 1640s, have been that of Giovanni Salzilli himself? It is a question that may be impossible to answer, but what is clear is that the showcasing of "Emblemes all relating to something of

---

[241] *Ibid.*, f. 48^v. Cf. Brookes, "Richard Symonds's Account," 98, who, however, erroneously mistranscribes "Alembeck" as two words "A l'embrice," regarding the second word as "illegible," and proposing "'l'embrice' = a shower of rain'" (139n 478). Actually, "l'humeroso" is an adjective, qualifying the academician in question, under which is Symonds' description (in English) of the depicted object, namely, an alembic (two vessels connected by a tube used for the distillation of chemicals). I am grateful to Tony Sheehan for the identification and interpretation of this noun.

[242] *Ibid.*, f. 48^v: "l'inalzato: a fountayne w[i]th this word. Vires ab ortu." Brookes, "Richard Symonds's Account," 98, mistranscribes "l'inalzato" as "l'malzato," and "ortu" as "ortii."

[243] *Ibid.*, f. 48^v: "Il Legiero. A spunge in the waters. Pondus ab undis." Cf. Brookes, "Richard Symonds's Account," 98.

[244] *Ibid.*, f. 48^v: "Lo Strepitoso. a Roaring fountayne like y^t at S Peters. Sonitus imitatur olympi." Cf. Brookes, "Richard Symonds's Account," 98. At 139n489, she mistranslates as "The roar of Olympus is imitated." At 139n488 (she interestingly suggests that "Symonds may have been referring to the fountain (the right-hand one of two; the left-hand one dates from 1677) by Carlo Maratti now in the Piazza San Pietro, dating from the time of Paul V, which (like its counterpart) is 46 feet high."

[245] *Ibid.*, f. 49^r. Cf. Brookes, "Richard Symonds's Account," 98.

[246] See 37.

humidum with Motos under them," and "of very many Emblemes all alluding to ye Humor" was central to the Umoristi's iconographical self-representation in its academic space. This invites a fresh reading of *Ad Salsillum* in relation to the Umoristi's *impresa* and motto, contemporary interpretations of the same, and the Lucretian subtext concerning the distillation of water by purging it of its natural salinity.

1.8 Academic Traditions

The metaphorical appropriation by the Umoristi of the Lucretian motto *redit agmine dulci* had been scrutinized and explicated in print by Girolamo Aleandro in his *Sopra l'Impresa degli Accademici Humoristi Discorso Detto nella Stessa Accademia*, published in Rome in 1611. This discourse is an important indicator of the contemporary reputation that the Umoristi had gained in Rome, and would prove influential upon subsequent interpretations of the academy's *impresa* and motto by Giovanni Ferro and Athanasius Kircher, among others.[247] In Aleandro's perceptive reading:

> sicome la Nuvola è condensata d'humorosi vapori levatisi dall' amarezza del mare, così l'Accademia de gli Humoristi è una raunanza di spiritosi ingegni, che dall' amarezza de' costumi mondani si sono separati.[248]

> just as the Cloud is condensed out of humorous vapors that have been raised aloft from the salinity of the sea, so the Accademia degli Humoristi constitutes an assembly of witty geniuses, who have been separated from the bitterness of worldly customs.

In this process "sicome quella, non ostante che da luogo così amaro habbia origine, se ne ritorna con abbondanza d'acque dolci" ("they, like this [the cloud], without revealing the salinity of their source, return with an abundance of sweet water").[249] Aleandro is careful to emphasize the

---

[247] See Giovanni Ferro, *Teatro d'Imprese*, 2 vols (Venice: Giacomo Sarzina. 1623), II, 518–520; Athanasius Kircher, *Oedipi Aegyptiaci Tomus Secundus. Gymnasium sive Phrontisterion Hieroglyphicum in Duodecim Classes Distributum* (Rome: Vitale Mascardi, 1653), 9. See also Marcellino de Pise, *Moralis Encyclopaedia Id Est Scientiarum Omnium Chorus* (Lyon: Laurentius Anisson, 1656), III, 323; Alessandro Sperelli, *Paradossi Morali* (Venice: Paolo Baglioni, 1666), II, 241.

[248] Girolamo Aleandro, *Sopra l'Impresa de gli Accademici Humoristi Discorso ... Detto nella Stessa Accademia* (Rome: Giacomo Mascardi, 1611), 8.

[249] Aleandro, *Sopra l'Impresa*, 8.

innate salinity of seawater ("l'acqua marina di sua natura salsa" ["seawater, salty by virtue of its own nature"]), stating that it is only through the force of elevation and purification by the sun that "acqua d'amara divenga dolce" ("bitter water becomes sweet").[250] Discussing the separation of the water and its return with the sweetness that it has acquired, he draws an explicit analogy with the "separazione" ("separation") from "gli studi, & costumi vulgari" ("the vulgar pursuits and customs") effected by the Academicians, and the consequential "vera dolcezza" ("true sweetness") that attends upon their "virtuose operazioni" ("virtuous undertakings").[251] He further expatiates upon that academic "sweetness" in a separate section entitled *DULCI*, viewing "la perfezione dell' operazioni" ("the perfection of their undertakings") as indicative that they "haver per conseguenza lasciata l'amarezza, o salsedine" ("have in consequence left behind them bitterness or salinity").[252] Aleandro also explains that the appellation "Humoristi" finds its origins, at least in part, in the term "humor,"[253] and is thus evocative of the four "humors" possessed by the human body: choleric, sanguine, phlegmatic, and melancholic.[254]

According to Hippocratic medicine the four humors consisted of black bile, yellow bile, phlegm, and blood, each of which corresponded to one of the four temperaments.[255] An excess or deficit of one of these humors resulted in disease, which was caused, it was believed, by the body's inhalation or absorption of vapors. As Lois Potter remarks:

> In the human body, the liquid element was supplied by the four *humours* which were extracted from food in the digestive tract. These were blood, phlegm, green bile (which came from the liver) and black bile (which came from the spleen). When these constantly moving liquids reached the

---

[250] Aleandro, *Sopra l'Impresa*, 15.

[251] Aleandro, *Sopra l'Impresa*, 42.

[252] Aleandro, *Sopra l'Impresa*, 63.

[253] Aleandro, *Sopra l'Impresa*, 32.

[254] Aleandro, *Sopra l'Impresa*, 34: "Quattro sono gli humori del corpo nostro, il colerico, il sanguigno, ... il flemmatico, & il malinconico ... Di questi quattro humori è contemprato il nostro corpo" ("Our body possesses four humors: the choleric, the sanguine, ... the phlegmatic, and the melancholic. ... It is in accordance with these four humors that our body is tempered").

[255] See Lawrence Babb, *The Elizabethan Malady: A Study of Melancholia in English Literature from 1580 to 1642* (East Lansing: Michigan State College Press, 1951).

> liver, the process of "concoction", or heating, caused them to evaporate and rise in the form of "spirits."[256]

The potential distillation and purification of "humors" seem to operate on a variety of levels in *Ad Salsillum*. England's *pessimus ... ventorum* (11) ("worst of winds") is strikingly personified in language evocative of a serious chest infection. Thus it is *Insanientis impotensque pulmonis* (12) ("powerless to control its madly heaving lungs") as *Pernix anhela ... exercet flabra* (13) ("it rapidly puffs its panting blasts"). But the traveling Milton has proven to be impervious to this by escaping such forces and arriving at *feraces Itali soli ad glebas* (14) ("the fertile clods of Italian soil"), that adjective *feraces* ("bearing rich crops, fertile, productive")[257] signaling the very antithesis of the destructive powers he has avoided. Later, the whole becomes internalized in the body of the sick Salzilli, in whose stomach is implanted an excessive humor, the *profunda bilis* (19) ("overflow of bile"), which assails his kidneys and "*breathes* its deadly breath" (*damnosum spirat* [20]).[258] The lines are aptly glossed by Bush:

> According to the physiological theory of the four humors, an excess of one—here—bile caused a corresponding disease.[259]

By contrast, Salzilli's envisaged healing is associated with an academic "sweetness," itself perhaps evocative of that Lucretian motto *redit agmine dulci* as adopted by the Umoristi and as interpreted in contemporary discourses on the subject:

> Sic ille caris *redditus* Musis
> Vicina *dulci* prata mulcebit cantu (31–32)[260]
>
> Thus *restored* once more to his beloved Muses,
> he will soothe the neighboring meadows with his *sweet* song.

In this reading the motto's verb *redire* ("to return") is punningly recast as *reddere* ("to give back, restore"), while the adjective (*dulcis* ["sweet"]), applied to seawater purged of its salinity, is retained to describe the restored (and renewed) sweetness of a recovered poet's song.

---

[256] Lois Potter, *A Preface to Milton* (London and New York: Routledge, 2013), 48.

[257] *OLD*, s.v. *ferax* 1.

[258] Emphasis is mine.

[259] Bush, *Variorum*, I, 265.

[260] Emphasis is mine.

And more than that. The trisyllabic *Sic ille* (31) mirrors *Salsillo* (6) and *Salsille* (17), as Milton seems to showcase upon Italian soil aspects of the "salting tradition"[261] epitomized by his sixth *Prolusio*, performed over a decade earlier in another *academia*, Cambridge University. Central to this was etymological play on *sal* ("salt") and on words beginning with, or related to, *sal*: *sal̲s̲amentarii*,[262] *sal̲tem*,[263] *in̲s̲ulsi*,[264] *sal̲utaris*, and *sal̲taturientes*.[265] This last, used to describe the Cambridge freshmen, functions as a macaronic pun, its clever combination of *sal* with the English "salt," enabling Milton, in the words of John Hale, to "give to the central salting idea a sudden and surprising new embodiment."[266]

---

[261] See Roslyn Richek, "Thomas Randolph's Salting (1627): Its Text, and John Milton's Sixth *Prolusion* as Another Salting," *ELR* 12 (1982): 102–131; John K. Hale, *Milton's Cambridge Latin: Performing in the Genres, 1625–1632* (Tempe, AZ: Medieval and Renaissance Texts and Studies, 2005), 195–219, especially 196: "Puns and jokes about salt are incessant, because the root idea is that speech, and social life as a whole, do not taste as good as they should unless they are 'seasoned' with 'salt,' to bring out their full and proper flavour. The metaphor is pervasive, almost obsessive."

[262] *epulas hasce ... nullo condiri sal̲e* ("these dishes ... unseasoned with *salt*" [*Prolusio* 6, 280–281]). *Quod ad sal̲es meos, non ego edentulos ... et veteres dicatis ... proinde credo neminem sal̲es meos dentatos inculpaturum ... Et certe in praesens ego exoptarem obtigisse mihi Horatii sortem, nempe ut sal̲samentarii filius; tunc enim sal̲es mihi essent ad unguem; vos etiam sal̲e ita pulchre defricatos dimitterem, ut nostros milites qui nuper ab Insula Reana capessere fugam non magis paeniteret sal̲is petiti* ("As to the *salt of my wit*, I don't want you to call it toothless and ancient ... I don't think anyone will find fault with my *wit* as having been too biting either ... For sure, I wish I had Horace's luck, born the son of a *fishwife*, for then I would have *salt wit* to perfection; yes, and I should send you off so well *seasoned* that you would regret asking for *salt*—like our army who got *salt* put on their tails as they fled from the *Salt* Islands" [*Prolusio* 6, 286–287]). All quotations are by page reference to Hale's edition in *Milton's Cambridge Latin*. Translations are, with minor modifications, those of Hale, who captures the wordplay very effectively. In all instances emphasis is mine.

[263] *quod vero non audemus sal̲tem non nisi in occulto* ("the role we do not risk, except *at least* in secret" [*Prolusio* 6, 280–281]). I have inserted "at least" to render *sal̲tem* (untranslated by Hale), itself possibly a macaronic pun.

[264] *Itane propria quae maribus femineo generi tribuunt in̲s̲ulsi grammaticastri?* ("Do these *witless* grammar-bunglers attribute to the feminine what is properly masculine?" [*Prolusio* 6, 282–283]).

[265] *hic quidem est novus et rarus magis quam sal̲utaris cibus ... has [sc. aves] igitur arbitror ego agasonibus utiliores futuras; nam cum sint naturae vividae, vegetae, et sal̲taturientes ...* ("Now these are a new dish, rare rather than *salutary* in fact ... These [birds], I think, will accordingly be more use to ostlers, because they are by nature lively and brisk and *prancing* creatures ... " [*Prolusio* 6, 278–279]).

[266] Hale, *Milton's Cambridge Latin*, 219.

Something strikingly similar seems to be at play in *Ad Salsillum*: *Salsillo* (6), *Salsille* (17), *Salus* (23), *salubre* (29); *salsa* (41),[267] with the possibility of a macaronic pun in *suras/Alternat* (4–5). Indeed, the envisaged healing of *Ioannes Salsillus* seems to be mirrored by the poem's linguistic purgation of the salinity inherent in his name: from *Salsillo* (6) to *Salsille* (17) to *Sic ille* (31) until the last line, which relegates *sal* to the outskirts of Rome—to the mouth of the Tiber: *Adusque curvi salsa regna Portumni* (41) "all the way up to the salted realms of curving Portumnus").[268] This type of wordplay, already evident in the Umoristi member's motto *Salus in salo*, found a natural home in the Italian academies, and Milton surely knew this to be the case.[269] It was central to the *cicalate* ("idle talks") regularly practiced in the Florentine Accademia della Crusca,[270] and (since 1636) adopted by the

---

[267] This emphasis upon *sal-* words may be enhanced by Milton's possible pun on *condere* ("to fashion") and *condire* ("to season") when describing Salzilli's poetic practices: *Romano/Tam cultus ore Lesbium condis melos* (21–22) ("So eloquently do you *fashion* the song of Lesbos upon Roman lips"). Cf. *Le Glorie degli Incogniti*, 66, s.v. Anton Giulio Brignole Sale Genovese: *SAL erit insulsum, salibus nisi condiat illud/Hic Ligur, ex ipso qui SALE nomen habet* ("*Salt* will be *lacking* in *salt* unless this Ligurian, who possesses a name derived from *salt* itself, *seasons* it with the *salt of his witticisms*"). Emphasis is mine. Cf. also, in a general sense, Milton, *Epistola Familiaris* 7 (to Charles Diodati) at *Epistolarum Familiarium Liber Unus*, 17: *Nae ipsum te nuper Salutis condum promum esse factum oportet, ita totum Salubritatis penum dilapidas* ("Truly, you must lately have been appointed the very *garnerer*, the very *steward*, of the *store* possessed by *Salus*—such is the ruin that you confer on *Salubrity*'s entire stock" [emphasis mine]), on which see *Epistolarum Familiarium Liber Unus and Uncollected Letters*, ed. Haan, 102–103, 108.

[268] Portumnus (Portunus) was the Roman god of harbors and gates. According to tradition, his temple was located at the mouth of the Tiber. Cf. Bush, *Variorum*, I, 267. The potential relegation of *sal* to the outskirts of Rome may assume additional force in light of the adjective *curvus* (41) used to describe the god. Although possibly alluding to the curved shore, *curvus* can also denote "stooping" (cf. *OLD* 3: " (of persons) Stooping, bowed, bent." In this reading, one of the effects of Salzilli's illness is transferred to Portumnus himself. Cf. *Tumidus ... Tibris* (36) ("the swollen Tiber"). See also 56, and 95–97.

[269] Several of Milton's other Latin poems associated with his Italian journey likewise pun on proper names. Thus *Mansus* plays on its addressee's name, Manso, and the Latin adjective *mansuetus* (60) ("gentle") (a pun preempted by the possibly anagrammatic *Manse tuae* [1]). *Epitaphium Damonis* puns on the "divine name" (*divinum nomen* [210]) *deo-datus* ("God-given") possessed by Charles Diodati, and on *Thyrso* (219) ("Bacchic wand") and Thyrsis, the Miltonic speaker of this pastoral elegy. On the ability of wordplay to enhance the epigrammatic "turn," whereby an "echo" of one word is achieved by altering a letter or a syllable at the beginning or middle of a subsequent word, see Jacobus Pontanus, *Poeticarum Institutionum Libri Tres* (Ingolstadt: Sartorius, 1594), 198.

[270] See Cinquemani, *Glad To Go For A Feast*, 23–24.

Accademia degli Apatisti,[271] an academy attended by Milton in 1638.[272] Of particular relevance to *Ad Salsillum* is an academic game known as the *lingua ionadattica* (or *lingua fagiana*), which involved the exchanging and interchanging of words with similar first syllables.[273] Or, as Eva Struhal succinctly puts it:

> *Lingua ionadattica*, a word of unclear etymological roots, is based on Florentine spoken dialect. However, in a burlesque, enigmatic, allusive, and playful way it substitutes one word for another in a manner that phonetically recalls the original term. Most often the new term is presented in such a way that it also points to a new aspect of its original meaning and entertains by stretching the relationship between designated object and word.[274]

That the practice was promoted as a demonstration of academic wit ("acutezza") is clear from Matteo Peregrini's pioneering tract *Delle Acutezze, che Altrimenti Spiriti, Vivezze e Concetti Volgarmente si Appellano* (1639). Here the *lingua ionadattica* is seen to evince its practitioner's alertness to "legamento artificioso" ("artificial linking"), whereby possible verbal correlations are signaled phonetically by syllabic iteration or by the skillful juxtaposition of words.[275] The continued

---

[271] See Elisa Goudriaan, *Florentine Patricians and Their Networks: Structures Behind the Cultural Success and the Political Representation of the Medici Court (1600–1660)* (Leiden: Brill, 2017), 208. Members of the Apatisti seem to have taken particular delight in wordplay, and invented anagrams of their own names, by which they were known in the academy, and under which their works were frequently published.

[272] For evidence of Milton's presence in the Apatisti in 1638, see 21.

[273] See Nardo, "Academic Interludes," 213, who does not, however, discuss *Ad Salsillum* in this context.

[274] Eva Struhal, "Reading with *Acutezza*: Lorenzo Lippi's Literary Culture," in *The Artist as Reader: On Education and Non-Education of Early Modern Artists*, eds. Heiko Damm, Michael Thimann, and Claus Zittel (Leiden: Brill, 2013), 105–127, at 121.

[275] See Matteo Peregrini, *Delle Acutezze, che Altrimenti Spiriti, Vivezze e Concetti Volgarmente si Appellano* (Genoa: Gio[vanni] Maria Farroni, Nicolò Pesagni, & Pier Francesco Barbieri, 1639), 34: "Il legamento artificioso di parole con parole consiste nella loro vicendevole collatione ... Quando poi l'artificio consiste in una determinata simmetria di due parti campeggianti l'una in faccia dell'altra; egli può havere alcuna rarità d'Acutezza considerabile" ("The artificial linking of words with words consists in their mutual juxtaposition ... When the artifice consists in a specific symmetry of two parts that stand out, one against the other, it can possess a certain rarity of wit that is considerable"). For an insightful reading of the practice as implemented by the

prevalence of the practice is indicated by Orazio Rucellai's "Cicalata della Lingua Ionadattica," delivered before the della Crusca in 1662, which discusses such instances as "solletico"/"sole," "vicario"/"vino," "federa"/"febbre," "gomitolo"/"gobbo," and "storpiato"/"Storione."[276]

In Milton's poem aspects of the *lingua ionadattica* seem to be recast in a Latin voice. The word *sal* at the heart of the name *Salsillus* ("the little salted one") is echoed phonetically in *Salus* (23), *salubre* (29), and *salsa* (41). And if Milton plays on the first syllable of his addressee's name, so too does he seem to play on its final two syllables ([s]*ille*) in such phrases as *sentis illud* (3), *ille* (8), *alumnus ille* (9) and *sic ille* (31).[277] In this last, *ille* is aptly preceded by *sic*, facilitating a macaronic pun on "sick," and thematically evoking the *aegrotans* of the poem's title. In all of this Milton demonstrates a wit (*sal*) of his own through employing the sort of etymological play so beloved of that academic world in which he participated.[278] In this sense his Latin verse capably epitomizes the syllabic scrutiny and semiotic versatility signaled by Richard Shoaf in relation to his vernacular writings:

> [N]o poet in English, except possibly Shakespeare, exploits the inside of words, their syllables, as Milton does. In Milton, semiosis, the *production* of signs and signification out of the elements of words, can be systematically mapped with results so extraordinary that they constitute in effect a new method for reading his poetry.[279]

A final word should be said about Milton's decision to employ the scazontic (or choliambic) meter. It is a decision that initially serves to surprise. Scazons, after all, were typically associated with satire or

---

poet, painter, and academician Lorenzo Lippi (1606–1665), see Struhal, "Reading with *Acutezza*," 120–121.

[276] See "Cicalata Settima della Lingua Ionadattica del Prior Orazio Rucellai," in *Prose Fiorentine Raccolte dallo Smarrito Accademico*, Part 1, vol. 6 (Florence: S[ua] A[ltezza] R[eale], 1723), 132–161, at 149.

[277] Emphasis is mine.

[278] The same practice may even underlie the predominance of "dis"- words in *Paradise Lost* 9.6-9: "foul *dis*trust, and breach/*Dis*loyal on the part of man, revolt,/And *dis*obedience: on the part of heaven/Now alienated, *dis*tance and *dis*taste." Emphasis is mine. See Christopher Ricks, *Milton's Grand Style* (Oxford: Oxford University Press, 1963), 69–72; Neil Forsyth, "Of Man's First Dis," in *Milton in Italy*, ed. Di Cesare, 345–369, neither of whom, however, relates the passage to Italian academic practice.

[279] R. A. Schoaf, *Milton, Poet of Duality: A Study of Semiosis in the Poetry and Prose Works* (Gainesville: University Press of Florida, 1993), x.

invective,[280] as is the case of Milton's only other use of the form in his Latin verses attacking Salmasius. Steven Oberhelman and John Mulryan candidly confess: "Milton's reason for selecting the choliamb is not clear to us."[281] The answer may reside, at least in part, in the limping effect produced by the scazontic meter (an iambic trimeter with the penultimate syllable reversed [u-u-u- u-u-/-x]),[282] thus aptly mirroring the potential lameness suffered by the poem's sick addressee.[283] But, when it comes to the matter of scrutinizing Milton's prosody, critics have been far from favorable. Thus, according to Landor, "[t]he scazons to Salzilli ... are full of false quantities."[284] Charles Symmons, observing that the fifth foot should always be an iambus, comments: "[i]n the poem before us ... Milton has violated this rule of Roman prosody in no less than twenty-one instances, by inserting either a spondee, or an anapest in the place in question. This is to be guilty, not of false quantity, but of an erroneous fabric of verse."[285] Similarly, Mackellar describes it as a rule that "Milton has not strictly observed,"[286] and Oberhelman and Mulryan remark that Milton has a spondee in the fifth foot in nineteen of the forty-one lines.[287] Might it be the case, however, that the so-called faults in question constitute Miltonic experimentation upon a given metrical form? It is surely more than a coincidence that one of these occurs in the line that describes Salzilli's own act of composing poetry: *Tam cultus ore*

---

[280] See Oberhelman and Mulryan, "Milton's Use of Classical Meters," 137.

[281] Oberhelman and Mulryan, "Milton's Use of Classical Meters," 137.

[282] For humanist discourses on the "lameness" afforded by the scazontic meter, see, among others, J. C. Scaliger, *Poetices Libri Septem* (Heidelberg: Pierre de St Andre, 1581), 150 (Book II, chapter IX, entitled IAMBICI SCAZONTES).

[283] Indeed meter is skillfully attuned to subject matter. The poem's fusion of the scazontic female *Musa* with the limping male deity Vulcan is comedic, even bathetic, in essence (cf. *Aeneid* 8. 408–415, where, as Vulcan rouses himself from sleep to approach his forge, Virgil compares him to a woman [*femina*] tending to her household chores). The tone seems to continue as she is invoked in language incorporating the colloquialisms of Roman comedy: the enclitic *dum* (*Adesdum* [6]) adding intensive force to the imperative (cf., for example, Plautus, *Manaechmi* 378; Terence, *Andria* 29), and the contracted *s'is* (6) (for *si vis*) (cf., for example, Plautus, *Casina* 203; Plautus, *Mostellaria* 1; Terence, *Heuton Timorumenos* 212; Terence, *Eunuchus* 311).

[284] Walter Savage Landor, "Imaginary Conversations," in *The Complete Works*, eds. Welby and Wheeler, V, 330.

[285] Charles Symmons, "Observations on Milton's Latin Poetry," *CJ* 9 (1814): 338–345, at 342.

[286] *Latin Poems*, ed. Mackeller, 57.

[287] Oberhelman and Mulryan, "Milton's Use of Classical Meters," 137.

Lesbium condis melos (22) ("so eloquently do you fashion the song of Lesbos upon Roman lips"). Here John Carey offers the interesting speculation that "[t]his regularly iambic line, among scazons, may be M[ilton]'s compliment to Salzilli's smoothness."[288] It is worth noting that the 1630s had witnessed the Umoristi's increased alertness to metrical versatility. Pietro Della Valle, for example, had, on 20 November 1633, recited before the academy his *Di Tre Nuove Maniere di Verso Sdrucciolo*,[289] expounding the merits of an Italian meter that concludes with an accent on the antepenultimate syllable. That tract would have been available to Milton in its 1634-printed version.[290] Certainly *Ad Salsillum Poetam Romanum Aegrotantem. Scazontes* provides a unique instance of a Miltonic title that actually signals the meter employed in the Latin poem proper, as both Salzilli and Scazons are (almost punningly?) juxtaposed. One senses that here, as elsewhere, he is showcasing his versatility to his addressee and, possibly, to a wider academic audience in seicento Rome.

1.9 The Topography of Rome

Ultimately, *Ad Salsillum* moves beyond the world of the Italian academy by drawing upon the topography of Rome. Invoking the city's hills (*vosque rore vinoso/Colles benigni* [27–28] ["and you, hills abounding in the dew of grapes"]), Milton expresses the hope that they might afford *levamen* (30) ("alleviation") to his sick addressee by bringing him *Siquid salubre vallibus frondet vestris* (29) ("any health-bringing plant that blooms in your valleys"). He then imagines the effect of the recovered

---

[288] John Milton, *Complete Shorter Poems*, ed. John Carey (London: Longman, 1968), 258.

[289] See Alemanno, "L'Accademia degli Umoristi," 117. The "sdrucciolo" or "sliding line" added an extra unstressed syllable to the single unaccented syllable ending a piano line. This "supernumerary syllable," as Michael Talbot observes, "is similarly ignored when classifying the metre." See Michael Talbot, *The Chamber Cantatas of Antonio Vivaldi* (Woodbridge: The Boydell Press, 2006), 35. Cayley regards it as "originally a genuine form of the Italian endecasillabo," and links it to the Latin *senarius*, which he compares to scazontes. See C. B. Cayley, "The Pedigree of English Heroic Verse," *Transactions of the Philological Society* 15 (1867): 43–54, at 51–52: "And if we consider on what conditions the senarius may be read as a regulated *sdrucciolo*, the principal or only ones seem to be that the line should contain no trisyllabic feet ... senarii ending in dissyllables would become bad scazons."

[290] Pietro Della Valle, *Di Tre Nuove Maniere di Verso Sdrucciolo* (Rome: Pietro Antonio Facciotti, 1634).

poet's song upon the neighboring regions. In so doing, he seems to zoom in upon one region in particular, predicting the amazement of one individual, Numa, the second of Rome's legendary kings, now situated in a quasi-pastoral setting of dark groves:

> Ipse inter atros emirabitur lucos
> Numa, ubi beatum degit otium aeternum,
> Suam reclivis semper Aegeriam spectans (33–35)

> Numa himself will be amazed, where amid the dark
> groves he spends a blessed eternity of repose, as he
> reclines, forever gazing upon his own Egeria.

It was from the water nymph Egeria,[291] one of the Camenae,[292] that Numa was purported to have acquired wisdom in the course of several nightly meetings.[293] Masson, while describing this "topographical allusion" as "interesting,"[294] speculates: "it might seem that Milton, while visiting the spots of classic interest about Rome, referred to his Livy and his Horace to help out the prosaic details of the guide-book."[295] Whether or not Milton used a guidebook in the course of his Italian travels remains unknown.[296] But what is known is that the grove or valley of Egeria, itself a famous beauty spot in the time of the Roman Empire,[297] had been greatly enhanced by Herodes Atticus into a *Nymphaeum Egeriae*, a grotto

---

[291] Cf. Ovid, *Fasti* 3.275-276: *Egeria est quae praebet aquas, dea grata Camenis:/illa Numae coniunx consiliumque fuit* ("It is Egeria who provides the water supply, that goddess pleasing to the Muses. She was Numa's wife and his counselor"). Cf. *Fasti* 3.261-262: *nympha, mone, nemori stagnoque operata Dianae;/nympha, Numae coniunx, ad tua facta veni* ("Advise me, Nymph, you who serve Diana's grove and lake, nymph, wife of Numa, come to me as I proclaim your deeds").

[292] See Ovid, *Met.* 15. 482–492; *Fasti* 3.261-284; 4.641–672; Cicero, *Rep.* 2.13–15; Plutarch, *Numa*, 4; Spenser, *Faerie Queene* 2.10.42.8.

[293] See Livy 1.19.5.

[294] Masson, *Life*, I, 755: "It is interesting to note, in this poem ... the topographical allusions to Rome and its neighbourhood—the vine-clad hills of Evander ... and the so-called fountain of Egeria, the supposed site of Numa's dusky grove."

[295] Masson, *Life*, I, 756.

[296] For the most part Milton seems to have relied on personal guides: Lucas Holstenius in Rome, and Giovanni Battista Manso in Naples. Indeed, where John Evelyn and his friends had to hire a coach to transport them through Naples (see *Diary*, ed. De Beer, II, 325), Milton could rely on Manso himself, who conducted him through the city and Viceroy's court (*Defensio Secunda*, 85. See Appendix 2.30–31).

[297] See, for example, Juvenal 3.12–20.

of Egeria, created in his sumptuous villa in the present day Valle della Caffarella. As part of the formalized restoration of the site, the grotto's main spring fed into large pools, one of which, known as the *Lacus Salutaris* ("Health-giving Lake"), was renowned for its curative powers.[298] Overlooked by the Church of Sant' Urbano alla Caffarella, originally a Roman temple, dedicated probably to Bacchus, the *Nymphaeum Egeriae* proved extremely popular to visitors to Rome in the seventeenth and eighteenth centuries, and especially to travelers undertaking the Grand Tour. Thus, according to Bernard de Montfaucon:

> Haud procul isto loco adscenditur in casam quae cum ad Cafarellos pertineat, *la Cafarella* dicitur. Ibi sub grandi fornice veteri fons visitur, qui etiam hodie usui est. Istic multi Romanorum aestivis mensibus conveniunt animi causa, ibique diem agunt.[299]
>
> Not far from that spot one ascends into a dwelling which is called "Caffarella" since it pertains to the Caffarelli. There, beneath a huge and ancient arch, one can go to see a spring, which is of use even today. In the summer months many people from Rome congregate in that place for their own gratification, and there they spend the day.

The site's popularity was largely on account of the widely held belief that it was here that Numa held regular nightly meetings with the nymph Egeria. De Montfaucon notes its association with the Egeria myth (*inscriptio autem ferebat fontem Egeriae esse, nymphisque dedicatum* ["an inscription stated that it was the spring of Egeria, and that it was dedicated to the nymphs"]), which he explicates by drawing upon Livy

---

[298] See Francesco Puccinotti, *Storia della Medicina* (Leghorn: Maximilian Wagner, 1850) I, 576: "Le leggi di Numa cominciarono così connesse all'idea della salute, che il suo sacro bosco, e la Egeria Ninfa e il sacro asilo delle Camene, erano in luogo dove scorreva il fiumicello Almone che presso allo speco formava un pelaghetto, da Rufo e Vittore chiamato *lacus salutaris*. Le acque erano minerali e valevano contro i mali della cute, e ritengono anche oggi il nome di *Acqua Santa*" ("Numa's laws began with their association with the idea of good health, namely, that his sacred wood, and the nymph Egeria, and the sacred sanctuary of the Muses were situated in a place from which there flowed the stream Almone, which formed near the cave a little lake termed by Rufus and Victor 'the health-giving lake.' The waters were of mineral, and had potency against maladies of the skin, and even today they retain the name of 'Holy Water'." See also Fabio Martini and Stefania Nardini, *Roma Nascosta: Una Guida Spigliata e Stimolante alla Riscoperta degli Insospettati Tesori di Una Roma Troppo Spesso Inaccessibile* (Rome: Newton Compton, 1984), 249.

[299] Bernard de Montfaucon, *Diarium Italicum sive Monumentorum Veterum, Bibliothecarum, Musaeorum, &c.* (Paris: Joannes Anisson, 1702), 152–153.

and Ovid.³⁰⁰ Itemized by Totti, the nearby Church of Sant' Urbano alla Caffarella was rediscovered in the Seicento as a Christian site associated with Pope Urban I (*d.* 230). Totti's "rather romantic"³⁰¹ description makes only minimal reference to the site's ancient history.³⁰² Instead, the whole is seen as a telling instance of Urban VIII's extensive restoration plans,³⁰³ realized in 1636 with the help of Francesco Barberini. These included, *inter alia*, the construction of large buttresses on the back and lateral walls, and additional brickwork covering the space between the columns of the portico.³⁰⁴ Francesco Piranesi produced a general plan of the environs, which he described as:

> l'area del Tempio che aveva innanzi, e le fabriche, che lo cingevano d'intorno: e inoltre il muro di sostruzione, che poneva la detta arca in piano nel declivio del monte che riguarda la valle Egeria.³⁰⁵
>
> the area of the Temple that was in front of it, and the constructions which surrounded it all about, and also the foundation wall beneath, which placed the said arch level on the slope of the mountain, which overlooks the valley of Egeria.

Eighteenth-century engravings give a good sense of the grotto's interior. That by Giovanni Battista Piranesi (*c.* 1766) shows the ruins of a recessed arch with a reclining statue (then, as now, missing its head), with water issuing from three pipes.³⁰⁶ The identity of the statue had given rise to

---

³⁰⁰ See De Montfaucon, *Diarium Italicum*, 153.

³⁰¹ Kirstin Noreen, "Sant'Urbano alla Caffarella, Rome: The Reconstruction of an Ancient Memorial," *Memoirs of the American Academy in Rome* 47 (2002): 57–82, at 57.

³⁰² See Kirstin Noreen, *Sant' Urbano alla Caffarella: Eleventh-Century Roman Wall Painting and the Sanctity of Martyrdom* (Ph.D thesis: Johns Hopkins University, 1998), and her "Lay Patronage and the Creation of Papal Sanctity during the Gregorian Reform: The case of Sant' Urbano alla Caffarella, Rome," *Gesta* 40 (2001): 39–59.

³⁰³ Totti, *Ritratto di Roma Moderna*, 128–129.

³⁰⁴ See Noreen, "Sant'Urbano alla Caffarella, Rome," 58, and her "Recording the Past: Seventeenth-Century Watercolor Drawings of Medieval Monuments," *Visual Resources* 16 (2000): 1–26.

³⁰⁵ Francesco Piranesi, *Raccolta dei Tempi Antichi* (Rome: F[rancesco] Piranesi, 1780), s.v. "Tempio dell' Onore e della Virtù," 3.

³⁰⁶ Giovanni Battista Piranesi, *Vedute di Roma*, 2 vols (Rome: Fausto Amedei, 1748–1778), reproduced in A. M. Hind, *Giovanni Battista Piranesi: A Critical Study, with a List of his Published Works and Detailed Catalogues of the Prisons and the Views of*

some misinterpretation in the Seicento and beyond. Lucas Holstenius, for example, in a letter to Peiresc (dated 2 May 1636), reported Francesco Barberini's interest in the church and its antiquities, and proceeded to state:

> Porro ecclesia illa de propinquo imminet fonti maximo, quam olim Camoenis sacrum fuisse credo. Tegitur enim fornice maxima antiqui Romani operis, cui adhuc imposita cernitur figura Nymphae, quam Egeriam esse facile adducar ut credam, cum qua Numa hoc in antro congressus dicitur.[307]

> That church moreover overlooks a very large spring close at hand, which, I believe, was once sacred to the Muses. For it is covered by a very large arch of ancient Roman

---

Rome (New York: E. Weyhe, 1922), no. 80; *Giovanni Battista Piranesi: The Complete Etchings*, ed. John Wilton-Ely (San Francisco: Alan Wofsy Fine Arts, 1994), no. 213.

[307] *Lucae Holstenii Epistolae ad Diversos*, ed. Jean-François Boissonade (Paris: J. Gratiot, 1817), 489–501, at 497. Holstenius conveys his interest in the ancient remains of the church and the grotto, stating that *circumcirca magna eruuntur antiquitatis vestigia* ("all about large traces of antiquity are being excavated"). He has no doubt that beneath the church there is an ancient cemetery. He relates that upon discovering many caves here, he sent skilled men to investigate and to see whether there might be access to the cemetery, *sed illi, lustratis omnibus me praesente, affirmarunt haec spiracula esse aquaeductus subterranei quo aqua a fonte, quem dixi, in lucum Camoenarum perducta iam olim fuit* (497–498) ("but they, surveying everything in my presence, reported that these fissures pertained to a subterranean aqueduct by which water was once conveyed from the aforementioned spring into the grove of the Muses"). Holstenius's interest in Egeria was earlier attested by his Latin epithalamium to Francesco's brother, Taddeo Barberini, and Anna Colonna, upon their wedding on 14 October 1627. Published in Rome in 1629, this piece, running to 146 Latin hendecasyllables, interestingly describes the nymph Egeria as "reclining" (*Antris Egeria abditis recumbens* [85] ["Egeria reclining in her secluded caves"]; *Antris haec dea roscidis recumbens* [143] ["this goddess reclining in her watery caves"]). See *Carmina Diversorum Auctorum in Nuptiis Illustrissimorum et Excellentissimorum D[ominorum] Thaddei Barberini et Annae Columnae* (Rome: R[everenda] Cam[era] Apost[olica], 1629), 162–166, at 164 and 166. Line-numbering is mine. It also alludes to the advice that she offered to Numa (*fatidicisque solvit ora/Verbis; consilium quibus Deorum/Et sacra edocuit prius maritum* [90–92] ["she opened her mouth to utter prophetic words with which she had in former times instructed her husband in the rites of the gods"]), but now her prophetic utterances are transmuted into a prediction of the happiness, and the future offspring that will bless this marriage (93–142). It was with some gratification, therefore, that Holstenius, writing to Peiresc on 3 November 1628, could quantify his announcement of the birth of a daughter (Lucrezia Barberini [1628–1699]) to the couple, by declaring with a retrospective glance: *Gaudeo Egeriam nostram non vanam fuisse vatem* ("I rejoice that our prophetess Egeria has not proved to be false") (*Epistolae ad Diversos*, ed. Boissonade, 109–114, at 114).

> workmanship, in which one can still see positioned the figure of a nymph, whom I could easily be adduced to believe was Egeria, with whom Numa is said to have met in this cave.

And even as late as 1790 John Bell's *New Pantheon* could offer only the most tentative of speculations:

> I never met with any true statue of Egeria; there is indeed the figure of a person reclined at the upper end of the grotto, called by her name near Rome, but it is so defaced by time, and by the water that gushes out all about it, that one cannot distinguish whether it was ever meant for her, or, indeed, whether it may be any water-goddess at all. It may as well have been the figure of an old Roman soldier, represented on the cover of some sarcophagus, in the manner that one often sees them; and, to say the truth, has more the air of such a figure than of a water-deity.[308]

In fact, the statue is clearly male, and in all likelihood that of the river-god Almo (the river Almo, the modern Almone, flows through the vale of Egeria).[309] But its ambivalent interpretation in the Seicento may provide an interesting context in which to read Milton's representation of Numa in an atypically recumbent position, and of the mesmerized male gaze, spellbound in enthrallment to the female nymph Egeria. Keightley suggests a possible debt to Lucretius' depiction of Mars and Venus at *De Rerum Natura* 1.31–37.[310] Freeman, although acknowledging this

---

[308] *Bell's New Pantheon; or, Historical Dictionary of the Gods, Demi-gods, Heroes, and Fabulous Personages of Antiquity* (London: J[ohn] Bell, 1790), I, 279.

[309] See Mariana Starke, *Information and Directions for Travellers on the Continent* (London: John Murray, 1828), 188: "At the upper end of a Grotto ... situated below the Temple of Bacchus, in the Valley of the Caffarella, (formerly *ad Camoenas*) are remains of a Recumbent Statue, called Egeria, though supposed, by antiquaries, to represent the Almo"; Mariano Vasi and Antonio Nibby, *New Guide of Rome and its Environs* (Rome: L[uigi] Piale, 1851), 347: "the ancient statue at the end of the nymphaeum, though deprived of its head, is evidently that of a man, nor can it be doubted from its character and garments that it represented a river god"; Karl Baedeker, *Italy: Handbook for Travellers. Second Part: Central Italy and Rome* (Leipzig: K[arl] Baedeker, 1875), 300: "The 'grotto' is a Nymphaeum, which was originally covered with marble, the shrine of the brook Almo, which flows past it in an artificial channel, and was erected at a somewhat late period. A niche in the posterior wall contains the mutilated statue of the river-god, standing on corbels from which water flows."

[310] *The Poems of John Milton*, ed. Thomas Keightley, 2 vols (London: Chapman and Hall, 1859), II, 450. Cf. Lucretius, *De Rerum Natura* 1. 33–37: *in gremium qui saepe tuum se/reiicit aeterno devictus vulnere amoris,/atque ita suspiciens tereti cervice reposta/pascit amore avidos inhians in te, dea, visus/eque tuo pendet resupini spiritus*

possibility, rightly points out that "Lucretius stresses the temporary nature of Mars' tranquility."[311] Milton's Numa, reclining and utterly transfixed in his eternal gaze, is perhaps more accurately describable as quasi-statuesque in essence. This idealistic rewriting of the legend may also reflect Milton's reinterpretation of its associated Roman topography. Likewise, the fact that the *nymphaeum Egeriae* was overlooked by what was formerly an ancient temple of Bacchus may lend additional force to his description of Rome's hills (*colles* [28]) as *rore vinoso/... benigni* (27–28) ("abounding in the dew of grapes"). Here their salutary power, an aspect highlighted by Livy, among others,[312] is intrinsically linked to their produce. In a striking personification,[313] they are urged to compete in rivalry (*certatim* [30]) with one another in their endeavor to afford Salzilli a remedy. The imagined remedy seems to constitute some sort of wine and herb-based concoction (*Siquid salubre vallibus frondet vestris* [29] ["if any health-bringing plant blooms in your valleys"]). Since ancient times wine was traditionally seen as possessing medicinal powers, with the Greek surgeon Dioscurides recommending as a medicinal aid a combination of fermenting must, herbs, flowers, and roots.[314] The purgative effects of wine were regarded as particularly effective in the treatment of bile—or, in Salzilli's case, the *profunda bilis* (19) ("overflow of bile") attacking his kidneys and deeply implanted in his stomach (19–20). That it was an enduring view is attested by such writers as the Swiss physician and botanist Gaspars Bauhin, who proclaimed in 1610:

---

ore ("he oft flings himself back upon thy lap, conquered by the eternal wound of love; and then pillowing his shapely neck upon thee and looking up he feeds with love his greedy eyes, gazing wistfully towards thee, while, as he lies back, his breath hangs upon thy lips"). Translation is that of *De Rerum Natura*, ed. Bailey, I, 177–179.

[311] Freeman, "Milton's Roman Connection," 103.

[312] Livy 5.54.4: *Non sine causa di hominesque hunc urbi condendae locum elegerunt, saluberrimos colles* ("It is not without reason that gods and men chose this spot for founding a city, the most health-giving hills"). Cf. Cicero, *Rep.* 2.5–10. See Caroline Vout, *The Hills of Rome: Signature of an Eternal City* (Cambridge: Cambridge University Press, 2012), 31.

[313] On the personification of mountains in general and of the hills of Rome in particular, see Vout, *The Hills of Rome*, 125–133. Cf. Milton's personification of the Lydian Mount Tmolus as *Tmolus Lydii montis Deus popularis* ("Tmolus, the native god of the Lydian mountain") in *Epistola Familiaris 2*, at *Epistolarum Familiarium Liber Unus*, 9–10, on which see *Epistolarum Familiarium Liber Unus and Uncollected Letters*, ed. Haan, 51–52, 57.

[314] See John M. Riddle, *Dioscurides on Pharmacy and Medicine* (Austin: University of Texas Press, 1985), 67; Stephen Charters, *Wine and Society: The Social and Cultural Context of a Drink* (Oxford: Butterworth-Heinemann, 2006), 246.

> Duplicia ergo sunt vina medicata: Quaedam enim solum alterant, quaedam vero humores praeparant, eosque sensim expurgant ... Quae vero purgant, vel expurgant humorem simplicem, vel mixtos. Simplicem, ut bilem flavam, vinum scammonites: bilem atram, vinum ex helleboro nigro.[315]

> And so there are two types of medicinal wines: some only cause alterations to the humors, but others get them into readiness and gradually purge them ... Those which have a purgative effect purge either an individual humor or a combination of humors: wine tasting of scammony, for an individual humor such as white bile; wine from black hellebore, for black bile.

The envisaged soothing of physical ailments is mirrored by the very landscape of the closing lines of *Ad Salsillum*, which reconfigure another aspect of Roman topography: the Tiber itself and its environs:

> Tumidusque et ipse Tibris hinc delinitus
> Spei favebit annuae colonorum,
> Nec in sepulchris ibit obsessum reges
> Nimium sinistro laxus irruens loro:
> Sed frena melius temperabit undarum,
> Adusque curvi salsa regna Portumni. (36–41)

> And the swollen Tiber himself, bewitched by this song, will favor the yearly hope of farmers, and will not proceed to besiege kings in their tombs by rushing along with his left rein too loose: instead, he will keep better rein upon his waves all the way up to the salted realms of curving Portumnus.

The passage counters Horace's grim vision of the river's inundation:

> vidimus flavum Tiberim retortis
> litore Etrusco violenter undis
> ire deiectum monumenta regis
>   templaque Vestae,
> Iliae dum se nimium querenti
> iactat ultorem, vagus et sinistra
> labitur ripa Iove non probante u-
>   xorius amnis.
>   (Horace, *Odes* 1.2.13–20)

---

[315] Caspar Bauhin, *De Compositione Medicamentorum sive Medicamentorum Componendorum Ratio et Methodus* (Offenbach: Conradus Nebenius, 1610), 134–135.

> We have seen the yellow Tiber, his waves hurled violently back from his Tuscan bank, advance to lay low the king's monument and Vesta's shrine, while he boasts that he is the avenger of Ilia's importunate complaints, and over his left bank glides far and wide, without the approval of Jupiter — a river too devoted to his wife.

Where the Horatian Tiber had turned against his own city, such will not be the case in Salzilli's Rome: *Nec in sepulchris ibit obsessum reges* (38) ("it will not proceed to besiege kings in their tombs"). The phrase, as Bush aptly notes, "corresponds to Horace's *monumenta regis*."[316] But with an important difference: Where Horace had described the Tiber flooding on the left bank (*vagus et sinistra/labitur ripa* [18–19] ["over his left bank glides far and wide"]), Milton states that this will not occur (*Nec ... ibit ... /Nimium sinistro laxus irruens loro* [38–39] ["he will not proceed ... rushing along with his left rein too loose"]).[317] The Horatian ill-omen,[318] "hinting," as Kenneth Quinn suggests, "at the misguided division of Roman against Roman,"[319] is hereby transformed into a symbol of harmony and calm in seicento Rome.[320] Most commentators agree that the flood alluded to by Horace was, in all likelihood, that described by the historian Dio Cassius, which occurred on 16–17 January 27 BC,[321] the very night after Octavian received the title "Augustus."[322] But the flood of Milton's poem can be read in a much more recent topographical context: that of an actual inundation of the Tiber in February 1637. On that occasion the river reached a level of 17.55

---

[316] Bush, *Variorum*, I, 267.

[317] With this reassurance that the inundation of the Tiber will not occur, cf. Marco Picarelli, "Per La S[ignora] D[etta] che non Teme l'alteratione del Tevere" (*Poesie de' Signori Accademici Fantastici*, 187).

[318] Inundations of the Tiber were viewed by the ancient Romans as portents of warning. The flood of AD 15 was termed an omen by Dio Cassius, at 57.14.7. Cf. Pliny *NH* 3.55. See J. W. Rich, *Cassius Dio: The Augustan Settlement (Roman History 53–55.9)* (Warminster: Aris and Phillips, 1990), 153.

[319] *Horace: The Odes*, ed. Kenneth Quinn (London: Macmillan, 1980), 122.

[320] The imagery of assuagement appropriately parallels the hoped-for physical calming of Salzilli's ailments graphically described in lines 19–20.

[321] See Dio Cassius, 53.20.1.

[322] See Raymond J. Clark, "Ilia's Excessive Complaint and The Flood in Horace, *Odes* 1.2," *CQ* 60 (May 2010): 262–267.

meters,[323] during which catastrophe, as Giacinto Gigli relates, Cardinal Francesco Barberini had asked to be punted through the flooded streets in order to distribute bread.[324] That it was still a vivid memory up to a year after the event is attested by Gian Lorenzo Bernini's *Inondazione della Tevere*, mounted for the Carnival of 1638.[325] This lavish production recreated the Tiber flood by presenting boats upon real water on the stage of the theater of the Palazzo Barberini.[326] It did so with a stunningly realistic hydraulic trick,[327] by which method Bernini, according to his biographers, "facesse comparir da lontano a poco a poco gran copia d'acque a romper gli argini" ("caused a huge supply of water, gradually making its way from afar, to break the levees"), thereby spilling out in the direction of the audience. Panic-stricken, they got up to flee, only to see to their amazement that a barrier had risen just in time to prevent the seeming misadventure.[328] As Pamela Smith notes, "[a]ll the audience had experienced the flood, but not a single onlooker had got wet."[329] Perhaps in *Ad Salsillum* metatheatrical ingenuity can be matched and even surpassed by the predicted power of poetry itself, whereby, in this instance too

Tumidus ... ipse Tibris ... frena melius temperabit undarum.

---

[323] See Silvia Enzi, "Le Inondazioni del Tevere a Roma tra il XVI e XVIII Secolo nelle Fonti Bibliotecarie del Tempo," *Mélanges de L'Ecole Française de Rome* 118 (2006): 13–20, at 17.

[324] Giacinto Gigli, *Diario di Roma*, ed. Manlio Barberito (Rome: Editore Colombo, 1994), 292–293.

[325] See Robert Fahmer and William Kleb, "The Theatrical Activity of Gianlorenzo Bernini," *Educational Theatre Journal* 25 (1973): 5–14, at 6–8; Irving Lavin, *Bernini and the Unity of the Visual Arts*, 2 vols (New York: Oxford University Press, 1980), I, 1541.

[326] The theater in question opened on 23 February 1632, and had a capacity for holding *c*. 3000 spectators.

[327] The trick was the work of the hydraulic engineer Giovanni Battista Aleotti. See Mary Ann Frese Witt, *Metatheater and Modernity: Baroque and Neobaroque* (Madison: Fairleigh Dickinson University Press, 2013), 81.

[328] Filippo Baldinucci, *Vita del Cavaliere Gio[vanni] Lorenzo Bernino* (Florence: Vincenzio Vangelisti, 1682), 76. Cf. Domenico Bernini, *Vita del Cavalier Gio[vanni] Lorenzo Bernini* (Rome: Rocco Bernabò, 1713), 55.

[329] Pamela H. Smith, *The Business of Alchemy: Science and Culture in the Holy Roman Empire* (Princeton, NJ: Princeton University Press, 1997), 267.

Chapter 2

Milton's Latin Epigrams to Leonora Baroni

By the time of Milton's arrival in Rome there was firmly established in the city a celebrated musical family, at least one of whom would come to leave a lasting impression upon him. The year 1633 had seen the migration from Naples to Rome of Adriana Basile Baroni, her husband, Mutio Baroni, and their children: a son Camillo, and two daughters, Leonora, and Caterina. Adriana, an extraordinarily gifted contralto and instrumentalist on the lira, harp, and Spanish guitar,[1] had already won acclaim throughout Italy. In 1610, for instance, none other than Claudio Monteverdi had proclaimed: "a Mantova la Signora Adriana benissimo cantare benissimo sonare et benissimo parlare ho udito" ("in Mantua I have heard the lady Adriana singing, playing, and speaking extremely well").[2] And in 1628 she had been honored by a volume of encomiastic verse, entitled *Il Teatro delle Glorie della Signora Adriana Basile*.[3] That she had already begun to make her mark in Italy's capital is evident from the testimony of Fulvio Testi, who, writing in 1634 to the Duke of Modena, asserted that Adriana "ha gusto di musica, e di musica da principe grande" ("has a great taste for music and for the principles of music").[4] Indeed it was Adriana's interpretation of the new monodic style that attested to her vocal technique. Eager to pass on her skills to her daughters, she had ensured that they received an education that incorporated both vocal and instrumental training.[5] Her efforts were

---

[1] See Alessandro Ademollo, *La Bella Adriana ed Altre Virtuose del Suo Tempo alla Corte di Mantova* (Città di Castello: Lapi, 1888); Kathryn Bosi, "Adriana's Harp: Paintings, Poetic Imagery, and Musical Tributes for the *Sirena di Posilipo*," *Imago Musicae* 30 (2019), 75–103. See also *Lettere di Diversi Principi alla Signora Adriana Basile Scritte* (Venice; rpt Naples: s.n., 1628).

[2] Claudio Monteverdi, *Lettere, Dediche e Prefazioni*, ed. Domenico De' Paoli (Rome: De Santis, 1973), 52.

[3] *Il Teatro delle Glorie della Signora Adriana Basile* (Venice; rpt Naples: s.n., 1628).

[4] Fulvio Testi, *Lettere*, ed. Maria Luisa Doglio, 2 vols (Bari: Laterza, 1967), II, 425.

[5] See Isabelle Emerson, *Five Centuries of Women Singers* (Westport, CT: Greenwood Publishing, 2005), 16–17.

stunningly realized in the musicianship of her daughter Leonora Baroni.[6] An outstanding soprano and a polished instrumentalist on theorbo, harp, and viol, Leonora enthralled audiences wherever she performed. Singing to her own accompaniment or to that of her mother (on lira) and her sister, Caterina (on harp), she eventually, in the words of Frederick Hammond, "eclipsed even her mother's fame."[7] Leonora was also a talented linguist, a composer of over thirty arias,[8] and, along with her sister, a minor Italian poet.[9]

Margaret Byard suggests that Leonora's performance would have given Milton "probably for the first time, an opportunity to hear a talented woman singing with professional skill and technique."[10] Although his epigrams are undated, the allusion to Tasso's madness in consequence of his love for another Leonora (*Ad Leonoram* 2.1–2) favors the return visit to Rome (January/February 1639), by which time he had met in Naples Giovanni Battista Manso, whose *Vita di Torquato Tasso* (1621) had promulgated the story that Tasso's insanity was the result of his love for Leonora d'Este.[11] Milton extols not only Leonora's vocal,[12]

---

[6] On Leonora Baroni, see Alessandro Ademollo, *La Leonora di Milton e di Clemente IX* (Milan: Ricordi, 1885); Eugene Schuyler, "Milton's Leonora," *Nation* 47 (18 October, 1888), 310–312; Mario Allessandrini, "Una Celebre Cantatrice alla Corte di Urbano VIII," *Scenario* 11 (April, 1942), 152–153; *The New Grove Dictionary of Music and Musicians*, ed. Stanley Sadie, 20 vols (London: Macmillan, 1980), II, 171–172; Liliana Pannella, "Baroni, Eleonora, Detta Anche l'Adrianella o l'Adrianetta," *DBI* 6 (1964): 456–458; B. M. Antolini, "Cantanti e Letterati a Roma nella Prima Metà del Seicento: Alcune Osservazioni," in *In Cantu et in Sermone: For Nino Pirrotta on his 80th Birthday*, eds. Fabrizio Della Seta and Franco Piperno (Florence: Olschki, 1989), 347–362; Amy Brosius, "'Il Suon, lo Sguardo, il Canto': The Function of Portraits of Mid-Seventeenth-Century Virtuose in Rome," *Italian Studies* 63 (2008): 17–39, at 33–38; Amy Brosius, *"Il Suon, lo Sguardo, il Canto": Virtuose of the Roman Conversazioni in the Mid-Seventeenth Century* (PhD thesis: New York University, 2009); Christine Jeanneret, "Gender Ambivalence and the Expression of Passions in the Performances of Early Roman Cantatas by Castrati and Female Singers," in *The Emotional Power of Music: Multidisciplinary Perspectives on Musical Arousal, Expression, and Social Control*, eds. Tom Cochrane, Bernardino Fantini, and Klaus R. Scherer (Oxford: Oxford University Press, 2013), 85–101.

[7] Hammond, *Music and Spectacle*, 86.

[8] See Hammond, *Music and Spectacle*, 86. Unfortunately, none of Leonora's musical compositions survive.

[9] See 102–104, 106–107.

[10] Byard, "'Adventrous Song,'" 322.

[11] See Manso, *Vita di Torquato Tasso*, 51–57; Haan, *From Academia to Amicitia*, 111–112.

[12] *Nam tua praesentem vox sonat ipsa Deum* (*Ad Leonoram* 1.4) ("for your very voice resonates the presence of God"); *Voce eadem poteras composuisse tua* (*Ad Leonoram*

but also her instrumental[13] talents, thereby suggesting that he has witnessed her perform firsthand. And there would have been ample opportunities for him to do so, given his connections with Lucas Holstenius[14] and the associated Barberini circle.[15] There are several possible venues at which he could have heard Leonora sing: perhaps in her own home, in which the family regularly put on concerts, or in one or more of the Roman academies with which she was evidently associated.

2.1 The Baroni Sisters and the Accademia degli Umoristi

Foremost among the academies of Rome was the Accademia degli Umoristi, which, as noted earlier, included among its membership another Italian addressee of Milton's Latin poetry, Giovanni Salzilli.[16] In regard to Leonora's role in the Umoristi, there has been a certain degree of confusion and consequential dissension among scholars. Frederick Hammond's assertion that she was the academy's "only female member"[17] overlooks the precedent of Francesca Caccini, who sang before them in 1623,[18] a precedent which may support the possibility that Leonora likewise performed for them.[19] Bianca Antolini is unequivocal in her belief that both Leonora and Caterina were full members.[20] On the other hand, Andrew Dell' Antonio underplays Leonora's academic status by stating that "it is unlikely that she fully participated in their gatherings on a regular basis, or even that the academicians truly considered her a full member of their court," preferring instead to view her membership as "honorific."[21] Evidence does exist, however, that both she and her sister were not only members of, but created no slight an impression upon, this learned male community. This is provided by an Italian sonnet authored

---

2.10) ("by means of your voice you could have afforded calm"); *Flexanimo cantu* (*Ad Leonoram* 2.12 ("by your soul-swaying song")).

[13] *Aurea maternae fila movere lyrae* (*Ad Leonoram* 2.6) ("as you plucked the golden strings of your mother's lyre").

[14] See Chapter 3.

[15] See 154–157, 169–172.

[16] See 35–40, 74–82.

[17] Hammond, *Music and Spectacle*, 86.

[18] See Ademollo, *La Bell' Adriana*, 119.

[19] See Brosius, "The Function of Portraits," 35.

[20] Antolini, "Cantanti e Letterati," 354.

[21] Dell'Antonio, *Listening as Spiritual Practice*, 86.

by Leonora herself, entitled "Alli Signori Accademici Humoristi con occasione, *che fù ricevuta nella loro Accademia*" ("To the Members of the Academy of the Umoristi *on the occasion that she was received into their Academy*").[22] The piece would see publication in *L'Idea della Veglia* (Rome, 1640),[23] along with six further poems by Leonora,[24] and no fewer than thirteen poems (eleven sonnets, a canzone, and a Madrigale) by her sister Caterina.[25] Here Leonora not only alludes to the academy's *impresa*,[26] but she also appropriates it imaginatively by addressing the Umoristi themselves as "Sacri Cigni" ("sacred swans"), "soavi del Tebro in sù le sponde/Stilla Nube immortal celesti humori" ("upon whom, on the pleasant banks of the Tiber, an immortal cloud drips celestial humors").[27] Significantly, she proceeds to thank them for affording her the privilege of moistening her lips in such beautiful waters, proclaiming: "Vostra Gloria ... /Spargerà su'l mio Nome aurei splendori" ("Your glory ... will sprinkle golden splendors upon my name").[28] Indeed Leonora's role (and her possible prominence?) may assume additional significance if a portrait of her by Fabio della Corgna[29] was, as Amy Brosius suggests, "commissioned by one of the members to hang in the space where the Accademia met,"[30] thereby functioning perhaps "as a surrogate for her performances."[31] Worthy of mention also is Caterina's accomplished sonnet in the same volume, entitled "Per l'Accademia de' Sig[nori] Humoristi, allude alla loro Impresa" ("For the Accademia of the

---

[22] Emphasis is mine.

[23] *L'Idea della Veglia* (Rome: Francesco Corbelletti, 1640), 220.

[24] Printed with a separate title page, Leonora's poems occur at *L'Idea*, 215–221. A further sonnet by Leonora, thanking its contributors, occurs at *Applausi*, 261.

[25] Printed with a separate title page, Caterina's poems occur at *L'Idea*, 223–236. A further sonnet by Caterina, thanking its contributors, occurs at *Applausi*, 262.

[26] On the *impresa* and motto of the Accademia degli Umoristi, see 75–82.

[27] *L'Idea*, 220, lines 1–4.

[28] *L'Idea*, 220, lines 7–8.

[29] On della Corgna's portrait, see Franca Trinchieri Camiz, "La Bella Cantatrice: I Ritratti di Leonora Barone e Barbara Strozzi a Confronto," in *Musica, Scienza e Idée nella Serenissima durante il Seicento Venezia*, ed. Francesco Passadore *et al* (Venice: Fondazione Ugo e Olga Levi, 1996), 285–294; Brosius, "The Function of Portraits"; Cristina Galassi, "La Virtuosa Eleonora Baroni in un Ritratto di Fabio della Corgna," *Kronos* 13 (2009): 177–183, reworked in her *Ritratto di Una Virtuosa Canterina: Eleonora Baroni e il Pittore Fabio della Corgna al Tempo dei Barberini* (Perugia: Aguaplano, 2017). See also 136.

[30] Brosius, "The Function of Portraits," 35.

[31] Brosius, "The Function of Portraits," 35.

Umoristi, with an allusion to their Emblem").[32] Further evidence of Caterina's membership of the Umoristi is evinced by the *Monumentum Romanum* (1638), commemorating (in January 1638) the death of Peiresc, and dedicated to Cardinal Francesco Barberini.[33] Among the 72 multilingual poems included therein[34] (only after careful vetting by the censors),[35] and described as having been recited at the Academy,[36] is an Italian sonnet by Caterina herself.[37] The placing of her piece (as third), preceded by those of none other than Camillo Colonna, Principal of the

---

[32] *L'Idea*, 223.

[33] See 36 and 76. For a concise overview of this volume, see Peter Rietbergen, *Power and Religion in Baroque Rome: Barberini Cultural Policies* (Leiden/Boston: Brill, 2006), 414–417.

[34] The volume, as noted by Rietbergen, *Power and Religion*, 417, constitutes "an extraordinary collection of short poems ... in almost every language known to Europe by the beginning of the 17th century." On its multilinguistic and multidialectical features, see also Testa, *Italian Academies*, 170.

[35] See the letter (to Camillo Colonna, Principal of the Umoristi) from the Censors (Censori) Fabio Leonida, Domenico Benigni, Gasparo de Simeonibus, Leone Allacci, Girolammo Rocco, and Bartolomeo Tortoletti, introducing "le Compositioni, con le quali da particolari Accademici, furono accompagnate l'Essequie del Signor di Peires [*sic*]" ("the compositions by particular Academicians, with which the Funeral Proceedings of Mr Peiresc were accompanied") (*Monumentum*, 33–34, at 33). See also Testa, *Italian Academies*, 170, who speculates that, "Barberini himself was in charge of corrections." As noted by Antolini, "Cantanti e Letterati," 357, these six censors would later reappear as contributors to the *Applausi*. See also 76–77.

[36] *Monumentum*, 35: "Componimenti Funerali Per la Memoria del Signor Di Peires [*sic*] Accademico Humorista Recitati nell' Accademia Romana" ("Funeral Compositions for the Memory of Peiresc, Member of the Umoristi Academy, Recited in the Academy of Rome").

[37] *Monumentum*, 36: "Di Caterina Baroni." *Incipit* "Tra bei Cigni di Pindo, e d'Hipprocene" ("By Caterina Baroni," commencing: "Amid the beautiful Swans of Pindus and of Hippocrene"). Antolini, "Cantanti e Letterati," 355, regards Caterina's contribution as an early display of her poetic talents. Among other contributors known to Milton were Lucas Holstenius (who provided a Latin elegiac poem [66], an *Epitaphium Saxonicum* [113], and a *Carmen Belgicum* [114]), Giovanni Battista Doni (who authored a Latin poem [63]), and Francesco Rovai (who contributed an Italian poem [105–106]). For Milton's links with Holstenius, see Chapter 3 in this volume. For his potential links with Doni, see Schleiner, "Milton, G.B. Doni." See also 125–130. For his possible acquaintance with Francesco Rovai, see Carlo Dati's description of him in his letter to Milton (22 October/1 November 1647) as one who "per quanto io credo da lei ben conosciuto" ("as far as I believe was well known to you") and his associated request that Milton compose a lament on the Italian academician's death. See *The Works of John Milton*, ed. Frank A. Patterson *et al*, 18 vols (New York: Columbia University Press, 1931–1940), XII, 296. The request seems to have remained unfulfilled. See Haan, *From Academia to Amicitia*, 61–71.

Academy, and Cardinal Berlingiero Gessi, is indicative of the likely esteem in which she was held. This would seem to set it apart from what Peter Rietbergen has viewed as the collection's "shallow versification of the kind produced by people who either did not know the deceased or did not care to put in an effort."[38] It is worth remarking, too, that Leonora and her sister are implicitly envisaged as integrated among, and immortalized by, the Umoristi in one of Domenico Benigni's poetic contributions to the *Applausi Poetici alle Glorie della Signora Leonora Baroni* (1639), a volume to which this discussion will return, and in language clearly evocative of that academy's *impresa*:

> Sacri Cigni Febei,
> Cui sù'l Tebro distilla auree rugiade
> NUBE, che dal Ciel cade.[39]

> Sacred Swans of Phoebus,
> upon whom on the Tiber a CLOUD distills
> golden dews, which fall from the sky.

Indeed, Benigni, one of the most celebrated librettists of his day,[40] seems to have been closely aligned to the Baroni sisters.[41] In a letter to Fulvio Di Costanzo, dated 1 June 1639, and published in *L'Idea*, he eloquently describes evenings in the Baroni household, some of which were devoted to music, others to eloquence, others to poetry. In regard to music, he states, the glories reside in Adriana, Leonora, and Caterina.[42] Benigni

---

[38] Rietbergen, *Power and Religion*, 415.

[39] *Applausi*, 100.

[40] See Jeanneret, "Gender Ambivalence," 86.

[41] Cf. Antolini, "Cantanti e Letterati," 357: "il Benigni, che appare particolarmente legato ... alle sorelle Baroni" ("Benigni, who appears to have had a particular bond ... with the Baroni sisters").

[42] *L'Idea*, 13–36, at 14–15: "La Casa del Signor Mutio Baroni, Barone di Piancerreto, gentil'huomo, che per le sue cortesi maniere hà saputo haver luogo nella gratia de i primi Principi d'Italia, in riguardo delle qualità virtuose della Signora Adriana Basile sua moglie, e delle Signore Leonora, e Caterina sue figliuole, che per esser più d'una, non mi concedono chiamarle Fenici del nostro secolo: hoggi è frequentata da primi Signori, e Virtuosi di questa Corte; prerogativa, che và del pari con quella di qualsivoglia più famosa Accademia c'honori la nostra Italia ... Delle sere, alcune si destinano alla Musica, altre all' eloquenza, & altre alla Poesia. Ne gli essercitii della Musica le glorie sono tutte delle Signore Adriana, Leonora, e Caterina" ("The house of Mr Mutio Baroni of Piancerreto [a gentleman, who by virtue of his courteous manners, has been able to hold a place of influence among the foremost Princes of Italy on account of the virtuous qualities of the Lady Adriana Basile, his wife, and of the misses Leonora and Caterina, his daughters, who on more than one occasion have

proceeds to single out Leonora for her preeminence, stating that she is known as "a little angel upon the earth," and "a celestial Siren," and highlighting the accolades bestowed upon her in the *Applausi*:

> la preeminenza della gloria si riposi nella Signora Leonora. Le lodi, che si danno al canto di questa Signora sono le più pellegrine, che possano cadere in pensasamento humano, tutte però inferiori al suo merito, e familiari al suo valore, i nomi di terrena Angeletta, e di celeste Sirena sono demostrationi vulgari della stima, con la quale altri la riveriscono, e come ogn' uno, secondo i propri sentimenti, s'ingegna di celebrarla, convengono però tutti, che sia il miracolo del canto, e della bellezza, alla quale confermano la sovranità di questo grado superiore all' Invidia, gli Applausi Poetici, che si preparano alle stampe.[43]

> The pre-eminence of glory resides in the lady Leonora. The praises that are given to this lady's singing are the most exotic that can occur to human thought. The names of "little angel upon the earth" and of "celestial Siren", all, however, inferior to her merit and intimately connected to her worth, are popular demonstrations of the esteem with which others revere her, and as each one tries to celebrate her in accordance with his own feelings, all are of the agreement of the existence in her of a miracle of song and of beauty. In confirmation of the sovereign power of this rank, superior to envy, are the *Applausi Poetici*, which they are preparing for publication.

Dell' Antonio has cast some doubt upon Leonora's ability to engage in "the neoclassical intellectual discourse to which Milton's encomium aspires."[44] This can be countered by her attested participation, along with her mother and sister, in a game entitled the "Oracle" (part of the *conversazioni* held in the Baroni household, and described by Benigni in *L'Idea*), which made imaginative recourse to philosophy, astrology and wordplay.[45] Furthermore, Benigni was particularly proactive in his endeavor to publish the poetry of both Leonora and her sister, Caterina.

---

permitted me to call them the phoenixes of our age] is frequented today by the leading Lords and Virtuosi of this Court, a privilege which equals that of any of the more famous Academies which honor our Italy ... Some evenings are dedicated to Music, others to eloquence, and others to Poetry. In terms of Musical proficiency all of the glories belong to the ladies Adriana, Leonora, and Caterina").

[43] *L'Idea*, 15–16.

[44] Dell' Antonio, *Listening as Spiritual Practice*, 86.

[45] See *L'Idea*, 16–36.

In introducing Leonora's poems in *L'Idea*, he conveys her reluctance to have her work published. Stating that her pieces contained therein are not many, and that he virtually had to steal them, he continues to proclaim that a single one would have been sufficient to immortalize her name.[46] Indeed, one should not exclude the possibility that among songs performed by Leonora were her musical settings of her own verse. Margaret Byard suggests that Leonora "probably sang her own compositions or those of composers popular at the time, of Monteverdi perhaps."[47] Christine Jeanneret includes both Leonora and Caterina among the number of "literate women (sometimes female singers themselves)" who "wrote texts to be set to music."[48] Among Leonora's poems included in *L'Idea* are several such candidates: a piece entitled "Canzonetta per Musica," or her sonnet "Un Cavaliero promette esser costante, quanto è più disprezzato," the latter perfectly epitomizing what Margaret Murata has identified as the "I–you" stance characteristic of the seventeenth-century madrigal:[49]

> Troppo son'io di tue bellezze amante,
>   Troppo sei tù ne l'amor mio crudele,
>   Troppo son'io nel mio servir fedele,
> Troppo sei tù nel variar costante.
>
> Io ti serbo nel duol fè di Diamante,
>   E tù sorda a ti mostri à mie querele,
>   Io di mia speme al Cielo alzo le vele,
>   E tù guidi mio legno in mar sonante (1–8)[50]
>
> Too loving am I of your beauties,
> Too cruel are you in your love for me,
> Too faithful am I in my servitude,
> Too constant are you in your fluctuation.

---

[46] *L'Idea*, 212: "Le prime sono della Signora LEONORA, sono poche, perche si sono havute di furto; ma una saria stata bastante all'immortalità del suo nome" ("The first ones belong to the lady Leonora. They are few because they have been an act of theft, but a single one would be sufficient for the immortality of her name").

[47] Byard, "'Adventrous Song,'" 323.

[48] Jeanneret, "Gender Ambivalence," 93. Other such female composers were Francesca Caccina, Brigida Bianchi, and Margherita Costa. See in general Giuliana Morandini, *Sospiri e Palpiti: Scrittrici Italiane del Seicento* (Genoa: Marietti, 2001).

[49] Margaret Murata, "Image and Eloquence: Secular Song," in *The Cambridge History of Seventeenth-Century Music*, eds. Tim Carter and John Butt (Cambridge: Cambridge University Press, 2005), 378–425, at 412–414.

[50] *L'Idea*, 216.

> I preserve you in grief made of Diamond,
> And you reveal yourself deaf to my complaints,
> I raise the sails of my hope towards Heaven,
> And you steer my boat into the roaring sea.

2.2 Contemporary Encomia of Leonora

Like her mother, Leonora was ultimately the recipient of a volume of poetry in her honor. Entitled *Applausi Poetici Alle Glorie della Signora Leonora Baroni*,[51] this collection, which would see publication in 1639, runs to some 267 pages, and contains poems in five languages (Italian for the most part, but also Latin, Greek, Spanish, and French). Marked by its extravagant exuberance, it lauds Leonora's voice, her musicianship, and her beauty, chastity, and moral character. Thus Berlingiero Gessi praises her under the three titles: "La Bellezza" ("Beauty"), "L'Honesta" ("Honesty"), and "La Musica" ("Music").[52] Leonora is also seen as a key force motivating and unifying the cosmos,[53] as a tenth muse, and as an idealized image of beauty, the latter associated in many instances with the fact that some of the poems are in praise of her portrait, painted by della Corgna.[54] And in 1640 Pietro della Valle would ask:

> Ci non và fuor di se sentendo cantare la signora Leonora col suo Arcileuto così francamente, e bizzarramente toccato?[55]
>
> Who is not transported outside his very self upon experiencing Leonora singing, with her Archlute plucked so freely and ingeniously?

It is a question that Milton may well have asked himself one year previously. That he witnessed Leonora in performance on at least one and

---

[51] See 45.

[52] See *Applausi*, 31–38, 39–46, and 47–54.

[53] See, for example, *Applausi*, 3 (by an anonymous author), in which Leonora's song is viewed as governing the harmony of the spheres, the sun, the moon, and the stars.

[54] Several of the poems are entitled "Per lo Ritratto della Signora Leonora Baroni fatto dal Sig[nore] D[on] Fabio della Cornia" ("On the Portrait of the Lady Leonora Baroni painted by Mr Fabio della Corgna"). See 136.

[55] Pietro della Valle, *Della Musica dell' Età Nostra che non è punto inferiora, anzi è migliore di quella dell' età passata* (Rome, 1640), in *Lyra Barberina Amphichordos: De' Trattati di Musica di Gio[vanni] Batista Doni*, ed. Anton Francesco Gori, 2 vols (Florence: Imperial Printer, 1763), II, 249–264, at 256. See Angelo Solerti, *Le Origini del Melodramma* (Turin: Bocca, 1903), 164.

possibly more occasions is attested by his three Latin epigrams composed in the course of either or both of his Roman sojourns, poems which, moreover, also seem to signal his awareness of her mother's musical,[56] and, potentially, her sister's poetical,[57] talents. The fact that his pieces did not appear in the *Applausi* is largely inconsequential in that it is unlikely that they were ever intended for that volume.[58] As Campbell and Corns aptly note, they "were written for the benefit of Milton's Roman friends, not for the lady herself."[59] Thus they would seem to fall into the category of those poems that he "patch[ed] up"[60] while in Italy (this time in response to a literary vogue current in Rome), and that he probably showed or recited to Italian fellow academicians. It is very possible, moreover, that several of the future *Applausi* contributions were circulating in manuscript at the time of his visits to Rome, perhaps receiving their trial performance in the city's foremost academies at a time when news of the planned volume was undoubtedly in the air. Interestingly, Milton's third Latin epigram describes Leonora as *Romulidum studiis ornata secundis* (7) ("adorned by the favorable enthusiasm of the sons of Romulus"). This acknowledgment may extend beyond the responses of those members of a Roman audience actually listening to her performance to embrace an essentially literary reaction—the latter reading rendered possible by the twofold meaning of *studium* as "enthusiasm" and "intellectual activity."[61]

It emerges in fact that several verse encomia of Leonora had already seen print by the time of Milton's Italian journey, and would have been easily accessible to him. As early as 1628 the aforementioned *Il Teatro* had included two poems of which the young Leonora is the sole addressee. There Michel' Arcangelo Alfonso Gaetano extols her as worthy of Jupiter's love, praising her charm and the impression she makes upon others when she sings or speaks or smiles, and concluding by hymning the "Cetra ... /In man di LEONORA" (11–12) ("the lyre ... in the hand of LEONORA").[62] Giorgio de le Monti, in the same volume, regards

---

[56] See 123, 132–134.

[57] See 115–116.

[58] Contrast Byard, "'Adventrous Song,'" 322–323: "the three Latin epigrams he wrote and intended for a volume of poetry dedicated to her."

[59] Campbell and Corns, *Life, Work, and Thought*, 123.

[60] Milton, *The Reason of Church Government*, 37, quoted at 19.

[61] *OLD*, *studium*, s.v. 2: "enthusiasm, eagerness (for)"; s.v. 7: "intellectual activity, esp. of a literary kind, or an instance of it, study."

[62] *Il Teatro*, 180: "Alla Sig[nora] Leonora Barone figliuola della detta Signora: Soggetto da Innamorar Giove."

her as in possession of musical powers that rival those of the cosmos itself. His sonnet, entitled "Canto più che divino" ("Song more than divine"), invites the heavens and the music of the spheres to come to a halt and listen to her singing. Emphasizing "L'Armonia suavissima" (6) ("the sweetest Harmony"), "La mano inimitabile, e gl'accenti" (8) ("her inimitable hand, and her tones"), it envisages Leonora as the "Mastra del coro Angelico" (13) ("Leader of an Angelic choir").[63] And another poem, by Oratio Amodeo, praises her along with her mother and sister.[64] These are high accolades indeed, given the fact that Leonora can have been no more than *c*. twelve years of age at the time. The possibility that Milton was familiar with *Il Teatro* is greatly strengthened by the fact that the volume was dedicated to none other than his Neapolitan acquaintance and host, Giovanni Battista Manso[65] (who also contributed one sonnet),[66] addressee of *Mansus*, and one in whose literary career Milton seems to have taken a particular interest.[67] And in 1630 two poems by Francesco Balducci, a member of the Umoristi, had seen publication in Rome. One,

---

[63] *Il Teatro*, 247: "Per La Sig[nora] Leonora Barona [*sic*] Figliuola della Sig[nora] Adr[iana]: Canto più che divino."

[64] *Il Teatro*, 52: "Loda la Sig[nora] Ad[riana] e le sue Signore Figliuole Maria, e Leonora." Maria is obviously a mistake for Caterina.

[65] See Domitio Bombarda's dedicatory letter "All' Illustriss[imo] Sig[nor] Mio, e Padrone sempre Colendiss[imo] Il Signor GIO[VANNI] BATTISTA MANSO MARCHESE DI VILLA," dated Venice, 1 April 1628, at *Il Teatro*, 3–14.

[66] *Il Teatro*, 16. Entitled "L'Armonia de' tre Mondi vinte dalla triplicata Armonia della Sig[nora] AD[RIANA]," Manso's contribution eloquently proclaims that the earth, the heavens, and the very seat of God are overcome by Adriana's beauty, kindly virtue and pleasing song, all three of which render her immortal.

[67] It was Manso who acted as Milton's guide in Naples, and visited him on more than one occasion at his lodgings. See *Defensio Secunda* 85, at Appendix 2.30–32. The headnote to *Mansus* reveals Milton's close interest in Manso's literary reputation, pointing out that he was the [eponymous] dedicatee of Tasso's *Il Manso, ovvero dell' Amicizia Dialogo* (Naples: Gio[vanni] Giacomo Carlino and Antonio Pace, 1596), and emphasizing that he was an extremely good friend of Tasso, by whom he was celebrated in *Gerusalemme Conquistata* (Rome: Guglielmo Facciotti, 1593), Book 20. The poem proper proclaims Manso as a biographer, alluding to his *Vita di Torquato Tasso* (Venice: Deuchino, 1621), a work with which the poem engages on an intertextual level (see Haan, *From Academia to Amicitia*, 179–184), and likewise acknowledging his biographical interests in Marino (*Mansus* 20–21). Noteworthy, too, is the likelihood that the *pocula ... bina* ("two cups") mentioned in *Epitaphium Damonis* 181–183 as having been gifted to Milton by Manso, and ekphrastically described therein at 185–197, constitute his *Erocallia* (1628) and *Poesie Nomiche* (1635). See De Filippis, "Milton and Manso: Cups or Books?" passim. See also 7. Appended to the *Poesie Nomiche* were multiple encomia of Manso, which seem to be echoed in *Mansus* itself, on which see Haan, *From Academia to Amicitia*, 137–148.

a Madrigal, entitled "Per la Sig[nora] Eleonora Barone, Musica Illustre," extols the captivating powers of her lyre-playing;[68] a second, a "Capitolo," entitled "L'Amor Costante," employs the extravagant language of love to describe her enchanting musicianship.[69] No fewer than three encomia of the more mature singer had appeared in the 1637 *Poesie dei Signori Fantastici di Roma*, a volume with which Milton seems to have been well acquainted,[70] suggesting perhaps her integration into and/or her performance before the Fantastici themselves. By then Leonora had clearly achieved celebrity status in the city. Thus Gabriel Marino, in a sonnet, entitled "Per la Sig[nora] Leonora Basile, Musica celebre," extols both her vocal and instrumental talents, to which Apollo himself yields,[71] and emphasizes the ennobling effect of her lyre-playing: "a la tua cetra/Sgombri da i cori ogni pensier più vile" (5–6) ("in response to your lyre every baser thought is dispelled from the human heart").[72] In short, her musicianship is viewed as an earthly manifestation of "l'armonia del Cielo" (14) ("the harmony of the Heavens").[73] Giovan Martino Longo, in an albeit conventional piece, entitled "Ad Amore, Per la Signora LEONORA BASILE: Musica celebre," sees in Leonora's very countenance the encapsulation of Cupid's bow and arrows.[74] More skillful perhaps is a French poem, entitled "Pour la Seignora LEONORA BASILE," by Giovanni Montreglio, which plays on the trope of Leonora as a modern reinvention of the Sirens, whose music lured listeners to their death. Now, in a metaphorical appropriation, she is envisaged as a "Syren de la mer d'Amour/Dont les airs emportent la Cour/Dans un volontaire naufrage" (1–3) ("Siren of the sea of love, whose music transports the heart into a voluntary shipwreck").[75] The poem would be reprinted in a slightly abridged form in the 1639 *Applausi*.[76]

---

[68] *Le Rime del Sig[no]r[e] Francesco Balducci* (Rome: Guiglielmo Facciotti, 1630), at *Rime Famigliari*, 21.

[69] Balducci, *Rime Famigliari*, 22. Both poems were reprinted in *Le Rime* (Rome: F[rancesco] Moneta, 1645), 407–408, and *Le Rime* (Venice: Baba, 1663), 362–363.

[70] See 45–46, 69–74.

[71] *Poesie*, 113: "Cede il canoro Dio, fregio de l'Etra,/Al tuo suono, al tuo canto" (1–2) ("The tuneful God, ornament of the harp, yields to your sound, to your singing").

[72] *Poesie*, 113.

[73] *Poesie*, 113.

[74] *Poesie*, 144.

[75] *Poesie*, 203–204, at 203.

[76] *Applausi*, 180–182. This clearly revised version alters "Bel arbitre de nostre sort" (4) to read "Abritre aimable de mon sort" (4), and omits in their entirety lines 31–36 and 43–48.

Other encomia of Leonora survive independently. The French viola da gambist André Maugars, upon hearing her singing one evening in 1639, and in the Baroni household no less, praises her understanding of music, her compositional skills, her perfect pronunciation and expression of words, and the high range and accuracy of her voice:

> elle l'entend parfaitement bien, voire mesme qu'elle y compose: ce qui fait qu'elle possède absolument ce quelle chante, et qu'elle prononce et exprime parfaitement bien le sens des paroles ... Elle chante ... avec une douce gravité. Sa voix est d'une haute estendüe, juste, sonore, harmonieuse ...[77]

> She understands [music] perfectly well, and even composes. All of this means that she has absolute control over what she sings, and that she pronounces and expresses the sense of the words perfectly ... She sings ... with gentle seriousness. Her voice is of high range, accurate, sonorous, harmonious ...

Maugars continues with the rapturous fantasy that Leonora's music

> me surprit si fort les sens et me porta dans un tel ravissement, que j'oubliay ma condition mortelle, et creuz estre desia parmy les anges, jouyssant des contentemens des bienheureux"

> had such an overwhelming effect on me and transported me into such ecstasy that I forgot my mortal condition and thought that I was already among the angels, enjoying the pleasures of the blessed.[78]

But perhaps most interesting is a Latin poem by Jean Jacques Bouchard, extant in manuscript in the Vatican Library.[79] Hymning Adriana, Leonora, and Caterina as Muses now transported from Mount Pindus to Rome, the piece is careful to itemize the particular talent possessed by each of the three performers: thus Adriana is praised for her lyre-playing, Leonora for her singing, and Caterina for her poetry:

---

[77] André Maugars, *Response Faite à un Curieux sur le Sentiment de la Musique d'Italie. Escrite à Rome le Premier Octobre 1639*, ed. Ernest Thoinan (Paris: A[natole] Claudin, 1865), 37. Translation is that of Walter H. Bishop, "Maugars' Response Faite à un Curieux sur le Sentiment de la Musique d'Italie," *Journal of the Viola da Gamba Society of America* 8 (1971): 5–17, at 13.

[78] *Response*, ed. Thoinan, 37–38, trans. Bishop, 13. That it was in the Baroni home that Maugars heard Leonora perform is attested by his reference to "cette vertueuse maison" ("this noble house") (*Response*, ed. Thoinan, 38).

[79] BAV Barb.lat. 2049, f. 52^r: *In Musas Romanas Adrianam, Eleonoram et Catharinam Epigramma Joannis Jacobi Bouchardi Parisiensis*.

> Ecce quirinalis clivi radicibus haeret
>   Sacra domus, Vatum concelebrata choris;
> Illuc Pieridas Pindo emigrare coegit
>   MUSAGETAE virtus, carminis arte polens.
> Heic Adriana fideis pulsat, Leonora canoros
>   Dat numeros, versus et Catharina facit (5–10).[80]

> Behold, contiguous to the foot of the slope of Quirinus there lies a sacred dwelling, celebrated by choruses of poets. To that spot the virtue of the guide of the Muses, powerful in the art of music, has forced the Pierides to emigrate from Pindus. Here Adriana plucks the strings, Leonora produces songful rhythms, and Caterina composes verses.

Importantly (and atypically) the poem bears a date: 1 February 1639,[81] thus indicating that the Baroni trio was flourishing and performing in Rome at the time of Milton's second sojourn in the city.[82] Finally, Paolo Giordano Orsini, in an undated "Idillio," inspired by the della Corgna portrait, emphasizes the portrait's paradoxical effect upon its viewer by reverting to a series of extravagant oxymorons. Thus, for example, Leonora is a Siren, who is not a Siren in virtue of her innocence; a swan, who is not a swan in that her song indicates the death not of the singer, but of the listener.[83]

Read alongside contemporary encomia of Leonora, Milton's three Latin epigrams are perhaps more noteworthy for their differences than for their similarities.[84] They do not mention Leonora's beauty or chastity, and even when they do praise her singing, the emphasis is more on the effects of her music (and perhaps also her poetry?) upon the sensibilities of the

---

[80] *Ibid.*, f. 52ʳ. *Musageta* denotes the Greek Μουσαγέτης ("guide of the Muses"), an epithet of Apollo as leader of the nine Muses. Bouchard uses the alternative, and rather archaic, forms of *heic* for *hic* and *fideis* for *fides*, for which see *OLD*.

[81] Bouchard's poem does not occur among those included in the 1639 *Applausi*, whose dedicatory letter, by Francesco Ronconi, is dated 1 September 1639.

[82] Gordon Campbell, *A Milton Chronology* (London: Macmillan, 1997), 64, suggests that Milton returned to Rome in January 1639, and probably stayed in the city until the end of February or the beginning of March.

[83] *Rime di Paolo Giordano II Duca di Bracciano* (Bracciano: Fei, 1648), (s.p.): "Bella ... /Sirena. A non Sirena .... Cigno. A non cigno" ("Beautiful Siren, but not a Siren. A swan, but not a swan").

[84] See Ademollo, *La Leonora*, 10. Bush, *Variorum*, I, 148, states: "[i]f he saw any of the poems that went into the *Applausi*, they do not seem to have left clear marks on his own."

listener, than on the quality of her voice *per se*. For Milton, this talented soprano serves to engender a series of intellectual discourses shared among peers.[85] Significantly these were Catholic peers. Foremost among the Umoristi's elite membership were several Cardinals, including Cardinal Giulio Rospigliosi (the future Pope Clement IX), Cardinal Francesco Barberini (who owned a personal copy of the *Applausi*),[86] and his brother Cardinal Antonio Barberini.[87] Milton certainly met Francesco Barberini in Rome at another musical event discussed in the text that follows, and he was even granted a private audience the following day.[88] This is attested by his Latin letter to Lucas Holstenius,[89] himself a contributor (of a Latin poem) to the *Applausi*.[90] In short, Milton's poems appear less effusive,[91] offering, instead, a series of variations on a theme, as it were. Thus Leonora's musicianship facilitates the interrogation and imaginative reinterpretation of Catholicism, of hermeticism, of current musicological theory, and of classical mythology.

2.3 From Catholicism to Hermeticism: *Ad Leonoram* 1[92]

Despite, or perhaps because of, the extravagant nature of the pieces included in the 1639 *Applausi*, religious analogies are virtually nonexistent therein. A typically conservative disclaimer, articulated in the volume's prefatory epistle to the "Lettor cortese" ("courteous Reader"), carefully defends the vocabulary employed, stressing that the use of such terms as "bless," "adore," "Idol," "Deity," "Divine," "Angelic," "Angel," "Paradise," and so on should be interpreted as attributes that signify the exceeding merit of the praised subject, as opposed to any supernatural

---

[85] On musicianship as initiating intellectual discourse, see Dell' Antonio, *Listening as Spiritual Practice*, 84–86.

[86] BAV Stamp. Barb. JJJ.VI.67.

[87] On the membership of Rospigliosi and the two Barberini Cardinals, see Maylender, *Storia*, V, 377 and 378. The Umoristi also included the celebrated musicologist Giovanni Battista Doni (Maylender, *Storia*, V, 378).

[88] See 154–157, 169–172.

[89] See Milton, *Epistola Familiaris* 9 at Appendix 1.3. See also Chapter 3.

[90] *Applausi*, 201–203. See also 126.

[91] Contrast Charles Lamb's rather blinkered viewpoint that "some of his addresses (*ad Leonoram* I mean) have rather erred on the farther side." See Charles Lamb, "Some Sonnets of Sir Philip Sidney," in *The Works of Charles and Mary Lamb*, ed. E. V. Lucas, 7 vols (London: Methuen, 1903–1905), II, 214.

[92] For Latin text and English translation, see Appendix 1.1(a).

entity.[93] It proceeds to offer the reassurance that "non è frà questi Autori chi habbia havuta intentione di allontanarsi punto dall' osservanza, che si deve alla vera Cattolica, e Romana Religione" ("it has not been the intention of these Authors to detract from the observance that is due to the true Catholic and Roman religion").[94] Praise of human song, and the language in which that praise is cast, should be regarded, not as a form of idolatry, but as mirroring on earth (yet not usurping) angelic praise of God.

Read in this context *Ad Leonoram* 1 emerges as a poem that is arguably more "Catholic" than those contained in the *Applausi*. Although dismissed by William Cowper as inferior to Milton's second and third epigrams on the subject,[95] this daringly defiant piece, as if in breach of the accepted theological discretion that would come to govern the published volume, seems to articulate a doctrine that is essentially Catholic. But it does so only by interrogating and recasting that doctrine in the language of hermeticism, perhaps as a means of bridging the divide between Catholicism and Protestantism. The opening pronouncement (*Angelus unicuique suus (sic credite gentes)/Obtigit aethereis ales ab ordinibus* [1–2] ["A winged angel from the heavenly ranks (believe this you nations) has been allotted to each individual"]), described by Masson as "[a] fancy in which I discern something characteristic of Milton,"[96] is in fact an audacious exemplification of, in the words of Robert West, Milton's use of "the Catholic idea" of the guardian angel.[97] By contrast, rarely in the *Applausi* is an angelic context invoked. And even when it is, the treatment is peripheral and highly conventional. Thus, for Francesco Carducci, Leonora is one "Quindi angelico suon spira la bocca" ("[whose] mouth breathes forth an angelic sound").[98] For Fulvio Testi,

---

[93] *Applausi*, sig. A5ᵛ: "di beare, adorare, Idolo, Deità, Divino, Angelico, Angelo, Paradiso, e somiglianti; sei pregato ad interpretarle per attributi significanti eccesso di merito nel soggetto lodato, e non altro di soprahumano" ("in regard to [such terms as] 'bless', 'adore,' 'Idol,' 'Deity,' 'Divine,' 'Angelic,' 'Angel,' 'Paradise,' and the like: you are asked to interpret them as attributes signifying the excess of merit in the praised subject, and not as anything pertaining to the superhuman").

[94] *Applausi*, sig. A5ᵛ.

[95] "I have translated only two of the three poetical compliments addressed to Leonora, as they appear to me far superior to what I have omitted" (*The Complete Poetical Works of William Cowper*, ed. H. S. Milford [Oxford: Oxford University Press, 1913], 598).

[96] Masson, ed., *Poetical Works*, III, 510.

[97] Robert H. West, *Milton and the Angels* (Athens: University of Georgia Press, 1955), 132.

[98] *Applausi*, 138.

Leonora is "l'Angioletta mia" ("my little Angel"), whose song, soaring heavenwards, enables its audience to forget earthly things.[99] According to Vincenzo Marescotti, her music replicates the angelic harmony that controls the motions of the spheres themselves.[100] But West's conviction that Milton's use of the idea is nothing more than "a fanciful compliment to Leonora's voice"[101] is the consequence of an overly simplistic reading. Milton in Rome is speaking in a voice that is carefully attuned to his Catholic audience.

Although the polarization between Catholic and Protestant theology concerning angels has been somewhat exaggerated, belief in guardian angels allocated to *individuals* (as opposed to places or communities) was, on balance, a Catholic tenet. As Joad Raymond observes, "[b]elief in individual guardian angels marked a clear, though not absolute, difference between Protestants and Roman Catholics."[102] An exemplification of that belief is provided by a sonnet entitled "A l'Angelo Custode." Its author, none other than Leonora's sister, Caterina Baroni, can confidently claim a guardian angel as her own:

> Solo tù puoi, ò mio Custode, e duce
> Mandato a me da gli stellanti Chori,
> Regger miei passi, e darmi vita, e luce.[103]

> You alone, o my Guardian and leader,
> Entrusted to me from the starry Choruses,
> Can guide my footsteps and give me life and light.

---

[99] *Applausi*, 156. In a letter, dated 24 March 1634, Testi had proclaimed of Leonora's musical talents: "Se gli angeli cantano in paradiso, bisogna credere che cantino com'ella" ("If the angels sing in paradise, we must believe that they sing as she does"). See Testi, *Lettere*, ed. Doglio, II, 129–130n660. Cf. André Maugars's praise (in 1639) of Leonora's song, which "me surprit si fort les sens et me porta dans un tel ravissement, que j'oubliay ma condition mortelle, et creuz estre desia parmy les anges" ("had such an overwhelming effect on me and transported me into such ecstasy that I forgot my mortal condition and thought that I was already among the angels") (*Response*, ed. Thoinan, 37–38; trans. Bishop, 13).

[100] *Applausi*, 260: "S'al moto armonioso/De l'angelo movente/Ogni sfera si volge" ("If every sphere turns in response to the harmonious motion of the angel that moves them").

[101] West, *Milton and the Angels*, 132.

[102] Joad Raymond, *Milton's Angels: The Early Modern Imagination* (Oxford: Oxford University Press, 2010), 232.

[103] *L'Idea*, 228, lines 9–11.

As the sonnet is undated, one can only speculate as to whether Milton was aware of its (possible?) existence. Certainly his inclusion of the doctrine in *Ad Leonoram* 1 would seem particularly apt, and thereby assume additional significance, if it contained a hidden compliment to her sister's poetical talents. That he, too, is signaling individual custodianship is highlighted by *unicuique* (1) ("to each individual").[104] But his seeming acknowledgment of Catholic doctrine is couched in language of ambiguity: *sic credite gentes* (1) ("believe this, you nations"). Raymond notes two possibilities afforded by Milton's parenthetical injunction:

> he could be suggesting that the belief in tutelary angels is one held by Leonora's audience at Rome, distancing himself from the belief; or the imperative *credite* might encourage the belief ("believe me").[105]

To this can be added the possibility that Milton, rather than distancing himself from the belief, is assuming a Catholic voice, whose articulation of Catholic doctrine challenges those of other religious persuasions (here pejoratively depicted as *gentes* in perhaps the noun's postclassical meaning of "gentiles" or "heathens")[106] to accept the professed tenet.

Addressing Leonora, Milton proclaims that she possesses a *gloria maior* (3) ("a glory that is greater") than that of individual angelic custodianship: *Nam tua praesentem vox sonat ipsa Deum* (4) ("for your very voice resonates the presence of God"). This is then followed by the suggestion that it is either God or the *mens tertia* (5) ("third mind") of a now empty heaven that secretly *serpit agens* (6) ("insinuates its motion") through her throat. *Serpit agens* is repeated (7) (the Miltonic syntax likewise entwining itself across the hexameter and pentameter lines) in language that is both corporeal and spiritual,[107] as this force teaches that

---

[104] Cf. Milton, *A Mask*, in which the Lady asserts her belief that "the Supreme good" (217) "Would send a glistring Guardian if need were/To keep my life and honour unassail'd" (219–220).

[105] Raymond, *Milton's Angels*, 235.

[106] See Lewis and Short, s.v. 2c: "In the ecc. fathers, *gentes*, like ἔθνος, opp. to Jews and Christians, pagan nations, heathens, gentiles." Cf. Lactantius, 2.13; Vulgate, Psalm 2.1, and Arnobius's eponymous *Adversus Gentes*.

[107] Interestingly, Milton's phrase, while lacking classical precedent, finds a parallel in the *Electrica* (Rome, 1767) of Giuseppe Maria Mazzolari (alias Josephus Marianus Parthenius), an Italian Jesuit and professor of rhetoric in Florence and Rome. Hymning, in book 5, the inspirational powers attendant upon intellectual endeavors (*furor philosophicus*), he states: *adeo vis ignea totis/Serpit agens se se venis, et pectore gliscit* ("to such an extent does the fiery force insinuate itself in every vein, and swell in the heart"). Text is that of *Josephi Mariani Parthenii Electricorum Libri VI* (Rome: Salomoni, 1767), 186. Yasmin Haskell, while not noticing the possible

mortal hearts can gradually become accustomed to an immortal sound.[108] And the theology changes from the Catholic to the pantheistic: *Quod si cuncta quidem Deus est per cunctaque fusus,/In te una loquitur; cetera mutus habet* (9–10) ("For if indeed God is all things, and through all things is diffused, it is in you alone that he speaks; the rest he holds in silence"). Charles Lamb remarked that in "thus apostrophis[ing] a singing-girl" Milton "came not much short of a religious indecorum," reading "something very like blasphemy in the last two verses."[109] But rather than blasphemy, this is a theological riddle, in which a Catholic tenet is voiced, questioned, and given an esoteric interpretation.

Milton's enigmatic *mens tertia* has been variously interpreted as the sphere of Venus,[110] one of the seraphim,[111] the last of three musical categories (as described by Boethius),[112] the Holy Spirit (as depicted by Saint Paul),[113] or the music of the spheres.[114] In support of the last of these readings one might adduce, perhaps, several of the *Applausi* encomiasts. Thus, in the words of Andrea Barbazza, Leonora's enticing notes "Portano in Terra le celesti Sfere" ("transport the heavenly spheres to the earth").[115] Likewise, according to Giovanni Bentivoglio:

> Se canti, ò LEONORA, ecco ci sueli
> Il concerto de' Cieli, à noi mal noto.
> Co'l tuo canto gentil, tù sol far puoi
> De l'armonia del Ciel fede trà noi.[116]

---

echo of Milton, remarks: "[Mazzolari's] description of the *furor philosophicus* in terms of a *vis ignea* might seem playfully to flirt with the idea of an electrical (i.e., material) spirit." See Y. A. Haskell, *Loyola's Bees: Ideology and Industry in Jesuit Latin Didactic Poetry* (Oxford: Oxford University Press, 2003), 235.

[108] Cf. Milton, "At a Solemn Musick" 17–18: "That we on Earth with undiscording voice/May rightly answer that melodious noise."

[109] Charles Lamb, "Some Sonnets of Sir Philip Sidney," in *Works*, ed. Lucas, II, 214.

[110] See, for example, *The Poems of John Milton*, ed. Keightley, II, 421.

[111] See Diane K. McColley, "Tongues of Men and Angels: *Ad Leonoram Romae Canentem*," *MS* 19 (1984): 127–148, at 139–142.

[112] See S. K. Heninger, *Touches of Sweet Harmony: Pythagorean Cosmology and Renaissance Poetics* (San Marino, CA: Huntington Library, 1974), 101–104. Cf. Boethius, *De Musica* 1.2: *tertia [gens] est musica, quae in quibusdam consistere dicitur instrumentis* ("the third [kind] pertains to music, which is said to reside in certain instruments").

[113] See Bush, *Variorum*, I, 149, who cites "the third heaven" of 2 Cor. 12.2.4.

[114] See Haan, *From Academia to Amicitia*, 108–109.

[115] *Applausi*, 19, line 6.

[116] *Applausi*, 174, lines 29–32.

> If you sing, o LEONORA, behold here on earth is the harmony of the heavens which is unfamiliar to us. With your noble singing you alone can make us believe that the harmony of the heavens is in our midst.

But that Milton is alluding to the Holy Spirit can now be attested by a parallel in a hermetic work by the sixteenth-century Franciscan, Hannibal Rosselli. A member of the Order of Capuchin Friars Minor, and Professor of theology at the Bernardine monastery on Castle Hill, Cracow,[117] Rosselli penned a huge six-book commentary on the *Pymander* and *Asclepius* of Hermes Trismegistus.[118] Familiarity with the *corpus hermeticum*, in which "fantastic, magical and theurgical elements were mixed in plentifully,"[119] was greatly facilitated by the appearance in 1471 of Ficino's Latin translation, entitled *Pimander*, the name of the first treatise in the collection.[120] The translation was hugely popular in Renaissance Italy. This, and the commentary tradition that it engendered, would have found a natural home in the Neoplatonic academies of Florence and Rome.

Rosselli's commentary was published between the years 1584 and 1590. In book 3, *De Ente, Materia, Forma, et Rebus Metaphysicis*,

---

[117] The Protestant John Dee records that on 19 April 1585, "I took Ghostly counsel of Doctor Hannibal, the great Divine, that had now set out some of his Commentaries upon Pymander, Hermitis Trismigisti," and that on the following day "I received the Communion at the Pernardines [*sic*], where that Doctor is a Professor." See *A True and Faithful Relation of What Passed for Many Yeers Between Dr. John Dee ... and Some Spirits* (London: D[avid] Maxwell, 1659), 397.

[118] Hermes Trismegistus is the *Ter magnus Hermes* ("thrice-mighty Hermes") of Milton's *De Idea Platonica* 33, where he is also described as *trino gloriosus nomine* (32) ("boasting in a threefold name") and as *arcani sciens* (33) ("skilled in mysteries"). Cf. "Il Penseroso" 88: "thrice great Hermes."

[119] Samuel Mintz, "The Motion of Thought: Intellectual and Philosophical Backgrounds," in *Backgrounds to Seventeenth-Century Literature*, eds. C. A. Patrides and Raymond B. Waddington (Manchester: Manchester University Press, 1980), 138–169, at 152.

[120] See *Mercurii Trismegisti Liber de Potestate et Sapientia Dei e Graeco in Latinum Traductus a Marsilio Ficino Florentino ad Cosmum Medicem Patriae Patrem. Pimander Incipit* (Treviso: Gerardus de Lisa, 1471). Among other translations or editions of the *corpus hermeticum* was a version in Italian by Tommaso Benci (*Il Pimandro di Mercurio Trimegisto* [Florence: Lorenzo Torrentino, 1548]), and a Latin rendering by Francesco Patrizi (*Nova de Universis Philosophia* [Ferrara: Benedictus Mammarellus, 1591]). It was not until 1650 and 1657 that John Everard's famous English translation would see print.

dedicated to Ferdinando de Medici, Grand Duke of Tuscany, he interprets the hermetic *deus est mens* ("God is mind")[121] as a *Divina substantia* ("a divine substance") that *tres habet descensus* ("has three types of descent"): the first is *altissimus deus* ("God most high"); the second is the *mens artificis* ("mind of the creator"); the third in the order of descent, the *anima mundi* ("world soul"), is named *mens tertia* by Trismegistus and specifically identified as the Holy Spirit:

> Deinceps est anima mundi, quae a Trismegisto *mens tertia* vocatur in primo Pymandri dicens: Pymandrum cum suo verbo peperisse aliam mentem, qui est *ignis sanctus, et spiritus numen.*[122]

> Next is the world soul, which is termed the *third mind* by Trismegistus in the first *Pymander*, where he says that Pymander with his word gave birth to another *mind* that is *holy fire and the divine power of the spirit.*

Indeed, Rosselli meticulously explicates the doctrine: *Pater igitur est prima mens, filius secunda, tertia spiritus sanctus* ("And so the first mind is the Father, the second the Son, the third the Holy Spirit").[123] In short, *deus est mens* denotes a trinity, whose *mens tertia* is explicitly equated with the Holy Spirit (*spiritus sanctus*).[124]

For the humanist hermeticist Lodovico Lazzarelli that Holy Spirit was essentially a spirit within. If Rosselli used the *corpus hermeticum* as an "interface between Christian and Platonic thinking,"[125] Lazzarelli's

---

[121] The Greek original has νοῦς ὁ θεός. See *Hermetis Trismegisti Poemander*, ed. Gustav Parthey (Berlin: Nicolai, 1854), 4.

[122] *Pymander Mercurii Trismegisti cum Commento Fratris Hannibalis Rosseli Calabri, Ordinis Minorum Regularis Observantiae, Theologiae et Philosophiae, ad S[anctum] Bernardinum Cracoviae Professoris. Liber III: De Ente, Materia, Forma, et Rebus Metaphysicis* (Cracow: Lazari, 1586), 364. Emphasis is mine.

[123] *Pymander Mercurii Trismegisti*, 364.

[124] *Pymander Mercurii Trismegisti*, 365: *Aliquando est spiritus sanctus, et omnes tres una mens, quia nimirum unus intellectus, una sapientia atque natura* ("Now at last is the Holy Spirit, and all three constitute a single mind, because presumably they possess a single intellect, a single wisdom and nature"). Cf. *Mercurii Trismegisti Liber*, trans. Ficino, f. 2^v: *Mens autem deus: utriusque sexus fecunditate plenissimus. vita et lux cum verbo suo mentem alteram opificem peperit: qui quidem deus ignis atque spiritus numen* ("Now the mind is God. Most replete with the fertility of either sex, Life and light, he gave birth with his own word to another creative mind, which indeed is God, the fire and divine power of the Spirit").

[125] Valery Rees, *From Gabriel to Lucifer: A Cultural History of Angels* (London: I. B. Tauris, 2013), 69.

Crater Hermetis (1505) offered a "Christianized compendium of the Hermetic texts."[126] Presented in the form of a dialogue between Lazzarelli and King Ferdinand of Aragon, this work, through inventive admixture of the poetic and the prosaic, reinvented hermeticism as a *crater* ("mixing bowl") filled with *mens* ("mind") sent down to earth by God. Now, for the first time, Pymander was explicitly identified as Jesus Christ,[127] whereby, as Jill Delsigne notes, "the human being ... [is] ensouled by God himself rather than a lesser angel or demon."[128] Lazzarelli conflates this with Pentecost, when the Holy Spirit descended upon the apostles, dwelling within them, and giving them the power to speak in other tongues.[129] Thus does the *mens* enable the individual to become the *aedes* ("temple") of the *Spiritus Sanctus*.[130] Central to Milton's conception of Leonora's voice is the divine presence that it both manifests and articulates: *Nam tua praesentem vox sonat ipsa Deum* (4) ("for your very voice resonates the presence of God"). This is developed in the poem's closing couplet. On the one hand, *si cuncta quidem Deus est per cunctaque fusus* (9) ("if indeed God is all things, and through all things is diffused") embraces "the optimist gnosis" of hermeticism, whereby "the universe is impregnated with God";[131] on the other, Leonora herself, as the unique vehicle for God's utterance, is endowed with a quasi-Pentecostal gift: *In te una loquitur; cetera mutus habet* (10) ("It is in you alone that [God] speaks; the rest he holds in silence").

"*Christianus ego sum o Rex: et Hermeticum simul esse non pudet*" ("'I am a Christian, Your Majesty, and at the same time I am not ashamed to be a Hermeticist'"), proclaims Lazzarelli.[132] Termed by James Ellison

---

[126] M. J. B. Allen, *Synoptic Art: Marsilio Ficino on the History of Platonic Interpretation* (Florence: Leo S. Olschki, 1998), 28.

[127] Lodovico Lazzarelli, *Ad Ferdinandum Regem Dialogus cui Titulus Crater Hermetis* (Paris: Henri Etienne, 1505), f. 60^v: *Ipse qui in Hermetis mente Pimander erat in me christus IHESUS* ("That very Pimander who existed in the mind of Hermes is in me JESUS Christ"). Cf. *Laudabo itaque christum IHESUM sub Pimandri nomine* ("And so I will praise JESUS Christ under the name of Pimander") (*Crater Hermetis*, f. 80^r).

[128] Jill Renée Delsigne, *Sacramental Magic and Animate Statues in Edmund Spenser, William Shakespeare, and John Milton* (PhD thesis: Rice University, 2012), 122.

[129] Cf. Acts 2:3–4: "And there appeared unto them cloven tongues like as of fire, and it sat upon each of them. And they were all filled with the Holy Ghost, and began to speak with other tongues, as the Spirit gave them utterance." Text is that of the King James Bible (Authorized Version).

[130] Lazzarelli, *Crater Hermetis*, f. 74^v.

[131] Mintz, "Motion of Thought," 152.

[132] Lazzarelli, *Crater Hermetis*, ff. 61^r–61^v.

the "international language of tolerance and ecumenism,"[133] hermeticism provided, in the words of Frances Yates, "a panacea for the religious situation of Europe."[134] Perhaps this was replicated in the case of Milton in Catholic Rome, who could now appeal to a "*prisca theologia*, a divine wisdom that was more ancient than denominational difference."[135] In a sense, then, hermeticism, like Latin, constituted a universal language.

2.4 "Soul-swaying Song": *Ad Leonoram 2*[136]

Milton's second Latin epigram conducts the reader on a hypothetical time-travel of sorts by imagining the consequences of Leonora's singing upon Torquato Tasso. The poem opens with a couplet marked by a starkly voiced realism: it was *Altera ... Leonora* (1) ("Another Leonora") who captivated the Italian poet, who in turn became mad on account of his insane love for her, and died. Milton's seemingly "factual" statement is set in sharp contrast to the series of hypotheses in the subsequent lines, as indicative gives way to subjunctive mood. If Tasso had heard Leonora Baroni singing, his madness could have been assuaged. Even if he had rolled his eyes more fiercely than Pentheus, Leonora's song could have soothed his aching heart, and restored him to his senses.[137] Although the connection between Tasso's madness and Leonora had been popularized even in England from an early date,[138] it was largely through Manso's

---

[133] James Ellison, "*The Winter's Tale* and the Religious Politics of Europe," in *New Casebooks: Shakespeare's Romances*, ed. Alison Thorne (New York: Palgrave Macmillan, 2003), 171–204, at 189.

[134] Frances Yates, *Giordano Bruno and the Hermetic Tradition* (London: Routledge and Kegan Paul, 1964), 179.

[135] Delsigne, *Sacramental Magic*, 120.

[136] For Latin text and English translation, see Appendix 1.1(b).

[137] The hypothetical strain of Milton's epigram finds a general parallel in the *Applausi*. Fabio Leonida imagines what would have happened if the tormenting forces of the underworld had heard Leonora singing: "S'udisse i vaghi suoi soavi accenti/L'augel di Titio, e d'Ission la rota;/L'un resterebbe satio, e l'altra immota:/E fine hauria'l martir di que' dolenti" ("If the bird of Tityos and the wheel of Ixion had heard her graceful, sweet tones, the one would have remained satisfied and the other motionless, and the torture of those sufferers would have ended") (*Applausi*, 119). Cf. Francesco Rapaccioli, who fantasizes about the effect that Leonora as Virgo would have had upon the signs of the zodiac (*Applausi*, 143–147).

[138] Cf. John Eliot, *Ortho-epia Gallica* (London: John Wolfe, 1593), 30: "This Youth fell mad for the love of an Italian lass, descended of a great house, when I was in Italie." Similarly Scipio Gentili seems to accept it in the hendecasyllabic verses prefixed to his Latin translation of the *Gerusalemme Liberata*. See *Scipii Gentilis*

Vita di Torquato Tasso (1621), that the story was most widely known.[139] Manso's erroneous and frequently false account was afforded greater credibility in that he had known Tasso personally. Manso states that while Tasso was staying with him at Naples he had the opportunity to examine his melancholy.[140] He describes his obsessive delusions, and links his name with Leonora d'Este. He was, in short, overcome by an "alto, e nobilissimo amore" ("a lofty and most noble love").[141] Milton's *Altera ... Leonora* assumes additional force when read alongside Manso's account of "Tre Leonore una delle quali fù l'amata di Tor[quato]" ("Three Leonoras, of one of whom Tor[quato] was enamored"):[142] 1) Leonora d'Este;[143] 2) Contessa San Vitale;[144] 3) a damigella of Leonora d'Este.[145]

But the envisaged scenario of Milton's poem is essentially anachronistic. The fact is that Tasso, having died in 1595, did *not* live in Leonora's age (*tuo ... aevo* [3] ["your lifetime"]). Temporally speaking, he missed her by a whole generation. The Miltonic fantasy, couched in a series of oxymorons (*miser ... felicius.../Perditus* [3–4] ["wretched ... more happily ... ruined"]), aptly, yet ironically, mirrors the insanity that it describes, its tonal shifts simultaneously wrong-footing the reader. At least until the reconciliatory statement that it is with a "Pierian voice" that Leonora sings (*te Pieria ... voce canentem* [5]). Several poets of the *Applausi* likewise associate Leonora with the Muses: at times she is a "canora Musa" ("tuneful Muse");[146] at others, a tenth Muse;[147] at others,

---

Solymeidos Libri Duo priores de Torquati Tassi Italicis expressi (London: John Wolfe, 1584).

[139] See C. P. Brand, *Torquato Tasso: A Study of the Poet and of his Contribution to English Literature* (Cambridge: Cambridge University Press, 1965), 207–209.

[140] Manso, *Vita di Torquato Tasso*, 72–76, offers an extravagant explanation of Tasso's madness: A close friend, Maddalo Fucci, gave the poet's love away at court. There followed a duel, in consequence of which Tasso was put into protective custody, but his associated sense of imprisonment marked the onset of his madness.

[141] Manso, *Vita di Torquato Tasso*, 48.

[142] Manso, *Vita di Torquato Tasso*, 50. Manso designates the respective Leonoras as "Prima" (51), "Seconda" (57), and "Terza" (59).

[143] Manso, *Vita di Torquato Tasso*, 51–57.

[144] Manso, *Vita di Torquato Tasso*, 57–59.

[145] Manso, *Vita di Torquato Tasso*, 59–62.

[146] Vincenzo Marescotti, at *Applausi*, 258.

[147] Thus Alfonso Pallavicini, at *Applausi*, 12, states: "Ma, perche chiare prove/Sian di ciò frà i Mortali,/Una Musa frà lor prende i natali/Aggiunta à l'altre nove,/Che le vince, E LE ONORA/Non men casta, e più bella e più canora" ("But so that there may

she is served by the Muses;[148] at others, her instrumental skills have been taught to her by the Pierides.[149] But Milton's Leonora, singing to her own accompaniment, is also very much her mother's daughter, suggested not only by the fact that she is playing her mother's instrument (*Aurea maternae fila movere lyrae* [6] ["as you plucked the golden strings of your mother's lyre"]), but also perhaps by the juxtaposition of *maternae* and *fila*, thus facilitating a possible pun on *filum* ("string") and *filia* ("daughter"). The association of Leonora's musicianship with that of Adriana Basile further augments the fantasy in that Adriana's *aevum* had indeed coincided with that of Tasso (she would have been c. fifteen years of age at the time of Tasso's death). Perhaps then, in another sort of flashback, we are invited to imagine the youthful Adriana (born c. 1580) performing in, say, Naples, where she was indeed active in the mid-1590s.[150] Furthermore, Milton's phraseology seems to transport us back to *Il Teatro* itself, in which Giovanni Battista Russo had proclaimed of Adriana:

> *Aurea* seu *citharae* percurris *fila*, Basilis,
>   Seu roseo ambrogium [*sic*] spargis ab ore sonum:
> Hinc trahis et fidibus mortalia corda canoris:
>   Hinc rapis ad superum cantibus illa melos.[151]

> Whether you pluck *the golden strings of the lyre*,
> Basile, or sprinkle an ambrosial sound from your
> rosy lips, on this side you sway mortal hearts with

---

be clear proofs of this among mortals, a Muse is born in their midst, is added to the other nine, who conquers and honors them and is no less chaste, but more beautiful and more musical"). Cf. Michael Marullus, *Ep.* 3.4 and *Ep.* 3.15, where Alessandra Scala is likewise envisaged as a tenth Muse.

[148] Thus Domenico Benigni, at *Applausi*, 108, proclaims: "Gran vanto è sì; ma che le Muse ancelle/Portino sù'l tuo crin toscano alloro,/Pregio è più bello" ("This is a great boast, yes; but it is a finer mark of esteem that the Muses, your handmaids, are placing Tuscan laurel on your hair").

[149] Thus Gregorio Porcio, at *Applausi*, 188 states: *Illic te Virtus artes, te turba Sororum/Pieridum docuit fila canora Lyrae* ("There Virtue taught you skills, the throng of the Pierian sisters instructed you in the tuneful strings of the lyre").

[150] Emerson, *Five Centuries of Women Singers*, 19, cites c. 1588–1610 as the period in which Adriana was active in Naples.

[151] *Il Teatro*, 242, lines 1–4. Emphasis is mine. With the phraseology, cf. also George Buchanan, *El.* 7.32: *aureaque Orpheae fila fuisse lyrae* ("and the strings of Orpheus' lyre were golden"). With Russo's *mortalia corda* (3) ("mortal hearts"), cf. Milton, *Ad Leonoram* 1.7–8: *facilisque docet mortalia corda/Sensim immortali assuescere posse sono* ("and readily teaches that mortal hearts can gradually become accustomed to an immortal sound").

your musical strings; on that, by your singing, you
transport them to heavenly song.

In Milton's hypothesis Tasso's madness is imagined as even more severe than that of Pentheus (*Quamvis Dircaeo torsisset lumina Pentheo /Saevior* [7–8] ["Even if he had rolled his eyes more fiercely than Dircaean Pentheus"]),[152] that pluperfect <u>tor</u>sisset (7) tonally incorporating <u>Torquatus</u> (1), whereby the poet is both literally and linguistically enveloped by the very symptoms of his insanity. Even so, Leonora's voice, Milton states, could have "composed" (*composuisse* [10]) his reeling senses; her singing would have had the power to appease his turmoil: *aegro spirans sub corde quietem* (11) ("breathing repose in the depths of his sick heart"). In all of this (and with a possible nod [in *composuisse*] to the fact that Leonora herself was an accomplished "composer"?),[153] Milton attributes to her song a hesychastic potential[154] in language that may be related to baroque musicology. The concept, while finding its origins in the tripartite division of music (into diastaltic, hesychastic, and systaltic) by such classical authors as Cleonides, Aristides, Quintilian, and Bryennius, had been revivified and reinterpreted in seicento Italy. Thus, for example, Monteverdi had included "molle" ("smooth") as one of three "generi" ("types") of which madrigal music consisted.[155] Particularly striking is the fact that the

---

[152] With *torsisset lumina* (7) ("had rolled his eyes") cf. Leonora Baroni's sonnet "Occhi belli, e crudeli" ("Beautiful and cruel Eyes") at *L'Idea*, 215, especially "Quando intorno girati i vostri lumi" (9) ("When you roll your eyes").

[153] See 100, 102, 106–107.

[154] Several of the *Applausi* poets likewise emphasize the soothing power of Leonora's *cantus*. Thus Fabio Leonida states: "Ma di questa Sirena è vero vanto/Placar la furia de le Furie stesse" ("But this Siren possesses the true boast that she placates the fury of the Furies themselves") (*Applausi*, 118). This is extended to embrace the fury of war. Gasparo de Simeonibus asserts that as a result of her singing "Fatti molli in un punto i ferri, e i cori" ("both swords and hearts are placated in a single instant" [*Applausi*, 167]).

[155] The other two "generi," in Monteverdi's view, were "concitato" ("agitated") and "temperato" ("moderate"). See Barbara Russano Hanning, "Monteverdi's Three Genera: A Study in Terminology," in *Musical Humanism and Its Legacy: Essays in Honor of Claude Palisca*, eds. Nancy Kovaleff Baker and Barbara Russano Hanning (Stuyvesant NY: Pendragon, 1992), 145–170. See also Tim Carter, "The Composer as Theorist? Genus and Genre in Monteverdi's *Combattimento di Tancredi e Clorinda*," in *Music in the Mirror: Reflections on the History of Music Theory and Literature for the Twenty-first Century*, eds. Andreas Giger and Thomas J. Mathiesen (Lincoln: University of Nebraska Press, 2002), 77–116, at 106; Richard Wistreich, "Of Mars I Sing: Monteverdi Voicing Virility," in *Masculinity and Western Musical Practice*, eds. Ian Biddle and Kirsten Gibson (Farnham: Ashgate, 2009), 67–94, at 68–71.

Florentine musicologist Giovanni Battista Doni, in his 1635 treatise *Compendio del Trattato de' Generi e de' Modi della Musica*, had given precedence to this hesychastic element, explicating it in some detail, and translating it by the verb *quietare*:

> E' da saper dunque, che, secondo i Greci Autori, la musica è di tre sorti: La prima, quella, che non induce alcun disordinato affetto, ò perturbatione vecmente; ma solo diletta piacevolmente l'animo; inducendo una moderata allegoria, e rasserenando con pensieri gravi, e tranquilli la mente; la quale dicevano *Hesychastica*, dal verbo ἡσυχάζειν, che vuol dire quietare.[156]

> It is therefore to be known that, according to the Greek authors, music is of three kinds: the first, that which does not induce any incoherent affection or vehement disturbance, but only pleasantly delights the mind, inducing a moderate alleviation and cheering it with deep contemplation, and calming the mind; that which they term *Hesychastica* from the verb ἡσυχάζειν, which means to afford calm.

Given Milton's attested musicological interests,[157] it is possible that, as Louis Schleiner has posited, he had read Doni's *Compendio* prior to, or in the course of, his Italian journey.[158] And he may even have had the opportunity to discuss such theories in person with Doni, who was in Rome at the time of Milton's second sojourn in the city.[159] Doni's tract was certainly read by Benedetto Fioretti (1579–1642),[160] President of the

---

[156] Giovanni Battista Doni, *Compendio del Trattato de' Generi de' Modi della Musica* (Rome: Andrea Fei, 1635), 54.

[157] Cf. *Defensio Secunda*, 83: *nonnunquam, rus urbe mutarem, aut coemendorum gratia librorum, aut novum quidpiam in Mathematicis, vel in Musicis, quibus tum oblectabar, addiscendi* ("sometimes I exchanged the country for the city in order either to purchase books or to learn something new in mathematics or in music, which were sources of enjoyment to me at that time"). Music scores, including works by Monteverdi, were among books that Milton would ship home from Venice. See Edward Phillips, *The Life of Mr. John Milton*, in *Early Lives*, ed. Darbishire, 59, quoted at 166.

[158] Schleiner, "Milton, G. B. Doni," 37.

[159] See Schleiner, "Milton, G. B. Doni," 38, and 42.

[160] That Fioretti owned a personal copy of the *Compendio*, gifted to him by its author, is attested by his letter to Doni of 5 July 1636, in which he sings the praises of the work, which he refers to as an "opera musicale, dono di V[ostro] S[ignore]" ("a musical work, the gift of your lordship"). See *Io[annis] Baptistae Donii Patricii Florentini Commercium Litterarium*, ed. Anton Francesco Gori (Florence: Caesario,

Florentine Accademia degli Apatisti, in which Milton had participated in 1638,[161] and by the budding Dutch musicologist Joan Albert Ban (Bannius) (1597–1644). Writing to Doni on 1 March 1639, Ban praises the *Compendio* (which had been recommended to him by Marin Mersenne): *Quem quum legissem, inveni profecto omnimoda eruditione refertissimum* ("When I had read it, I certainly discovered it to be most replete with every type of erudition").[162] Ban, however, had developed a theory of his own, which may not be unrelated to the musicological dimension of Milton's epigram.

The hypothetical account of the potential restoration of Tasso's sanity by Leonora's soothing musicianship is, in Milton's view, rooted in the fact that her song is *flexanimus* (12) ("soul-swaying"). Read in its context, this would seem to denote her ability to "turn" the Tassonian mind in ways essentially antithetical to the professed insanity that led to his death. The rare compound adjective *flexanimus* likewise occurs in Lucas Holstenius's Latin encomium of Leonora included in the *Applausi*:

> ... roseoque fingit ori
> Carmen flexanimum, diserta verba,
> Dulces blanditias, iocosque doctos.[163]

> ... and upon her rosy lips she composes
> a soul-swaying song, skillful words,
> sweet blandishments, and learned jokes.

The parallel, dismissed by Bush as "insignificant,"[164] merits consideration in relation to seicento musicological theory. *Flexanimus* in its primary sense of something "that bends or sways the mind"[165] is first found in Pacuvius, where it is applied to oratory (*o flexanima atque omnium regina oratio*) ["o eloquence, soul-swaying and queen of all things"]),[166]

1754), appended to Ang[elo] Mar[ia] Bandini, *Commentariorum De Vita et Scriptis Ioannis Bapt[istae] Doni ... Libri Quinque* (Florence: Caesario, 1755), 122.

[161] See Haan, *From Academia to Amicitia*, 29–37.

[162] *Commercium Litterarium*, ed. Gori, 128–130, at 128 (misnumbered 144).

[163] *Applausi*, 202. Cf. Maffeo Barberini, *In Psalmum CXXXVI. Paraphrasis*: *Flexanimum nobis ... dicite carmen* ("proclaim to us a soul-swaying song"), in *Maphaei S[anctae] R[omanae] E[cclesiae] Card[inalis] Barberini Nunc Urbani Papae VIII Poemata* (Rome: Rev[erenda] Cam[era] Apost[olica], 1640), 39.

[164] Bush, *Variorum*, I, 148.

[165] *OLD*, s.v. *flexanimus* 1.

[166] Pacuvius, *Trag.* 177. Cf. Catullus 64. 330: [*coniunx*] *quae tibi flexanimo mentem perfundat amore* ("[your wife] who may imbue your consciousness with soul-swaying love") where *flexanimus* denotes the ability of marital love to "turn one's thoughts

a phrase quoted by Cicero in *De Oratore*.[167] In the seventeenth century, however, it had come to be appropriated to describe music itself. Thus the term *musica flexanima* was coined by Ban to encapsulate his theory that true expression of the text was achievable only by adhering to stringent rules concerning melody, rhythm, and concord. Central to Ban's system is the exact size of each melodic interval, which, he believed, conveyed a particular emotional effect. Thus minor intervals denote sadness, whereas major intervals signal robustness.[168] This theory had already seen print in Ban's *Dissertatio Epistolica, de Musicae Natura*, published in 1637 at Leiden, and reprinted alongside dissertations by Hugo Grotius and others.[169] To some degree it was the product of the "musical humanism"[170] of the Seicento. As Erwin Panofsky acutely observes:

> once musical theory had turned "humanistic", it was not doubted that music addressed itself to man as well as God and that its purposes were, not only to delight the ear of the

---

aside from other things." See *Catullus: The Poems*, ed. Kenneth Quinn (London: Macmillan; New York: St Martin's Press, 1970), 342. Cf. Virgil, *Georgics* 4.516: *nulla Venus, non ulli animum flexere hymenaei* ("no thoughts of passion, no thoughts of marriage-rites distracted his mind"); *Aeneid* 4. 22: *solus hic inflexit sensus* ("this man alone has caused my feelings to swerve").

[167] Cicero, *De Oratore* 2.187: *Sed tantam vim habet illa, quae recte a bono poeta dicta est flexanima atque omnium regina rerum oratio, ut non modo inclinantem excipere aut stantem inclinare, sed etiam adversantem ac repugnantem, ut imperator fortis ac bonus, capere possit* ("but eloquence, which has rightly been termed by a good poet 'soul-swaying' and 'the queen of all things,' has such great force that it has the power not only to raise up the one who stoops or to bend the one who stands, but also, like a brave and good commander, to capture the one who opposes and resists").

[168] See, among others, J. P. N. Land, "Joan Albert Ban en de Theorie der Toonkunst," *Tijdschrift van de Vereniging voor Nederlandse Muziekgeschiedenis* 1 (1883): 95–111; 3 (1891): 204–218; Rudolf A. Rasch, "Ban's Intonation," *Tijdschrift van de Vereniging voor Nederlandse Muziekgeschiedenis* 33 (1983): 75–99; Rudolf A. Rasch, "Six Seventeenth-Century Dutch Scientists and their Knowledge of Music," in *Music and Science in the Age of Galileo*, ed. Victor Coelho (Dordrecht: Kluwer Academic Publishers, 2010), 185–210, at 192–195. See also David Damschroder and David Russell Williams, *Music Theory from Zarlino to Schenker: A Bibliography and Guide* (Stuyvesant, NY: Pendragon Press, 1990), 21.

[169] *Dissertatio Epistolica, de Musicae Natura*, printed with separate title page and pagination in *Hugonis Grotii et Aliorum De Omni Genere Studiorum Recte Instituendo Dissertationes* (Leiden: Isaac Commelin, 1637).

[170] See D. P. Walker, "Musical Humanism in the 16th and Early 17th Centuries," *MR* 2 (1941): 1–13, 111–121, 220–227, 288–308; 3 (1942): 55–71. See also Geneviève Rodis-Lewis, "Musique et Passions au XVIIe Siècle: Monteverdi et Descartes," *XVIIe Siècle* 92 (1971): 81–98.

listener, but also to influence his soul—emotionally, intellectually and morally.[171]

Ban firmly believed that music constituted another form of oratory, albeit in a different medium. Writing to William Boswell on 15 December 1637, he cites Pacuvius, via Cicero, to proclaim:

> Musicam flexanimam instaurandam volo, illamque oratoriam, cuius ego tibi nuper ideam ostendi "illam omnium reginam rerum musicam, quae" (verba Ciceronis sunt 2 De Oratore) "tantam vim habet, ut non modo inclinantem erigere aut stantem inclinare, sed etiam adversantem et repugnantem, ut bonus ac fortis imperator, capere possit."[172]

> It is my wish to reinstate [the theory of] "music as soul-swaying", and as pertaining to oratory, the idea of which I have recently pointed out: "[Music], that queen of all things" (the words are those of Cicero, *De Oratore*, bk 2) "has such great force that it possesses the ability not only to raise up the one who stoops or to bend the one who stands, but also, like a brave and good commander, to capture the one who opposes and resists."

He proceeds to emphasize the interrelationship, based, in his view, upon a shared aim: *finis musicae est docere, delectare et movere. Is musico cum oratore communis est, licet aliis mediis utatur musicus quam orator* ("the goal of music is to teach, to please, and to move. This is a goal shared by the musician and the orator, even though the musician uses media that differ from the orator").[173] Perhaps most interesting in this regard is Ban's correspondence with Doni in 1639–1640. Thus, in his aforementioned letter of 1 March 1639, he reveals something of his unwavering belief in the novelty and validity of his theory:

> Ego qui Musicae studio subsecivis horis, dum a seriis occupationibus nonnihil licet deflectere, plane adductus sum; plurimum laboravi, ut eam flexanimam (qualem nunquam vidi, sed tantum temerarie laudatam legi) redderem.[174]

---

[171] Erwin Panofsky, *Galileo as a Critic of the Arts* (The Hague: Martinus Nijhoff, 1954), 10.

[172] Ban, autograph letter to William Boswell (15 December 1637), Leiden University Library Cod. Hug. 37, ff. 1–12, at f. 1ʳ.

[173] *Ibid.*, f. 3ʳ.

[174] *Commercium Literarium*, ed. Gori, 128.

> I, who have obviously been subjected to the captivating powers afforded by my musical studies undertaken in my spare hours (since I derive no small pleasure in being distracted from serious business), have been working chiefly with the purpose of rendering that [theory of] "music as soul-swaying" (the like of which I have never seen, but have only read as having been the object of accidental praise).

In a further letter to Doni, dated 1 July 1639, he candidly describes the struggles associated with his attempted promotion of *musica flexamina* to his contemporaries: *me proprio marte ad Musicae flexanimae virtutem eruendam aliquid conantem* ("as in a warfare of my own I make some attempt with regard to unearthing the virtue of 'music as soul-swaying'").[175] That they exchanged works and ideas is evinced by Doni's letter to Ban of 15 October 1639,[176] and by Ban's undated epistle addressed to a certain *Philomusus* (i.e., Doni as interpreted by Gori),[177] which seems to contain a synopsis of a manuscript work sent to him by

---

[175] *Commercium Literarium*, ed. Gori, 132–133, at 132. In 1638 Ban had entered into correspondence with Marin Mersenne, who had dismissed his theory as outmoded and inconsequential. As a result, Mersenne would, in 1640, set up a competition between Ban and Antoine Boësset, in which both musicians were challenged with the task of setting the same French poem. See D. P. Walker, "Joan Albert Ban and Marsenne's Musical Competition of 1640," *Music and Letters* 57 (1976): 233–255. Although losing the competition, Ban continued to persist in his convictions in regard to the validity of *musica flexanima*. Later, Mersenne praises both Ban and Doni in an interesting juxtaposition of their theories. See Mersenne, *Cogitata Physico Mathematica* (Paris: Antonius Bertier, 1644), 356: *Porro quod ad modos attinet omnium optime Ioannes Baptista Doni (magnum Italiae decus) in illis restituendis laboravit; cuius tractatus et discursus omnes ab omnibus Harmoniae amantibus legi velim: ut in flexanima Musica vir clarissimus Albertus Bannius, annorum, ut audio, fere quadringentorum prosapia nobilis, a quo in dies expectamus libros in illa materia incomparabiles* ("Furthermore as regards musical measures, Giovanni Battista Doni [the great glory of Italy] devoted the greatest labors of all to their restitution. I should like his tracts and all of his discourses to be read by all those who are lovers of Harmony: likewise in the field of 'soul-swaying music' Albert Ban, a most famous man, noble by virtue of his lineage which, so I hear, spans roughly four hundred years, from whom we are daily awaiting unequalled books on that subject").

[176] *Commercium Literarium*, ed. Gori, 134–135, at 135: *Adiunxi his literulis Musici cuiusdam nostratis μελύδριον* ("I have appended to this letter 'a tune' by a fellow native musician").

[177] *Commercium Literarium*, ed. Gori, 136–141. Cf. Gori's note at 135–136: *Est, ut videtur, Synopsis Musicae operis MS. Ad Donium trasmissa* [sic], *ut iudicium suum ferret, quam nolui praetermittere* ("This, it seems, is a synopsis of a work in manuscript sent to Doni for him to offer his judgment, and one which I did not wish to overlook").

Ban. Here he clearly articulates his belief in the efficacy of *musica flexanima* as akin to that of oratory:

> Musicam nostram eo modo construximus, Philomuse, ut flexanima foret: efficax nimirum, oratorio more ad docendum, delectandum, et movendum.[178]

> Lover of the Muse, we have constructed our music in such a way that it should prove to be soul-swaying, with the evident capacity to teach, to please and to move in the manner of the orator.

In short, *modulamentum anima est Musicae flexanimae; eoque solo omnis eloquentia Musica exigitur* ("modulation is the soul of soul-swaying music, and from that alone is every form of Musical eloquence executed").[179]

Read in its contemporary contexts, Milton's second Latin epigram takes as its point of departure an Italian poet's reputed insanity only to propose a remedy that is literally in tune with current musicological theory, one that is effected by the musicianship of Leonora Baroni, but also perhaps by the vacillating tonalities of the poem's Latin voice.

2.5 From Naples to Rome: *Ad Leonoram* 3[180]

The tonalities of Milton's encomia of Leonora continue to shift. His third Latin epigram seems to situate her performance in a mythological context. It emerges, however, that ancient mythology is invoked only to be developed, transformed, and molded to suit the context of seicento Rome. The poem's implicit equation of Leonora's singing with that of one of the Sirens (*liquidam Sirena* [1] ["clear-voiced Siren"]), famous in antiquity for the alluring power of their song,[181] is a motif that pervades the *Applausi*. Thus Leonora is variously described as "bella Sirena" ("beautiful Siren"),[182] "questa Sirena" ("this Siren"),[183] "vaga Siren" ("lovely Siren"),[184] *Ut notis Siren caneres superbis* ("So that as a Siren

---

[178] *Commercium Literarium*, ed. Gori, 136.

[179] *Commercium Literarium*, ed. Gori, 137.

[180] For Latin text and English translation, see Appendix 1.1(c).

[181] See Homer, *Odyssey* 12, 184–192.

[182] *Applausi*, 19.

[183] *Applausi*, 118.

[184] *Applausi*, 121.

you might sing with lofty notes"),[185] "La Sirena immortale" ("The immortal Siren"),[186] "dolce Sirena" ("sweet Siren"),[187] "Fastosetta Sirena" ("Magnificent Siren"),[188] "pudica Siren" ("modest Siren"),[189] and "Syrene de la mer d'amour" ("Siren of the sea of love").[190] In essence this recurring leitmotif perfectly epitomizes what Dell'Antonio has described as "the quasi-interactive 'dialogic' interplay of the poems" in the collection as a whole.[191]

For Milton, however, Leonora is also a second Parthenope,[192] who has exchanged a less attractive Naples for the serenity of Rome: *Illa quidem vivitque, et amoena Tibridis unda/Mutavit rauci murmura Pausilipi* (5–6) ("She is, in fact, alive, and has exchanged the murmurings of the raucous Posillipo for Tiber's pleasant waters").[193] The lines find a close *Applausi* parallel in Fulvio Testi's salutation:

> Fastosetta Sirena,
>   Che da Partenopei liti odiosi
> Sù la Romana arena
> Se' venuta à turbar gli altrui riposi.[194]

---

[185] *Applausi*, 146.

[186] *Applausi*, 155.

[187] *Applausi*, 129 and 185.

[188] *Applausi*, 157.

[189] *Applausi*, 201.

[190] *Applausi*, 180. For further instances of this recurring leitmotif, see *Applausi*, 43 (misnumbered 51), 89, 99, 100, 117, 149, 196, 239, 250, 252, 259. See also Haan, *From Academia to Amicitia*, 114–116.

[191] Dell'Antonio, *Listening as Spiritual Practice*, 86.

[192] Cf. Milton, *A Mask* 878–879: "And the songs of Sirens sweet,/By dead Parthenope's dear tomb."

[193] With Milton's emphasis upon the fact that this Siren is not dead, but actually living in the person of Leonora (*Illa quidem vivitque* [5] ["she is, in fact, alive"]), cf. Giulio Rospigliosi, at *Applausi*, 185 (on the della Corgna portrait), who praises the artist's ability to bring the Siren to life in the form of Leonora as depicted therein: "Per te questa de' cor dolce Sirena/Non è finta, *ma vive*; e i lumi ardenti/Scoccan dal vago ciglio amabil pena" ("On your account this Siren with her sweet heart is not feigned, *but is alive*, and her blazing eyes dart from their graceful lids a lovely pain"). Emphasis is mine.

[194] *Applausi*, 157. Cf. Lucas Holstenius, at *Applausi*, 201: *pulchrae Parthenopes canora proles* ("the tuneful offspring of beautiful Parthenope"). See also Gregorio Porcio, at *Applausi*, 188: *Mox te Parthenope blandas Sirenas, et inter/Sebethi Nymphas fovit amica sinu* ("Soon Parthenope nursed you in her kindly bosom amongst the charming Sirens and the Nymphs of the Sebeto").

> Magnificent Siren,
> you who have come from the unpleasant
> shores of Parthenope to Roman sand
> in order to disturb the repose of others.

But Milton's topography is more specific in its reference to Posillipo (6), the birthplace *not* of Leonora (who was born in Mantua), but of her mother, famously known as the "Siren of Posillipo." Indeed, it was as the daughter of Parthenope that Adriana was universally acclaimed in *Il Teatro*. This is acknowledged by Domitio Bombarda in his dedicatory letter, prefixed to the volume,[195] and by several encomiasts therein,[196] who also highlight the landscape of her birthplace as if in acknowledgment of its etymological origins in "pausilipon" ("the place where one forgets cares" = "sans souci"). Thus the contribution by the "Principe di Stigliano, Duca di Sabioneta," specifically entitled "Meraviglie della Signora Adr[iana] nella gioconda Riva di Pausilippo operate" ("The wonders of the Lady Adr[iana] performed on the joyful bank of Posillipo") praises the "tranquillo Mare,/Di questa piaggia amena" (1–2) ("tranquil sea of this pleasant beach"), the origin of "Bella, e vaga Sirena" (4) ("a beautiful and lovely Siren").[197] Francesco Rasi, while tracing Adriana's birth back to "piacevolissimo grembo della vaga Partenope" ("the most pleasant womb of the lovely Parthenope") is careful to qualify the location as pertaining not to that associated with the Syrtes, proverbially dangerous to sailors, but to the spot "dove bagnano l'onde Tirrhene il verdeggiante Pausilippo" ("where the Tyrrhenian waves lap the verdant Posillipo"). It is Adriana's voice that rescues her storm-tossed listeners, and places them "in tranquillo porto di soavità" ("in a tranquil harbor of sweetness").[198] Adriana's birthplace, although

---

[195] *Il Teatro*, 9: "altri la Nobil PARTENOPE di questa innocente SIRENA inclita Genitrice avventurosa chiamavano" ("others have daringly named the noble PARTHENOPE as the renowned mother of this innocent SIREN").

[196] Cf. "Ma Partenope bella udinne il canto / ... / Di Partenope havesse il tuo bel Regno" ("But the beautiful Partenope heard your song ... You possessed as your own the beautiful realm of Parthenope") (*Il Teatro* 106); "Partenope, onde entro sue vive spoglie/Chiuder tuo vago spirto" ("Parthenope, where among her living remains is enclosed your lovely spirit" (*Il Teatro*, 108); "Rivedrà pur costei Mantoa famosa,/Di Partenope gloria, e'immortal face" ("On account of this woman famous Mantua will behold again the glory and the immortal face of Parthenope") (*Il Teatro*, 164); "nova Partenope" ("a new Parthenope") (*Il Teatro*, 170); "A las selvas de Partenope En Alabança de la S[eñora] Andriana [sic]" (*Il Teatro*, 206) ("To the woods of Parthenope in Defense of the Lady Adriana").

[197] *Il Teatro*, 17.

[198] *Il Teatro*, 90.

not occurring in the *Applausi*, is interestingly signaled by Milton in the seemingly pejorative *rauci murmura Pausilipi* (6) ("the murmurings of the raucous Posillipo"), which he associates not with serene tranquility, but with noise, be it of traffic in the tunnel underneath the mountain[199] or, more likely, the splashing of waves beneath the mountain cliff.[200] But now that adjective "amena"/*amoenus* ("pleasant") pertains not to Posillipo, but to Rome, symbolized by the Tiber itself: *amoena Tibridis unda* ("Tiber's pleasant waters").[201] Milton's depiction of Parthenope as a Naiad (*Litoreamque tua defunctam Naiada ripa* [3] "a Naiad of the shore, dead upon your river bank" [3]) is unattested in classical literature.[202] Bush's speculation that he "is using the term [*sc.* Naiad] loosely"[203] may indeed be true, but it is worth remarking that Milton's phrase <u>NAIADA Ripa</u>[204] affords an anagrammatic potential with *ADRIANA*. That his epigram may be embracing *Il Teatro* at this precise point is perhaps hinted at by the poem's opening question: *Credula quid liquidam Sirena, Neapoli, iactas* (1) ("Credulous Naples, why do you boast of your clear-voiced Siren").[205] In fact, wordplay on the name Adriana Basile is a recurring feature in *Il Teatro*. Although evident to some degree in the Italian poems included therein,[206] it is a much more prevalent characteristic of the Latin encomia. Thus Bernardino Palmerio, in a piece entitled *Naiadum Lusus pro Adriana Basili Dithyrambus*, discusses the potential origin of the name Adriana Basile, offering witty puns on the Latin nouns *Adria* (the

---

[199] The mountain is pierced by a tunnel (now called the Old Grotto) through which traffic on the Via Atiniana passes.

[200] Cf. Pacuvius, *Trag.* 417 and Cicero, *De Orat.* 3.161: *murmur maris* ("the murmur of the sea"); Ovid, *Met.* 2.455: *cum murmure labens ... rivus* ("a stream ... gliding with a murmur").

[201] Cf. Virgil, *Aen.* 7.30: *fluvio Tiberinus amoeno* ("Tiber with his pleasant river"); 8.31: *deus ipse loci fluvio Tiberinus amoeno* ("The very deity of the place, Tiber with his pleasant river").

[202] Cf. Bush, *Variorum*, I, 151: "Editors have not found classical authority for calling Parthenope a naiad."

[203] Bush, *Variorum*, I, 151, who compares *A Mask* 252-253, noting Ovid's general use of *nymphae* (*Heroides* 1.27; 9. 103; 16. 128).

[204] Emphasis is mine.

[205] With this concept and phraseology, cf. Quilletto Francese at *Applausi*, 247: *Tuas quid Graecia iactas/Aonidas, ficti numina vana Chori?* ("Why, Greece, do you boast of your Theban women, and of the insubstantial divinities of a feigned Chorus?").

[206] See, for example, the punning on "Adriana"/"Arianna" (*Il Teatro*, 31); on "Adriana"/"Adria" (*Il Teatro*, 59); on "Basile"/"Basi" (*Il Teatro*, 44).

Adriatic Sea) and *Basis* (foundation/basis).²⁰⁷ Anagrammatic play on Adriana's name likewise lies at the heart of Giovanni Thomas Giovini's contribution, explicitly entitled ANDRIANA BASILIS ANAGRAMMA. BINAS DIANA LIRAS.²⁰⁸ The most sophisticated instance is provided by Pier Francesco Massa, whose Latin poem contains double acrostics on Adriana's husband and herself: thus the left acrostic spells MUTIUS BARONIUS; the right spells ADRIANA BASILIS.²⁰⁹ Although it would be unwise to succumb to a methodology akin to that of Francis Bacon (whose blighted reading of Milton's Italian sonnets argued for hidden acrostic allusions to Leonora),²¹⁰ it is just possible that Milton's epigram thematically and linguistically embraces a modern Neapolitan Siren, Adriana herself, of whom, in this reading, *Il Teatro* had indeed boasted throughout.

The potential rivalry between Naples and Rome signaled in Milton's poem would come to be embodied by the textual, and especially the paratextual, relationships between *Il Teatro* and the *Applausi*. Here, Amy Brosius's speculation that *Il Teatro* "surely served as the model for the *Applausi*"²¹¹ merits further investigation. A comparison of the layout, presentation and organization of the two volumes seems to suggest a conscious endeavor on the part of Francesco Ronconi, the *Applausi*'s editor, to match and outshine its maternal literary ancestor. In contrast to the rather plain title page of its predecessor, the *Applausi* is adorned with an ornate frontispiece, which seems to seek to achieve a reconciliation between the celestial and the terrestrial. Here, the coat of arms of the family of de Melo/Moura is held aloft, not, as in the family crest, by two military, spear-wielding warriors, but by two winged angels. Beneath, there stand two Muses: one classical and laureate, gazing in wonderment at a new earthly Muse, who holds a viol, and treads underfoot the Muses' customary instruments—in all likelihood Leonora herself as a tenth Muse. This figure, human yet mythological, classical yet contemporary,

---

[207] *Il Teatro*, 222–226, at 224: *Quod nomen tumido sumpsit ab Adria/Quamvis aequore maius,/Maius et Orbe/ADRIANA BASILIS/Basis honorum,/Basis et sapientia*e ("ADRIANA BASILE, the *basis* of honors, and the *basis* of wisdom, has derived from the *Adriatic*, a name greater than the albeit swollen sea, and greater than the world"). Emphasis is mine.

[208] *Il Teatro*, 240. The anagram (*Andriana Basilis/Binas Diana Liras*) is explicated in lines 9–10: *Aonidum assensere Deae; nam Delius unam/Temperat, at* BINAS, *nostra* DIANA LIRAS ("The divine Muses gave their approval; for the god of Delos tunes a single lyre, but our DIANA tunes TWO LYRES").

[209] *Il Teatro*, 219.

[210] See *Some Acrostic Signatures of Francis Bacon*, ed. William Stone Booth (Boston: Houghton Mifflin, 1909), 557–563.

[211] Brosius, "The Function of Portraits," 33.

is the object of gazes both angelic and Roman. The address to the reader is particularly self-conscious in its contextualization of the volume alongside *Il Teatro*, in its presentation of Leonora as the worthy successor of Adriana, and in its emphasis upon the care with which the *Applausi* poems have been "selected," as opposed to merely "collected":

> Haurai goduto gli anni addietro il Teatro delle Compositioni, che fù stampato in lode della Signora Adriana Basile Baronessa di Pian Cerreto, Madre della Signora Leonora Baroni: godi hora le Glorie della medesima Signora Leonora Baroni, che ti presento, raccolte, ò per meglio dire, scelte in questo Volume, trà infinite, che ne sono state composte: non ammirar con minori applausi il trionfo della Figliuola, di quel, che tù habbia ammirato quel della Madre.[212]

> Having enjoyed some years ago the Theater of Compositions that was printed in praise of the lady Adriana Basile, Baroness of Piancerreto, mother of the lady Leonora Baroni, enjoy today the Glories of the same lady Leonora Baroni, which I present to you, collected, or to speak more accurately, chosen, in this Volume, from among the infinite numbers that have been composed. Admire the triumph of the Daughter with an applause no less than that with which you have admired that of the Mother.

Just as *Il Teatro* is dedicated to a Marquis (Giovanni Battista Manso),[213] so the *Applausi* is dedicated to a Marquess and Spanish ambassadress, but this dedicatee is rather fortuitously named *Eleonora* de Melo.[214] In consequence, encomia of "Leonora" can conveniently reflect positively on the Marquess "Eleonora,"[215] praises of whom neatly bookend the *Applausi* as a whole.[216] Whereas *Il Teatro* showcased a single engraving

---

[212] *Applausi*, sig. A5ʳ.

[213] See 109.

[214] Emphasis is mine. See Francesco Ronconi's dedicatory letter (dated Rome, 1 September 1639) "All' Illustrissima, et Eccellentissima Signora, e Padrona Colendissima La Signora D[onna] Eleonora de Melo, Marchesa di Castel Rodrigo, Ambasciatrice di S[ua] Maestà Cattolica in Roma," at *Applausi*, sig. A2ʳ–A4ᵛ.

[215] At *ibid.*, sig. A2ʳ, Ronconi dedicates "al *nome*" ("to the *name*") of the Marquess, his collection, which, he continues, is intended "per eternare con sì degni Applausi poetici le glorie della Signora *Leonora* Baroni" ("to immortalize with such worthy poetic Applauses the glories of the Lady *Leonora* Baroni"). Emphasis is mine.

[216] Thus Ronconi's dedicatory letter is balanced by the volume's concluding piece, an extravagant canzone by Domenico Benigni, addressed "All' Ill[ustrissi]ma, et Eccellentissima Sig[no]ra, DONNA LEONORA DI MELO, MARCHESA DI CASTEL RODRIGO, Ambasciatrice di S[ua] Maestà Cattolica in Roma" (*Applausi*, 263–267).

of its subject (by Claude Mellan), the iconographical subtext of the *Applausi* is, by comparison, much more complex. Not only does it present an engraved miniature of the della Corgna portrait, but it also contains a paratextual description and interpretation of the actual full-length painting:

> un Ritratto di questa Signora, dipinto dal Sig[nore] D[on] Fabio della Corgna, il quale la rappresenta tutta intiera, in piedi, con habito di color di cenere, e che s'attiene con la sinistra ad una Lira, e con la destra sostenta la l'arco di essa, à cui Amore, rimirando lei in viso, furtivamente accomoda un de' suoi strali, per ferir con l'arco musicale della medesima quei cuori, che non haveva potuto impiagar con l'arco proprio; che però rotto in più pezzi, si rimira a' piedi di quella, come singolar trofeo delle sue glorie.[217]

> a Portrait of this Lady, painted by Mr Fabio della Corgna, which represents her entirely standing, with an ash-colored dress, and she holds a Lira in her left hand, and in her right hand raises a bow, to which Cupid, gazing at her face, furtively notches one of his arrows in order to strike with the bow of this same lady's music those hearts which he has been unable to pierce with his own bow. This, however, can be seen, broken into several pieces, at her feet, as a singular trophy of her glories.[218]

And among the contributions are no fewer than twenty-two poems, which this painting has inspired.[219] A further two pieces look to a portrait of

---

[217] *Applausi*, sig. A5ʳ–A5ᵛ.

[218] As noted by Brosius, "The Function of Portraits," 37, "Cupid's broken bow indicates that his once autonomous power to induce love is now completely dependent upon the chastely depicted beloved, Leonora. It is only through Leonora's music and, more literally, her 'musical' bow, that the power of love can be wielded."

[219] *Applausi*, 1, 2 (two poems by an unknown author); 6–16 (by Alfonso Pallavicini); 21 (by Andrea Barbazza); 26–29 (by Annibale Bentivoglio); 58–60 (by Camillo Colonna); 113–116 (by della Corgna himself); 123–126 (by Ferdinando Orsino); 127–131 (by Flavio Orsino); 183 (by Gio[vanni] Antonio Orsino); 185 (by Giulio Rospigliosi); 186 (by Giulio Cesare Raggioli); 191–195 (by Lelio Guidiccioni); 204–211 (by Ludovico d'Agliè); 215–219 (by Mario Sforza); 220 and 221–226 (by Oddo Savelli Palombara); 227 (by Paolo Emilio Orsino); 230 and 231 (by Pier Francesco Pauli); 234–243 (by Pompeo Colonna); 253–259 (by Vincenzo Marescotti). On the significance of the della Corgna portrait as the only instance of a full-length, life-size depiction of a female singer, see Brosius, "The Function of Portraits," 35. The fact that Camillo Colonna, the President of the Umoristi, chose to compose his piece in celebration of the della Corgna painting may lend further support to the possibility that it hung in that Academy, on which see 102.

Leonora by Guido Reni,[220] and a bust of her by Gian Lorenzo Bernini,[221] neither of which artifacts seem to have survived. Whereas the poems in *Il Teatro* are presented in a quite random fashion, requiring an index ("Tavola") of authors, those in the *Applausi*, as explicitly signaled in the address to the reader, are neatly arranged in alphabetical order according to author.[222]

Ultimately, perhaps, Milton's poem reconciles the Neapolitan and the Roman by suggesting and celebrating a Siren who undergoes, as it were, a series of emulatory births and rebirths: Parthenope, Adriana, Leonora, one whose migration from Naples to Rome mirrors the history of the Baroni family since 1633.

---

[220] See *Applausi*, 22–24, by Andrea Barbazza, addressed to Guido Reni.

[221] See *Applausi*, 85–92, by Domenico Benigni, addressed to Gian Lorenzo Bernini.

[222] *Applausi*, sig. A5^r: "Quel fine medesimo, che mi mosse à dispor queste Poesie per ordine d'Alfabeto, secondo il nome di ciascuno de gli Autori" ("It is this same purpose that has motivated me to arrange these poems in alphabetical order, according to the name of each of the authors").

Chapter 3

Milton, Lucas Holstenius, and the Culture of Rome

Where the Latin epigrams in praise of Leonora Baroni demonstrate Milton's creative experimentalism in response to an encomiastic vogue current in seicento Rome, *Epistola Familiaris* 9 attests to his presence in the very hub of Catholicism, the Vatican itself. And it does so by articulating an associated sense of inclusion, integration, even wonderment, that never ceases to surprise. Extant (in a very clean holograph) in the Vatican Library,[1] the letter is addressed to Lucas Holstenius (Holste), Librarian of the Barberini Library (1636), of Cardinal Francesco Barberini (1638), and subsequently of the Vatican Library (first custodian, 1641; second custodian, 1653).[2] Holstenius, although a convert to Catholicism, did not limit his scholarly contacts to fellow Catholics. Indeed, as Blom observes, he "had quite a few correspondents in the Protestant countries of Europe including England."[3] He was also an important avenue to both Catholic and Protestant scholars seeking access to the Barberini and Vatican libraries,[4] and a major point of contact for English booksellers forever on the hunt for manuscripts that might see publication.

---

[1] BAV Barb.lat. 2181, ff. 57^r–58^v, where, however, it is dated 29 March 1639, in contrast to *Epistolarum Familiarium Liber Unus*, 28, which prints 30 March 1639. In view of this discrepancy, it is tempting to suggest that the text printed in 1674 was based on another draft (or copy) made the next day, and revised at a later date. For Latin text and English translation, see Appendix 1.3.

[2] On Lucas Holstenius's work and life, see Peter Fuchs, "Holste, Lukas," *NDB* 9 (Berlin, 1972), 548–550; Roberto Almagià, *L'Opera Geografica di Luca Holstenio*, Studi e Testi 102 (Vatican City: Biblioteca Apostolica Vaticana, 1942); F. J. Blom, "Lucas Holstenius (1596–1661) and England," in *Studies in Seventeenth-Century English Literature, History and Bibliography*, eds. G. A. M. Janssens and F. G. A. M. Aarts (Amsterdam: Rodopi, 1984), 25–39, and, especially, Rietbergen, *Power and Religion*, 256–295.

[3] Blom, "Lucas Holstenius," 25.

[4] See L. G. Pélissier, "Les Amis d'Holstenius," *Revue des Langues Romanes* 5 (1891): 321–378; Rietbergen, *Power and Religion*, 268–269.

Exactly how Holstenius came to hear of Milton remains something of a mystery. Parker's speculation that, upon his arrival in Rome, Milton "probably carried letters of introduction from his Florentine friends"[5] cannot apply in this particular instance, given Milton's attested mystification about how Holstenius had become aware of his presence in the city. It is, of course, not impossible that, unbeknownst to him, they had passed along their recommendations. Milton wonders whether it was as a consequence of comments made by Alessandro Cherubini,[6] an interesting speculation in that it suggests his personal acquaintance with this youthful Roman prodigy. Son of the eminent lawyer, Laertius Cherubini (1556–c.1626),[7] Alessandro certainly had scholarly interests (in Platonic philosophy, its associated commentary tradition, and the translation of Greek texts into Latin) akin to those of Holstenius himself, and may well have been the avenue of introduction, even if at the time of Milton's Roman sojourns he was mortally ill and probably bedridden. He would die prematurely (in 1640) at the age of c. twenty-eight.[8] Another

---

[5] Parker, *Biography*, I, 173.

[6] Milton, *Epistola Familiaris* 9: *nisi si quid forte ab Alexandro Cherubino dictum de me prius fuerat* ("unless some mention of me happened to have been made in advance by Alessandro Cherubini"). Milton seems to indicate his awareness of the existence of an avenue of communication between the two scholars.

[7] Alessandro was the second of a total of five Cherubini children: four boys (Fausto, Alessandro, Angelo Maria, and Flavio) and one girl. See Marco Palma, "Cherubini, Laerzio," *DBI* 24 (1980): 434–435.

[8] Although apparently leaving no published writings, Alessandro Cherubini was highly praised by Rossi for his immensely wide reading, his scholarly knowledge, his particular devotion to Plato, and his talents as a translator. See Rossi, *Pinacotheca*, 180–181: *Nihil erat in unaquaque liberalium disciplinarum arte, quod ille non nosset; nullus liber ... in lucem editus, quem ille attente non legisset, omniaque eius dicta non meminisset ... ad Philosophiam praesertim contulit suam operam, et ad eam inprimis, in qua princeps est Plato ... quo factum est, ut multos libros Graecos Latine reddiderit* ("There was not a single aspect of any of the liberal arts of which he did not possess knowledge. There was no published book that he had not read with close attention or had failed to remember its every word. ... It was to philosophy in particular that he applied his own efforts and, above all, to that branch in which Plato is pre-eminent. ... The result was that he rendered many Greek books into Latin"). Although Rossi does not provide dates, he states that Alessandro died *cum ille vix octavum et vigesimum annum attigerit* ("when he had scarcely reached his twenty-eighth year"), remarking that for the final three years of his life he was wracked with pain and, in fact, closer to death than to life (*ibid.*, 180). This does not preclude the possibility that Milton had visited the young scholar. Alessandro's death can now be pinpointed rather more closely. That it occurred some time between 14 April and 9 September 1640 is attested by two documents: (1) an agreement, dated 14 April 1640, between the brothers Flavio and Alessandro Cherubini and the Head of the Cathedral of Frascati in regard to a vineyard which they possessed (Archivio di Stato di Roma,

possibility is Patrick Young, who was "the most intimate acquaintance of Holstenius's in England,"[9] and who maintained a regular epistolary correspondence with him until 1652.[10] The fact that Young had been Prebend and Treasurer of St Paul's Cathedral, London (1621–1624), and, possibly, one of Milton's early tutors,[11] makes this an attractive

---

NF, G. Longus prot. 76, f. 313); (2) a posthumous inventory of Alessandro Cherubini's possessions, dated 9 September 1640 (Archivio di Stato di Roma, AC, C. Colonna, prot. 2076, ff. 578ff.). See M. B. Guerrieri Borsoi, "Tra Le Ville e La Città: Tre Casini Seicenteschi a Frascati," in *Il Tesoro della Città. Strenna dell' Associazione Storia della Città* (Rome: Kappa, 2008–2010), VI, 190–214, at 194. Some evidence of Alessandro's scholarly interests around the time of Milton's Roman sojourns is provided by his recorded donation to Federico Ubaldini (1610-1657), Secretary to Cardinal Francesco Barberini, of an anonymous medieval manuscript of metrical arguments to Statius' *Thebaid*. Extant as BAV Barb.lat. 74, the manuscript's internal plate bears the inscription: "1639 a di 3 maggio questo manoscritto fu donata da sig[nore] Alessandro Cherubini a mons[ignore] Federico Ubaldini in Roma" ("on 3 May 1639 this manuscript was donated by Mr Alessandro Cherubini to Monsignor Federico Ubaldini in Rome"). On the work in question, see Harald Anderson, "Newly Discovered Metrical Arguments to the *Thebaid*," *Medieval Studies* 62 (2000): 219–253.

[9] Blom, "Lucas Holstenius," 29.

[10] See *Epistolae ad Diversos*, ed. Boissonade, 161; Johannes Kemke, *Patricius Junius, Bibliothekar der Könige Jacob I. und Carl I. von England: Mitteilungen aus Seinem Briefwechsel* (Leipzig: M[ax] Spirgatis, 1896; rpt Wiesbaden: Otto Harrassowitz, 1969), 52–64, 105–106; Blom, "Lucas Holstenius," 29–34.

[11] See Campbell and Corns, *Life, Work, and Thought*, 18, 123. Thus Isaac Vossius, in a letter (8 July 1651) to his regular correspondent, Nicolas Heinsius, reports that he had heard from his uncle Junius that Milton was a pupil of Patrick Young: *iam certior factus sum ab avunculo meo Iunio, qui cum eo familiaritatem colit. Is me significavit eum ... discipulum Patricii Iunii* ("I have received information from my uncle Junius, who cultivated a close friendship with him. He has indicated to me that he [Milton] ... was the pupil of Patrick Young") (*Sylloges Epistolarum a Viris Illustribus Scriptarum*, ed. Pieter Burman, 5 vols [Leiden: Samuel Luchtmans, 1727], III, 618). Although it is not impossible that "Patrick" is a slip for "Thomas," it seems very unlikely, as Campbell and Corns, *Life, Work, and Thought*, 389, aptly point out, that the otherwise astute Francis Junius would have "confused his fellow scholar-librarian Patrick Young with the Smectymnuan Thomas Young, who did not move in such circles." On Patrick Young's petitioning of Holstenius to make available to him the resources of the Vatican and Barberini Libraries, see Thomas Smith, *Vitae Quorundam Eruditissimorum et Illustrium Virorum* (London: David Mortier, 1707), s.v. *Vita Patricii Iunii*, 32: *Holstenium, imprimis sibi longo amicitiae usu coniunctissimum, cui Bibliothecae Vaticanae et Barberinae adyta reserata fuerant, crebris literis rogat, ut quicquid inibi elici possit, quod editioni suae ornandae conducat, et praesertim lectiones admodum vetusti codicis in Bibliotheca Barberina, XII Prophetas, una cum veterum Interpretum versionibus ad oram appositis, continentis, illico transmittantur* ("In frequent letters he requests of Holstenius [who had a particularly close and long-standing friendship with him, and to whom the

suggestion. Whatever the means of introduction, Milton took no small pride in the meeting. Later, in *Defensio Secunda*, when briefly describing his reception into intellectual circles in Rome, he would carefully single Holstenius out by name.[12] As Campbell and Corns remark, "the common interest in Hellenic scholarship seems to have been more powerful than the religious difference."[13] It is likely, too, that in the course of his Roman sojourns Milton had familiarized himself with several of Holstenius's published works in a manner not dissimilar to his practice in Florence,[14] and, especially, in Naples.[15] And they had other shared literary interests: Holstenius would contribute a Latin poem to the 1639 *Applausi Poetici alle Glorie della Signora Leonora Baroni*,[16] in praise of which soprano Milton, as we have seen, composed three Latin epigrams.[17]

---

sanctuaries of the Vatican and Barberini libraries had been made accessible] that anything that can be fetched from that place that might prove advantageous to the adorning of his own edition, and, especially, the readings of quite an ancient codex in the Barberini Library, containing the twelve Prophets, together with the marginal glosses of ancient interpreters, should there and then be sent along to him"). Milton would later send Patrick Young a volume (extant in Dublin: Trinity College, R.dd.39) containing ten of his tracts.

[12] Milton, *Defensio Secunda*, 84–85. See Appendix 2.23–26.

[13] Campbell and Corns, *Life, Work, and Thought*, 123.

[14] In Florence, Milton demonstrated his familiarity with the writings of Benedetto Buonmattei, addressee of *Epistola Familiaris* 8. See *Epistolarum Familiarium Liber Unus*, 20–25; *Epistolarum Familiarium Liber Unus and Uncollected Letters*, ed. Haan, 116–139, and, for the possibility that Milton had read works by Buonmattei, *ibid.*, 118, 132, 135. See also Cinquemani, *Glad to Go For a Feast*, 13–19; Haan, *Bilingualism*, 109, 113.

[15] In Naples, Milton seems to have taken particular care to familiarize himself with several volumes by Giovanni Battista Manso, addressee of *Mansus*. See 109.

[16] *Applausi*, 201–203.

[17] See Appendix 1.1(a)–1(c) and Chapter 2. Just as Holstenius views Leonora as a Siren (*pudica Siren* [1] ["modest Siren"]) and as the *Pulchrae Parthenopes canora proles* (2) ("tuneful offspring of beautiful Parthenope"), so Milton wonders *Credula quid liquidam Sirena, Neapoli, iactas,/Claraque Parthenopes fana Acheloidos? (Ad Leon.* 3. 1–2) ("Credulous Naples, why do you boast of your clear-voiced Siren, and of the famous shrine of Parthenope, daughter of Achelous?"), when, in fact, she has exchanged the murmurs of Posillipo for the pleasant waters of the Tiber (*Ad Leon.* 3. 5–6). In Holstenius's eyes, she possesses a *carmen flexanimum* (21) ("soul-swaying song"); for Milton, she could heal even Tasso's insanity by virtue of her *Flexanimo cantu* (*Ad Leon.* 2. 12) ("soul-swaying song"), on which see 126–130.

3.1 Milton in the Vatican

Certainly Milton seems to rejoice in Holstenius's hospitality, which included granting him admission to the Vatican Library.[18] Housed in Domenico Fontana's building, this was a Library that did not fail to impress foreign visitors. As John Evelyn proclaims:

> This Library is doubtlesse the most nobly built, furnish'd, and beautified in the World, ample, stately, light and cherefull, looking into a most pleasant Garden: The Walls and roofe are painted; not with Antiques, and Grotesc's (like our Bodlean at Oxford) but Emblemes, Figurs, Diagramms.[19]

Milton witnessed, and probably availed of, the Library's rich bibliographical resources, or, as he puts it, its *conquisitissimam librorum supellectilem* (8) ("most choice collection of books").[20] Here he would have had the opportunity to view precious codices regularly on display, among which were those of Virgil, the Bible, Terence, and Petrarch.[21]

---

[18] Milton, *Epistola Familiaris* 9: *in Musaeum comiter admisso* ("upon being granted courteous access to the Museum").

[19] John Evelyn, *Diary*, ed. De Beer, II, 300. Evelyn's account, here and elsewhere, is closely indebted to the description provided by Johann Heinrich von Pflaumern. Cf. Von Pflaumern, *Mercurius Italicus* (Augsburg: Andreas Aperger, 1625), 204: *Summe hilaris locus est et Musarum digna sedes. lucem amplissimis fenestris copiosam accipit, et e propinquis hortis suavem auram, quae libros legentesque recreat* ("The place is extremely cheerful, and the worthy dwelling-place of the Muses. It receives an abundance of light through its very large windows, and a sweet breeze from the nearby gardens, which refreshes the books and their readers"). See also note 21, with which cf. Evelyn, *Diary*, ed. De Beer, II, 301–302, quoted at 152.

[20] On the library's history, see, among others, Eugene Muentz and Paul Fabre, *La Bibliothèque du Vatican au XVe Siècle*, Bibliothèque des Écoles Françaises d'Athènes et de Rome, 48 (Paris: Thorin, 1887); Leonard Boyle, "Sixtus IV and the Vatican Library," in *Rome: Tradition, Innovation, and Renewal*, eds. Clifford M. Brown, John Osborne, and W. Chandler Kirwin (Victoria, BC: University of Victoria, 1991), 65–73; Leonard Boyle, "Niccolò V Fondatore della Biblioteca Vaticana," in *Niccolò V nel Sesto Centenario della Nascita*, eds. Franco Bonatti and Antonio Manfredi, Studi e Testi 397 (Vatican City: Biblioteca Apostolica Vaticana, 2000), 3–8; Carmela Vircillo Franklin, "'Pro Communi Doctorum Virorum Commodo': The Vatican Library and its Service to Scholarship," *Proceedings of the American Philosophical Society* 146 (2002): 363–384; Christopher S. Celenza and Bridget Pupillo, "Le Grandi Biblioteche 'Pubbliche' del XV Secolo," in *Atlante Storico della Letteratura Italiana*, eds. S. Luzzatto and G. Pedullà, 3 vols (Turin: Einaudi, 2010–2012), I, 312–321.

[21] See Von Pflaumern, *Mercurius Italicus*, 204: *binos Virgilios in membranis amplius mille ante annos scriptos; eiusdem vetustatis Terentium ... Biblia Graeca vetustissima in membranis exarata; Petrarchae epigrammata ipsiusmet manu scripta* ("two

And more than that: he was afforded the privilege of examining *permultos ... manuscriptos auctores Graecos* ("a great number of Greek authors in manuscript"), enhanced by Holstenius's painstaking annotations (*tuis lucubrationibus exornatos*), some of which, we are told, *expeditas modo typographi manus et μαιευτικὴν poscere videbantur*[22] ("seemed to be demanding the agile hands and the 'midwifery' of the printer"). Among these yet-to-be-printed volumes was, in all likelihood, Holstenius's Latin rendering (with copious annotation) of Arrian's Greek treatise on hunting. This work, which was currently in progress, would eventually see publication in Paris some five years later (in 1644).[23] Milton recounts, with a clear sense of pride, that he was presented with a *duplici dono* (16) ("a twofold gift") of one of Holstenius's printed works. Leo Miller made a very eloquent and seemingly persuasive case for the argument that the gifted volume in question was Holstenius's recently

---

volumes of Virgil in vellum written more than a thousand years previously, a Terence of the same archaic quality, ... an extremely ancient Greek bible inscribed on vellum, Petrarch's epigrams written in his very own hand").

[22] Milton, *Epistola Familiaris* 9. See Appendix 1.3.8–14. On Holstenius's meticulous editorial practices, especially in regard to annotation and commentary, cf. his address to the reader in *Sallustii Philosophi de Diis et Mundo* (Rome: Mascardi, 1638), 113: *Pauculis hisce foliis explendis loca quaedam ex Platonicis Philosophis, maxime autem Proclo, annotare libuit, quae uberrimi commentarii loco esse poterunt ad eruditum et elegantissimum hoc Opusculum illustrandum* ("In filling out these few little pages it has been my wish to annotate certain passages from the Platonic philosophers, but mostly from Proclus, which will be able to serve in the place of a most copious commentary, in order to illustrate this learned and most elegant little work"). On his linguistic talents, and, especially, his expertise in Greek, cf. Gabriel Naudaeus's letter to Holstenius in *Sallustii*, 3–10, at 8: *linguae siquidem Graecae peritissimus es* ("seeing that you are most skilled in the Greek language"); Jean-Pierre Nicéron, *Mémoires pour Servir à l'Histoire des Hommes Illustres dans la République des Lettres*, 44 vols (Paris: Briasson, 1727–1745), XXXI, 237–238: *varias quoque linguas* [sc. *tenuit*], *praeter Graecam Latinamque, quarum scriptoribus plurimum lucis attulit* ("[he possessed] also a variety of languages, besides Greek and Latin, upon whose writers he shed a great deal of light").

[23] Ἀρριανός Κυνηγετικός: *Arrianus De Venatione Luca Holstenio Interprete* (Paris: Sébastien and Gabriel Cramoisy, 1644). That Holstenius was probably still working on this project at the time of Milton's visit is suggested by the fact that the manuscript, extant as BAV Barb.gr.201, contains a dedicatory letter (ff. 1ʳ–2ᵛ) to Cardinal Antonio Barberini, dated just one year later (15 May 1640). However, the majority of Holstenius's editions would fail to see print. Cf. *The Literary Gazette, and Journal of the Belles Lettres*, 50 (January 3, 1818), 6: "the number of his publications does not answer to the prodigious extent of his knowledge ... he hurried, by the vivacity of his imagination, from one work scarcely sketched out, to another of a different kind." Holstenius bequeathed the bulk of his manuscripts to Cardinal Francesco Barberini.

published *Demophili Democratis et Secundi, Veterum Philosophorum Sententiae Morales* (Rome, 1638), his Latin rendering of the axioms of the later Pythagoreans.[24] Miller based his argument on his interpretation of the adjective *duplex* as Greek with facing Latin translation,[25] and also on his belief that this was "the only recent publication by Holstenius, and this after a lapse of eight years."[26] But several aspects of Milton's letter would seem to suggest Holstenius's *Porphyrii Philosophi Liber de Vita Pythagorae*, published in Rome in 1630,[27] as a more likely candidate. Also printed in type duplex,[28] this much more substantial volume contained materials pertaining (both directly and indirectly) to a *single* author (Porphyry), hence fitting more accurately Milton's description of the gift as *unius* (16) (sc. *auctoris*), as opposed to the multiauthored *Demophili Democratis et Secundi*. And it was *duplex* in another sense too, namely, its bipartite division into (i) Holstenius's Latin renderings of the Greek works in question, and (ii) Holstenius's original contributions: his *Dissertatio* on Porphyry's life and writings, and his notes on Porphyry's *Vita Pythagorae*. Thus Part 1 consists of Holstenius's Latin translation (on facing pages) of the following Greek works: (a) Porphyry, *De Vita Pythagorae*;[29] (b) an anonymous Greek life of Pythagoras;[30] (c) Porphyry, *Sententiae ad Intelligibilia Ducentes*, the second part of which is proudly announced as having been unearthed by Holstenius from among the holdings of the Vatican Library;[31] (d) Porphyry, *De Antro*

---

[24] This slim volume contains a dedicatory letter (to Carlo and Maffeo Barberini), dated 5 December 1638.

[25] Miller, "Milton and Holstenius," 574.

[26] Miller, "Milton and Holstenius," 574. In fact, Holstenius had also recently seen through press the *Sallustii Philosophi de Diis et Mundo* (1638), a Latin rendering (by Leone Allacci) of a treatise on the gods and the cosmos by the fourth-century philosopher Sallustius, augmented (at 113–119) by Hostenius's notes. See also note 22.

[27] Lucas Holstenius, *Porphyrii Vita Pythagorae* (Rome: Typis Vaticanis, 1630).

[28] Ancient Greek occurs on the even-numbered pages with Holstenius's facing Latin translation on the odd-numbered pages.

[29] *Porphyrii Philosophi sive Malchi De Vita Pythagorae Liber L[uca] Hostenio Interp[rete]* (1–42).

[30] *Incertus De Vita Pythagorae. Ex Photii Bibliotheca, Codice CCLIX. L[uca] Holstenio interp[rete]* (43–56).

[31] Entitled (with a separate title page) *Porphyrii Philosophi Sententiae ad intelligibilia ducentes. Quorum altera pars nunc primum prodit ex Bibliotheca Vaticana, Studio atque opera Lucae Holstenii* (57–98).

Nympharum;³² (e) *Alia Appendix Sententiarum*;³³ f) Porphyry, *De Styge*.³⁴ These constitute a mini-volume in their own right, followed, as they are, by an *Index Auctorum*³⁵ and *Index Rerum et Verborum Memorabilium*.³⁶ Then, in Part 2, carefully differentiated by separate title pages and pagination, there occur Holstenius's *Dissertatio de Vita et Scriptis Porphyrii Philosophi*,³⁷ and his *Observationes ad Vitam Pythagorae a Porphyrio Scriptam*.³⁸ It is alongside this volume in general, and Holstenius's *Observationes* in particular, that the quasi-Pythagoreanism of Milton's letter, and its occasional incorporation of Greek terms, can fruitfully be read.

Itemizing his experiences in Rome, Milton describes his attendance at a musical event, further discussed in the text that follows.³⁹ Without identifying the actual performance, he refers to it as ἀκρόαμα illud musicum ("that musical 'entertainment'").⁴⁰ The Greek noun, derived from ἀκροάομαι ("to listen"), occurs here in the sense of "anything heard, esp. with pleasure, piece read, recited, played or sung."⁴¹ A few sentences later, Milton wonders whether he is alone in experiencing his host's hospitality or whether, in respect of Holstenius devoting three (actually two) years to his literary studies at Oxford, it is his inclination to honor all Englishmen with courtesies of that nature. If the latter, then he is handsomely repaying to England the debts of his "schooling," here denoted by the Greek noun διδασκάλια (31) ("teaching" or "instruction").⁴² Milton's incorporation of these two Greek words is undoubtedly a compliment to his philhellenic addressee. But it also seems to assume additional force when examined in the more specific context of one of Holstenius's *Observationes*. It emerges that Holstenius

---

³² Entitled (with a separate title page) *Porphyrius Philosophus De Antro Nympharum libro XIII. Odysseae. Luca Holstenio Interprete* (99–135).

³³ *Alia Appendix Sententiarum sive graduum ad intelligibilia. Eruta ex M.S. codice, quem Cl[arissimus] V[ir] Aloysius Lolinus Belluensis Episcopus Bibliothecae Vaticanae legavit* (136–147).

³⁴ *Porphyrii Locus ex Libro De Styge* (149–153).

³⁵ *Ibid.*, 154–155.

³⁶ *Ibid.*, 156–169.

³⁷ *Ibid.*, [Part 2], 1–91.

³⁸ *Ibid.*, [Part 2], 93–122.

³⁹ See 154–165.

⁴⁰ See Appendix 1.3.19.

⁴¹ Liddell and Scott, s.v. 1.

⁴² See Appendix 1.3.27–31.

had in fact singled out these terms, and had commented on their associated etymology, and their implementation by a range of classical authors, including Nicomachus and Iamblichus:

> διδασκαλεῖον) ... nam Pythagorae scholam proprie διδασκαλεῖον appellant, ut Platonis Academiam, Aristotelis Lycaeum vel περίπατον, Epicuri hortos, Zenonis porticum. hinc sectatores Pythagorae οἱ ἀπὸ τοῦ Πυθαγορεικοῦ διδασκαλείου Nicomacho lib[ro] 1 harm[onici] [enchiridii] et Iamb[licho] lib[ro] i. c[apite] 23 et 28. atque alibi. sed ut a docendo διδασκαλεῖον, ita ab audiendo seu auscultando τὴν ἀκρόασιν τοῦ Πυθαγόρου vocat c[apite] 29 et saepius ὁμακόϊον.[43]

> διδασκαλεῖον) ... For they appropriately term the school of Pythagoras a διδασκαλεῖον, just as that of Plato an "Academy," that of Aristotle a Lycaeum or περίπατον, that of Epicurus "gardens," that of Zeno a "colonnade." Hence followers of Pythagoras are "those pertaining to the school of Pythagoras" in Nicomachus in book 1 of his *Enchiridion* and in Iamblichus in book 1, chapter 23 and 28, and elsewhere. But just as he terms it a διδασκαλεῖον after the verb "teaching," so he terms the "audience of Pythagoras" an ἀκρόασιν after the verb "hearing" or "listening" in chapter 29, and more frequently an ὁμακόϊον.

Holstenius's note is keyed to the noun διδασκαλεῖον, a term used by Porphyry to describe the "school" which was opened by Pythagoras in his native land, Ionia, upon his return from Egypt.[44] Now, however, in Milton's possible appropriation, that Pythagorean school is, as it were, Anglicized. This is achieved by its transmutation into the wide range of educational opportunities that were afforded Holstenius *outside* his native

---

[43] *Observationes*, 103–104. With Milton's choice of the adjective *musicum* (19) to describe the ἀκρόαμα in question, cf. Holstenius's rendering of τὸν κανόνα as *canonem musicum* at Porphyry, *De Vita Pythagorae*, 3, and his accompanying gloss at *Observationes*, 98, explaining his amplification by reference to Pythagoras's mathematical theory of music: τὸν κανόνα) *musicum scilicet. quod et in versione explicationis causa addidi. nam Laertius testatur Pythagoram canonem unius chordae invenisse* ("τὸν κανόνα] namely, of music. I have added this in my translation for the sake of explanation. For Laertius attests that Pythagoras invented the theory of a single chord"). Holstenius further explicates his rendering by recourse to a *Ms. Codex graecorum musicorum, quem Illustrissimi Card[inalis] Barberini instructissima bibliotheca mihi suppeditavit* (*Observationes*, 99) ("a Manuscript Codex of Greek music, with which the extremely well-equipped Library of the most distinguished Cardinal Barberini supplied me").

[44] Porphyry, *De Vita Pythagorae*, 6: ἐπανελθόντα δ'εἰς τὴν Ἰωνίαν, κατασκευάσαι ἐν τῇ πατρίδι διδασκαλεῖον, rendered by Holstenius as *Reversum autem in Ioniam, ludum in patria aperuisse* ("but having returned to Ionia, he opened a school in his native land").

land by England in general and by Oxford in particular during a two-year sojourn (1622–1624).⁴⁵ Likewise, that "audience of Pythagoras" is hereby recast as collective listeners to a seicento musical performance. Milton's implicit self-fashioning is as a scrupulous reader of Holstenius's work.

3.2 From *Katabasis* to *Anabasis*

But Milton's tribute moves beyond the linguistic to incorporate Holstenius's literary, and, more specifically, his Pythagorean interests. On this occasion, however, Pythagoras is read through a Virgilian lens.⁴⁶

---

[45] Arriving in Oxford on 27 June 1622, Holstenius was admitted to the Bodleian Library (Bodleian Library, MS Wood E5, f. 94), where for the next two years he undertook intensive research in connection with his planned edition of Greek geographers, a long-standing project, on which see Blom, "Lucas Holstenius," passim; Rietbergen, *Power and Religion*, 259–260. In the course of his residency at Oxford he collected the autograph of (*inter alios*) the Bodleian Librarian, John Rouse (to whom Milton would later send copies of his own poems and tracts). The autograph indicates that Holstenius was working in the Bodleian Library *c*. June–December 1622: *Habe, doctissime Luca, qualecunque amicitiae nostrae perpetuo uti spero duraturae symbolum; sed cum hoc, ut memor Bodleyanae quae te cultorem nobilem et assiduum per aliquot menses habuit lenias aliquando nobis desiderium tui, illius operis editione quod hic foeliciter meditatus es. Hoc a te rei pub[licae] literariae nomine peto Jo[annes] Rous inclytae Bodleyanae apud Oxon[iam] Custos Decemb[ris] 2 1622* (Österreichische Nationalbibliothek, Vienna: Sign. Cod. 9660, f. 177ʳ) ("Accept, most learned Lucas, a symbol of our friendship, which, as is my hope, will last for eternity; but with this condition: that mindful of the Bodleian, which has had you as its noble and constant inhabitant for some months, you may eventually alleviate my desire for you by the publication of that work which in this place you have been happily planning. This I ask of you in the name of the republic of letters, John Rouse, Guardian of the famous Bodleian at Oxford 2 December 1622"). Holstenius remained in England until October 1624. In a letter to Johannes Meursius, he summarizes with pleasure, and in idealistic language, his time in the Bodleian, and his associated investigation of Greek and Latin manuscripts: *Post meum a vobis discessum, Britannia suis deliciis ita me detinuit ut ad Lotophagos accessisse videar. Delitui ut plurimum in Oxoniensium bibliothecis, veteres codices Graecos Latinosque sedulo excutiens* (*Epistolae ad Diversos*, ed. Boissonade, 6–22, at 10) ("After my departure from you, Britain detained me with her delights in such a way that it seemed that I had reached the Lotus-eaters. For the most part I buried myself in the libraries of Oxford, assiduously scrutinizing ancient Greek and Latin codices"). Likewise, on 2 November 1624, he wrote from Paris to Patrick Young, describing with much enthusiasm the warm hospitality that he had received in London. See *Patricius Junius*, ed. Kemke, 52.

[46] Holstenius would doubtlessly have picked up Milton's Virgilianisms. For his own knowledge of the Virgilian corpus, see, for example, his citation of the *Aeneid* at *De Vita et Scriptis Porphyrii*, 49, and of the *Georgics* and the *Aeneid* at *Observationes*,

This is achieved by a reconfiguration of the *katabasis/anabasis* motifs in Virgil's *Aeneid*,[47] a subtext explicitly signaled by quotation of *Aeneid* 6. 679-680.[48] Thus the purported "reason" (*causa* [5]) for Milton's "ascent" (*Cum ... ascenderem* [5]) of the Vatican (namely, to see Holstenius)[49] is described in language that is evocative of Aeneas' experiences in the course of his "descent" into the underworld, a descent motivated by his express wish to see his father Anchises.[50] The fact that Milton, so he tells us, was *ignotum prorsus* (6) ("absolutely unknown") to his host serves perhaps to reinforce the analogy, as if in counter response to the question tellingly posed by Anchises to his son: *"datur ora tueri,/nate, tua et notas audire et reddere voces?"* (*Aen.* 6. 688-689) ("'Am I permitted to behold your face, my son, and to listen and reply to your *well-known*

108–109. Further, anecdotal, evidence is provided by Gilles Ménage, *Menagiana, ou Les Bons Mots*, ed. Bernard de la Monnoye, 4 vols (Paris: Veuve Delaulne, 1729), I, 222. Holstenius, while attending one of Cardinal Francesco Barberini's feasts, is purported to have broken wind. In response, the Cardinal smiled, as did the other guests, upon which Holstenius turned to him and uttered the Virgilian phrase: *Tu das epulis accumbere Divum* ("You grant me the right to recline at the feasts of the gods") (spoken by Aeolus, god of the winds, to Juno at *Aen.* 1.79), remarking that this tag was appropriate, but certainly not the following (adapted) Virgilian phrase: *Ventorum facis, tempestatumque potentem* ("You give me power over winds and storms"). The original reads *nimborumque facis tempestatumque potentem* (*Aen.* 1. 80) ("You give me power over clouds and storms"). The point of the joke resides in the substitution of Virgil's clouds by winds, over which Holstenius, a seventeenth-century Aeolus, seated though he is at the feasts of the gods (i.e., the Barberini), has no control!

[47] Cf. Virgil, *Aen.* 6. 126–129: *facilis descensus Averno/ ... /sed revocare gradum superasque evadere ad auras,/hoc opus, hic labor est* ("The descent to Avernus is easy ... but to retrace one's steps and to escape to the upper air, this is the task, this the toil"). For Milton's later reworking of these lines, cf. Moloch's misguided statements at *Paradise Lost* 2. 75–77: "That in our proper motion we *ascend*/Up to our native seat: *descent* and fall/To us is adverse", and, especially, 2. 81: "The *ascent* is *easy* then." Emphasis is mine. The motifs occur frequently in Petrarch's Latin letters. Cf., for example, *Rerum Familiarium* 1.3: *scio me ascendere ut descendam* ("I know that I am ascending in order to descend"); 7.7: *quamdiu hic sumus, cadimus quidem et resurgimus, descendimus et ascendimus* ("for as long as we are here, we do indeed fall and rise up again; we descend and ascend").

[48] See Appendix 1.3.12–13, and 150–153. On Milton's adaptation of these motifs in his hymn to light at *Paradise Lost* 3. 1–55, see Estelle Haan, "'Both English and Latin': Milton's Bilingual Muse," *RS* 21 (2007): 679–700, at 696–700; Haan, *Bilingualism*, 175–180.

[49] Appendix 1.3.5: *Cum enim tui conveniendi causa in Vaticanum ascenderem* ("For when I went up to the Vatican for the purpose of meeting you").

[50] Cf. Virgil, *Aen.* 6. 487–488: *iuvat ... / ... veniendi discere causas* ("they [souls of the Trojan dead] take delight ... in learning the reasons for his [Aeneas's] coming").

voice?'").[51] The Virgilian context is further suggested, and indeed enhanced, by the occurrence of a combination of several associated motifs: (a) receiving/admitting (*recepisti* [7]; *admisso* [8]; *admiserit* [21]);[52] (b) expecting/awaiting (*exspectans* [21]);[53] (c) virtual clasping by the hand (*paene manu prehensum* [21] ["almost clasping me by the hand"]);[54] (d) dismissal (*dimittor* [16] ["I am dispatched"]),[55] and (e) almost verbatim quotation of *Aen*. 6. 679–680. Thus manuscripts, annotated by Holstenius, and eagerly anticipated by his readers, resemble Virgilian souls, lingering by the river Lethe as they await rebirth:

> penitus convalle virenti
> inclusae animae, superumque ad limen iturae   (12–13)

> souls shut up deep within a green valley, and about
> to approach the threshold of the upper world.

---

[51] Emphasis is mine.

[52] Milton is "admitted" twice: by (1) Holstenius (to the Vatican Library); (2) Cardinal Francesco Barberini (to the theater of the Palazzo Barberini), on which see 154. Cf. the multiple "admissions" granted to Aeneas and others in the underworld: (1) Anchises to Aeneas at *Aen*. 6. 692–693: *"quas ego te terras et quanta per aequora vectum/accipio!"* ("'I receive you, borne through what lands and over how many seas!'"); (2) Charon at (a) *Aen*. 6. 315: *navita sed tristis nunc hos nunc accipit illos* ("but the stern boatman admits [to his boat] now some, now others"); (b) *Aen*. 6. 392–393: *"nec vero Alciden me sum laetatus euntem/accepisse lacu"* ("'and it gave me no joy to have received upon the lake even Hercules when he came here'"); (c) *Aen*. 6. 412–413: *accipit alveo/ingentem Aenean* ("he admitted on board his boat Aeneas in his bulk").

[53] Milton is "expected" by Cardinal Francesco Barberini at the theater door. Cf. Anchises to Aeneas at *Aen*. 6. 687–688: *"venisti tandem, tuaque exspectata parenti/vicit iter durum pietas?"* ("'Have you come at last, and has your sense of duty, awaited by your father, overcome the tough journey?'").

[54] The handshake is between Milton and Cardinal Francesco Barberini. Cf. Aeneas to Anchises at *Aen*. 6. 697–698: *"da iungere dextram,/da, genitor, teque amplexu ne subtrahe nostro"* ("'Father, let me, oh let me clasp your hand, and do not withdraw from my embrace'"). Milton's use of the adverb *paene* (21) ("virtually") to describe the handshake may also subtly evoke the elusive nature of Aeneas's attempted clasping of his father's ghostly shade at *Aen*. 6.700–702.

[55] Milton is "dispatched" from the Library by Holstenius, having been presented with one of his published books (perhaps as a parting gift). Cf. the final dispatching (through the ivory gate) of Aeneas and the Sibyl by Anchises, at *Aen*. 6. 897–898: *his ibi tum natum Anchises unaque Sibyllam/prosequitur dictis portaque emittit eburna* ("With these words Anchises accompanied his son there together with the Sibyl, and sent them out through the ivory gate"). Contrast Ovid, *Met*. 3. 695: *corpora tormentis Stygiae dimittite morti* ("Send the body of the tormented man [Acoetes] down to Stygian death").

In Milton's quotation, however, the Virgilian *lumen* ("light") is cited as *limen* ("threshold"). Although the confusion between *lumen* and *limen* is attested elsewhere in the Virgilian manuscript tradition,[56] all manuscripts are unequivocal in reading *ad lumen ituras* at 680. The Yale editors attempt to explain the seeming discrepancy by remarking: "It is impossible to say whether Milton's 'limen' is a misprint or a misquotation; the sense is different from Virgil's, but satisfactory."[57] But, given Milton's careful adaptation of Virgil's lines to accommodate his own Latin syntax,[58] it is likely that this is an adaptation, especially since the reading *limen* (not *lumen*) is clearly legible in the Vatican holograph of the present letter. If so, several interpretations are possible.

Perhaps the substitution (if such it is) may be influenced by the fact that *ad limen ituras* had occurred in Stephanus Depleurre, *Aeneis Sacra* (1618), in the context of a punning description of Limbo and its inhabitants.[59] Or perhaps, as John Hale speculates, *limen* denotes "books (personified) coming out of a private interior, over its threshold and out into the public world; or even undergoing a rite of passage."[60] Alternatively, the textual change, if such it is, might suggest, and indeed foreshadow, a Miltonic alertness to printing procedures that would manifest itself most conspicuously in *Areopagitica* (1644). Holstenius's manuscripts, envisaged as on the verge of engaging with the printing press, are hereby depicted as ready to succumb to the printing impression physically imposed from above (*superum ... limen*). If so, Milton may be appropriating the Roman lintel (termed *limen superum* to distinguish it from the door-sill/threshold (termed *limen inferum*)[61] to describe the wooden rectangular platen, which was screwed down from above and

---

[56] See, for example, Virgil, *Aen.* 6. 255: *ecce autem primi sub lumina solis et ortus* ("then, behold, just before the first gleam of the sun's rising"), where some manuscripts read *limina*.

[57] *Milton's Private Correspondence*, eds. Arthur Turner and Alberta T. Turner in *The Complete Prose Works of John Milton*, ed. Don M. Wolfe, 8 vols (New Haven, CT: Yale University Press, 1953) I, 333.

[58] Virgil's accusatives are transformed into nominatives.

[59] See Stephanus Depleurre, *Aeneis Sacra Continens Acta Domini Nostri Iesu Christi* (Paris: Adrian Taupinart, 1618), 24.

[60] John K. Hale, "Milton's reading of Virgil's *Aeneid* VI. 680 in his Letter to the Vatican Librarian," *N&Q* 49 (2002): 336.

[61] Cf. Plautus, *Most.* 5.1.1: *limen superum inferumque salve* ("Hail, lintel and door-sill!").

pressed against the inked paper, which, in turn, was pressed over the letters placed within a form.[62]

The description of the manuscripts/souls as *inclusae* ("shut up") may also hint at the Vatican Library's practice of locking up and segregating its precious holdings,[63] or, as John Evelyn relates:

> As to the ranging of the bookes, they are all shut up in Presses of Wainscot, and not expos'd on shelves to the naked ayre; nor are the most precious mix'd amongst the more ordinary, which are shew'd to the curious onely; Such as are those two Virgils written in Parchment, of more then a thousand yeares old; the like a Terence: The Acts of the Apostles in Golden Capital Letters: Petrarchs Epigramms written with his owne hand: Also an Hebrew Parchment made up in the antient manner from whence they were first cal'd Volumina.[64]

In Milton's appropriation Vatican manuscripts are envisaged as pregnant souls demanding purification by the hands of the printer as midwife, and eventual delivery into the world as printed books (*expeditas modo typographi manus et μαιευτικὴν poscere videbantur* [14] ["they seemed to be demanding the agile hands and the 'midwifery' of the printer"]). The analogy is enhanced by the description of a further category of manuscripts (those edited by Holstenius) as *tua opera etiamnum editi* (15) ("already edited by your endeavors"). This may draw upon the twofold meaning of the verb *edere* as "To bring forth (offspring), give birth to; so *edere in lucem*"[65] and "(of an author or editor) To publish (writings)."[66] The whole develops perhaps Anchises's quasi-Pythagorean explication of the doctrine of the transmigration of souls as *"animae, quibus altera fato/corpora debentur"* (*Aen.* 6. 713–714) ("'souls, to whom a second body is owed by fate'"). After all, as Milton would later proclaim:

---

[62] On the use of *limen* in a printing context, cf. Andrew Marvell, *Dignissimo Suo Amico Doctori Wittie* 17, who, in a wish for the safe-keeping of his page, proclaims: *hunc subeas librum sancti ceu limen asyli* ("may you enter this book as though it were the threshold of a hallowed sanctuary"). See Haan, *Andrew Marvell's Latin Poetry*, 107.

[63] Cf. Von Pflaumern, *Mercurius Italicus*, 204: *Pretiosissimi ac vetustissimi Codices, separati a reliquo grege, ligneis armariis clausi asservantur* ("The most precious and most ancient codices are separated from the rest of the stock, and are protected, shut up in wooden book-presses").

[64] John Evelyn, *Diary*, ed. De Beer, II, 301–302.

[65] *OLD*, s.v. 2a.

[66] *OLD*, s.v. 9.

> Books are not absolutely dead things, but doe contain a potencie of life in them to be as active as that soule was whose progeny they are; nay they do preserve as in a violl the purest efficacie and extraction of that living intellect that bred them.[67]

It is worth emphasizing, too, that midwifery frequently functions as a Platonic metaphor for the philosopher's dialectical method of bringing to birth the ideas of others.[68] Thus Socrates, in the *Theaetetus*, describes himself as the son of a midwife and as "midwife" to Theaetetus and to other youths who are philosophically "pregnant."[69] Likewise, in the *Symposium*, he repeats the suggestion of Diotima of Mantinea that the soul is pregnant with prudence and virtue, begotten by poets *inter alia*, and eager to deliver, but that the delivery of a long-felt conception requires assistance.[70] One senses that the inference would not have been missed by Holstenius as someone forever interested in Socratic, Platonic, and Neoplatonic writings.

The lines may assume one final, additional, force when read in a more contemporary context. The disorganized state of the *Typographia Vaticana*, the Vatican Library's Press, had recently raised the concerns of both Cardinal Francesco Barberini and Holstenius, the latter voicing his complaints in a letter (dated 4 December 1636) to his friend Peiresc.[71] This in turn had resulted in a Barberini initiative in 1638 to establish a Latin and Greek Press, the director of which was to be Holstenius himself.[72]

---

[67] *Areopagitica*, 4.

[68] See David Sedley, *The Midwife of Platonism: Text and Subtext in Plato's Theaetetus* (Oxford: Clarendon Press, 2006); J. B. McMinn, "Plato's Mantic Myths in the Service of Socrates' Maieutic art," *Kernos* 3 (1990): 219–234; K. M. Sayre, "A Maieutic View of Five Late Dialogues," in *Methods of Interpreting Plato and his Dialogues*, eds. J. C. Klagge and N. D. Smith (Oxford: Clarendon Press, 1992), 221–243; Fiona Leigh, "Platonic Dialogue, Maieutic Method, and Critical Thinking," *Journal of Philosophy of Education* 41 (2007): 209–223. Cf. also Milton, *The Doctrine and Discipline of Divorce* (London: T.P. and M.S., 1644), sig. A2^v: "till Time the Midwife rather than the mother of Truth, have washt and salted the Infant, declar'd her legitimat, and Churcht the father of his young Minerva, from the needlesse causes of his purgation."

[69] Plato, *Theaetetus*, 149e–151e.

[70] Plato, *Symposium* 209 a–c.

[71] See *Epistolae ad Diversos*, ed. Boissonade, 274–280. As suggested by Rietbergen, *Power and Religion*, 273, Holstenius was "perhaps, complaining on the basis of his experiences with his Porphyrius-edition."

[72] Although some doubt still remains in regard to the precise details surrounding the printing initiative in question, it is clear that the planned location of the Latin and Greek Press was to be none other than Cardinal Francesco Barberini's official

3.3 Milton at the Opera

Milton's letter also places its author among Rome's elite musical circles. This is attested by his aforementioned revelation that he attended an ἀκρόαμα ... *musicum* (19) ("musical 'entertainment'"), which, he states, was presented to the public *magnificentia vere Romana* (19-20) ("with truly Roman magnificence"). The reference is, in all likelihood, to the comedic pastoral opera *Chi Soffre Speri* ("He who suffers, may hope"), which was lavishly put on by Cardinal Antonio Barberini on 17/27 February 1639 to inaugurate the recently completed theater contiguous to the Palazzo Barberini at the Quattro Fontane.[73] The realization of this building project was certainly a cause of celebration, and much more. It served as a strong statement of, and ample testimony to, the prestigious status of the Barberini, who, as Frederick Hammond notes, "by constructing a monumental court theater ... proclaimed themselves a ruling house ranking with the Medici and the Farnese."[74] But it also signaled papal power.

In the immediate weeks leading up to the production there was undoubtedly an air of excitement in the city. Rehearsals (to lute accompaniment) were being held on a regular basis,[75] while the final touches were being put to the set. This was designed by none other than the masterful craftsman Bernini himself, and painted in the Vatican, before being transported across to the theater only at the last minute, probably to preserve the element of surprise.[76] Milton's term *magnificentia* (19), encapsulating the extravagance surrounding the production, is one that was employed by other eyewitnesses, such as Lelio Guidiccioni, who offers glowing praise of the lavish performance

---

residence, the Palazzo della Cancellaria. Holstenius was requested to investigate the costs of running the project, and wrote to Barberini, estimating the sum of 400 *scudi*. See Rietbergen, *Power and Religion*, 272–273. Interestingly, the holograph of Milton's letter is addressed: "Holstenio nel Palazzo / Roma" ("To Holstenius in the Palace / Rome") which, as noted by Bottkol, "Holograph," 623, signals "not ... the Palazzo Barberini in the Via delle Quattro Fontane, but rather the official residence of Cardinal Francesco Barberini in the Cancellaria, near the Campo de' Fiori."

[73] See Leila Zammar, *Scenography at the Barberini Court in Rome: 1628–1656* (PhD thesis: University of Warwick, 2017), 163–164, 175–182.

[74] Hammond, *Music and Spectacle*, 235.

[75] See Lorenzo Bianconi and Thomas Walker, "Production, Consumption and Political Function of Seventeenth-Century Opera," *Early Music History* 4 (1984): 209–296, at 219.

[76] See Lewis, "*Chi Soffre Speri*," 85; Zammar, *Scenography at the Barberini Court*, 180–181.

and its spectacular staging.⁷⁷ Because of the significance of the 1639 occasion we are fortunate to have a host of important records of expenditure that offer an interesting glimpse into the staging, the acting, and the music. Bills are recorded for clouds, painted perspectives, and dimmers for lights, and expenditure on shoes and hats suggests that there were at least twenty-four singers and dancers.⁷⁸ The extravaganza was certainly *musicum*, as described by Milton, enhanced, as it was, by its incorporation of instrumental combinations that were, to say the least, imaginatively wide-ranging. This is evinced by records pertaining to continuo instruments, two harpsichords, two violoni, two lutes, a harp, a cetra, violins, players on the cittern, bagpipe, cifalo, Jews' harp, and even "one who whistles like a nightingale."⁷⁹ As for the opera itself, this had been revised and substantially augmented from its first production on 12 February 1637.⁸⁰ It consisted of libretto by Cardinal Giulio Rospigliosi (the future Pope Clement IX), and music by the highly esteemed composer, Virgilio Mazzocchi, whose contribution was very substantial,⁸¹ in collaboration with Marco Marazzoli, whose input amounted to at least the music for the *intermedio* to Act II.⁸² Extant in a

---

⁷⁷ See Lelio Guidiccioni, *Cardinalis Antonii Barberini Magnificentia: Scenica Spectacula Exhibet*, in Girolamo Teti, *Aedes Barberinae ad Quirinalem* (Rome: Mascardus, 1642), 123–124.

⁷⁸ See Frederick Hammond, "Bernini and the 'Fiera di Farfa,'" in *Gianlorenzo Bernini: New Aspects of his Art and Thought*, ed. Irving Lavin (University Park, PA: Pennsylvania State University Press, 1985), 115–125, at 119.

⁷⁹ Hammond, "Bernini and the 'Fiera di Farfa,'" 119.

⁸⁰ See Murata, *Operas*, 32–34, and, for cast and plot summary of the 1639 version, and a list of documents pertaining to both the 1637 and 1639 performances, *ibid.*, Appendix I: D, at 258–288. See also Hugo Goldschmidt, *Studien zur Geschichte der Italienischen Oper im 17. Jahrhundert* (Leipzig: Breitkopf and Härtel, 1901), I, 90–92; Stuart Reiner, "Collaboration in *Chi Soffre Speri*," *MR* 22 (1961): 265–282.

⁸¹ Virgilio Mazzocchi (1597–1646) was both talented and prolific. In addition to his contribution to *Chi Soffre Speri*, he composed music for the sacred opera *L'innocenza Difesa* (1641), likewise performed at the Palazzo Barberini. Among his other music is a series of concertato motets (*Sacrae Flores*, 1640) and double-choir liturgical music (*Psalmi Vespertini*, 1648), as well as a wide range of madrigals, oratorios, and operas. See Julie Anne Sadie, *Companion to Baroque Music* (Berkeley: University of California Press, 1998), 66.

⁸² Marco Marazzoli (1602–1662) was a priest who was highly regarded for the breadth and quality of his musicianship. A talented singer, and virtuoso harpist, he was also the composer of cantatas, of which no fewer than 379 survive. In 1631 he had become attached to the musical establishment of Cardinal Antonio Barberini in Rome, eventually settling there in 1637 upon his appointment to a post in the papal chapel. In addition to his collaborative contribution to *Chi Soffre Speri*, Marazzoli would later compose an opera *L'Armida* (1641), a "festa teatrale," entitled *Gli Amori*

clean manuscript score,[83] together with the 1639 printed *Argomento*,[84] and a 1667 manuscript libretto,[85] this lengthy entertainment both captivated and mesmerized its audience. Or, as the *Avvisi* proclaim: "ancorchè duri per lo spatio di 5 hore nondimeno pare a' spettatori un momento tanto"[86] ("even though it lasted for five hours, it seemed nonetheless but a moment to the spectators").

The event certainly stretched the newly built theater's seating capacity (of up to 4,000) to breaking point, and it did so not without some chaos. One eye-witness, Raimondo Montecuccoli, emissary of the Duke of Modena, estimated that audience-numbers amounted to some 3,500, and proceeded to describe how Cardinal Antonio stood in person at the door because of the extent of the crowd, while both he and his brother Cardinal Francesco made every effort to accommodate as many people as possible.[87] Thus, he reports, Francesco went from row to row, politely ensuring that everyone squeezed up as tightly as possible, and, in so doing, he facilitated the accommodation of a further 600 people.[88] And

---

di Giasone e d'Issifile (1642), *La Pretensioni del Tebro e del Po* (1643), and *Il Capricio* (1643). See Sadie, *Companion to Baroque Music*, 65–66.

[83] BAV Barb.lat. 4386. For a facsimile, see Virgilio Mazzocchi and Marco Marazzoli, *L'Egisto overo Chi Soffre Speri*, intro. Howard Mayer Brown, *Italian Opera, 1640–1770*, ser. 2, vol. 61 (New York: Garland, 1982).

[84] *Argomento et Allegoria della Comedia Musicale Intitolata Chi Soffre Speri* (Rome: Camera Apostolica, 1639).

[85] BAV Vat.lat. 13340. For facsimiles of the libretto and the 1639 *Argomento*, see *Italian Opera Librettos: 1640–1770*, vol. 14, ed. Howard Mayer Brown (New York: Garland, 1983).

[86] BAV Urb.lat.1107: *Avvisi di Roma*, f. 39ᵛ (5 March 1639). See Alessandro Ademollo, *I Teatri di Roma nel Secolo Decimosettimo* (Rome: Pasqualucci, 1888), 29.

[87] Raimondo Montecuccoli, Letter (2 March 1639) to the Duke of Modena: "Cardinale Antonio, che stava in persona alla porta, per una grandissima calca … Il sig[nor] Card[inale] Barberino et il sig[nor] Card[inale] Antonio travagliarono assaissimo per accomodar quanta più gente fusse possibile, e si figura, ch' ascendessero a 3m[ille] e cinquecento persone" ("Cardinal Antonio, who stood in person at the door; on account of the huge crowd … Cardinal Barberini and Cardinal Antonio labored very hard to accommodate as many people as possible, which, it is estimated, rose to three thousand, five hundred"). See Ademollo, *Teatri*, 28–29.

[88] Raimondo Montecuccoli, Letter (2 March 1639): "il sig[nor] card[inale] Barberino (Francesco) il quale andato a banco per banco et con modi humanissimi, e di somma cortesia, fece, per quanto era possibile, stringer ognuno, che fu cagione, che vi capirono da 600 persone di più" ("Cardinal Barberini [Francesco] who proceeded from bench to bench and with the most dignified manners and the utmost courtesy made everyone squeeze up as much as possible, which was the reason that a further 600 people were accommodated"). See Ademollo, *Teatri*, 30–31.

Antonio was even seen beating with a stick a well-dressed young man, whom he accused of insolence![89] According to Milton, however, it was Francesco who waited at the door, seeking him out *tanta in turba* (20) ("in so great a crowd"), shaking his hand, and granting him admission in an extremely courteous manner (*persane honorifice intro admiserit* [21]).[90] As the unofficial Cardinal patron of England and Scotland, Francesco was certainly proactive in his hospitable reception of English travelers to Rome.[91] And the present instance seems to have been no exception.

No doubt Milton was supplied with one of the 3,980 copies of the opera's libretto printed for the occasion, and bound in colored paper,[92] or perhaps, singled out, as he seems to have been, he was the privileged recipient of one of the 100 more expensive copies of the printed *Argomento*, presented to the more distinguished members of the audience.[93] These were adorned with gilt ornamentation and bound in "carta turchesa." Caroline Castiglione observes that "[a] copy of the libretto might have been handy for following the plot," which, in her view, "like other operas of the period, lacked 'linear logic.'"[94] Perhaps, however, it had much to offer the author of *Arcades* and *A Mask*, not least in terms of dramaturgical potential.

---

[89] Raimondo Montecuccoli, Letter (2 March 1639): "Io vedemmo di li a poco entrare nel salone et quasi subito uscirne con uno che si andava spingendo innanzi et bravandogli aspramente e sentii in particolare che gli disse: ti insegnerò ben io di far l'insolente; e poi di suo pugno lo battè assai forte con un bastone che haveva in mano e furono cinque o sei colpi" ("A little later I saw him enter the hall and almost immediately come out with someone who was pushing his way forward and behaving with roughness and bravado, and I noticed in particular that he said to him 'I will teach you a good lesson on how to be insolent'; and then he beat him very hard with a stick that he had in his hand, and there were five or six strokes"). See Ademollo, *Teatri*, 30.

[90] See Appendix 1.3.20–21.

[91] Thus Thomas Windebank, writing from Rome to his father on 10 September 1636, states: "I have been to visit the Cardinal Barberino, who, having notice of my arrival here, sent to visit me first. He is so obliging and courteous to all our nation that I have the less wonder at the honour he doth me." See Masson, *Life*, I, 748.

[92] Hammond, "Bernini and the 'Fiera di Farfa,'" 119.

[93] Lewis, "*Chi Soffre Speri*," 85.

[94] Caroline Castiglione, *Patrons and Adversaries: Nobles and Villagers in Italian Politics, 1640–1760* (Oxford: Oxford University Press, 2005), 27.

3.4 *Magnificentia Romana* and Metatheater

Milton's description of the production of the opera in question tellingly qualifies the noun *magnificentia* by the adjective *Romana*. Margaret Byard imagines his "amazement ... as he would inevitably contrast the splendor of the Barberini theater with any similar structure in London."[95] Rome, after all, afforded dramatists the opportunity to create and replicate effects unachievable in seventeenth-century London or Ludlow. Although Inigo Jones had traveled to Italy just one year earlier, and had returned to England with imaginative theatrical sketches and theories, it would take some time for their acceptance and eventual realization.[96] Central to Roman spectacle was verisimilitude. And central to verisimilitude was the innovative stagecraft of Bernini. During the carnival season of 1638, for example, Bernini's *Inondazione della Tevere*, as noted earlier, had presented boats sailing on real water upon a recreated Tiber in inundation, submerging houses, and seeming to spill out over terrified spectators,[97] all this just one year after the actual flooding of the river. But, according to his biographer, Filippo Baldinucci, it was his stage design for the "Fiera di Farfa" of *Chi Soffre Speri* that would earn Bernini eternal fame:

> Vivera sempre al Mondo la fama della sua Commedia della Fiera, fatta per il Cardin[ale] Antonio in tempo di Urbano.[98]

> The fame of his Comedy of the Fair produced for Cardinal Antonio in the time of [Pope] Urban, will always live in the world.

Involving figurines representing actual people, and presenting live animals on stage, "the entire spectacle," as Hammond remarks "was designed to involve the viewer by its verisimilitude, which was sometimes carried to the point of seeming to threaten him with real physical danger."[99] In short, it provided for its large audience an experience that was essentially metatheatrical.

---

[95] Byard, "'Adventrous Song,'" 316.

[96] See John G. Demaray, *Milton's Theatrical Epic: The Invention and Design of Paradise Lost* (Cambridge MA: Harvard University Press, 1980), 25.

[97] See 96–97.

[98] Baldinucci, *Vita del Cavaliere Gio[vanni] Lorenzo Bernino*, 77. As Hammond observes, Baldinucco was the first to attribute the staging to Bernini. See Hammond, "Bernini and the 'Fiera di Farfa,'" 117.

[99] Hammond, "Bernini and the 'Fiera di Farfa,'" 119.

Following the three-act structure of secular plays of the Commedia dell' arte, *Chi Soffre Speri* is loosely based on a scene in Boccaccio, *Decameron* 9. Set in fourteenth-century Tuscany, it takes as its focal point Boccaccio's impoverished hero Egisto (whose sole possessions amount to his land, a very ugly tower, and a beloved falcon) and his love for the wealthy widow Alvida, whose son is dying. Although hitherto rejecting Egisto's suit, Alvida announces her wish to dine with him. Eager to provide a feast for his visitor, Egisto orders the sacrifice of his falcon. Upon her arrival, Alvida expresses her horror at Egisto's tower, in response to which he has it torn down. It is only after dinner that the real motivation for her visit becomes apparent: her wish to acquire the falcon for her son. Egisto is overwhelmed by grief at the sheer futility of his sacrificial act. To this main plot are added several subplots concerning unrequited love: that of Dorillo for Eurilla (who is in love with Armindo), that of Armindo (in reality a disguised woman Lucinda) for Egisto. Hearing that Alvida is dining with Egisto, Armindo/Lucinda decides to commit suicide, and falls down senseless. When this news reaches Egisto, he fears the worst, believing that all hope is lost. But in a sudden turn of events his misfortunes are stunningly reversed. Thus, in a series of seemingly magical discoveries, a gleaming bloodstone is found in the breast of the dead falcon. This is discovered to be a heliotrope with restorative powers, which is brought to Alvida's son, who thereupon recovers.[100] Then Egisto suddenly uncovers a trove of precious jewels among the ruins of his tower. This solves his financial worries.[101] It also emerges that Armindo/Lucinda is not in fact dead, but has merely fainted. These unexpected outcomes resoundingly attest to the eponymous adage "Chi Soffre Speri," as is aptly summarized in the *Argomento* to Act III, sc. 13:

---

[100] See *Argomento*, 14: "SCENA NONA. *Clori, & i medesimi*. Vien portata una lucidissima gemma trovatasi nel petto dell' estinte Falcone: E si riconosce per Elitropio di singolar virtù contro l'infermità; che però è subito inviato al figliolo d'Alvida" ("NINTH SCENE: *Chloris and the same characters*. There is brought forth a most shining gem, found in the breast of the deceased Falcon. And this is recognized as a Heliotrope of exceptional power in the face of infirmity, but it is immediately sent to Alvida's son").

[101] See *Argomento*, 15: "SCENA DECIMA. *Egisto, e sopradetti*. Riceve Egisto una ricchissima Arca scoperta pur all'hora fra le ruine della sua Torre, & apertala vi trova gran quantità di pretiosissime gemme, con una memoria postavi dal Padre" ("TENTH SCENE: *Egisto and the aforementioned characters*. Egisto is the recipient of a very rich chest discovered even at the hour amidst the ruins of his Tower, and when he opens it, he finds a large quantity of very precious jewels, together with a memento placed there by his Father").

> S'intende da lui, come per occulta forza dell' Elitropio il figliolo d'Alvida era restato libero dalla sua grave infirmità; onde tutti si muovono lieti per vederlo, e per ritrovar Lucinda; concludendo per tanti, e sì nuovi accidenti d'Amore, e di Fortuna, che in qualsivoglia successo CHI SOFFRE SPERI.[102]
>
> It is understood from this how by the hidden force of a Heliotrope Alvida's son had remained free from his serious infirmity; whence all proceed with joy in order to see him and to find Lucinda; with the conclusion, in view of so many and so unprecedented accidents of Love and of Fortune, that in any outcome HE WHO SUFFERS MAY HOPE.

Finally, Alvida is so touched by Egisto's acts of sacrifice that she declares her love. As both lovers plan to marry, the whole ends happily in a celebratory *intermedio*, entitled "Fiori," for which some 5,000 flowers were procured.[103] In short, the opera never fails to surprise its audience, and it does so on a variety of levels.

Drawing upon such Renaissance entertainments as the *intermedio* (a spectacular celebration of marriage etc.), the *pastorale* (a bucolic drama abounding in song and dance), and the *mascherata* (featuring festive dancing combined with drama),[104] *Chi Soffre Speri* experiments with genre in ways that are both creative and surreal.[105] Advertised in its printed *Argomento* as a "comedia musicale,"[106] and variously described by critics as a "comic opera,"[107] a "sentimental tragicomedy,"[108] and a "transference of the mask tradition of the Commedia dell' arte into opera,"[109] the piece's vacillating generic status is helpfully elucidated by Emily Wilbourne:

> Strictly speaking, *Chi soffre speri* is not a "comedy," which would require an urban setting. More properly, the story

---

[102] *Argomento*, 15.

[103] As is indicated by the expense records for the 1639 production.

[104] See Lewis, "*Chi Soffre Speri*," 10–11.

[105] See Simona Santacroce, "Un Melodramma Ridicoloso del 'Papa Comico': *Chi Soffre Speri*," *SS* 53 (2012): 53–88.

[106] Title page of the 1639 *Argomento*.

[107] Lewalski, *Life*, 100; Campbell and Corns, *Life, Work, and Thought*, 122.

[108] Hammond, *Music and Spectacle*, 226.

[109] Nino Pirrotta, "Commedia dell' arte and Opera," in his *Music and Culture in Italy From the Middle Ages to the Baroque: A Collection of Essays* (Cambridge MA: Harvard University Press, 1984), 343–360, at 355.

> belongs to a genre that Andreini would have labeled "commedia boschereccia," in which fields and glades substitute for the streets and windows of the comic stage sets, and shepherds and shepherdesses for the folk of the town. Such plays lay midway between the comedy proper and the pastoral play (which was set in Arcadia and included gods, heroes, nymphs and satyrs among the cast).[110]

But perhaps it was the opera's lavish theatrical effects that seem to have left the greatest impression upon the audience. The 1639 production capably demonstrated the *magnificentia* afforded by splendid costumes, excellent acting ability, dancing (closing each of the *intermedi*), highly elaborate staging, and, above all, the essential verisimilitude achievable on dramaturgical, linguistic, and musical levels.[111] Thus Montecuccoli praises the whole

> per la vaghezza della scena, per la varietà, bizzarria e ricchezza de' vestiti, per l'esquisitezza de' recitanti, e musici ... per la novità et artificio delle prospettive.[112]

> for the beauty of the set, for the variety, eccentricity, and richness of the costumes, for the exquisiteness of the performers and musicians ... for the novelty and artifice of the perspective scenes.

Likewise, the *Avvisi di Roma* (5 March 1639) attest to "l'ecc[ellenz]a de recitanti, ricchezze d'habiti, vaghezze delle scene, et mutatione d'intermedii"[113] ("the excellence of the performers, the richness of the costumes, the beauty of the scenery, and the variety of *intermedi*"). In fact, the staging created quite a sensation in its day, not least in its realistic portrayal of a spectacular thunderstorm:

> Vi fu anche un improviso imbunimento d'aria con lampi, tuoni, et un fulmine, che passò per la scena, e successe parimente grandine, e pioggia.[114]

---

[110] Emily Wilbourne, *Seventeenth-Century Opera and the Sound of the Commedia dell'Arte* (Chicago: The University of Chicago Press, 2016), 202.

[111] See *Enciclopedia dello Spettacolo*, eds. Silvio D'Amico and Sandro D'Amico, 9 vols (Rome: Casa Editrice Le Maschere, 1954), II, 374–375.

[112] Raimondo Montecuccoli, Letter (2 March 1639). See Ademollo, *Teatri*, 28.

[113] *Avvisi di Roma*: 5 March 1639. See Ademollo, *Teatri*, 29.

[114] Raimondo Montecuccoli, Letter (2 March 1639). See Ademollo, *Teatri*, 28.

> There was also an unexpected darkening of the air with lightning, thunder, and a lightning-bolt which crossed the stage, followed equally by hail and rain.

But of particular note was a magnificent "Fair of Farfa," which was composed especially for the 1639 production.[115] This, according to the *Avvisi* was:

> così ben disposta che contiene artisti et mercanti d'ogni sorte, che parlando in musica vanno procurando di vendere le merci, et opere loro, ma di più vi vengono alcuni mercanti a cavallo parimente veri, vi si vede parimente il passaggio di carrozze et il corso d'un palio[116]

> so well arranged that it contains artisans and merchants of every kind, who, speaking in music, go about trying to sell their wares and their products, but there are also some merchants on horseback, who are equally real; one can see the procession of carriages and the running of a *palio*

or as Montecuccoli puts it:

> un carro tirato da buovi, una lettiga condotta da muli con un persona dentro, uno sopra un cavallo che la seguitava et ogni cosa era vera e viva.[117]

> a wagon drawn by oxen, a litter carried by mules with a person inside, someone who followed it on horseback, and everything true and life-like.

Further details are provided by *Avvisi* records extant in the Biblioteca Nazionale, Naples:

> apparente prospettive et intermedii meravigliosi e gustosissimi con balli di ninfe e pastori, mutationi di tempi in grandini et in pioggia et in particolare fu rappresentata una

---

[115] This fair (the *intermedio* to Act II) replaced the May festival *intermedio* of the 1637 production. See Hammond, "Bernini and the 'Fiera di Farfa,'" passim; Zammar, *Scenography at the Barberini Court*, 183–190.

[116] *Avvisi di Roma*: 5 March 1639. See Ademollo, *Teatri*, 29; Hammond, "Girolamo Frescobaldi and a Decade of Music," 113.

[117] Raimondo Montecuccoli, Letter (2 March 1639). See Ademollo, *Teatri*, 28. The essential realism of the whole, as aptly noted by Hammond, was enhanced by the fact that Cardinal Francesco Barberini was Abbot of the great Benedictine abbey of Farfa, and that items for his household were actually purchased at the real fair of Farfa. See Hammond, "Bernini and the 'Fiera di Farfa,'" 119.

> fiera col concorso di varie genti anche in carozza et a cavallo con conversatione per accidente nati in un ballo e questione con spade di filo e prospettive di distanza lontanissima illuminate da un sole che sol suo giro a poco a poco.[118]

> perspective scenes and wonderful and pleasing *intermedi* with dances of nymphs and shepherds, and the change of the weather into hail and rain. And, in particular, there was represented a fair with the concourse of various people both in carriages and on horseback with a conversation arising by chance during a dance, and a quarrel with thin swords, and perspective scenes of the farthest distances illuminated by a sun which, as it turned, descended little by little.

Indeed, it was the representation of a rising and setting sun that constituted one of the most stunning aspects of the staging:

> vidisses exorientem primo Solem, nocturnasque tenebras fugantem; mox se paulatim ex undis attollentem, atque adeo artificiose omnia illustrantem, ut qui modo Theatrum ingressi, eundem vere occidentem reliquerant, retrogradum facile crederent; quasi novas Nundinas, quae ibi iucundissime, ad veri ipsissimam imaginem, exhibebantur, lustraturus.[119]

> you would have seen the Sun first of all rising, and chasing away night's darkness; next, raising itself gradually from the waves, and artfully illuminating everything to such an extent that those who had just entered the theater, having in reality left the sun setting, might easily believe that it was advancing behind them, as if about to shine on new markets, which were exhibited there most delightfully in the very same image of reality.

This special effect was rendered possible by Bernini's ingenious creation of a machine which, as Zammar suggests, "probably consisted of a painted *lontananza* (backdrop) of the sky, illuminated by eight torches placed into *canali ad uso di casetta* (ducts used as boxes) that could be moved thanks to a mechanical device made to raise and lower the torches."[120]

---

[118] Naples: Biblioteca Nazionale, MS XII, b.40 ("Avvisi Pubblici [da Roma] dell' anno 1639").

[119] Girolamo Teti, *Aedes Barberinae ad Quirinalem*, 35.

[120] Zammar, *Scenography at the Barberini Court*, 184. See also her "Gian Lorenzo Bernini: A Hypothesis about his Machine of the Rising Sun," in *La Dimensione del Tragico nella Cultura Moderna e Contemporanea*, ed. Erica Faccioli (Rome: UniversItalia, 2014), 233–252.

Equally impressive was an exact recreation of the Palazzo Barberini gardens.[121] Thus, according to the *Avvisi*:

> et nell' est[rem]o intermedio si vede l'apparenza del giardino del medemo Palazzo de sig[nori] Barberini con il gioco della pilotta, passaggio di carrozze, cavalli et lettighe, et cose simili che recano gran stupore tal che universalmente è stato stimato artificio raro et meglio inteso di quanti mai ne siano stati veduti in questa città.[122]

> In the last *intermedio* one sees the appearance of the garden of the same Palace of the signori Barberini with the game of *pilotta*, the passage of carriages, horses and litters, and similar things, which arouse such great wonder that it has been universally regarded as a rare artifice, and the best of those which have ever been seen in this city.

But "machinery" could also operate on a wide range of other levels. Baroque opera afforded a sense of community, reflected in, and encapsulated by, shared and frequently vocalized audience reaction. It constituted, in the words of Erika Fischer-Lichte, "a kind of machinery that worked on the senses of the spectators and produced different kinds of emotion in them," offering them "a liminal experience, for it transformed all those who underwent it and, at the same time, strengthened their sense of *communitas*, their common identity as members of the court."[123]

3.5 Musical Experimentalism

Musically, too, *Chi Soffre Speri* was experimental for its day, not least in exemplifying the fact that expressiveness in a recitative soliloquy resides in its musical harmonies.[124] Thus, for example, as Margaret Murata has

---

[121] The garden scenery had taken no fewer than forty-three days to be completed. See Zammar, *Scenography at the Barberini Court*, 180.

[122] *Avvisi di Roma*: 5 March 1639. See Ademollo, *Teatri*, 29–30.

[123] Erika Fischer-Lichte, "Transforming Spectators into Viri Perculsi: Baroque Theatre as Machinery for Producing Affects," in *Performativity and Performance in Baroque Rome*, eds. Peter Gillgren and Mårten Snickare (Farnham: Ashgate, 2012), 87–97, at 94.

[124] For a detailed analysis of the opera's libretto and musical setting, see Maria Anne Purciello, *And Dionysus Laughed: Opera, Comedy and Carnival in Seventeenth-Century Venice and Rome* (PhD thesis: Princeton University, 2005), 194–245.

carefully demonstrated,[125] Armindo's soliloquy from the final act is framed by harmonic relationships, which "enable the harmony to convey the same sense of disjunction expressed by the text."[126] Here the text's fluctuations of mood, its emotional indulgence, and its sense of imbalance are mirrored by Mazzocchi's recourse to harmonic variety, his associated expansion of chord pairs, and, ultimately, by downward phrases, whose effect "accumulates into a general feeling of melodic stasis and a sense of the oppressiveness of Armindo's impossible situation."[127] The opera's experimentalism is equally discernible in the libretto's imaginative recreation of contrasting dialects. Thus comic servants speak in regional dialects, in the language of everyday speech, which in turn spills over into their music.[128] More serious characters, meanwhile, voice their sentiments in a more educated Italian.[129] These "specific linguistic hallmarks of residual orality," as Wilbourne points out, "invoke commedia dell'arte practice."[130] They also facilitate wordplay and a sonic iteration[131] that is reflected both orally and musically.[132]

In regard to the potential impact of the performance upon Milton, only speculation is possible. His interest in Italian music at this time is attested by Edward Phillips, according to whom he shipped home from Venice:

---

[125] See Murata, *Operas*, 164–166.

[126] Murata, *Operas*, 165.

[127] Murata, *Operas*, 166. For musical illustrations, see *ibid.*, Appendix 1: D.

[128] Murata, describing the opera's recitative texture, observes that "all characters sing repeated notes over sustained bass notes, but Zanni's manner is more singsong, while Egisto's loftier speech reflects his upper-class locution and more coherent language." See Margaret Murata, "Chi soffre speri," *The New Grove Dictionary of Opera*, Grove Music Online (Oxford: Oxford University Press): http://www.oxfordmusiconline.com/subscriber/article/grove/ music/O008004

[129] See Wilbourne, *Seventeenth-Century Opera*, 111.

[130] Wilbourne, *Seventeenth-Century Opera*, 113.

[131] Wilbourne, *Seventeenth-Century Opera*, 115, discussing Lucinda/Armindo's lament in Act III, scene 3, notes sonic wordplay on "spero" ("I hope") in the rapid succession of "pensiero"/"spero"/"dispero"/"io spero"/"ab disperanza."

[132] Willbourne, *Seventeenth-Century Opera*, 118, offers an interesting discussion of the contrasting, yet mirroring, voices of the hopeful Egisto and the despairing Lucinda/Armindo: "Just as the structure and wording of Armindo/Lucinda's material relies on the model provided by Egisto, the melodic and rhythmic realization of each of her statements is based upon his music." See also her Example 3.4, at 119.

> a Chest or two of choice Musick-books of our best Masters flourishing about that time in Italy, namely Luca Marenzo [sic], Monte Verde, Horatio Vecchi, Cifa [sic], the Prince of Venosa, and several others.[133]

Milton was a long-term believer in the interrelationship between music and words. Hence his injunction to the "Sphear-born harmonious Sisters, Voice, and Vers" to "Wed your divine sounds, and mixt power employ."[134] Likewise in *Ad Patrem*, a piece in which a father's musicianship is both complimented and complemented by the speaker's poetic voice, Milton asks: *Denique quid vocis modulamen inane iuvabit/ Verborum sensusque vacans, numerique loquacis?* (50–51) ("In short, what will the hollow modulation of the voice avail—devoid of words, feeling and the rhythm of speech?"). Later, in 1646, he would bestow lavish praise upon Henry Lawes for his ability to set words to music in such a way that verbal meaning was not obscured:

> Harry whose tuneful and well measur'd Song
> First taught our English Musick how to span
> Words with just note and accent, not to scan
> With Midas Ears, committing short and long.[135]

In short, the relationship between words and music is reciprocal: "Thou honour'st Verse, and Verse must lend her wing/To honour thee."[136] And in the closing tercet Lawes's musical achievements in England are interestingly envisaged as surpassing those of the Italian composer, Casella, who had set some of Dante's *Canzoni* to music:

> Dante shall give Fame leave to set thee higher
> Then his Casella, whom he woo'd to sing,
> Met in the milder shades of Purgatory.[137]

---

[133] Edward Phillips, *The Life of Mr. John Milton*, in *Early Lives*, ed. Darbishire, 59. The itemized list is both impressive and seemingly indicative of the travelling Milton's proactive quest to secure copies of music by the best contemporary Italian composers.

[134] *At A Solemn Musick*, 2–3.

[135] Sonnet 13 "To Mr. H[enry] Lawes, on his Aires," 1–4. The Trinity manuscript of the sonnet is dated 9 February 1645 (i.e. 1646). See Lewalski and Haan, 547.

[136] Sonnet 13, 9–10.

[137] Sonnet 13, 12–14. In *Purgatorio* 2. 7–119 Dante meets the shade of the Italian composer Casella, who, upon being asked to sing, responds with the canzone "Amor che nella mente mi ragiona" ("Love that employs reason in my mind"). See Amilcare Iannucci, "Casella's Song and the Tuning of the Soul," *Thought* 65 (1990): 27–46; Alessandra Fiori, "Il Canto di Casella: Esegesi Dantesche a Confronto," in *Trent'*

3.6 The Theatrical Milton

A Janus-like glance at Milton's own theatrical interests and experiences reveals that he had in all probability attended plays in London. His self-fashioning in *Elegia Prima* (c. 1626) as student/spectator of comedy and tragedy (27-46), and, more specifically, his description of the venue in which such plays were staged as London's *sinuosum ... theatrum* (27) ("curving theater") suggest the curved auditorium of the Blackfriars theater, and, perhaps, the teenage Milton's attendance at a production of Ben Jonson's *The Staple of News*, a Blackfriars staging of which is attested for February 1626.[138] The fact that John Milton senior, as Herbert Berry uncovered, was one of that theater's trustees can only reinforce the possibility.[139] Cambridge too had doubtlessly afforded him

---

Anni di Ricerche Musicologiche: Studi in Onore di F. Alberto Gallo, eds. Patrizia Dalla Vecchia and Donatella Restani (Rome: Torre D'Orfeo, 1996), 283–289. Milton's reference would seem to be particularly appropriate, given the fact that Lawes cultivated the "aria parlante." See N. C. Carpenter, "Milton and Music: Henry Lawes, Dante, and Casella," *ELR* 2 (1972): 237–242.

[138] See Alfred Harbage, *Annals of English Drama 975–1700: An Analytical Record of All Plays, Extant or Lost, Chronologically Arranged and Indexed by Authors, Titles, Dramatic Companies &c*, rev. S. Schoenbaum (Philadelphia: University of Pennsylvania Press, 1964), 122. See also *Ben Jonson, Vol. 9: An Historical Survey of the Text; The Stage History of the Plays; Commentary on the Plays*, eds. C. H. Herford, Percy Simpson, and Evelyn Simpson (Oxford: Clarendon Press, 1950), 251; Ben Jonson, *The Staple of News*, ed. Anthony Parr (Manchester: Manchester University Press, 1988), 49. The allusions to a *catus ... senior* (29) ("shrewd old man"), *prodigus haeres* (29) ("prodigal heir"), and *miles* (30) ("soldier") seem, at first glance, to suggest several of the stock characters of Plautine and Terentian drama, in which case Milton may be describing his reading of Roman comedy. The lines, however, may have a more contemporary import. Thus Timothy Burbury makes a convincing and eloquent argument that they refer to Pennyboy Canter, Pennyboy Junior, and Captain Sunfield in Jonson's *The Staple of News*. Furthermore, the pejorative description of a vociferous advocate (*Sive decennali fecundus lite patronus/Detonat inculto barbara verba foro* [31–32] ["whether an advocate, profiting from a ten-year-old suit, thunders his uncouth words before an uncivilized courtroom"]) may allude to the legalistic Picklock. See T. J. Burbery, "John Milton, Blackfriars Spectator?: 'Elegia Prima' and Ben Jonson's *The Staple of News*," *Ben Jonson Journal* 10 (2003): 57–76; T. J. Burbery, *Milton The Dramatist* (Pittsburgh: Duquesne University Press, 2007), 6–14. It is also possible, though perhaps less likely, that the reference is to George Ruggle's neo-Latin play *Ignoramus*. Although acted in Cambridge in 1615, there is no record of a performance in London. The work was not published until 1630, but it is not impossible that Milton had read it in manuscript.

[139] Herbert Berry, "The Miltons and the Blackfriars Playhouse," *MP* 89 (1992): 510–514. See also Gordon Campbell, "Shakespeare and the Youth of Milton," passim. Campbell makes the very interesting proposition that John Milton senior may have

ample opportunity to witness and participate in theatrical (or quasi-theatrical) activities. This is particularly true of the vacation festivities at Christ's College Hall, Cambridge in July 1628, where Milton presents himself as father of theatrical activities that involved students passing through flames.[140] And, as playwright, he had demonstrated an alertness to staging effects and the consequential verisimilitude that they might afford: the illuminated regal throne of *Arcades* (*c.* 1632) whereby nymphs and shepherds are surprised by a "sudden blaze of majesty" (2). More striking, *A Mask Presented at Ludlow Castle*, first staged on 29 September 1634, had stretched verisimilitude to its extreme by presenting a setting that was actual, as opposed to fictional: the forests of Ludlow itself. At the same time, the masque had imaginatively shifted between the sylvan and the palatial, not least in the replacing of Comus's "wild wood" by a "stately Palace," which in turn gives way to "Ludlow Town and the President's Castle." Nonetheless, the potential for dramatic effect was seriously curtailed by the small staging area afforded by Ludlow Castle, and by the practical difficulty of securing stage machinery. Scholars have remarked on the open-endedness of the stage direction "The Attendant Spirit descends or enters," matched and complemented by his claim that he can fly or run back to heaven (1013–1017). The simple fact, as Burbury observes, was that "Milton did not know if machinery would be available to lower and raise" the performing actor.[141] Other effects, such as the Lady's vision of the figures of Conscience, Faith, Hope, and Chastity (212–215) and/or her registering of the silver lining gleaming from the sable cloud (221–225), may well have been narrated, rather than staged, in view of "the difficulty of obtaining cloud machines and other devices in a remote area such as Wales."[142]

In short, *Chi Soffre Speri* capably demonstrated to its audience a new and exciting theatrical potential that, ultimately, may not have been lost on the future poet of *Paradise Lost, Paradise Regained*, and *Samson Agonistes*. For the later Milton, however, it was a potential that could be realized most effectively through the power of words and colorful imagery. Demaray traces the epic's interrelated prophetic shows and theatrical triumphs back to the "grand Continental staged spectacle, the

---

been the author of one of the tributes to Shakespeare for the First Folio (1623). This, he convincingly argues, might help to explain the inclusion of Milton's "On Shakespeare" in the Second Folio (1630).

[140] See Demaray, *Milton's Theatrical Epic*, 1.

[141] Burbury, *Milton The Dramatist*, 48.

[142] Burbury, *Milton The Dramatist*, 47.

last often performed against designs of the universe with 'infinite' perspectives."[143] And although one cannot but help contrasting the visual drama of Bernini's ingeniously crafted rising and setting sun with what Burbury describes as "the ... single lighting effect" of *Samson Agonistes*: the "sun rising while the captive walks away from the prison,"[144] one wonders to what extent the staged Barberini garden might go some way toward understanding the "sylvan scene, ... / ... a woody theatre/Of stateliest view" (*Paradise Lost* 4.140–142) that would become the Edenic setting for Satan's entrapment of Eve, or the "woody Scene" (*Paradise Regained* 2.294) with its surrounding vistas and the associated perspective afforded by "alleys brown/That open'd in the midst" (2.293–294), a scene in which Christ's temptation would be dramatically staged.[145] As David Quint remarks, "[i]t is unclear whether the 'woody scene' itself is part of the stage set or a particularly attractive natural *locus amoenus*."[146] One senses, however, that it is a contrived artifice intended to entice Christ onto a perverse theatrical set designed by Satan himself.[147] It is a part that Christ declines.

3.7 An Audience with a Cardinal

Just one day after attending the performance in question, Milton was granted a private audience with Cardinal Francesco Barberini. The privilege, he tells us, was the consequence of Holstenius's actions.[148] In the absence of any independent record, it is impossible to determine what was discussed. Perhaps, as Campbell and Corns suggest, the meeting was

---

[143] Demaray, *Milton's Theatrical Epic*, xv.

[144] *Samson Agonistes* 9–11: "here I feel amends,/The breath of Heav'n fresh-blowing, pure and sweet,/With day-spring born" (9–11), lines in which, as remarked by Burbury, *Milton The Dramatist*, 168, the rising sun is "conveyed effectively." Text is that of *The Complete Works*, Vol. II, ed. Knoppers.

[145] See John Dixon Hunt, *Garden and Grove: The Italian Renaissance Garden in the English Imagination 1600–1750* (Philadelphia: University of Pennsylvania Press, 1986), 174.

[146] David Quint, "The Disenchanted World of *Paradise Regained*," *HLQ* 76 (2013): 181–194, at 187.

[147] See Brendan Prawdzik, *Theatrical Milton, Politics and Poetics of the Staged Body* (Edinburgh: Edinburgh University Press, 2017), 188–189.

[148] Appendix 1.3.22–23: *Qua ego gratia cum illum postridie salutatum accessissem, tute idem rursus is eras qui et aditum mihi fecisti et colloquendi copiam* ("When, for this reason, I had approached him the next day in order to pay my respects, again it was you who afforded me both access and opportunity for a conversation with him").

entirely formal.[149] That it was more than amicable is suggested by the lavish praise, which, toward the end of the letter, Milton bestows upon a Cardinal, who, after all, had served as one of the ten judges in the trial of Galileo.[150] Carefully referring to Francesco by the official title "Eminenza" ("his Eminence"), first conferred upon Cardinals by the Barberini,[151] Milton proclaims his pre-eminence over the Italian families of d'Este, Farnese, and Medici, all of whom were famous in the Renaissance for their generous patronage of the arts. It is certainly a very great compliment. But the Cardinal epitomizes much more than patronage or power. He possesses other, equally enduring, qualities, which Milton proceeds to hymn. Thus his *magnae virtutes* (48–49) ("great virtues") and *recti ... studium* (49) ("devotion to what is right"), excellently epitomized also by his promotion of all the liberal arts, are, we read, forever present before Milton's eyes. And so is *illa mitis et, ut ita dicam, submissa animi celsitudo* (50–51) ("that gentle and, so to speak, humble loftiness of mind") *quae sola se deprimendo attollere didicit* (51–52) ("which alone has learnt to attain elevation through submissiveness"). The oxymoronic language is amplified by adaptation of Callimachus, *Hymn* 6.58: Demeter's epiphanic revelation of her godhead, as reflected in the contrast between her steps, which cling to the ground, and her head, which touches Olympus:

---

[149] Campbell and Corns, *Life, Work, and Thought*, 123.

[150] Whether or not Milton was aware of this fact remains a mystery. At *Areopagitica*, 24, recalling his Italian sojourn, he would famously claim: "There it was that I found and visited the famous Galileo grown old, a prisner to the Inquisition, for thinking in Astronomy otherwise then the Franciscan and Dominican licencers thought." The claim, although much contested, is probably true.

[151] Appendix 1.3.47–48: *De cetero, novo beneficio devinxeris si Eminentissimum Cardinalem quanta potest observantia meo nomine salutes* ("As for the rest, you will have bound me by a new bond of good favor if you convey to his Eminence the Cardinal greetings in my name, and with the greatest possible respect"). Cf. H. J. Todd, *Some Account of the Life and Writings of John Milton* (London: C[harles] and J[ohn] Rivington, 1826), 38: "Milton, it may be observed, is careful not to omit the title first applied to the Cardinals by Barberini: since whose time, Dr Bargrave relates, 'the title of Padrone continueth to the Pope's chiefe Nephew, and the title of *Eminenza* to all the Cardinalls ... The title of Excellency belonging to soveraine Princes in Italy they [Barberini] strove to find out something that should not be inferior to it; and canvassing many titles, at length they pitched upon *Eminency*, which the Princes hearing of, they took upon themselves the title of Highness'." Cf. Gabriel Naudaeus to Holstenius at *Sallustii*, 7: *Eminentissimo tuo Principi FRANCESCO BARBERINO maximo ... gratissimus merito acceptissimusque haberis* ("You are deservedly regarded as most pleasing and acceptable ... to your prince, the most Eminent FRANCESCO BARBERINI").

> de qua [sc. submissa animi celsitudine] vere dici potest quod
> de Cerere apud Callimachum est, diversa tamen sententia:
> ἴθματα μὲν χέρσω κεφαλὰ δὲ οἱ ἅπτετ' ὀλύμπω [152]
>
> concerning which [sc. humble loftiness of mind] it can truly
> be said, as it is of Ceres in Callimachus, though in a different
> sense: "Feet still cling to the earth, while the head touched
> Olympus."

Despite, or perhaps because of, Milton's effusive hyperbole, one detects a self-conscious irony when the quotation is examined in its original context. It is an irony that could hardly have been missed by the philhellenic Holstenius. In Callimachus's hymn,[153] Demeter is presented in a hallowed grove. It is here that she nourishes many, and bestows fair laws on cities (a role now mirrored perhaps by that of the Barberini in Rome). But this idealized, quasi-utopian, world order is not without the threat of disruption and potential corruption. As Neil Hopkinson notes, "the grove becomes a *locus amoenus*. ... The scene is idyllic; but its peace is already undermined by a violence latent in the language and imagery."[154] For suddenly and shamelessly her grove is invaded by an outsider, the deranged Erysichthon, along with twenty servants. In an act of hubris, they threaten to deface and defile the *locus amoenus* by felling its precious trees.[155] Demeter, assuming the guise of priestess Nicippe, addresses her invader in gentle tones, emphasizing that the grove is a sanctified space. Undeterred, Erysichthon becomes even fiercer, whereupon Demeter, now enraged, resumes her godlike shape (in the line quoted by Milton), an epiphany that causes the servants to run away, leaving their bronze tools in the trees. Rebuking Erysichthon for his evil speech, the goddess inflicts on the intruder the eternal punishment of

---

[152] Appendix 1.3.52–53 (Milton has changed the original aorist ἄψατ to the imperfect ἅπτετ). Cf. Homer, *Iliad* 4.443 (of Eris); Virgil, *Aeneid* 4. 177 (of *Fama*): *ingrediturque solo et caput inter nubila condit* ("she walks upon the ground and buries her heads amid the clouds"); likewise of Orion at *Aeneid* 10. 767.

[153] See, in general, Peter Bing, "Callimachus and the Hymn to Demeter," *Syllecta Classica* 6 (1995): 29–42, and, for a metapoetic reading, C. W. Müller, *Erysichthon. Der Mythos als narrative Metapher im Demeterhymnos des Kallimachos* (Stuttgart: Franz Steiner, 1987), 27–45.

[154] *Callimachus: Hymn to Demeter*, ed. Neil Hopkinson (Cambridge: Cambridge University Press, 1984), 5.

[155] See Jackie Murray, "The Metamorphosis of Erysichthon: Callimachus, Apollonius, and Ovid," in *Hellenistica Groningana 7: Callimachus II*, eds. M. A. Harder, R. F. Regtuit, and G. C. Wakker (Leuven: Peeters, 2004), 207–242.

hunger and disease—all this in contrast to the perpetual feasting enjoyed by the gods.[156]

Milton's appropriation of the verse from Callimachus to describe Francesco Barberini is effected, he points out, *diversa ... sententia* (53) ("in a different sense"). The phrase seems to signal its allegorical import, with a nod perhaps to Holstenius's regular implementation of the term *sententia* in the titles of his Latin translations, not least, his eponymous Latin rendering of Porphyry's Ἀφορμαὶ πρὸς τὰ Νοητά as *Sententiae ad Intelligibilia Ducentes*[157] in the volume that was possibly gifted by him to Milton.[158] When the whole is read allegorically, Milton's good-humored self-fashioning is perhaps as an intruder of a sacred (in this instance, Catholic) space, noted indeed for the sumptuous banquets hosted in the Casa Barberini, where both Cardinals were renowned for "keeping a free table in the princely manner."[159] And, by a further equation, Francesco Barberini is the priest[ess]/Demeter figure. The allegory is enhanced by the fact that Porphyry, in the *De Antro Nympharum* as translated by Holstenius (a work likewise included in the potentially gifted volume), had explicitly stated that the priestesses of Demeter, when initiated into the rites of the Earth-goddess, were termed "bees" by the ancients: *Cereris sacerdotes ... apes antiqui appellabant*[160] ("The ancients used to call the priestesses of Ceres 'bees'"). The fact that bees constituted the heraldic symbol of the Barberini family may serve to re-enforce the equation.

But if the Protestant Milton is indeed an "intruder," *Epistola Familiaris* 9 depicts its author as a humanist among fellow humanists, as one who can reveal that he has been commissioned by his addressee to inspect a manuscript among the Medicean codices in the Biblioteca Laurenziana in Florence, even if has been unable to fulfill the commission because of that library's reputation for its particularly strict

---

[156] Cf. *Callimachus: Hymn to Demeter*, ed. Hopkinson, 9: "Erysichthon's prophecy of perpetual feasting is horribly fulfilled." See also Andrew Faulkner, "Fast, Famine, and Feast: Food for Thought in Callimachus' Hymn to Demeter," *HSCP* 106 (2011): 75–95.

[157] See Porphyry, Ἀφορμαὶ πρὸς τὰ Νοητά, trans. Holstenius, at *Porphyrii Philosophi Liber de Vita Pythagorae*, 57–98. On Holstenius's regular use of the eponymous noun *sententia*, cf. also *Alia Appendix Sententiarum* at ibid., 136–147. See also *Demophili Democratis et Secundi, Veterum Philosophorum Sententiae Morales* (1638), passim.

[158] See 144–148.

[159] Rietbergen, *Power and Religion*, 388.

[160] Porphyrius, *De Antro Nympharum*, trans. Holstenius, 99–135, at 119.

rules.[161] Milton can, however, do the next best thing: recommend that Holstenius utilize for this purpose the services of Giovanni Battista Doni,[162] who is expected to be in Florence any time soon.

In conclusion, here, as elsewhere, the traveling Milton of the late 1630s presents himself as one who is very much in tune with the comings and goings of those within spaces, both literal and literary, in which he has found a welcome and comfortable place. Whether in the city's leading academies or in the Vatican Library or in the theater of the Palazzo Barberini, he stands alongside Catholic literati as a Protestant, whose "invasion" of Rome's "sacred grove" is both a proactive integration into that world and a celebration of its academicians, its manuscripts, its music, and its culture—in short

magnificentia vere Romana.

---

[161] Appendix 1.3. 38–40: *In illa bibliotheca, nisi impetrata prius venia, nihil posse exscribi, ne stilum quidem scriptorium admovisse tabulis permissum* ("In that library, they say, nothing can be transcribed unless prior permission has been obtained upon request; it is not permitted even to bring a writing implement to the tables"). Milton may be reporting a ban on note-taking (although this is unattested in other such complaints); alternatively, perhaps the point is that the use of ink was forbidden at the tables. David Colvillus, Scotus in his ms letter to Holstenius (in the same Vatican collection as the holograph of Milton's present letter) complains about the library's index, which he describes as *nec ordine alphabeto* [sic] ("not in alphabetical order"). Likewise, Holstenius, in a letter (dated 16 December 1629) to Giovanni Battista Doni, sharply criticizes the library's haphazard and unreliable indexing system, and the inability of the staff (*meri ... librorum custodes* ["mere custodians of books"]) to comprehend the names of authors (*Epistolae ad Diversos*, ed. Boissonade, 178–181, at 179).

[162] On Doni, see 125–130.

APPENDICES

EDITORIAL POLICY

Copy-texts

Poemata (London, 1645) Queen's University Library, Belfast, Percy/584.

Pro Populo Anglicano Defensio Secunda (London, 1654) Biblioteca Nazionale Centrale, Rome, BVEE032246.

Epistolarum Familiarium Liber Unus (London, 1674) Henry E. Huntington Library and Art Gallery, 105620.

In all instances the printer's spacing errors and wrong-turned and wrong-font letters have been silently corrected, and "&" has been expanded to "et," and enclitic "q;" to "que." Punctuation and orthography have been standardized and modernized. Thus "j" has been regularized as "i," and Latin spelling has been normalized in accordance with the forms recommended in Lewis and Short, *A Latin Dictionary*. Likewise, redundant capitals have been normalized, and accents, such as those denoting the ablative case (â), adverb (è), or contracted verbs (ê), are omitted. In the interest of clarity, abbreviations of proper names or dates have been expanded, and are indicated by the use of angle brackets. All other departures from the copy-texts are acknowledged in the apparatus criticus.

The lemma represents this edition and follows the indicated copy-text, unless otherwise noted. Collation of *Ad Leonoram* 1, 2, and 3, and of *Ad Salsillum* in the 1645 *Poemata* is with *Poems, &c Upon Several Occasions Both English and Latin, &c., Compos'd at Several Times by Mr John Milton* (London: Thomas Dring, 1673). Collation of *Epistola Familiaris* 9 in *Epistolarum Familiarium Liber Unus* (London: Brabazon Aylmer, 1674) is with BAV MS Barb. lat. 2181, ff. 57^r-58^v. Unless otherwise stated, the changes called for in the 1645 and 1674 *Errata* have been made in the text, and are indicated in the apparatus criticus.

Appendix 1

Milton's Roman Sojourns, 1638–1639
The Latin Writings

1 (a)   Ad Leonoram Romae Canentem

Angelus unicuique suus (sic credite gentes)
    Obtigit aethereis ales ab ordinibus.
Quid mirum, Leonora, tibi si gloria maior,
    Nam tua praesentem vox sonat ipsa Deum?
5   Aut Deus aut vacui certe mens tertia coeli
    Per tua secreto guttura serpit agens;
Serpit agens, facilisque docet mortalia corda
    Sensim immortali assuescere posse sono.
Quod si cuncta quidem Deus est per cunctaque fusus,
10   In te una loquitur; cetera mutus habet.

1 (b)   Ad Eandem

Altera Torquatum cepit Leonora poetam,
    Cuius ab insano cessit amore furens.
Ah miser ille tuo quanto felicius aevo
5   Perditus et propter te, Leonora, foret!
Et te Pieria sensisset voce canentem
    Aurea maternae fila movere lyrae,
Quamvis Dircaeo torsisset lumina Pentheo
    Saevior, aut totus desipuisset iners,
10 Tu tamen errantes caeca vertigine sensus
    Voce eadem poteras composuisse tua;
Et poteras aegro spirans sub corde quietem
    Flexanimo cantu restituisse sibi.

      5 canentem] canentam [*Corrected from the Errata*]
      8 desipuisset] desipuiiset 1645 desipulisset 1673 [*Corrected from the Errata*]

1 (c)   Ad Eandem

Credula quid liquidam Sirena, Neapoli, iactas,
    Claraque Parthenopes fana Acheloiados,
Litoreamque tua defunctam Naiada ripa
5   Corpora Chalcidico sacra dedisse rogo?
Illa quidem vivitque, et amoena Tibridis unda
    Mutavit rauci murmura Pausilipi.
Illic Romulidum studiis ornata secundis
    Atque homines cantu detinet atque deos.

To Leonora Singing at Rome

A winged angel from the heavenly ranks has been allotted to each individual (believe this, you nations). What wonder then, Leonora, if you possess a greater glory, for your very voice resonates the presence of God; either God or at least the third mind of a now empty heaven secretly insinuates its motion through your throat. Its motion it insinuates, and readily teaches that mortal hearts can gradually become accustomed to an immortal sound. For if indeed God is all things, and through all things is diffused, it is in you alone that he speaks; the rest he holds in silence.

To the Same

Another Leonora captivated the poet Torquato, who became insane as a consequence of his mad love for her. Ah how much more happily would that wretched man have met his ruin in your lifetime and on your account, Leonora! And he would have felt the effect of your singing with a Pierian voice, as you plucked the golden strings of your mother's lyre. Even if he had rolled his eyes more fiercely than Dircaean Pentheus or had totally lost his senses and his reason, you, nonetheless, by means of your voice could have calmed those senses reeling and blindly spinning, and breathing repose in the depths of his sick heart, through your soul-swaying song you could have restored him to himself.

To the Same

Credulous Naples, why do you boast of your clear-voiced Siren, and of the famous shrine of Parthenope, daughter of Achelous, and that when she, a Naiad of the shore, died on your river bank, you committed her sacred body to a Chalcidian pyre? She is, in fact, alive, and has exchanged the murmurings of the raucous Posillipo for Tiber's pleasant waters. There, adorned by the favorable enthusiasm of the sons of Romulus, by her song she takes hold of both men and gods.

2. Ad Salsillum Poetam Romanum Aegrotantem: Scazontes

O Musa, gressum quae volens trahis claudum
Vulcanioque tarda gaudes incessu,
Nec sentis illud in loco minus gratum
Quam cum decentes flava Deiope suras
5 Alternat aureum ante Iunonis lectum,
Adesdum et haec s'is verba pauca Salsillo
Refer, camoena nostra cui tantum est cordi,
Quamque ille magnis praetulit immerito divis.
Haec ergo alumnus ille Londini Milto,
10 Diebus hisce qui suum linquens nidum
Polique tractum (pessimus ubi ventorum
Insanientis impotensque pulmonis
Pernix anhela sub Iove exercet flabra)
Venit feraces Itali soli ad glebas
15 Visum superba cognitas urbes fama
Virosque doctaeque indolem iuventutis,
Tibi optat idem hic fausta multa, Salsille,
Habitumque fesso corpori penitus sanum;
Cui nunc profunda bilis infestat renes,
20 Praecordiisque fixa damnosum spirat,
Nec id pepercit impia quod tu Romano
Tam cultus ore Lesbium condis melos.
O dulce divum munus, O Salus Hebes
Germana, tuque, Phoebe, morborum terror
25 Pythone caeso, sive tu magis Paean
Libenter audis, hic tuus sacerdos est.
Querceta Fauni, vosque rore vinoso
Colles benigni, mitis Evandri sedes,
Siquid salubre vallibus frondet vestris,
30 Levamen aegro ferte certatim vati.
Sic ille caris redditus rursum Musis
Vicina dulci prata mulcebit cantu.
Ipse inter atros emirabitur lucos
Numa, ubi beatum degit otium aeternum,
35 Suam reclivis semper Aegeriam spectans.
Tumidusque et ipse Tibris hinc delinitus
Spei favebit annuae colonorum,
Nec in sepulchris ibit obsessum reges
Nimium sinistro laxus irruens loro:
40 Sed frena melius temperabit undarum,
Adusque curvi salsa regna Portumni.

23 O Salus] O salus 1673 Osalus 1645
28 Evandri 1673] Euandri 1645

To Salzilli, a Poet of Rome, in his Illness: Scazons

O Muse, who drag a lame foot willingly, and, despite your tardy progress, rejoice in the gait of Vulcan, unaware that in its place this is less charming than when Deiopea, golden-haired, and with seemly ankles, dances trippingly before Juno's couch of gold. Come then and convey, if you will, these few words to Salzilli, to whose heart my poetry is so dear, and which he preferred, though undeservedly, to the mighty gods. Convey then these words sent by that foster-child of London, Milton, who in recent days has left his own nest and tract of the heavens (where the worst of winds, losing control of its madly raging lungs, rapidly puffs its panting blasts beneath the sky), and has come to the fertile clods of Italy's soil to behold cities known by proud reputation, and the men and excellence of its learned youth.

To you, Salzilli, this same person wishes many good fortunes and the fullness of good health for your weary body. An overflow of bile is presently assailing your kidneys, and, implanted in the depths of your stomach, is breathing its deadly breath; in its irreverence it has failed to show consideration for the fact that you so eloquently fashion the song of Lesbos upon Roman lips.

O sweet gift of the gods, o Health, sister of Hebe, and you, Phoebus, terror of diseases ever since your slaying of Python (or whether you give ear more readily as Paean), this man is your priest. Oak-groves of Faunus, and you, hills abounding in the dew of grapes, the abode of gentle Evander, if any health-bringing plant blooms in your valleys, bring it eagerly to relieve a sick poet.

Thus restored once more to his beloved Muses, he will soothe the neighboring meadows with his sweet song. Numa himself will be amazed, where amid the dark groves he spends a blessed eternity of repose, as he reclines, forever gazing upon his own Egeria. And the swollen Tiber himself, bewitched by this song, will favor the yearly hope of farmers, and will not proceed to besiege kings in their tombs by rushing along with his left rein too loose: instead, he will keep better rein upon his waves all the way up to the salted realms of curving Portumnus.

3. Epistola Familiaris 9: Lucae Holstenio Romae in Vaticano

[1] Tametsi multa in hoc meo Italiae transcursu multorum in me humaniter et peramice facta et possum et saepe soleo recordari, tamen pro tam brevi notitia, haud scio an iure dicam ullius maiora exstitisse in me benevolentiae indicia quam ea quae mihi abs te profecta sunt.

[2] Cum enim tui conveniendi causa in Vaticanum ascenderem, ignotum prorsus (nisi si quid forte ab Alexandro Cherubino dictum de me prius fuerat) summa cum humanitate recepisti; mox in Musaeum comiter admisso, et conquisitissimam librorum supellectilem et permultos insuper manuscriptos auctores Graecos tuis lucubrationibus exornatos adspicere licuit, quorum partim nostro saeculo nondum visi, quasi in procinctu, velut illae apud Maronem

>   penitus convalle virenti
> inclusae animae, superumque ad limen iturae

expeditas modo typographi manus et μαιευτικὴν poscere videbantur; partim tua opera etiamnum editi passim ab eruditis avide arripiuntur, quorum et unius etiam duplici dono abs te auctus dimittor.

[3] Tum nec aliter crediderim quam quae tu de me verba feceris ad praestantissimum Cardin[alem] Franc[iscum] Barberinum, iis factum esse ut cum ille paucis post diebus ἀκρόαμα illud musicum magnificentia vere Romana publice exhiberet, ipse me tanta in turba quaesitum ad fores exspectans, et paene manu prehensum persane honorifice intro admiserit.

[4] Qua ego gratia cum illum postridie salutatum accessissem, tute idem rursus is eras qui et aditum mihi fecisti et colloquendi copiam; quae quidem cum tanto viro (quo etiam in summo dignitatis fastigio nihil benignius, nihil humanius) pro loci et temporis ratione largiuscula profecto potius erat, quam nimis parca.

[5] Atque ego, doctissime Holsteni, utrum ipse sim solus tam te amicum et hospitem expertus an omnes Anglos, id spectans scilicet quod triennium Oxoniae litteris operam dederis, istiusmodi officiis

---

Lectiones editionis 1674 cum codice Vaticano MS Barb. lat. 2181, fols 57ʳ-58ᵛ collatae.
Tit. Lucae Holstenio Romae in Vaticano] Ioannes Miltonius Lucae Holstenio. Romae. VAT

5 ascenderem] ascenderam VAT   15 tua opera] tuo opere VAT   arripiuntur VAT] accipiuntur 1674   16 dimittor] demittor VAT   18 Cardin[alem] Franc[iscum] Barberinum] Cardinalem Barberinum VAT   20 publice] populo VAT
22 accessissem] accesseram VAT   27 doctissime VAT] Doctissime 1674

Appendix 1

Familiar Letter 9: To Lucas Holstenius in the Vatican at Rome

[1] Although I both can, and frequently do, recall the many kindly and most friendly courtesies bestowed upon me by many in the course of this journey of mine through Italy, I do not know, nonetheless, if I can justly say that from anyone have there appeared greater tokens of good will towards me than those which have emanated from you to me, given the briefness of our acquaintance.

[2] For when I went up to the Vatican for the purpose of meeting you, you received me with the utmost kindness, despite the fact that I was absolutely unknown to you (unless some mention of me happened to have been made in advance by Alessandro Cherubini). Later, upon being granted courteous access to the Museum, I was permitted to look over its most choice collection of books and, furthermore, its great number of Greek authors in manuscript, adorned by your painstaking labors. Some of these, not yet seen by our generation, stood as if in array— just as in Virgil those

> souls shut up deep within a green valley
> and about to approach the threshold of the upper world

and seemed to be demanding the agile hands and the "midwifery" of the printer. Others, already edited by your endeavors, are everywhere being snapped up eagerly by scholars. And I too was dispatched, enriched by a twofold gift from you of one of these.

[3] Next, I could not help believing that it was in consequence of your comments about me to the most excellent Cardinal Francesco Barberini that when, a few days later, he presented to the public, and with truly Roman magnificence, that musical "entertainment," he personally waited for me at the door, and singling me out in so great a crowd, and virtually clasping me by the hand, he admitted me inside in an extremely courteous manner.

[4] When, for this reason, I had approached him the next day in order to pay my respects, again it was you who afforded me both access and opportunity for a conversation with him — an opportunity indeed which, given the greatness of the man (one than whom there is nothing even in the highest pinnacle of dignity more kind, nothing more courteous), was undoubtedly rather too generous than too sparing, considering time and location.

[5] And for sure, most learned Holstenius, I do not know whether I am alone in finding you so friendly and hospitable, or whether, in respect presumably of your devoting three years to your literary studies at Oxford, it is your inclination to honor

quoscunque prosequi studium sit certe nescio. Si hoc est, pulchre tu quidem Angliae nostrae ex parte etiam tuae διδασκάλια persolvis; privatoque nostrum cuiusque nomine et patriae publico parem utrobique gratiam promereris. Sin est illud, eximium me tibi prae ceteris habitum dignumque adeo visum quicum velis ζενίαν ποιεῖσθαι, et mihi gratulor de tuo iudicio et tuum simul candorem prae meo merito pono.

[6] Iam illud vero quod mihi negotium dedisse videbare de inspiciendo codice Mediceo, sedulo ad amicos retuli, qui quidem eius rei efficiendae spem perexiguam in praesens ostendunt. In illa bibliotheca, nisi impetrata prius venia, nihil posse exscribi, ne stilum quidem scriptorium admovisse tabulis permissum; esse tamen aiunt Romae Ioannem Baptistam Donium (is ad legendas publice Graecas litteras Florentiam vocatus indies exspectatur), per eum ut consequi possis quae velis facile esse; quamquam id sane mihi pergratum accidisset si res tam praesertim optanda quae sit mea potius opella saltem aliquanto plus promovisset, cum sit indignum tam tibi honesta et praeclara suscipienti non omnes undicunque homines et rationes et res favere.

[7] De cetero, novo beneficio devinxeris si Eminentissimum Cardinalem quanta potest observantia meo nomine salutes, cuius magnae virtutes rectique studium ad provehendas item omnes artes liberales egregie comparatum semper mihi ob oculos versantur; tum illa mitis et, ut ita dicam, submissa animi celsitudo, quae sola se deprimendo attollere didicit; de qua vere dici potest quod de Cerere apud Callimachum est, diversa tamen sententia: ἴθματα μὲν χέρσῳ κεφαλὰ δὲ οἱ ἅπτετ' ὀλύμπῳ. Quod ceteris fere principibus documento esse potest triste illud supercilium et aulici fastus quam longe a vera magnanimitate discrepantes et alieni sint. Nec puto fore, dum ille vivit, Estenses, Farnesios aut Mediceos, olim doctorum hominum fautores, ut quis amplius desideret.

[8] Vale, doctissime Holsteni, et si quis tui tuorumque studiorum amantior est, illi me quoque, si id esse tanti existimas, ubicumque sim gentium futurus, velim annumeres.

Florentiae, Mart[ii] 30 1639

37 efficiendae] efficiundae VAT   40 Ioannem Baptistam Donium] Ioan[nem] Baptist[am] Donium VAT   46 favere] favere simul, et quasi congruere VAT
47 Eminentissimum] Eminentiss[imum] VAT   49 liberales] liberas VAT
59 doctissime VAT] Doctissime 1674   62 Mart[ii] 30 1639] mart[ii] 29 1639 VAT
Aversa pagina Miltonii manu add. "Al molto illustre Sig[nor] il Sig[nor] Luca / Holstenio nel Palazzo / Roma." VAT

all Englishmen with courtesies of that sort. If it is the latter, you are indeed handsomely repaying to our England (yours also in part) your debts of "schooling," and you deserve equal thanks on both counts — privately in the name of each of us; and publicly in the name of our country. If it is the former: that you have regarded me as distinctly above the rest, and that I should seem so worthy of your desire to "form an interchange of friendship," I both offer myself congratulations on this judgment of yours, and at the same time I rank your kind disposition above my own merit.

[6] Now, in regard to that commission which you seemed to have set me concerning the inspection of a Medicean codex, I earnestly relayed it to my friends; but indeed they are holding out for the present only the slimmest hope of accomplishing that matter. In that library, they say, nothing can be transcribed unless prior permission has been obtained upon request; it is not permitted even to bring a writing implement to the tables. They do report, however, that Giovanni Battista Doni is in Rome (he has been called to Florence to the public lectureship in Greek, and is expected any day now), and that through his agency you can easily achieve your wish. Nonetheless, it would truly have been a fortune most welcome for me if a topic so especially desirable had rather seen, at least to some degree, some advancement by the little effort that is mine; since it is a shame that not all men or methods or materials are everywhere at your disposal in your undertaking matters so honorable and distinguished.

[7] As for the rest, you will have bound me by a new bond of good favor if you convey to his Eminence the Cardinal greetings in my name, and with the greatest possible respect. Forever present before my eyes are his great virtues, and devotion to what is right, excellently epitomized also by his promotion of all the liberal arts; and, moreover, that gentle and, so to speak, humble loftiness of mind, which alone has learnt to attain elevation through submissiveness. Concerning which it can truly be said, as it is of Ceres in Callimachus, though in a different sense: "Feet still cling to the earth, while the head touched Olympus." This can serve to prove to other princes as a rule how much at odds with, and alien to, true magnanimity are that surly haughtiness and courtly pride. Nor do I think that, while he is alive, will anyone yearn any more for the d'Este, the Farnese, or the Medici, once the patrons of learned men.

[8] Farewell, most learned Holstenius, and, wheresoever in the world I am destined to be, if there is anyone who has very high regard for you and for your studies, my wish should be that you count me in his company, should you think it worth the effort.

Florence, March 30 1639

Appendix 2

Milton's Italian Journey

Defensio Secunda **(1654)**

Defensio Secunda

[1] Exacto in hunc modum quinquennio, post matris obitum regiones exteras et Italiam potissimum videndi cupidus, exorato patre, uno cum famulo profectus sum. Abeuntem vir clarissimus Henricus Woottonus, qui ad Venetos Orator Iacobi regis diu fuerat, et votis et praeceptis eunti peregre sane utilissimis eleganti epistola perscriptis me amicissime prosecutus est.

[2] Commendatum ab aliis nobilissimus vir Thomas Scudamorus, vicecomes Slegonensis, Caroli regis Legatus, Parisiis humanissime accepit, meque Hugoni Grotio, viro eruditissimo, ab Regina Suecorum tunc temporis ad Galliae regem Legato, quem invisere cupiebam, suo nomine et suorum uno atque altero deducente commendavit. Discedenti post dies aliquot Italiam versus litteras ad mercatores Anglos, qua iter eram facturus, dedit ut quibus possent officiis mihi praesto essent.

[3] Niceaea solvens Genuam perveni; mox Liburnum et Pisas, inde Florentiam. Illa in urbe, quam prae ceteris propter elegantiam cum linguae tum ingeniorum semper colui, ad duos circiter menses substiti; illic multorum et nobilium sane et doctorum hominum familiaritatem statim contraxi, quorum etiam privatas academias (qui mos illic cum ad litteras humaniores tum ad amicitias conservandas laudatissimus est) assidue frequentavi. Tui enim, Iacobe Gaddi, Carole Dati, Frescobalde, Cultelline, Bonmatthaei, Clementille, Francine, aliorumque plurium memoriam apud me semper gratam atque iucundam nulla dies delebit.

[4] Florentia Senas, inde Romam profectus, postquam illius urbis antiquitas et prisca fama me ad bimestre fere spatium tenuisset (ubi et Luca Holstenio aliisque viris cum doctis tum ingeniosis sum usus humanissime) Neapolim perrexi. Illic per Eremitam quendam, quicum Roma iter feceram, ad Ioannem Baptistam Mansum, Marchionem Villensem, virum nobilissimum atque gravissimum (ad quem Torquatus Tassus insignis poeta Italus de amicitia scripsit) sum introductus; eodemque usus, quamdiu illic fui, sane amicissimo; qui et ipse me per urbis loca et Proregis aulam circumduxit, et visendi gratia haud semel ipse ad hospitium venit. Discedenti serio excusavit se, tametsi multo plura detulisse mihi officia maxime cupiebat, non potuisse illa in urbe propterea quod nolebam in religione esse tectior.

[5] In Siciliam quoque et Graeciam traiicere volentem me tristis ex Anglia belli civilis nuntius revocavit: turpe enim existimabam, dum mei cives domi de libertate dimicarent, me animi causa otiose peregrinari. Romam autem reversurum monebant mercatores se didicisse per litteras parari mihi ab Iesuitis Anglis insidias si Romam reverterem, eo quod de religione nimis libere locutus essem.

Second Defense

[1] Having passed five years in this way, I was eager, after the death of my mother, to see foreign parts, and Italy, above all. Prevailing upon my father, I set out along with one servant. Upon my departure, Sir Henry Wotton, a most distinguished gentleman, who had served for a long time as King James' Ambassador to the Venetians, treated me in the most friendly manner by writing an elegant letter, conveying good wishes and precepts of the utmost use to one traveling abroad.

[2] Upon the recommendation of others, the most noble Thomas Scudamore, Viscount of Sligo, and Ambassador of King Charles, received me at Paris with the greatest courtesy, and of his own accord, and accompanied by several from among his entourage, he recommended me to Hugo Grotius, a most learned man, who at that moment in time was serving as Ambassador from the Queen of Sweden to the King of France, and whom I was longing to visit. Some days later, as I was departing for Italy, he gave me letters to the English merchants, who were on the route I was about to take, requesting that they might offer me whatever services were in their power.

[3] Setting sail from Nice, I reached Genoa; soon afterwards Leghorn and Pisa, and from there Florence. In that city, which I have always revered above the rest on account of the elegance of both its tongue and its men of genius, I remained for about two months. There straightaway I made the acquaintance of many men of rank and of learning, and I even frequented with regularity of attendance their private academies (a custom there that is worthy of the highest praise, designed, as it is, to preserve not only polite letters, but also the bonds of friendship). Why, no time will erase the forever pleasing and delightful memory of you, Jacopo Gaddi, Carlo Dati, Frescobaldi, Coltellino, Buonmattei, Clementillo, Francini, and a great many others.

[4] From Florence I set out for Siena, and from there to Rome. After the antiquity of that city and its renown of old had detained me for a period of roughly two months (where I made the very friendly acquaintance of Lucas Holstenius and of many other men of learning and of genius), I proceeded to Naples. There I was introduced by a certain Eremite friar, with whom I had journeyed from Rome, to Giovanni Battista Manso, Marquis of Villa, a most noble and influential man (to whom the illustrious Italian poet Torquato Tasso addressed his work on friendship). For the duration of my time there I was treated by him in a most friendly manner: for he conducted me in person through the regions of the city and the Viceroy's court, and more than once paid me a personal visit at my lodgings. As I was leaving, he extended an earnest apology for failing to offer me greater services, stating that, although that was his foremost desire, he had been unable to do so in that city on account of the fact that I refused to be more guarded on the subject of religion.

[5] Although it was my intention to pass over also into Sicily and Greece, the grim news from England of the civil war summoned me home: for I regarded it as shameful to be traveling abroad at my leisure, and for the improvement of my mind, while my fellow-citizens were fighting at home for freedom. As I was on the point of returning to Rome, the merchants warned me that they had learnt from their letters that, should I return to Rome, the English Jesuits were setting a plot for me, on account of the fact that I had spoken too liberally on the topic of religion.

[6] Sic enim mecum statueram de religione quidem iis in locis sermones ultro non inferre; interrogatus de fide, quicquid essem passurus, nihil dissimulare. Romam itaque nihilo minus redii. Quid essem, si quis interrogabat, neminem celavi; si quis adoriebatur, in ipsa urbe Pontificis alteros prope duos menses, orthodoxam religionem, ut antea, liberrime tuebar, Deoque sic volente incolumis Florentiam rursus perveni, haud minus mei cupientes revisens ac si in patriam revertissem. Illic totidem quot prius menses libenter commoratus (nisi quod ad paucos dies Lucam excucurri) transcenso Apennino, per Bononiam et Ferraram Venetias contendi. Cui urbi lustrandae cum mensem unum impendissem et libros quos per Italiam conquisiveram in navem imponendos curassem, per Veronam ac Mediolanum et Paeninas Alpes, Lacu denique Lemanno, Genevam delatus sum.

Appendix 2

[6] For I had made it my resolution not to initiate conversation on the subject of religion in those regions, but, if interrogated about my faith, to dissimulate nothing irrespective of consequential suffering. And so, notwithstanding, I returned to Rome: I concealed what I was from nobody who asked me; if anyone attacked me, I defended most liberally, as before, the orthodox faith for almost another two months in the very city of the Pontiff. And thus by the will of God I reached Florence again in safety, revisiting those who were no less eager to see me than if I had returned to my own country. There I lingered with pleasure for as many months as previously (with the exception of an excursion for a few days to Lucca); then, crossing the Apennines, I hastened, via Bologna and Ferrara, to Venice. Having spent one month surveying this city, and seeing to the shipping of the books which I had acquired in Italy, I was borne by way of Verona, Milan, and the Pennine Alps, and finally, along Lake Lemano, to Geneva.

Bibliography

1. **MANUSCRIPTS**

BOLOGNA
Biblioteca di San Francesco Dei Frati Minori Conventuali
MS. 42.

CAMBRIDGE
Trinity College
MS R. 3.4.

DUBLIN
Trinity College
R.dd.39.

FLORENCE
Biblioteca Marucelliana
MS A.36.

Biblioteca Nazionale Centrale
MSS Magliabecchiana, MSS. II. IV. 22 (formerly Magl. Cl. XXV 524).
MSS Magliabecchiana, MSS. Cl. IX, cod. 60.

HARVARD
Houghton Library
MS Sumner 84.

LEIDEN
University Library
Cod. Hug. 37.

LONDON
British Library
Egerton MS 1635.

NAPLES
Biblioteca Nazionale
MS XII, b.40.

OXFORD
Bodleian Library
MS Wood E5.

ROME
Archivio di Stato di Roma
AC, C. Colonna, prot. 2076.
NF, G. Longus prot. 76.

Biblioteca Apostolica Vaticana
Barb.gr.201.
Barb. lat. 74.
Barb. lat. 2049.
Barb. lat. 2181.
Barb. lat. 4386.
Urb.lat.1107.
Vat. lat. 6910.
Vat. lat. 13340.

Biblioteca Nazionale Vittorio Emanuele
MS 71.2.A.13.

VENICE
Biblioteca Nazionale Marciana
MS. Ital. XI. LXI (6792).

VIENNA
Österreichische Nationalbibliothek
Sign. Cod. 9660.

2.   MILTON: TEXTS

Milton, John. *An Apology Against a Pamphlet Call'd A Modest Confutation of the Animadversions Upon the Remonstrant against Smectymnuus* (London: John Rothwell, 1642).
———. *Areopagitica: A speech of Mr. John Milton for the Liberty of Unlicenc'd Printing, to the Parliament of England* (London: s.n., 1644).
———. *Complete Prose Works*, ed. Don M. Wolfe *et al*, 8 vols (New Haven, CT: Yale University Press, 1953–1982).
———. *Complete Shorter Poems*, ed. John Carey (London: Longman, 1968; reprint 1997).
———. *Epistolarum Familiarium Liber Unus and Uncollected Letters*, ed. Estelle Haan, Supplementa Humanistica Lovaniensia XLIV (Leuven: Leuven University Press, 2019).
———. *Epistolarum Familiarium Liber Unus: Quibus Accesserunt, Eiusdem, Iam Olim in Collegio Adolescentis, Prolusiones* (London: Brabazon Aylmer, 1674).
———. *Paradise Lost*, ed. Alastair Fowler (London: Longman, 1998).
———. *Paradise Regained*, in *The Complete Works of John Milton: Volume II: The 1671 Poems: Paradise Regain'd and Samson Agonistes*, ed. Laura Lunger Knoppers (Oxford: Oxford University Press, 2008).

———. *Poems*, ed. Thomas Keightley, 2 vols (London: Chapman and Hall, 1859).
———. *Poems ... Both English and Latin, Compos'd at Several times* (London: Humphrey Moseley, 1645).
———. *Poems, &c. Upon Several Occasions ... Both English and Latin, &c. ... With a Small Tractate of Education* (London: Thomas Dring, 1673).
———. *Poetical Works*, ed. David Masson, 3 vols (London: Macmillan, 1874).
———. *Pro Populo Anglicano Defensio Secunda. Contra Infamem Libellum Anonymum cui Titulus, Regii Sanguinis Clamor ad Coelum Adversus Parricidas Anglicanos* (London: Thomas Newcomb, 1654).
———. *Shorter Poems*, in *The Complete Works of John Milton: Volume III*, eds. Barbara Kiefer Lewalski and Estelle Haan (Oxford: Oxford University Press, 2012; rev. 2014).
———. *The Doctrine and Discipline of Divorce: Restor'd to the Good of Both Sexes, from the Bondage of Canon Law, and Other Mistakes, to Christian Freedom, Guided by the Rule of Charity* (London: T.P. and M.S., 1643).
———. *The History of Britain* (London: James Allestry, 1670).
———, *The Latin Poems*, ed. Walter Mackellar (New Haven, CT: Yale University Press, 1930).
———.*The Reason of Church-Government Urg'd Against Prelaty. In Two Books* (London: John Rothwell, 1641).
———. *Works*, ed. Frank A. Patterson *et al*, 18 vols (New York: Columbia University Press, 1931–1940).

3. MILTON: COMMENTARIES

BUSH, Douglas. *A Variorum Commentary on the Poems of John Milton: Volume I: The Latin and Greek Poems* (New York: Columbia University Press, 1970).
WOODHOUSE, A. P. S., and BUSH, Douglas, *A Variorum Commentary on the Poems of John Milton: The Minor Poems* (New York: Columbia University Press, 1972), II.1.

4. MILTON: BIOGRAPHIES AND BIOGRAPHICAL RESOURCES

CAMPBELL, Gordon. *A Milton Chronology* (London: Macmillan, 1997).
———, and CORNS, Thomas N. *John Milton: Life, Work, and Thought* (Oxford: Oxford University Press, 2008).
DARBISHIRE, Helen, ed. *The Early Lives of Milton* (London: Constable & Co. Ltd, 1932).
LEWALSKI, Barbara K. *The Life of John Milton: A Critical Biography* (Oxford: Blackwell, 2000).
MASSON, David. *The Life of John Milton: Narrated in Connexion with the Political, Ecclesiastical, and Literary History of his Time*, 7 vols (London: Macmillan, 1881–1894; reprint Gloucester, MA: Peter Smith, 1965).
PARKER, W. R. *Milton: A Biography*, 2 vols (Oxford: Oxford University Press, 1968; rev. Gordon Campbell, 1996).

5. OTHER PRIMARY TEXTS AND ANTHOLOGIES

Academia Tenuta da Fantastici a 12 di Maggio 1655. In Applauso della Santità di Nostro Signore Alesandro VII (Rome: Vitale Mascardi, 1655).

ACHILLINI, Claudio. *Due Lettere: L'Una del Mascardi all'Achillini, L'Altra dell' Achillini al Mascardi sopra le Presenti Calamità* (Rome: Lodovico Grignani, 1631).

―――. *Mercurio, e Marte* (Parma: Seth and Erasmo Viotti, 1628).

―――. *Poesie* (Bologna: Clemente Ferroni, 1632).

―――. *Rime e Prose* (Venice: Nicolò Pezzana, 1673).

―――. *Teti e Flora* (Parma: Seth and Erasmo Viotti, 1628).

ALBERTINI, Francesco. *Opusculum de Mirabilibus Novae et Veteris Urbis Romae* (Rome: Jacobus Mazochius, 1510).

ALEANDRO, Girolamo. *Sopra l'Impresa de gli Accademici Humoristi Discorso ... Detto nella Stessa Accademia* (Rome: Giacomo Mascardi, 1611).

ALLACCI, Leone. *Sallustii Philosophi de Diis et Mundo*, ed. Lucas Holstenius (Rome: Mascardi, 1638).

Applausi Poetici alle Glorie della Signora Leonora Baroni, ed. Francesco Ronconi (Braccciano: Giovanni Battista Cavario, 1639).

Argomento et Allegoria della Comedia Musicale Intitolata Chi Soffre Speri (Rome: Camera Apostolica, 1639).

ASCHAM, Roger. *The Scholemaster* (London: John Daye, 1570).

A True and Faithful Relation of What Passed for Many Yeers Between Dr. John Dee ... and Some Spirits (London: David Maxwell, 1659).

BAEDEKER, Karl. *Italy: Handbook for Travellers. Second Part: Central Italy and Rome* (Leipzig: Karl Baedeker, 1875).

BALDINUCCI, Filippo. *Vita del Cavaliere Giovanni Lorenzo Bernino Scultore, Architetto, e Pittore* (Florence: Vincenzio Vangelisti, 1682).

BALDUCCI, Francesco. *Rime* (Rome: Guiglielmo Facciotti, 1630).

―――. *Rime* (Rome: Francesco Moneta, 1645).

―――. *Rime* (Venice: Baba, 1663).

BAN, Joan Albert. *Dissertatio Epistolica, de Musicae Natura*, in *Hugonis Grotii et Aliorum De Omni Genere Studiorum Recte Instituendo Dissertationes* (Leiden: Isaac Commelin, 1637).

BARBERINI, Maffeo. *Poemata* (Rome: Reverenda Camera Apostolica, 1640).

BAUHIN, Caspar. *De Compositione Medicamentorum sive Medicamentorum Componendorum Ratio et Methodus* (Offenbach: Conradus Nebenius, 1610).

BEDE. *Ecclesiastical History*, eds. Bertram Colgrave and R. A. B. Mynors (Oxford: Oxford University Press, 1969).

BELL, John. *Bell's New Pantheon; or, Historical Dictionary of the Gods, Demi-gods, Heroes, and Fabulous Personages of Antiquity*, 2 vols (London: John Bell, 1790).

BERNINI, Domenico. *Vita del Cavalier Giovanni Lorenzo Bernini* (Rome: Rocco Bernabò, 1713).

CALLIMACHUS. *Hymn to Demeter*, ed. Neil Hopkinson (Cambridge: Cambridge University Press, 1984).

CANCELLIERI, Francesco. *Storia de' Solenni Possessi de' Sommi Pontefici Detti Anticamente Processi o Processioni dopo la loro Coronazione dalla Basilica Vaticana alla Lateranense* (Rome: Luigi Lazzarini, 1802).

Carmina Diversorum Auctorum in Nuptiis Illustrissimorum et Excellentissimorum Dominorum Thaddei Barberini et Annae Columnae (Rome: Reverenda Camera Apostolica, 1629).

CATULLUS. *Poems*, ed. Kenneth Quinn (London: Macmillan; New York: St Martin's Press, 1970).

CENNINI, Cennino. *Il Libro delle' Arte o Trattato della Pittura*, eds. Gaetano and Carlo Milanesi (Florence: Felice Le Monnier, 1859).

CEULI, Tiberio. *La Penna Canzone* (Rome: Paolo Moneta, 1670).

———. *L'Oriente Conquistato Poema Heroico* (Rome: Filippo Maria Mancini, 1672).

———. *Per la Morte di Monsignor Agostino Mascardi Oratione di Tiberio Ceuli, da lui Recitata nell'Accademia de' Signori Humoristi di Roma* (Rome: Francesco Moneta, 1641).

CHIABRERA, Gabriel. *Rime* (Milan: Società Tipografica de' Classici Italiani, 1807).

COWPER, William. *Complete Poetical Works*, ed. H. S. Milford (Oxford: Oxford University Press, 1913).

DELLA VALLE, Pietro. *Della Musica dell' Età Nostra che Non È Punto Inferiora, Anzi È Migliore di Quella dell' Età Passata* (Rome, 1640), in *Lyra Barberina Amphichordos: De' Trattati di Musica di Giovanni Batista Doni*, ed. Anton Francesco Gori, 2 vols (Florence: Imperial Printer, 1763), II, 249–264.

———. *Di Tre Nuove Maniere di Verso Sdrucciolo* (Rome: Pietro Antonio Facciotto, 1634).

DE MONTFAUCON, Bernard. *Diarium Italicum sive Monumentorum Veterum, Bibliothecarum, Musaeorum, &c.* (Paris: Joannes Anisson, 1702).

DE PISE, Marcellino. *Moralis Encyclopaedia Id Est Scientiarum Omnium Chorus* (Lyon: Laurentius Anisson, 1656).

DEPLEURRE, Stephanus. *Aeneis Sacra Continens Acta Domini Nostri Iesu Christi* (Paris: Adrian Taupinart, 1618).

DONI, Giovanni Battista. *Commercium Litterarium*, ed. Anton Francesco Gori (Florence: Caesario, 1754), appended to Angelo Maria Bandini, *Commentariorum De Vita et Scriptis Ioannis Baptistae Doni ... Libri Quinque* (Florence: Caesario, 1755).

———. *Compendio del Trattato de' Generi de' Modi della Musica* (Rome: Andrea Fei, 1635).

DU BELLAY, Joachim. *Les Regrets et Autres Oeuvres Poëtiques*, eds. J. Joliffe and M. A. Screech (Geneva: Droz, 1974).

DU MOULIN, Peter. *Regii Sanguinis Clamor ad Coelum Adversus Parricidas Anglicanos* (The Hague: Adrian Vlacq, 1652).

ELIOT, John. *Ortho-epia Gallica* (London: John Wolfe, 1593).

EVELYN, John. *Diary*, ed. E. S. De Beer, 6 vols (Oxford: Clarendon Press, 1955).

FANTUZZI, Giovanni. *Notizie degli Scrittori Bolognesi* (Bologna: St Thomas Aquinas Press, 1781).

Fasti dell' Accademia degl' Intrecciati (Rome: Reverenda Camera Apostolica, 1673).

FERRO, Giovanni. *Teatro d'Imprese*, 2 vols (Venice: Giacomo Sarzina, 1623).

FLETCHER, Phineas. *Locustae vel Pietas Iesuitica*, ed. Estelle Haan, Supplementa Humanistica Lovaniensia IX (Leuven: Leuven University Press, 1996).

FORCELLA, Vincenzo. *Iscrizioni delle Chiese e d'Altri Edificii di Roma* (Rome: Ludovico Cecchini, 1877).

GARUFFI, Giuseppe Malatesta. *Italia Accademica* (Rimini: Dandi, 1688).

GIGLI, Giacinto. *Diario di Roma*, ed. Manlio Barberito (Rome: Editore Columbo, 1994).
GIL, Alexander. *Parerga: sive Poetici Conatus* (London: Robert Milborne, 1632).
GIMMA, Giacinto. *Elogi Accademici della Società degli Spensierati di Rossano* (Naples: Carlo Troise, 1703).
GROTIUS, Hugo. *Poemata Collecta* (Leiden: Andreas Clocquius, 1617).
GUIDICCIONI, Lelio. *Cardinalis Antonii Barberini Magnificentia: Scenica Spectacula Exhibet*, in Teti, *Aedes Barberinae ad Quirinalem*, 123–124.
HERBERT, Edward. *Autobiography* (Strawberry Hill, 1764).
HERBERT, George. *Poetical Works*, ed. A. B. Grosart (London: George Bell and Sons, 1876).
HERRING, Francis. *Pietas Pontificia*, ed. Estelle Haan, *Humanistica Lovaniensia* 41 (1992): 251–295.
HOLSTENIUS, Lucas. *Αρριανός Κυνηγετικός: Arrianus De Venatione Luca Holstenio Interprete* (Paris: Cramoisy, 1644).
———. *Democratis et Secundi, Veterum Philosophorum Sententiae Morales* (Rome: Mascardi, 1638).
———. *Epistolae ad Diversos*, ed. Jean-François Boissonade (Paris: J. Gratiot, 1817).
———. *Porphyrii Vita Pythagorae* (Rome: Typis Vaticanis, 1630).
HORACE. *Odes*, ed. Kenneth Quinn (London: Macmillan, 1980).
———. *Odes Book II*, ed. Stephen Harrison (Cambridge: Cambridge University Press, 2017).
———. *Opera*, ed. E. C. Wickham (Oxford: Clarendon Press, 1957).
HOWELL, James. *Instructions for Forreine Travell* (London: Humphrey Moseley, 1642).
Il Teatro delle Glorie della Signora Adriana Basile (Venice; reprint Naples: s.n., 1628).
Italian Opera Librettos: 1640–1770, vol. 14, ed. Howard Mayer Brown (New York: Garland, 1983).
JAMES VI and I, King. *An Apologie for the Oath of Allegiance* (London: Robert Barker, 1609).
JONSON, Ben, eds., C.H. Herford, Percy Simpson, and Evelyn Simpson, 11 vols. (Oxford: Clarendon Press, 1925–1952).
———. *The Staple of News*, ed. Anthony Parr (Manchester: Manchester University Press, 1988).
KIRCHER, Athanasius. *Oedipi Aegyptiaci Tomus Secundus. Gymnasium sive Phrontisterion Hieroglyphicum in Duodecim Classes Distributum* (Rome: Vitalis Mascardus, 1653).
LAMB, Charles and LAMB, Mary. *Works*, ed. E. V. Lucas, 7 vols (London: Methuen, 1903).
LANDOR, Walter Savage. *The Complete Works*, eds. T. E. Welby and Stephen Wheeler, 16 vols (London: Chapman and Hall, 1927–1936).
LAZZARELLI, Lodovico. *Ad Ferdinandum Regem Dialogus cui Titulus Crater Hermetis* (Paris: Henri Etienne, 1505).
L'Egisto overo Chi Soffre Speri, intro. Howard Mayer Brown, *Italian Opera, 1640–1770*, ser. 2, vol. 61 (New York: Garland, 1982).
Le Glorie degli Incogniti (Venice: Francesco Valuasense, 1647).
Lettere di Diversi Principi alla Signora Adriana Basile Scritte (Venice; reprint Naples: s.n., 1628).

L'Idea della Veglia (Rome: Francesco Corbelletti, 1640).

LITHGOW, William. *The Totall Discourse of the Rare Adventures and Painefull Peregrinations of Long Nineteene Yeares Travayles from Scotland to the Most Famous Kingdomes in Europe, Asia and Affrica* (London: Nicholas Okes, 1632).

LUCRETIUS. *De Rerum Natura Libri Sex*, ed. Cyril Bailey, 3 vols (Oxford: Clarendon Press, 1946–1949).

MABILLON, Jean, and GERMAIN, Michel. *Musaeum Italicum seu Collectio Veterum Scriptorum in Bibliothecis Italicis* (Paris: Edmund Martin, Johannes Boudot, & Stephanus Martin, 1687).

MALATESTI, Antonio. *La Tina: Equivoci Rusticali*, ed. Davide Messina, (London: Modern Humanities Research Association, 2014).

MANSO, Giovanni Battista. *Erocallia ovvero dell'Amore e della Belleza* (Venice: Deuchino, 1628).

———. *Poesie Nomiche* (Venice: Francesco Baba, 1635).

———. *Vita di Torquato Tasso* (Venice: Deuchino, 1621).

MASCARDI, Agostino. *Discorsi Morali su La Tavola di Cebete Tebano* (Venice: Antonio Pinelli, 1627).

———. *La Congiura del Conte Giovanni Luigi de' Fieschi* (Venice: Giacomo Scaglia, 1629).

———. *Orazioni* (Genoa: Giuseppe Pavoni, 1622).

———. *Prose Vulgari* (Venice: Bartolomeo Fontana, 1626).

MAUGARS, André. *Response Faite à un Curieux sur le Sentiment de la Musique d'Italie. Escrite à Rome le Premier Octobre 1639*, ed. Ernest Thoinan (Paris: Anatole Claudin, 1865).

MAZZOLARI, Giuseppe Maria (alias Josephus Marianus Parthenius). *Electricorum Libri VI* (Rome: Salomoni, 1767).

Memorie de' Viaggi per l'Europa Christiana, Scritte à Diversi in Occasion de' Suoi Ministeri dall' Abate Giovanni Battista Pacichelli: Parte Terza (Naples: Giacomo Raillard, 1685).

MÉNAGE, Gilles. *Menagiana, ou Les Bons Mots*, ed. Bernard de La Monnoye, 4 vols (Paris: Veuve Delaulne, 1729).

MERSENNE, Marin. *Cogitata Physico Mathematica* (Paris: Antonius Bertier, 1644).

MONTAIGNE, Michel de. *Journal de Voyage*, ed. François Rigolot (Paris: Presses Universitaires de France, 1992).

MONTEVERDI, Claudio. *Lettere, Dediche e Prefazioni*, ed. Domenico De' Paoli (Rome: De Santis, 1973).

Monumentum Romanum Nicolao Claudio Fabricio Perescio Senatori Aquensi (Rome: Typis Vaticanis 1638).

MORYSON, Fynes. *An Itinerary ... Containing His Ten Yeeres Travell through the Twelve Dominions of Germany, Bohmerland, Sweitzerland, Netherland, Denmarke, Poland, Italy, Turky, France, England, Scotland & Ireland* (London: John Beale, 1617).

MUNDAY, Antony. *The English Romayne Lyfe, 1582*, ed. G. B. Harrison (Edinburgh: Edinburgh University Press, 1966).

NICÉRON, Jean-Pierre. *Mémoires Pour Servir à l'Histoire des Hommes Illustres dans la République des Lettres*, 44 vols (Paris: Briasson, 1727–1745).

ORSINI, Paolo Giordano. *Rime* (Bracciano: Fei, 1648).

PATRIZI, Francesco. *Nova de Universis Philosophia* (Ferrara: Benedictus Mammarellus, 1591).

PEREGRINI, Matteo. *Delle Acutezze, che Altrimenti Spiriti, Vivezze e Concetti Volgarmente si Appellano* (Genoa: Giovanni Maria Farroni, Nicolò Pesagni, & Pier Francesco Barbieri, 1639).
PETRARCH, Francesco. *Bucolicum Carmen*, ed. Thomas G. Bergin (New Haven, CT: Yale University Press, 1974).
———. *Collatio Laureationis*, ed. Carlo Godi, *Italia Medioevale e Umanistica* 13 (1970): 13–27.
———. *Le Familiari*, ed. Vittorio Rossi, 4 vols (Florence: Sansoni, 1933–1942).
PIAZZA, Bartolomeo. *Eusevologio Romano* (Rome: Giovanni Andreoli, 1690).
PIRANESI, Francesco. *Raccolta dei Tempi Antichi* (Rome: Francesco Piranesi, 1780).
PIRANESI, Giovanni Battista. *The Complete Etchings*, ed. John Wilton-Ely (San Francisco: Alan Wofsy Fine Arts, 1994).
———. *Vedute di Roma*, 2 vols (Rome: Fausto Amedei, 1748–1778).
Poesie de' Signori Accademici Fantastici di Roma (Rome: Grignano, 1637).
PONTANUS, Jacobus. *Poeticarum Institutionum Libri Tres* (Ingolstadt: Sartorius, 1594).
PUCCINOTTI, Francesco. *Storia della Medicina* (Leghorn: Maximilian Wagner, 1850).
QUEVEDO, Francisco de. *Obra Poética*, ed. J. M. Blecua, 3 vols (Madrid: Castalia, 1969–1971).
RODOLFINI, Angelo. *L'Epistole d'Ovidio in Terza Rima del Signor Angelo Rodolfini con gli Argomenti del Signor Ippolito Aurispa* (Macerata: Giuseppe Piccini, 1682).
———. *Sonetti* (Rome: Tinassi, 1688).
ROSSI, Giovanni Vittorio (pseud. Janus Nicius Erythraeus). *Pinacotheca Imaginum Illustrium, Doctrinae vel Ingenii Laude, Virorum* (Cologne: Iodocus Kalcovius, 1645).
RUCCELLAI, Orazio. "Cicalata Settima della Lingua Ionadattica," in *Prose Fiorentine Raccolte dallo Smarrito Accademico*, Part 1, vol. 6 (Florence: Sua Altezza Reale, 1723), 132–161.
RUGGLE, George. *Ignoramus* (London: J. S. Hawkins, 1630).
SANDYS, George. *Travels, Containing an History of the ... Turkish Empire* (London: William Barrett, 1615).
SCALIGER, J. C. *Poetices Libri Septem* (Heidelberg: Pierre de St Andre, 1581).
Selectae Christianae Orbis Deliciae ex Urbibus, Templis, Bibliothecis, et Aliunde, ed. Pierre François Sweerts (Cologne: Bernardus Gualterus, 1625).
SMITH, Thomas. *Vitae Quorundam Eruditissimorum et Illustrium Virorum* (London: David Mortier, 1707).
SPERELLI, Alessandro. *Paradossi Morali* (Venice: Paolo Baglioni, 1666).
STARKE, Mariana. *Information and Directions for Travellers on the Continent* (London: John Murray, 1828).
STIGLIANI, Tommaso. *Lettere* (Rome: Angelo Bernabo, 1664).
STRADLING, John. *A Direction For Travailers. Taken Out of Iustus Lipsius, and Enlarged for the Behoofe of the Right Honorable Lord, the Yong Earle of Bedford, Being Now Ready to Travell* (London: Cuthbert Burbie, 1592).
Sylloges Epistolarum a Viris Illustribus Scriptarum, ed. Pieter Burman, 5 vols (Leiden: Samuel Luchtmans, 1727).
TASSO, Torquato. *Gerusalemme Conquistata* (Rome: Guglielmo Facciotti, 1593).
———. *Il Manso, ovvero dell' Amicizia Dialogo* (Naples: Giovanni Giacomo Carlino and Antonio Pace, 1596).

———. *Solymeidos Libri Duo Priores*, trans. Scipio Gentili (London: John Wolfe, 1584).
TENNYSON, Alfred. *The Poems*, ed. Christopher Ricks, 3 vols (London: Longman, 1987).
TESTI, Fulvio. *Lettere*, ed. Maria Luisa Doglio, 2 vols (Bari: Laterza, 1967).
———. *Poesie Liriche et Alcina Tragedia* (Modena: Pompilio Totti, 1636).
———. *Rime* (Modena: Soliani, 1617).
TETI, Girolamo. *Aedes Barberinae ad Quirinalem* (Rome: Mascardi, 1642).
TIRABOSCHI, Girolamo. *Storia della Letteratura Italiana*, 13 vols (Modena: Società Tipografica, 1772–1782).
TODD, H. J. *Some Account of the Life and Writings of John Milton* (London: Charles and John Rivington, 1826).
TOTTI, Pompilio. *Ritratto di Roma Antica* (Rome: Andrea Fei, 1627).
———. *Ritratto di Roma Moderna* (Rome: Mascardi, 1638).
TRISMEGISTUS, Hermes. *Il Pimandro*, trans. Tommaso Benci (Florence: Lorenzo Torrentino, 1548).
———. *Liber de Potestate et Sapientia Dei e Graeco in Latinum Traductus a Marsilio Ficino Florentino ad Cosmum Medicem Patriae Patrem. Pimander Incipit* (Treviso: Gerardus de Lisa, 1471).
———. *Poemander*, ed. Gustav Parthey (Berlin: Nicolai, 1854).
———. *Pymander Mercurii Trismegisti cum Commento Fratris Hannibalis Rosseli Calabri, Ordinis Minorum Regularis Observantiae, Theologiae et Philosophiae, ad Sanctum Bernardinum Cracoviae Professoris. Liber III: De Ente, Materia, Forma, et Rebus Metaphysicis* (Cracow: Lazari, 1586).
VIRGIL. *Aeneid: Books 7–12*, ed. R.D. Williams (Basingstoke: St Martins Press, 1973).
———. *Eclogues*, ed. Robert Coleman (Cambridge: Cambridge University Press, 1977).
———. *Opera*, ed. F.A. Hirtzel (Oxford: Clarendon Press, 1942).
VITALIS, Jean. *Romanae Ecclesiae Elogia* (Rome: Valerius & Aloysius Doricus, 1553).
VON PFLAUMERN, Johann Heinrich. *Mercurius Italicus* (Augsburg: Andreas Aperger, 1625).
WALLACE, Michael. *In Serenissimi Regis Iacobi . . . Liberationem*, ed. Estelle Haan, *Humanistica Lovaniensia* 42 (1993): 368–401.
WEBBE, Edward. *Edward Webbe, Chief Master Gunner, His Travailes. 1590*, ed. Edward Arber (London: Alex Murray & Son, 1869).
WOOD, Anthony à. *Athenae Oxonienses*, ed. Philip Bliss, 4 vols (London: Rivington et al, 1813–1820).
YOUNG, Patrick (Junius, Patricius). *Patricius Junius, Bibliothekar der Könige Jacob I. und Carl I. von England: Mitteilungen aus Seinem Briefwechsel*, ed. Johannes Kemke, (Leipzig: Max Spirgatis, 1896; reprint Wiesbaden: Otto Harrassowitz, 1969).

6. WORKS OF REFERENCE

A Greek–English Lexicon, eds. H. G. Liddell, R. Scott, and H. S. Jones (Oxford: Clarendon Press, 1940).
A Latin Dictionary, eds. C. T. Lewis and Charles Short (Oxford: Clarendon Press, 1955).
Dizionario Biografico degli Italiani (Rome: Istituto della Enciclopedia Italiana, 1960–).
Inventari dei Manoscritti delle Biblioteche d'Italia, eds. Giuseppe Mazzatinti, Albano Sorbelli, and Luigi Ferrari, 113 vols (Forlì, Luigi Bordandini, 1890–).
Oxford Dictionary of National Biography, 60 vols (Oxford: Oxford University Press, 2004).
Oxford Latin Dictionary, ed. P. G. W. Glare (Oxford: Clarendon Press, 1968–1982).
The Literary Gazette and Journal of the Belles Lettres (London: H. Colburn, 1818–1836).
The New Grove Dictionary of Music and Musicians, ed. Stanley Sadie, 20 vols (London: Macmillan, 1980).

7. SECONDARY LITERATURE

ACHINSTEIN, Sharon and SAUER, Elizabeth, eds., *Milton and Toleration* (Oxford: Oxford University Press, 2007).
ACKERMAN, James S. "The Planning of Renaissance Rome, 1450–1580," in *Rome in the Renaissance*, ed. Ramsey, 3–17.
ADEMOLLO, Alessandro. *I Teatri di Roma nel Secolo Decimosettimo* (Rome: Pasqualucci, 1888).
———. *La Bella Adriana ed Altre Virtuose del Suo Tempo alla Corte di Mantova* (Città di Castello: Lapi, 1888).
———. *La Leonora di Milton e di Clemente IX* (Milan: Ricordi, 1885).
ALEMANNO, Laura. "L'Accademia degli Umoristi," *Roma Moderna e Contemporanea* 3 (1995): 97–120.
ALLEN, M. J. B. *Synoptic Art: Marsilio Ficino on the History of Platonic Interpretation* (Florence: Leo S. Olschki, 1998).
ALLESSANDRINI, Mario. "Una Celebre Cantatrice alla Corte di Urbano VIII," *Scenario* 11 (April, 1942): 152–153.
ALLODOLI, Ettore. *Giovanni Milton e l'Italia* (Prato: Vestri & Spighi, 1907).
ALMAGIÀ, Roberto. *L'Opera Geografica di Luca Holstenio*, Studi e Testi 102 (Vatican City: Biblioteca Apostolica Vaticana, 1942).
AMENDOLA, Nadia. *La Poesia di Giovanni Pietro Monesio, Giovanni Lotti e Lelio Orsini nella Cantata da Camera del XVII Secolo* (PhD thesis: University of Johannes Gutenberg, Mainz, 2017).
ANDERSON, Harald. "Newly Discovered Metrical Arguments to the *Thebaid*," *Medieval Studies* 62 (2000): 219–253.
ANTOLINI, B. M. "Cantanti e Letterati a Roma nella Prima Metà del Seicento: Alcune Osservazioni," in *In Cantu et in Sermone: For Nino Pirrotta on his 80th Birthday*, eds. Fabrizio Della Seta and Franco Piperno (Florence: Olschki, 1989), 347–362.
AVELLINI, Luisa. "Tra 'Umoristi' e 'Gelati,'" *Studi Secenteschi* 23 (1982): 109–137.

AYLWARD, K. J. *Milton's Latin Versification: The Hexameter* (PhD thesis: Columbia University, 1966).
BABB, Lawrence. *The Elizabethan Malady: A Study of Melancholia in English Literature from 1580 to 1642* (East Lansing: Michigan State College Press, 1951).
BACON, Francis. *Some Acrostic Signatures*, ed. William Stone Booth (Boston: Houghton Mifflin, 1909).
BEAL, Mary. *A Study of Richard Symonds: His Italian Notebooks and Their Relevance to Seventeenth-Century Painting Techniques* (New York: Garland, 1984).
BELLINI, Eraldo. *Agostino Mascardi tra "Ars Poetica" e "Ars Historica"* (Milan: V&P Università, 2002).
———. "Mascardi, Agostino," *Dizionario Biografico degli Italiani* 71 (2008): 525–532.
BENET, Diana Treviño. "The Escape From Rome: Milton's Second Defense and a Renaissance Genre," in *Milton in Italy*, ed. Di Cesare, 29–49.
BERNÈS, Anne-Catherine. "René-François de Sluse et Italie," in *Congrès de Namur (XLIX Congrès de la Fédération des Cercles d'Archéologie et d'Histoire de Belgique)* (Namur: Presses Universitaires de Namur, 1990), III, 305–317.
BERRY, Herbert. "The Miltons and the Blackfriars Playhouse," *Modern Philology* 89 (1992): 510–514.
BIANCONI, Lorenzo and WALKER, Thomas. "Production, Consumption and Political Function of Seventeenth-Century Opera," *Early Music History* 4 (1984): 209–296.
BING, Peter. "Callimachus and the Hymn to Demeter," *Syllecta Classica* 6 (1995): 29–42.
BISHOP, Walter H. "Maugars' Response Faite à un Curieux sur le Sentiment de la Musique d'Italie," *Journal of the Viola da Gamba Society of America* 8 (1971): 5–17.
BLOM, F. J. "Lucas Holstenius (1596–1661) and England," in *Studies in Seventeenth-century English Literature, History and Bibliography*, eds. G. A. M. Janssens and F. G. A. M. Aarts (Amsterdam: Rodopi, 1984), 25–39.
BORSOI, M. B. Guerrieri. "Tra Le Ville e La Città: Tre Casini Seicenteschi a Frascati," in *Il Tesoro della Città. Strenna dell' Associazione Storia della Città* (Rome: Kappa, 2008–2010), VI, 190–214.
BOSI, Kathryn. "Adriana's Harp: Paintings, Poetic Imagery, and Musical Tributes for the *Sirena di Posilipo*," *Imago Musicae* 30 (2019): 75–103.
BOW, Douglas. *Doctors, Ambassadors, Secretaries: Humanism and Professions in Renaissance Italy* (Chicago: The University of Chicago Press, 2002).
BOYLE, Leonard. "Niccolò V Fondatore della Biblioteca Vaticana," in *Niccolò V nel Sesto Centenario della Nascita*, eds. Franco Bonatti and Antonio Manfredi, Studi e Testi 397 (Vatican City: Biblioteca Apostolica Vaticana, 2000), 3–8.
———. "Sixtus IV and the Vatican Library," in *Rome: Tradition, Innovation, and Renewal*, eds. Clifford M. Brown, John Osborne, and W. Chandler Kirwin (Victoria, BC: University of Victoria, 1991), 65–73.
BRAND, C. P. *Torquato Tasso: A Study of the Poet and of his Contribution to English Literature* (Cambridge: Cambridge University Press, 1965), 207–209.
BRILL, Mary Campbell. *Milton and Ovid* (PhD thesis: Cornell University, 1935).
BROOKES, Anne. *Richard Symonds in Rome, 1649–1651* (PhD thesis: University of Nottingham, 2000).

———. "Richard Symonds's Account of his Visit to Rome in 1649–1651," *Walpole Society* 69 (2007): 1–183.

BROSIUS, Amy. "'Il Suon, lo Sguardo, il Canto': The Function of Portraits of Mid-Seventeenth-Century Virtuose in Rome," *Italian Studies* 63 (2008): 17–39.

———. *"Il Suon, lo Sguardo, il Canto": Virtuose of the Roman Conversazioni in the Mid-Seventeenth Century* (PhD thesis: New York University, 2009).

BRYDGES, Egerton. *Res Literariae: For May 1821 to February 1822* (Geneva: William Fick, 1822).

BUELOW, George J. *A History of Baroque Music* (Bloomington: Indiana University Press, 2004).

BURBERY, J. T. "John Milton, Blackfriars Spectator?: 'Elegia Prima' and Ben Jonson's *The Staple of News*," *Ben Jonson Journal* 10 (2003): 57–76.

———. *Milton the Dramatist* (Pittsburgh: Duquesne University Press, 2007).

BYARD, Margaret. "'Adventrous Song': Milton and the Music of Rome," in *Milton in Italy*, ed. Di Cesare, 305–328.

———. "Divine Wisdom—Urania," *Milton Quarterly* 12 (1978): 134–137.

———. "Note on the Illustration: St. Peter's and Pandaemonium?" *Milton Quarterly* 9 (1975): 65–66.

CÀLLARI, Luigi. *I Palazzi di Roma, e le Case d'Importanze Storica e Artistica* (Rome: Bardi, 1968).

CAMIZ, Franca Trinchieri. "La Bella Cantatrice: I Ritratti di Leonora Barone e Barbara Strozzi a Confronto," in *Musica, Scienza e Idée nella Serenissima durante il Seicento Venezia*, ed. Francesco Passadore *et al* (Venice: Fondazione Ugo e Olga Levi, 1996), 285–294.

CAMPBELL, Gordon. "Diodati, Charles (1609/10–1638)," *Oxford Dictionary of National Biography* 16 (2004), 252.

———. "Shakespeare and the Youth of Milton," *Milton Quarterly* 33 (1999): 95–105.

CARPENTER, N. C. "Milton and Music: Henry Lawes, Dante, and Casella," *English Literary Review* 2 (1972): 237–242.

CARTER, Tim. "The Composer as Theorist? Genus and Genre in Monteverdi's *Combattimento di Tancredi e Clorinda*," in *Music in the Mirror: Reflections on the History of Music Theory and Literature for the Twenty-first Century*, eds. Andreas Giger and Thomas J. Mathiesen (Lincoln: University of Nebraska Press, 2002), 77–116.

CASTAGNA, Luigi. "Il Pindarismo Mediato di Orazio," *Aevum Antiquum* 2 (1989): 183–214.

———. "Pindaro, Le Origini del Pindarismo e Gabriello Chiabrera," *Aevum* 65 (1991): 523–542.

CASTIGLIONE, Caroline. *Patrons and Adversaries: Nobles and Villagers in Italian Politics, 1640–1760* (Oxford: Oxford University Press, 2005).

CAYLEY, C. B. "The Pedigree of English Heroic Verse," *Transactions of the Philological Society* 15 (1867): 43–54.

CELENZA, Christopher S. and PUPILLO, Bridget. "Le Grandi Biblioteche 'Pubbliche' del XV Secolo," in *Atlante Storico della Letteratura Italiana*, eds. S. Luzzatto and G. Pedullà, 3 vols (Turin: Einaudi, 2010–2012), I, 312–321.

CHANEY, Edward. *The Evolution of the Grand Tour: Anglo-Italian Cultural Relations Since the Renaissance* (London: Frank Cass, 1998).

———. *The Grand Tour and the Great Rebellion: Richard Lassels and "The Voyage of Italy" in the Seventeenth Century* (Geneva: Slatkine, 1985).

———. "The Visit to Vallombrosa: A Literary Tradition," in *Milton in Italy*, ed. Di Cesare, 113–146.

CHARTERS, Stephen. *Wine and Society: The Social and Cultural Context of a Drink* (Oxford: Butterworth-Heinemann, 2006).

CINQUEMANI, A. M. *Glad To Go For A Feast: Milton, Buonmattei, and the Florentine Accademici* (New York: Peter Lang, 1998).

CLARK, D. L. *John Milton at St. Paul's School: A Study of Ancient Rhetoric in English Renaissance Education* (New York: Columbia University Press, 1948).

CLARK, Raymond J. "Ilia's Excessive Complaint and The Flood in Horace, *Odes* 1.2," *Classical Quarterly* 60 (May 2010): 262–267.

CLAVERING, Rose and SHAWCROSS, John T. "Milton's European Itinerary and his Return Home," *Studies in English Literature* 5 (1965): 49–59.

COCHRANE, Eric W. *Tradition and Enlightenment in the Tuscan Academies 1690–1800* (Chicago: University of Chicago Press, 1961).

COFFEY, John. *Persecution and Toleration in Protestant England, 1558–1689* (Harlow: Longman, 2000).

COLE, Spencer. "The Dynamics of Deification in Horace's *Odes* 1–3," in *Between Magic and Religion: Interdisciplinary Studies in Ancient Mediterranean Religion and Society*, eds. S. R. Asirvatham, C. O. Pache, and John Watrous (Oxford: Rowman & Littlefield, 2001), 67–91.

COLOMBO, Angelo. *I "Riposi di Pindo": Studi di Claudio Achillini (1574–1640)* (Florence: Olschki, 1988).

———. "Sul Plagio: Una Rettifica della Bibliografia di Claudio Achillini (e di G. B. Marino)," *Studi Secenteschi* 25 (1984): 101–113.

———. "Tra 'Incogniti' e 'Lincei': Per la Biografia di Claudio Achillini," *Studi Secenteschi* 26 (1985): 141–176.

CONDEE, Ralph W. "Ovid's Exile and Milton's Rustication," *Philological Quarterly* 37 (1958): 498–502.

———. *Structure in Milton's Poetry: From the Foundation to the Pinnacles* (University Park: Pennsylvania State University Press, 1974).

CURRAN, John E. *Roman Invasions: The British History, Protestant Anti-Romanism, and the Historical Imagination in England, 1530–1600* (Newark: University of Delaware Press/London: Associated University Presses, 2002).

D'AMICO, Silvio, and D'AMICO, Sandro, eds. *Enciclopedia dello Spettacolo*, 9 vols (Rome: Casa Editrice Le Maschere, 1954).

DAMSCHRODER, David, and WILLIAMS, David Russell. *Music Theory from Zarlino to Schenker: A Bibliography and Guide* (Stuyvesant, NY: Pendragon Press, 1990).

DAVIES, Stevie, and HUNTER, William B. "Milton's Urania: 'The Meaning Not the Name I Call,'" *Studies in English Literature* 28 (1988): 95–111.

DE FILIPPIS, Michele. "Milton and Manso: Cups or Books?" *Publications of the Modern Language Association of America* 51 (1936): 745–746.

DELBEKE, Maarten. "An Unstable Sublime: Milton's Pandemonium and the Baldacchino at St. Peter's in Rome," *Lias* 43 (2016): 281–296.

DELL'ANTONIO, Andrew. *Listening as Spiritual Practice in Early Modern Italy* (Berkeley: University of California Press, 2011).

DELSIGNE, Jill Renée. *Sacramental Magic and Animate Statues in Edmund Spenser, William Shakespeare, and John Milton* (PhD thesis: Rice University, 2012).

DEMARAY, John G. *Milton's Theatrical Epic: The Invention and Design of Paradise Lost* (Cambridge MA and London: Harvard University Press, 1980).

DE MATTEI, Rodolfo. "Dispute Filosofico-Politiche nelle Accademie Romane del Seicento," *Studi Romani* 9 (1961): 148–167.

DI CESARE, Mario A., ed. *Milton in Italy: Contexts, Images, Contradictions* (Binghamton, NY: Medieval and Renaissance Texts and Studies, 1991).

DOLLOFF, Matthew K. *Mediating the Muse: Milton and the Metamorphoses of Urania* (University of Texas, 2006).

DORIAN, D. C. *The English Diodatis* (New Brunswick, NJ: Rutgers University Press, 1950).

DUBOWY, Norbert. "'Al Tavolino Medesimo del Compositor della Musica': Notes on Text and Context in Alessandro Scarlatti's *Cantate da Camera*," in *Aspects of the Secular Cantata in Late Baroque Italy*, ed. Michael Talbot (London: Routledge, 2016), 111–134.

DUCKWORTH, G. E. "Milton's Hexameter Patterns — Vergilian or Ovidian?" *American Journal of Philology* 93 (1972): 52–60.

DUNN, Francis. "Horace's Sacred Spring (*Odes* I, 1)," *Latomus* 48 (1989): 97–109.

ELLISON, James. "*The Winter's Tale* and the Religious Politics of Europe," in *New Casebooks: Shakespeare's Romances*, ed. Alison Thorne (New York: Palgrave Macmillan, 2003), 171–204.

EMERSON, Isabelle. *Five Centuries of Women Singers* (Westport, CT: Greenwood Publishing, 2005).

ENZI, Silvia. "Le Inondazioni del Tevere a Roma tra il XVI e XVIII Secolo nelle Fonti Bibliotecarie del Tempo," *Mélanges de L'Ecole Française de Rome* 118 (2006): 13–20.

FAHMER, Robert and KLEB, William. "The Theatrical Activity of Gianlorenzo Bernini," *Educational Theatre Journal* 25 (1973): 5–14.

FASSÒ, Luigi. "Stigliani, Tommaso," in *Enciclopedia Italiana di Scienze, Lettere ed Arti* 32 (Rome: Istituto dell' Enciclopedia Italiana, 1936).

FAULKNER, Andrew. "Fast, Famine, and Feast: Food for Thought in Callimachus' Hymn to Demeter," *Harvard Studies in Classical Philology* 106 (2011): 75–95.

FIORI, Alessandra. "Il Canto di Casella: Esegesi Dantesche a Confronto," in *Trent' Anni di Ricerche Musicologiche: Studi in Onore di F. Alberto Gallo*, eds. Patrizia Dalla Vecchia and Donatella Restani (Rome: Torre D'Orfeo, 1996), 283–289.

FISCHER-LICHTE, Erika. "Transforming Spectators into Viri Perculsi: Baroque Theatre as Machinery for Producing Affects," in *Performativity and Performance in Baroque Rome*, eds. Peter Gillgren and Mårten Snickare (Farnham: Ashgate, 2012), 87–97.

FITZGERALD, William. *Variety: The Life of a Roman Concept* (Chicago: The University of Chicago Press, 2016).

FLETCHER, Harris F. "Milton's *Apologus* and its Mantuan Model," *Journal of English and Germanic Philology* 55 (1956): 230–233.

FLOOD, John. *Poets Laureate in the Holy Roman Empire: A Bio-bibliographical Handbook* (Berlin: Walter de Gruyter, 2006).

FORMICHETTI, Cianfranco. "Doni, Giovanni Battista," *Dizionario Biografico degli Italiani* 41 (1992): 167–170.

FORSYTH, Neil. "Of Man's First Dis," in *Milton in Italy*, ed. Di Cesare, 345–369.

FRANKLIN, Carmela Vircillo. "'Pro Communi Doctorum Virorum Commodo': The Vatican Library and its Service to Scholarship," *Proceedings of the American Philosophical Society* 146 (2002): 363–384.

FREEMAN, James A. *Milton and the Martial Muse: Paradise Lost and European Traditions of War* (Princeton, NJ: Princeton University Press, 1980).

———. "Milton's Roman Connection: Giovanni Salzilli," *Milton Studies* 19 (1984): 87–104.

FRYE, Roland Mushat. *Milton's Imagery and the Visual Arts: Iconographic Tradition in the Epic Poems* (Princeton, NJ: Princeton University Press, 1978).

FUCHS, Peter. "Holste, Lukas," *Neue Deutsche Biographie* 9 (Berlin: Duncker & Humblot, 1972), 548–550.

GABRIELE, Giuseppe. "Accademie Romane. Gli Umoristi," *Roma* 13 (1935): 173–184.

GALASSI, Cristina. "La Virtuosa Eleonora Baroni in un Ritratto di Fabio della Corgna," *Kronos* 13 (2009): 177–183.

———. *Ritratto di Una Virtuosa Canterina: Eleonora Baroni e il Pittore Fabio della Corgna al Tempo dei Barberini* (Perugia: Aguaplano, 2017).

GALLO, Marco. "Orazio Borgianni, L'Accademia di S. Luca e L'Accademia degli Humoristi: Documenti e Nuove Datazioni," *Storia dell' Arte* 76 (1992): 296–345.

GOLD, Barbara K. "Openings in Horace's Satires and Odes: Poet, Patron, and Audience," in *Beginnings in Classical Literature*, eds. Francis M. Dunn and Thomas Cole, Yale Classical Studies 29 (Cambridge: Cambridge University Press, 1992), 161–186.

GOLDSCHMIDT, Hugo. *Studien zur Geschichte der Italienischen Oper im 17. Jahrhundert* (Leipzig: Breitkopf and Härtel, 1901).

GOODE, James. "Milton and Sannazaro," *Times Literary Supplement* (13 August 1931): 621.

GOUDRIAAN, Elisa. *Florentine Patricians and Their Networks: Structures Behind the Cultural Success and the Political Representation of the Medici Court (1600–1660)* (Leiden: Brill, 2017).

GRACIOTTI, Sante. "La Fortuna di Una Elegia di Giano Vitale, o le Rovine di Roma nella Poesia Polacca," *Aevum* 34 (1960): 122–136.

GRAVIT, F. W. "The Accademia degli Umoristi and its French Relationships," *Papers of the Michigan Academy* 29 (1935): 501–521.

GREENE, Thomas G. "Resurrecting Rome: The Double Task of the Humanist Imagination," in *Rome in the Renaissance*, ed. Ramsey, 41–54.

HAAN, Estelle. *Andrew Marvell's Latin Poetry: From Text to Context* (Brussels: Collection Latomus, 2003).

———. *Both English and Latin: Bilingualism and Biculturalism in Milton's Neo-Latin Writings* (Philadelphia: American Philosophical Society, 2012).

———. "'Both English and Latin': Milton's Bilingual Muse," *Renaissance Studies* 21 (2007): 679–700.

———. "'Coelum Non Animum Muto'? Milton's Neo-Latin Poetry and Catholic Italy," in *Milton and Catholicism*, eds. Ronald Corthell and Thomas N. Corns (Notre Dame, IN: University of Notre Dame Press, 2017), 131–167.

———. "England, Neo-Latin and the Continental Journey," in *Political Turmoil: Early Modern British Literature in Transition, 1623–1660*, ed. Stephen B. Dobranski (Cambridge: Cambridge University Press, 2019), 322–338.

———. *From Academia to Amicitia: Milton's Latin Writings and the Italian Academies* (Philadelphia: American Philosophical Society, 1998).

———. "From Helicon to Heaven: Milton's Urania and Vida," *Renaissance Studies* 7 (1993): 115–136.

———. "'Heaven's Purest Light': Milton's *Paradise Lost* 3 and Vida," *Comparative Literature Studies* 30 (1993): 115–136.

———. "*Mansueti ... Chironis*: Milton, Manso, and Ovid's Chiron," *Classical and Modern Literature* 17 (1997): 251–264.

———. "Mantuan, Milton and 'The Fruit of that Forbidden Tree,'" *Medievalia et Humanistica* 25 (1998): 75–92.

———. "Milton's *Elegia Quarta* and Ovid: Another Cross-comparison," *Notes and Queries* 54 (2007): 400–405.

———. "Milton's *In Quintum Novembris* and the Anglo-Latin Gunpowder Epic," *Humanistica Lovaniensia* 41 (1992): 221–250.

———. "Milton's Latin Poetry and Vida," *Humanistica Lovaniensia* 44 (1995): 282–304.

———. "Milton's *Paradise Regained* and Vida's *Christiad*," in *From Erudition to Inspiration: A Booklet for Michael*, ed. Estelle Haan (Belfast: Belfast Byzantine Texts and Translations, 1992), 53–77.

———. "Pastoral," in *A Guide to Neo-Latin Literature*, ed. Victoria Moul (Cambridge: Cambridge University Press, 2017), 163–179.

HADFIELD, Andrew. "Milton and Catholicism," in *Milton and Toleration*, eds. Achinstein and Sauer, 186–202.

———. "The English and Other Peoples," in *A Companion to Milton*, ed. Thomas N. Corns (Oxford: Blackwell, 2001, 2003), 174–190.

HALE, John K. "Milton and the Gunpowder Plot: *In Quintum Novembris* Reconsidered," *Humanistica Lovaniensia* 50 (2001): 351–366.

———. "Milton Playing with Ovid," *Milton Studies* 25 (1989): 3–19.

———. *Milton's Cambridge Latin: Performing in the Genres, 1625–1632* (Tempe, AZ: Medieval and Renaissance Texts and Studies, 2005).

———. *Milton's Languages: The Impact of Multilingualism on Style* (Cambridge: Cambridge University Press, 1997).

———. "Milton's Reading of Virgil's *Aeneid* VI. 680 in his Letter to the Vatican Librarian," *Notes and Queries* 49 (2002): 336.

HAMMOND, Frederick. "Bernini and the 'Fiera di Farfa,'" in *Gianlorenzo Bernini: New Aspects of his Art and Thought*, ed. Irving Lavin (University Park, PA: Pennsylvania State University Press, 1985), 115–125.

———. "Girolamo Frescobaldi and a Decade of Music in Casa Barberini: 1634–1643," *Analecta Musicologica* 19 (1980): 94–124.

———. *Music and Spectacle in Baroque Rome* (New Haven, CT: Yale University Press, 1994).

HANNING, Barbara Russano. "Monteverdi's Three Genera: A Study in Terminology," in *Musical Humanism and Its Legacy: Essays in Honor of Claude Palisca*, eds. Nancy Kovaleff Baker and Barbara Russano Hanning (Stuyvesant, NY: Pendragon, 1992), 145–170.

HANSES, Mathias. "Love's letters: An Amor-Roma Telestich at Ovid, *Ars Amatoria* 3.507-10," in *Wordplay and Powerplay in Latin Poetry*, eds. Phillip Mitsis and Ioannis Ziogas (Berlin: Walter de Gruyter, 2016), 199–212.

HARBAGE, Alfred. *Annals of English Drama 975–1700: An Analytical Record of All Plays, Extant or Lost, Chronologically Arranged and Indexed by Authors,*

Titles, Dramatic Companies &c, rev. S. Schoenbaum (Philadelphia: University of Pennsylvania Press, 1964).
HARDIE, Philip. "Milton's *Epitaphium Damonis* and the Virgilian Career," in *Pastoral Palimpsests: Essays on the Reception of Theocritus and Virgil*, ed. Michael Paschalis (Herakleion: Crete University Press, 2007), 79–100.
HARDIN, R. F. "The Early Poetry of the Gunpowder Plot: Myth in the Making," *English Literary Review* 22 (1992): 62–79.
HARDING, Davis P. *Milton and the Renaissance Ovid* (Urbana: University of Illinois Press, 1946).
HARRIS, Neil. "Galileo as Symbol: The 'Tuscan Artist' in *Paradise Lost*," *Annali dell' Istituto e Museo di Storio della Scienza di Firenze* 10 (1985): 3–29.
———. "The Vallombrosa Simile and the Image of the Poet in *Paradise Lost*," in *Milton in Italy*, ed. Di Cesare, 71–94.
HARRISON, Thomas P. "The Latin Pastorals of Milton and Castiglione," *Publications of the Modern Language Association of America* 50 (1935): 480–493.
HASKELL, Y. A. *Loyola's Bees: Ideology and Industry in Jesuit Latin Didactic Poetry* (Oxford: Oxford University Press, 2003).
HENINGER, S. K. *Touches of Sweet Harmony: Pythagorean Cosmology and Renaissance Poetics* (San Marino, CA: Huntington Library, 1974).
HIND, A. M. *Giovanni Battista Piranesi: A Critical Study, with a List of his Published Works and Detailed Catalogues of the Prisons and the Views of Rome* (New York: E. Weyhe, 1922).
HOPKINS, David. "Milton and the Classics," in *John Milton: Life, Writing, Reputation*, eds. Paul Hammond and Blair Worden (Oxford: Oxford University Press, 2010), 23–41.
HUI, Andrew. *The Poetics of Ruins in Renaissance Literature* (New York: Fordham University Press, 2016).
HUNT, John Dixon. *Garden and Grove: The Italian Renaissance Garden in the English Imagination 1600–1750* (Philadelphia: University of Pennsylvania Press, 1986).
HUNTER, William B. "Milton's Urania," *Studies in English Literature* 4 (1964): 35–42.
———. *The Descent of Urania: Studies in Milton, 1946–1988* (Lewisburg, PA: Bucknell University Press, 1989).
HUTCHINSON, G. O. *Talking Books: Readings in Hellenistic and Roman Books of Poetry* (Oxford: Oxford University Press, 2008).
HUTTAR, Charles A. "Vallombrosa Revisited," in *Milton in Italy*, ed. Di Cesare, 95–111.
IANNUCCI, Amilcare. "Casella's Song and the Tuning of the Soul," *Thought* 65 (1990): 27–46.
JEANNERET, Christine. "Gender Ambivalence and the Expression of Passions in the Performances of Early Roman Cantatas by Castrati and Female Singers," in *The Emotional Power of Music: Multidisciplinary Perspectives on Musical Arousal, Expression, and Social Control*, eds. Tom Cochrane, Bernardino Fantini, and Klaus R. Scherer (Oxford: Oxford University Press, 2013), 85–101.
KEMP, Martin. "From *Mimesis* to *Fantasia*: The Quattrocento Vocabulary of Creation, Inspiration and Genius in the Visual Arts," *Viator* 8 (1977): 347–398.
KILGOUR, Maggie. *Milton and the Metamorphosis of Ovid* (Oxford: Oxford University Press, 2012).

KIMMICH, P. E. *John Milton's Technical Handling of the Latin Elegy* (PhD thesis: University of Illinois, 1958).

KING, John N. *Milton and Religious Controversy: Satire and Polemic in Paradise Lost* (Cambridge: Cambridge University Press, 2000).

KNEDLIK, J. L. "High Pastoral Art in *Epitaphium Damonis*," *Milton Studies* 19 (1984): 149–163.

KNOPPERS, Laura Lunger. "Satan and the Papacy in *Paradise Regained*," *Milton Studies* 42 (2002): 68–85.

LAND, J. P. N. "Joan Albert Ban en de Theorie der Toonkunst," *Tijdschrift van de Vereniging voor Nederlandse Muziekgeschiedenis* 1 (1883): 95–111; 3 (1891): 204–218.

LAVIN, Irving. *Bernini and the Unity of the Visual Arts*, 2 vols (New York: Oxford University Press, 1980).

LAVIN, M. A. *Seventeenth-Century Barberini Documents and Inventories of Art* (New York: New York University Press, 1975).

LAZZERI, Allessandro. *Intellettuali e Consenso nella Toscana del Seicento: L'Accademia degli Apatisti* (Milan: A. Giuffrè, 1983).

LEIGH, Fiona. "Platonic Dialogue, Maieutic Method, and Critical Thinking," *Journal of Philosophy of Education* 41 (2007): 209–223.

LEIGH, Matthew. "The Garland of Maecenas (Horace, *Odes* 1.1.35)," *Classical Quarterly* 60 (2010): 268–271.

LEWALSKI, Barbara K. *Milton's Brief Epic: The Genre, Meaning, and Art of Paradise Regained* (Providence, Rhode Island: Brown University Press/Methuen, 1966).

LEWIS, Susan Gail. *"Chi Soffre Speri" and the Influence of the "Commedia dell' Arte" on the Development of Roman Opera* (M. Mus. Thesis: University of Arizona, 1995).

LIEB, Michael. *Milton and the Culture of Violence* (Ithaca, NY: Cornell University Press, 1994).

LOW, Anthony. "*Mansus*: In its Context," *Milton Studies* 19 (1984): 105–126.

LUNN, David. *The English Benedictines, 1540–1688* (London: Barnes & Noble, 1980).

MACDONALD, William L. *The Pantheon: Design, Meaning, and Progeny* (London: Penguin Books, 1976).

MACKELLAR, Walter. "Milton, James I and Purgatory," *Modern Language Review* 18 (1923): 472–473.

MARTIN, Catherine Gimelli. *Milton's Italy: Anglo-Italian Literature, Travel, and Religion in Seventeenth-Century England* (New York: Routledge, 2017).

MARTINDALE, Charles. *Redeeming the Text: Latin Poetry and the Hermeneutics of Reception* (Cambridge: Cambridge University Press, 1993).

———. "Unlocking the Word-Hoard: In Praise of Metaphrase," *Comparative Criticism* 6 (1984): 47–72.

MARTINI, Antonio, and CASANOVA, M. L. *SS Nome di Maria*, Le Chiese di Roma Illustrate 70 (Rome: Marietti, 1962).

MARTINI, Fabio, and NARDINI, Stefania. *Roma Nascosta: Una Guida Spigliata e Stimolante alla Riscoperta degli Insospettati Tesori di Una Roma Troppo Spesso Inaccessibile* (Rome: Newton Compton, 1984).

MAXWELL, Catherine. *The Female Sublime From Milton to Swinburne: Bearing Blindness* (Manchester: Manchester University Press, 2001).

MAYER, Thomas F. *The Roman Inquisition: A Papal Bureaucracy and its Laws in the Age of Galileo* (Philadelphia: University of Pennsylvania Press, 2013).
MAYLENDER, Michele. *Storia delle Accademie d'Italia*, 5 vols (Bologna: Capelli, 1926–1930).
MCCLUNG, William A. "The Architecture of Pandaemonium," *Milton Quarterly* 15 (1981): 109–112.
MCCOLLEY, Diane K. "Tongues of Men and Angels: *Ad Leonoram Romae Canentem*," *Milton Studies* 19 (1984): 127–148.
MCMINN, J. B. "Plato's Mantic Myths in the Service of Socrates' Maieutic art," *Kernos* 3 (1990): 219–234.
MELEHY, Hassan. *The Poetics of Literary Transfer in Early Modern France and England* (London: Routledge, 2010).
MENGHINI, Mario. *Tommaso Stigliani: Contributo all Storia Letteraria del Secolo XVII* (Modena: Sarasino, 1890).
MESSINA, Davide. "*La Tina* Regained," *Milton Quarterly* 45 (2011): 118–122.
MILLER, Leo. "Milton Dines at the Jesuit College: Reconstructing the Evening of October 30, 1638," *Milton Quarterly* 13 (1979): 142–146.
MINTZ, Samuel. "The Motion of Thought: Intellectual and Philosophical Backgrounds," in *Backgrounds to Seventeenth-Century Literature*, eds. C. A. Patrides and Raymond B. Waddington (Manchester: Manchester University Press, 1980), 138–169.
MONTALTI, Lina. *Un Mecenate in Roma Barocca: Il Cardinale Benedetto Pamphili (1653–1730)* (Florence: Sansoni, 1955).
MORANDINI, Giuliana. *Sospiri e Palpiti: Scrittrici Italiane del Seicento* (Genoa: Marietti, 2001).
MUENTZ, Eugene, and FABRE, Paul. *La Bibliothèque du Vatican au XVe Siècle*, Bibliothèque des Écoles Françaises d'Athènes et de Rome, 48 (Paris: Thorin, 1887).
MULDER, John R. "Shades and Substance," in *Milton in Italy*, ed. Di Cesare, 61–69.
MÜLLER, C. W. *Erysichthon. Der Mythos als narrative Metapher im Demeterhymnos des Kallimachos* (Stuttgart: Franz Steiner, 1987).
MURATA, Margaret. "Chi soffre speri," *The New Grove Dictionary of Opera*, Grove Music Online (Oxford University Press). Available at http://www.oxfordmusiconline.com/subscriber/article/grove/music/O008004
———. "Image and Eloquence: Secular Song," in *The Cambridge History of Seventeenth-Century Music*, eds. Tim Carter and John Butt (Cambridge: Cambridge University Press, 2005), 378–425.
———. *Operas For The Papal Court 1631–1668* (Ann Arbor, Michigan: UMI Research Press, 1981).
———. "Why the First Opera Given in Paris Wasn't Roman," *Cambridge Opera Journal* 7 (1995): 87–105.
MURPHY, Stephen. *The Gift of Immortality: Myths of Power and Humanist Poetics* (London: Associated University Presses, 1997).
MURRAY, Jackie. "The Metamorphosis of Erysichthon: Callimachus, Apollonius, and Ovid," in *Hellenistica Groningana 7: Callimachus II*, eds. M. A. Harder, R. F. Regtuit, and G. C. Wakker (Leuven: Peeters, 2004), 207–242.
MUSURILLO, Herbert. "The Poet's Apotheosis: Horace, *Odes* 1.1," *Transactions and Proceedings of the American Philological Association* 93 (1962): 230–239.
NARDO, Anna K. "Academic Interludes in *Paradise Lost*," *Milton Studies* 27 (1991): 209–241.

NICOLSON, M. H., *John Milton: A Reader's Guide to his Poetry* (London: Thames and Hudson, 1964), 196–198.
———. "Milton's Hell and the Phlegraean Fields," *University of Toronto Quarterly* 7 (1938): 500–513.
NISBET, R. G. M., and RUDD, Niall. *A Commentary on Horace: Odes Book III* (Oxford: Oxford University Press, 2004).
NOREEN, Kirstin. "Lay Patronage and the Creation of Papal Sanctity during the Gregorian Reform: The case of Sant' Urbano alla Caffarella, Rome," *Gesta* 40 (2001): 39–59.
———. "Recording the Past: Seventeenth-Century Watercolor Drawings of Medieval Monuments," *Visual Resources* 16 (2000): 1–26.
———. *Sant' Urbano alla Caffarella: Eleventh-Century Roman Wall Painting and the Sanctity of Martyrdom* (Ph.D thesis: Johns Hopkins University, 1998).
———. "Sant'Urbano alla Caffarella, Rome: The Reconstruction of an Ancient Memorial," *Memoirs of the American Academy in Rome* 47 (2002): 57–82.
OBERHELMAN, S. M., and MULRYAN, John. "Milton's Use of Classical Meters in the *Sylvarum Liber*," *Modern Philology* 81 (1983): 131–145.
PALMA, Marco. "Cherubini, Laerzio," *Dizionario Biografico degli Italiani* 24 (1980): 434–435.
PANNELLA, Liliana. "Baroni, Eleonora, Detta Anche l'Adrianella o l'Adrianetta," *Dizionario Biografico degli Italiani* 6 (1964): 456–458.
PANOFSKY, Erwin. *Galileo as a Critic of the Arts* (The Hague: Martinus Nijhoff, 1954).
PARKER, W. R. "Milton and the News of Charles Diodati's Death," *Modern Language Notes* 72 (1957): 486–488.
PASCHALIS, Michael. *Virgil's Aeneid: Semantic Relations and Proper Names* (Oxford: Clarendon Press, 1997).
PASTOR, Ludwig. *The History of the Popes*, trans. Dom Ernest Graf, 40 vols (London: Kegan Paul, 1923–1953).
PÉLISSIER, L. G. "Les amis d'Holstenius," *Revue des Langues Romanes* 5 (1891): 321–378.
PIRROTTA, Nino. *Music and Culture in Italy From the Middle Ages to the Baroque: A Collection of Essays* (Cambridge MA: Harvard University Press, 1984).
POLLITT, J. J. *The Art of Rome c. 753 B.C–A.D. 337: Sources and Documents* (Cambridge: Cambridge University Press, 1983).
POOLE, William. *Milton and the Making of Paradise Lost* (Cambridge MA: Harvard University Press, 2017).
POTTER, Lois. *A Preface to Milton* (London: Routledge, 2013).
PRAWDZIK, Brendan. *Theatrical Milton, Politics and Poetics of the Staged Body* (Edinburgh: Edinburgh University Press, 2017).
PRITCHARD, Allan. "Milton in Rome: According to Wood," *Milton Quarterly* 14 (1980): 92–97.
PURCIELLO, Maria Anne. *And Dionysus Laughed: Opera, Comedy and Carnival in Seventeenth-Century Venice and Rome* (PhD thesis: Princeton University, 2005).
PUTNAM, Michael C. J. *Essays on Latin Lyric, Elegy, and Epic* (Princeton, NJ: Princeton University Press, 1982).
———. "Horace *C*.3.30: The Lyricist as Hero," *Ramus* 2 (1973): 1–19.
QUINT, David. "Milton, Fletcher and the Gunpowder Plot," *Journal of the Warburg and Courtauld Institutes* 54 (1991): 261–268.

———. "The Disenchanted World of *Paradise Regained*," *Huntington Library Quarterly* 76 (2013): 181–194.

RACE, W. H. *The Classical Priamel from Homer to Boethius*, Mnemosyne Supplement 74 (Leiden: Brill, 1982).

RAMSEY, P. A., ed. *Rome in the Renaissance: The City and the Myth* (Binghamton, NY: Medieval and Renaissance Texts and Studies, 1982).

RASCH, Rudolf A. "Ban's Intonation," *Tijdschrift van de Vereniging voor Nederlandse Muziekgeschiedenis* 33 (1983): 75–99.

———. "Six Seventeenth-Century Dutch Scientists and their Knowledge of Music," in *Music and Science in the Age of Galileo*, ed. Victor Coelho (Dordrecht: Kluwer Academic Publishers, 2010), 185–210.

RAYMOND, Joad. *Milton's Angels: The Early Modern Imagination* (Oxford: Oxford University Press, 2010).

REED, Jay. "*Mora* in the *Aeneid*," in *Wordplay and Powerplay in Latin Poetry*, eds Phillip Mitsis and Ioannis Ziogas (Berlin: Walter de Gruyter, 2016), 87–106.

REES, Valery. *From Gabriel to Lucifer: A Cultural History of Angels* (London: I. B. Tauris, 2013).

REINER, Stuart. "Collaboration in *Chi Soffre Speri*," *Music Review* 22 (1961): 265–282.

REVARD, Stella P. "Milton and Classical Rome: The Political Context of *Paradise Regained*," in *Rome in the Renaissance*, ed. Ramsey, 409–419.

———. *Milton and the Tangles of Neaera's Hair: The Making of the 1645 Poems* (Columbia: University of Missouri Press, 1997).

———. *Pindar and the Renaissance Hymn-Ode 1450–1700* (Tempe: Arizona Center for Medieval and Renaissance Studies, 2001).

RHODES, Dennis E. "Pompilio Totti: Publisher, Engraver, Roman Antiquary," *Papers of the British School at Rome* 37 (1969): 161–172.

RICH, J. W. *Cassius Dio: The Augustan Settlement (Roman History 53–55.9)* (Warminster: Aris and Phillips, 1990).

RICHEK, Roslyn. "Thomas Randolph's Salting (1627): Its Text, and John Milton's Sixth *Prolusion* as Another Salting," *English Literary Review* 12 (1982): 102–131.

RICKS, Christopher. *Milton's Grand Style* (Oxford: Oxford University Press, 1963).

RIDDLE, John M. *Dioscurides on Pharmacy and Medicine* (Austin: University of Texas Press, 1985).

RIETBERGEN, Peter. *Power and Religion in Baroque Rome: Barberini Cultural Policies* (Leiden: Brill, 2006).

RILEY, E. H. *The Virgilian Element in the Works of Milton* (PhD thesis: Cornell University, 1925).

RIZZI, Fortunato. "Claudio Achillini e il Soggiorno Parmense," *Aurea Parma* 36 (1952): 3–13.

RODIS-LEWIS, Geneviève. "Musique et Passions au XVIIe Siècle: Monteverdi et Descartes," *XVIIe Siècle* 92 (1971): 81–98.

ROSA, Alberto Asor. "Achillini, Claudio," *Dizionario Biografico degli Italiani* 1 (1960): 145–148.

RUSSO, Piera. "L'Accademia degli Umoristi. Fondazione, Strutte e Leggi: Il Primo Decennio di Attività," *Esperienze Letterarie* 4 (1979): 47–61.

RYAN, Lawrence V. "Milton's *Epitaphium Damonis* and B. Zanchi's Elegy on Baldassare Castiglione," *Humanistica Lovaniensia* 30 (1981): 108–123.

SADIE, Julie Anne. *Companion to Baroque Music* (Berkeley: University of California Press, 1998).
SANTACROCE, Simona. "Un Melodramma Ridicoloso del 'Papa Comico': *Chi Soffre Speri*," *Studi Secenteschi* 53 (2012): 53–88.
SANTIROCCO, Matthew S. *Unity and Design in Horace's Odes* (Chapel Hill: University of North Carolina Press, 1986).
SAYRE, K. M. "A Maieutic View of Five Late Dialogues," in *Methods of Interpreting Plato and his Dialogues*, eds. J. C. Klagge and N. D. Smith (Oxford: Clarendon Press, 1992), 221–243.
SCHLEINER, Louise. "Milton, G.B. Doni, and the Dating of Doni's Works," *Milton Quarterly* 16 (1982): 36–42.
SCHOAF, R. A. *Milton, Poet of Duality: A Study of Semiosis in the Poetry and Prose Works* (Gainesville: University Press of Florida, 1993).
SCHUYLER, Eugene. "Milton's Leonora," *Nation* 47 (18 October, 1888): 310–312.
SEDLEY, David. *The Midwife of Platonism: Text and Subtext in Plato's Theaetetus* (Oxford: Clarendon Press, 2006).
SEDLEY, David L. *Sublimity and Skepticism in Montaigne and Milton* (Ann Arbor: University of Michigan Press, 2005).
SETAIOLO, Aldo. "Il Proemio dei Carmina Oraziani," *Atti e Memorie dell' Accademia Toscana di Scienze e Lettere "La Columbaria"* 38 (1973): 1–59.
SHAFER, Robert. *The English Ode to 1660: An Essay in Literary History* (New York: Haskell House, 1966).
SHAWCROSS, John T. "*Epitaphium Damonis*: Lines 9–13 and the Date of Composition," *Modern Language Notes* 71 (1956): 322–324.
———. "Milton's European Itinerary and his Return Home," *Studies in English Literature* 5 (1965): 49–59.
SHEY, H. J. "The Poet's Progress: Horace *Ode* 1.1," *Arethusa* 4 (1971): 185–196.
SKYRME, Raymond. "Quevedo, Du Bellay, and Janus Vitalis," *Comparative Literature Studies* 19 (1982): 281–295.
SLADE, Paul. *Italia Conquistata: The Role of Italy in Milton's Early Poetic Development* (PhD thesis: University of Exeter, 2017).
SMITH, Malcolm C. "Janus Vitalis Revisited," *Revue de Littérature Comparée* 63 (1989): 69–75.
———. "Looking for Rome in Rome: Janus Vitalis and his Disciples," *Revue de Littérature Comparée* 51 (1977): 510–527.
SMITH, Pamela H. *The Business of Alchemy: Science and Culture in the Holy Roman Empire* (Princeton, NJ: Princeton University Press, 1997).
SMITH, Rebecca W. "The Source of Milton's Pandaemonium," *Modern Philology* 29 (1931): 187–198.
SOLERTI, Angelo. *Le Origini del Melodramma* (Turin: Bocca, 1903).
STRUHAL, Eva. "Reading with Acutezza: Lorenzo Lippi's Literary Culture," in *The Artist as Reader: On Education and Non-Education of Early Modern Artists*, eds. Heiko Damm, Michael Thimann, and Claus Zittel (Leiden: Brill, 2013), 105–127.
SUERBAUM, Werner. "Poeta Laureatus et Triumphans. Die Dichterkrönung Petrarcas Stellung und sein Ennius-Bild," *Poetica* 5 (1972): 293–328.
SUTTON, Dana F. "Milton's *In Quintum Novembris, Anno Aetatis 17* (1626): Choices and Intentions," in *Qui Miscuit Utile Dulci: Festschrift Essays for Paul Lachlan MacKendrick*, eds. Gareth Schmeling and Jon D. Mikalson (Wauconda: Bolchazy-Carducci, 1998), 349–375.

SYMMONS, Charles, "Observations on Milton's Latin Poetry," *Classical Journal* 9 (1814): 338–345.
TALBOT, Michael. *The Chamber Cantatas of Antonio Vivaldi* (Woodbridge: Boydell Press, 2006).
TESTA, Simone. *Italian Academies and their Networks, 1525–1700: From Local to Global* (Basingstoke: Palgrave Macmillan, 2015).
TOMLINSON, Charles. "The Poet as Painter," in *Essays by Divers Hands: Innovation in Contemporary Literature*, ed. Vincent Cronin, Transactions of the Royal Society of Literature 40 (Woodbridge: Boydell Press, 1979), 147–162.
TREIP, Mindele Anne. *"Descend from Heav'n Urania": Milton's Paradise Lost and Raphael's Cycle in the Stanza della Segnatura* (Victoria: University of Victoria, 1985).
TUCKER, G. H. "Sur les *Elogia* (1553) de Janus Vitalis et les *Antiquitez de Rome* de Joachim Du Bellay," *Bibliothèque d'Humanisme et Renaissance* 47 (1985): 103–112.
TUMBLESON, Raymond D. "Of True Religion and False Politics: Milton and the Uses of Anti-Catholicism," *Prose Studies* 15 (1992): 253–270.
TUMMINELLO, Girolamo. "Giano Vitale, Umanista del Secolo XVI," *Archivio Storico Siciliano*, n.s. 8 (Palermo, 1883): 59–60.
TURNER, Amy Lee. "Arts and Design, Milton and the," in *A Milton Encyclopedia*, ed. William B. Hunter *et al* (Lewisburg, PA: Bucknell University Press, 1978), I, 90–102.
TUTINO, Stefania. *Shadows of Doubt: Language and Truth in Post-Reformation Catholic Culture* (Oxford: Oxford University Press, 2014).
VASI, Mariano, and NIBBY, Antonio. *New Guide of Rome and its Environs* (Rome: Luigi Piale, 1851).
VOUT, Caroline. *The Hills of Rome: Signature of an Eternal City* (Cambridge: Cambridge University Press, 2012).
VRETSKA, Karl. "Horatius, *Carm*. I.1," *Hermes* 99 (1971): 323–335.
WADDY, Patricia. *Seventeenth-Century Roman Palaces: Use and the Art of the Plan* (New York: The Architectural History Foundation/Cambridge MA: The Mit Press, 1990).
WALKER, D. P. "Joan Albert Ban and Marsenne's Musical Competition of 1640," *Music and Letters* 57 (1976): 233–255.
———. "Musical Humanism in the 16th and Early 17th Centuries," *The Music Review* 2 (1941): 1–13, 111–121, 220–227, 288–308; 3 (1942): 55–71.
WALSHAM, Alexandra. *Charitable Hatred: Tolerance and Intolerance in England, 1500–1700* (Manchester: Manchester University Press, 2006).
WARNEKE, Sara. *Images of the Educational Traveller in Early Modern England* (Leiden: Brill, 1995).
WATT, Mary Alexandra. *Dante, Columbus and the Prophetic Tradition: Spiritual Imperialism in the Italian Imagination* (Oxford: Routledge, 2017).
WEINRICH, Harald. *On Borrowed Time: The Art and Economy of Living with Deadlines*, trans. Steven Rendall (Chicago: The University of Chicago Press, 2005).
WEST, Robert H. *Milton and the Angels* (Athens: University of Georgia Press, 1955).
WILBOURNE, Emily. *Seventeenth-Century Opera and the Sound of the Commedia dell'Arte* (Chicago: The University of Chicago Press, 2016).

WISTREICH, Richard. "Of Mars I Sing: Monteverdi Voicing Virility," in *Masculinity and Western Musical Practice*, eds. Ian Biddle and Kirsten Gibson (Farnham: Ashgate, 2009), 67–69.

WITT, Mary Ann Frese. *Metatheater and Modernity: Baroque and Neobaroque* (Madison, NJ: Fairleigh Dickinson University Press, 2013).

WOODMAN, Tony. "*Exegi monumentum*: Horace, *Odes* 3.30," in *Quality and Pleasure in Latin Poetry*, eds. Tony Woodman and David West (Cambridge: Cambridge University Press, 1974), 115–128.

WOODS, Susanne. "'That Freedom of Discussion Which I Loved': Italy and Milton's Cultural Self Definition," in *Milton in Italy*, ed. Di Cesare, 9–18.

YATES, Frances. *Giordano Bruno and the Hermetic Tradition* (London: Routledge and Kegan Paul, 1964).

ZAMMAR, Leila. "Gian Lorenzo Bernini: A Hypothesis about his Machine of the Rising Sun," in *La Dimensione del Tragico nella Cultura Moderna e Contemporanea*, ed. Erica Faccioli (Rome: UniversItalia, 2014): 233–252.

———. *Scenography at the Barberini Court in Rome: 1628–1656* (PhD thesis: University of Warwick, 2017).

INDEX NOMINUM ET LOCORUM

Academia Tenuta di Fantastici (1655), 34, 35, 42
Accademia
  degli Apatisti, *see s.v.* Florence
  degli Incogniti, *see s.v.* Venice
  degli Innominati, *see s.v.* Parma
  degli Intrecciati, *see s.v.* Rome
  degli Intrepidi, *see s.v.* Ferrara
  degli Oziosi, *see s.v.* Naples
  degli Spensierati, *see s.v.* Rossano
  degli Svogliati, *see s.v.* Florence
  degli Umoristi, *see s.v.* Rome
  dei Fantastici, *see s.v.* Rome
  dei Filoponi, *see s.v.* Faenza
  dei Gelati, *see s.v.* Bologna
  della Crusca, *see s.v.* Florence
  della Notte, *see s.v.* Bologna
  di San Luca, *see s.v.* Rome
  Nazionale dei Lincei, *see s.v.* Rome
Achelous, 142
Achilles, 51, 53
Achillini, Claudio, 41–42
Acoetes, 150
Adriatic Sea, 133, 134
Aeneas, 32, 51, 58, 59, 149, 150
Aeolia, 67
Aeolic dialect, 67
Aeolus, 58, 149
Aetna, Mount, 57
Africa, 18, 48
Agnes, Saint, 43
Agrippa, 24
Albertini, Francesco, 4
Alcaeus, 57, 60, 67, 68
Alcides, *see* Hercules
Alcina, Island of, 42
Aleandro, Girolamo, 80–81
Aleotti, Giovanni Battista, 97
Alessandro VII, Pope, *see* Chigi, Fabio
Alighieri, Dante, 31, 166, 167
Allaci, Leone, 36, 77, 103, 145
Allestry, James, 13
All Saints, Feast of, 21
All Souls, Feast of, 21
Almo(ne), 90, 93
Alps, 1, 19
Alvida, 159–160
Amedei, Fausto, 91
Amodeo, Oratio, 109
Anabasis, 148–153

Anaximander, 75
Anchises, 149, 150, 152
Andreini, Giovanni Battista, 161
Andreoli, Giovanni, 61
Angels, 17, 21, 22, 24, 105, 109, 113, 114–116, 119, 120, 134, 135
Anisson
  Joannes, 90
  Laurentius, 80
Aonia, 133, 134
Aperger, Andreas, 143
Aphrodite, *see* Venus
Apollo, 30, 42, 50, 57, 65, 67, 68, 69, 70, 72, 74, 104, 110, 112
Apollonius Rhodius, 171
Applausi Poetici alle Glorie della Signora Leonora Baroni (1639), 45, 77, 102, 103, 104, 105, 107–108, 110, 112, 113–115, 117–118, 121, 122–123, 124, 126, 130–132, 133, 134–137, 142
Apuleius, 24
Aquilo, 66, 69
Aquinas, Thomas, 41, 43
Aragon, 120
Arcadia, 161
Archilochus, 60, 68
Ares, *see* Mars
Aria Parlante, 167
Ariosto, Ludovico, 53
Aristides, 124
Aristophanes, 75
Aristotle, 75, 147
Armida, 155
Armindo, 159, 165
Arno, 5
Arnobius, 116
Arrian, 144
Arthur, King, 53
Ascension, Feast of the, 33
Ascham, Roger, 16
Asclepiad, Lesser, 66
Asclepius, 63, 70, 118
Asia, 18
Astraea, 38, 49, 63
Athena, 38
Athens, 14, 114
Atticus, Herodes, 89
Aufidus, 67
Augsburg, 143

Augustus, *see s.v.* Caesar
Aurispa, Ippolito, 38
Avellino, 31
Avernus, 149
Avvisi di Roma, 156, 161, 162, 163, 164
Aylmer, Brabazon, 14, 176

Baba, Francesco, 5, 110
Babel, Tower of, 47
Babylon, 15
Bacchus, 84, 90, 93, 94
Bacchylides, 63
Baedeker, Karl, 93
Baglioni, Paolo, 80
Baldinucci, Filippo, 97, 158
Balducci, Francesco, 41, 109–110
Ban, Joan Albert, 126–130
Bandini, Angelo Maria, 126
Barbazza, Andrea, 41, 43, 117, 136, 137
Barberini
  Antonio, Cardinal, 10, 26, 75, 113, 144, 154, 155, 156, 157, 158, 172
  Carlo, 145
  Court of, 154, 162, 163, 164
  family of, 11, 26, 101, 102, 103, 149, 153, 154, 164, 169, 170, 171, 172
  Francesco, Cardinal, 18, 75, 91, 92, 97, 103, 113, 139, 141, 144, 147, 149, 150, 153, 154, 156, 157, 162, 169–172
  Library of, 139, 141–142, 147
  Lucrezia, 92
  Maffeo, 145
  Maffeo (Pope Urban VIII), 21, 22, 26, 91, 100, 126, 158
  Palazzo of, 19, 26, 150, 154, 155, 164, 169, 173
  Press of, 153–154
  Taddeo, 92
  Theater of (1632), 97
  Theater of (1639), 150, 154, 156–157, 158, 173
Barbieri, Pier Francesco, 85
Bargrave, John, 170
Bari, 99
Baroni

Camillo, 99
Caterina, 75, 76, 99, 100, 101, 102, 103, 104, 105, 106, 108, 109, 111, 112, 115, 116
  home of, 101, 105, 111, 112
Leonora, 19, 28, 45, 75, 77, 99–137, 139, 142
Mutio, 99, 104, 134
Barrett, William, 17
Basile, Adriana, 99–100, 101, 104, 105, 108, 109, 111, 112, 123, 132–134, 135, 137
Bauhin, Gaspars, 94–95
Beale, John, 17
Bede, 17
Bedford, Earl of, 3
Beelzebub, 22
Belgium, 39, 103
Bell
  George, 7
  John, 93
Bembo, Pietro, 53
Benci, Tommaso, 118
Benedictines, Order of, 19, 162
Benetti
  Benedetto, 41, 43
  Francesco, 41, 43, 46
Benigni, Domenico, 36, 75, 76, 103, 104–106, 123, 135, 137
Bentivoglio
  Annibale, 136
  Giovanni, 117
Berlin, 119, 139
Bernabò, Rocco, 97
Bernarbo, Angelo, 31
Bernard, Saint, 118, 119
Bernini
  Domenico, 97
  Gian Lorenzo, 97, 137, 154, 155, 157, 158, 162, 163, 169
Bertier, Antonius, 129
Bianchi, Brigida, 106
Bible, 25, 143
  versions of,
    AV (Authorized Version), 120
    Greek, 143–144
    Hebrew, 141–142, 152
    Vulgate, 116
  books of,
    Psalms, 116, 126, 155

Index Nominum et Locorum

Acts, 120, 152
  Corinthians, 117
  Revelation, 14
Bilingualism, 20, 21, 68, 142, 149
Biondo, Flavio, 11
Boccaccio, Giovanni, 159
  Decameron, 159
Boësset, Antoine, 129
Boethius, 63, 117
Bohemia, 17, 39
Bologna, 33, 41, 44
  Accademia dei Gelati, 75
  Accademia della Notte, 41
  Biblioteca di San Francesco de Frati
    Minori Conventuali, 44
  University of, 41
Bombarda, Domitio, 109, 132
Boniface, Saint, 26
Bordandini, Luigi, 35
Borghese, Scipio, 32
Borgianni, Orazio, 75
Boswell, William, 128
Bouchard, Jean Jacques, 111–112
Boudot, Johannes, 4
Bracciano, 45, 112
Briasson, Anton–Claude, 144
Britain, 13, 148
Bruni, Antonio, 41, 44
Bruno, Giordano, 121
Brussels, 69
Bryennius, 124
Buchanan, George, 123
Buonmattei, Benedetto, 20–21, 142
Burbie, Cuthburt, 3
Burman, Pieter, 141

Caccini, Francesca, 101, 106
Caesar
  Augustus, 68, 69, 96
  Julius, 69
Caffarella, *see s.v.* Rome
Callimachus, 66, 170–172
Calvinism, 27
Cam, 69
Cambridge, 12, 68, 167
  University of, 12–13, 15, 16,
    83, 167–168
    Christ's College, 168
    Trinity College, 53, 166

Camenae, 55, 89, 90, 92, 93; *see also*
  Muses
Campania, 31
Cancellieri, Francesco, 34
Capitol, *see s.v.* Rome
Capponi, Luigi, Cardinal, 78
Capuchins, Order of, 118
Cardoini, Camillo, 27
Carducci, Francesco, 41, 44, 114
Carey, Patrick, 18
Carlino, Giovanni Giacomo, 109
Caroli, Giovanni Battista, 41
Carpani, Giusppe, 33
Casella, 166, 167
Cassius, Dio, 24, 96
Castel Roderigo, 135
Castiglione, Baldassare, 13
Castor, 72
Catherine, Saint, 43
Catholicism, *see s.v.* Roman
Catullus, Gaius Valerius, 65, 126–127
Cavario, Giovanni Battista, 45
Cecchini, Ludovico, 40
Cennini, Cennino, 61
Ceres, 171, 172; *see also* Demeter
Cesarini
  Alessandro, Cardinal, 43
  Virginio, 32
Ceuli, Tiberio, 30, 41, 42, 43, 44, 46
Charles I, King, 68, 141
Charles V, King, 43
Charon, 150
Cherubini
  Alessandro, 20, 41, 140–141
  Angelo Maria, 140
  Fausto, 140
  Flavio, 140
  Laertius, 140
Chiabrera, Gabriello, 33–34, 75
Chigi, Fabio, 33, 42, 44; *see also*
  Alessandro VII, Pope
Chiron, 12
Chi Soffre Speri, 26, 154–165, 168
Chloris, 159
Choliambic meter, *see* Scazons
Christ, 25, 33, 43, 46, 49, 120, 151,
  169
Christianity, 6, 11, 14, 32, 39, 91, 116,
  119–120

Church Fathers, 25
Cicalate, 84, 86
Cicero, Marcus Tullius, 56, 89, 94, 127, 128, 133
Cifra, Antonio, 166
Circe, 16
Cittadonio, Paolo, 41
Claudin, Anatole, 111
Clement IX, Pope, *see* Rospigliosi, Giulio
Cleonides, 124
Clio, 38
Clocquius, Andreas, 57
Clorinda, 124
Codner, David, 19–20
Cologne, 6, 33
Colonna
  Anna, 92
  Camillo, 36, 103, 136
  Pietro, 43
  Pompeo, 32, 136
Colosseum, *see s.v.* Rome
Columbus, Christopher, 31–32, 43
Colvillus, David, 173
Commedia
  Boschereccia, 161
  dell' Arte, 26, 159, 160, 161, 165
Commelin, Isaac, 127
Comus, 58, 168; *see also s.v.* Milton, *Mask, A*
Confidati, Alfonso, 41, 43
Constantinople
  Photius of, 145
Corbelletti, Francesco, 102
Corinthian order (of architecture), 22
Corner, Federico, Cardinal, 26
Costa, Margherita, 106
Cowper, William, 114
Cracow, 118, 119
Cramoisy
  Gabriel, 144
  Sébastien, 144
Cupid, 7, 110, 136
Cytherea, 53; *see also* Venus

D'Agliè, Ludovico, 136
Dal Pozzo, Cassiano, 75
Damon, 1–7; *see also* Diodati, Charles
Da Montevecchio, Giulio, 35
Dandi, Giovan Felice, 42
Dante, *see* Alighieri
Dati, Carlo, 10, 15, 41, 48, 103
Davila, Enrico Caterino, 32
Daye, John, 16
De Brass, Henri, 14
Dee, John, 118
Deiopea, 57, 58, 62, 71
De la Monnoye, 149
Delaulne, Veuve, 149
De le Monti, Giorgio, 108–109
De Lisa, Gerardus, 118
Delius, *see* Apollo
Della Corgna, Fabio, 75, 102, 107, 112, 131, 136
Della Valle, Pietro, 75, 88, 107
Delos, 42, 134
De Maura, *see* De Melo
De Medici
  Cosimo, 118
  Court of, 85
  family of, 154, 170, 172
  Ferdinando, 119
  Margherita, 41
De Melo
  Eleonora, 135
  family of, 134
Demeter, 170, 171, 172; *see also* Ceres
Democrates, 145, 172
De Montfaucon, Bernard, 90–91
Demophilus, 145, 172
Denmark, 17
De Pise, Marcellino, 80
Depleurre, Stephanus, 151
De' Rossi, Giovanni Maria, 41
Descartes, René, 127
De Simeonibus, Gasparo, 36, 76–77, 103, 124
De Sluse, René François, 39
De St Andre, Pierre, 87
D'Este
  family of, 170
  Leonora, 100, 122
De Totis, Giuseppe, 35
Deuchino, Evangelista, 7, 49, 109
Diana, 89, 134
Di Costanzo, Fulvio, 104
Diodati
  Charles, 2, 5, 6, 55, 84
  Isabel, 5
  Philadelphia, 5

Dionysus, 164; *see also* Bacchus
Dioscurides, 94
Dirce, 124
Dominicans, Order of, 170
Doni, Giovanni Battista, 20, 75, 103, 107, 113, 125–129, 173
Doric order (of architecture), 22
Doricus
   Aloysius, 5
   Valerius, 5
Dorillo, 159
Dring, Thomas, 176
Du Bellay, Joachim, 4, 6, 7
Dublin, 142
   Trinity College, 142
Du Moulin, Peter Jr, 16, 18
Dutch, 39, 126, 127

Eden, 169
Egeria, 62, 89–94
   Nymphaeum of, 89–94
Egisto, 156, 159–160, 165
Egypt, 80, 147
Egyptians, 21
Eliot, John, 121
Elizabeth I, Queen, 81
England, 3, 4, 13, 14, 16, 17, 18, 20, 27, 28, 47, 48, 56, 58, 72, 121, 139, 141, 146, 148, 157, 158, 166
English (language), 53, 79, 118
Epicurus, 147
Epiphany, Feast of the, 33
Eris, 171
Erysichthon, 171–172
Erythraeus, Janus Nicius, *see* Rossi, Giovanni Vittorio
Etienne, Henri, 120
Etruria, 24, 52
Etruscan, 9, 95, 96
Eurilla, 159
Euripides, 63
Europe, 5, 17, 39, 103, 121, 139
Evander, 59, 89
Evangelista, Bernardo, 41, 43
Eve, 169
Evelyn, John, 10, 22, 77–78, 89, 143, 152
Everard, John, 118

Fabri, Alberto, 41, 61

Facciotti
   Guiglielmo, 109, 110
   Pietro Antonio, 88
Faenza, 36
   Accademia dei Filoponi, 36
Falcidio, 32
Falkland, Viscount, 18
Fama, 171
Fantuzzi, Giovanni, 41
Farfa, 26, 155, 157, 158, 162
   Benedictine abbey of, 162
Farnese
   Court of, 41
   family of, 154, 170
   Odoardo, 41
Farroni, Giovanni Maria, 85
Fauns, 59
Faunus, 59
Fei, Andrea, 10, 112, 125
Ferdinand, King, 120
Ferrara, 41, 118
   Accademia degli Intrepidi, 41
Ferretti, Giuseppe, 41
Ferro, Giovanni, 80
Ferroni, Clemente, 41
Ficino, Marsilio, 118, 119, 120
Fick, William, 38
Fieschi, Giovanni Luigi, 52
Fiesole, 24
Fioretti, Benedetto, 125
Fletcher, Phineas, 14, 15
Flora, 41
Florence, 3, 5, 8, 9, 10, 15, 18, 20, 21, 24, 34–35, 41, 42, 46, 47, 61, 84, 85, 86, 97, 100, 107, 116, 118, 120, 125, 126, 140, 142, 172, 173
   Accademia degli Apatisti, 20–21, 85, 126
   Accademia degli Svogliati, 20, 46
   Accademia della Crusca, 84, 86
   Biblioteca Laurenziana, 172–173
   Biblioteca Marucelliana, 21
   Biblioteca Nazionale Centrale, 20, 34–35
Fontana
   Bartolomeo, 52
   Domenico, 143
Fontescue
   John, 18
   Nicholas 18,

Forcella, Vincenzo, 40
Forlì, 35
France, 4, 17, 41, 43, 47–48, 121
  Dauphin of, 41
Francese, Quilletto, 133
Francini, Antonio, 47, 56
Franciscans, Order of, 14, 15, 118, 170
Frascati, 140, 141
French
  Ambassador, 78
  language, 45, 49, 107, 110, 129
Frescobaldi, Girolamo, 26, 162
Fucci, Maddalo, 122
Furies, 124

Gabriel, Angel, 119
Gaetano, Michel' Arcangelo Alfonso, 108
Galilei, Galileo, 24, 46, 75, 127, 128, 170
Gallus, 2
Garopoli, Girolamo, 41
Garuffi, Giuseppe Malatesta, 42, 61
Gawen, Thomas, 20
Geneva, 4, 27, 38
Genoa, 52, 84, 85
Gentiles, 32, 116
Gentili, Scipio, 121
Germain, Michel, 4
Germany, 17
Gessi, Berlingiero, Cardinal, 43, 104, 107
Gesualdo, Carlo, 166
Gigli, Giacinto, 97
Gil, Alexander Jr, 62
Gimma, Giacinta, 35–36
Giobbe, Giovanni Battista, 41
Giovini, Giovanni Thomas, 134
God, 100, 109, 114, 116, 117, 119, 120, 127
Goffredi, Giovanni Antonio, 41, 44
Gori, Anton Francesco, 21, 107, 125, 126, 128, 129
Gradi, Stefano, 34
Grand Tour, 90
Gratiot, J., 92
Greece, 5, 20, 47–48, 52, 133
Greek (language), 24, 47, 49, 55, 57, 59, 107, 112, 140, 144, 145, 146, 148
Greeks, 21, 64

Gregory XV, Pope, 17, 91
Grignano, Lodovico, 41
Grotius, Hugo, 56, 127
Gualterus, Bernardus, 6
Guarini, Battista, 43, 75, 77
Guglielmi, Giacomo, 41
Guidiccioni, Lelio, 136, 154–155
Gunpowder Plot, 14–15

Hague, The, 16, 128
Hammersmith, 13
Harvard, 27
  Houghton Library, 27
Heaven, 7, 9, 13, 24, 25, 58, 65, 68, 86, 106, 107, 109, 110, 114, 115, 116, 117, 118, 169
Hebe, 30, 57, 71
Hebrew (language), 49, 152
Hebrews, 14; *see also* Jews
Heidelberg, 87
Heinsius, Nicolas, 141
Helicon, 13, 25
Hell, 23, 34
Hellenism, 142, 146, 171
Hendecasyllables, 88, 92, 121
Hera, 38; *see also* Juno
Herbert
  Edward, 18
  George, 7
Hercules, 43, 150
Hermes, 118, 120
Hermeticism, 113, 114, 118–121
Herring, Francis, 15
Hesiod, 57
  Theogony, 57
Hesperus, 2
Hippocrates, 81
Hippocrene, 71, 103
Holden, Henry, 18
Holstenius, Lucas, 8, 9, 19, 27, 34, 89, 92, 101, 103, 113, 126, 131, 139–153, 169, 170, 171, 172, 173
Holy Spirit, 25, 117, 118–120
Homer, 20, 38, 50, 51, 52, 53, 54, 57, 63, 67, 130, 171
  Iliad, 38, 171
  Odyssey, 57, 130, 146
Horace, 9, 27, 32, 34, 55, 59–69, 83, 89, 95–96
  Ars Poetica, 32, 61

Epistles, 27, 60, 63
Epodes, 63
Odes, 55, 60, 63–69, 95–96
Satires, 63
Howell, James, 3
Hypnerotomachia Poliphili (1499), 3
Hypsipyle, 156

Iamblichus, 147
Ida, Mount, 55
Ilia, 95, 96
Il Teatro delle Glorie delle Signora Adriana Basile (1628), 99, 108–109, 123, 132–134, 135, 137
Inachus, 53
Inghirami, Valerio, 33
Ingolstadt, 84
Inquisition, 17, 170
Intermedio, 155, 160, 161, 162, 163, 164
Ionia, 147
Ireland, 17
Italian
  academies, 17, 19, 20–21, 24, 36–37, 46, 52, 54, 62, 76, 84, 88, 103, 108, 118, 173
  journey, 1, 2, 3, 11, 13, 15, 18, 23, 24, 27, 28, 30, 54, 56, 62, 68, 84, 89, 90, 108, 125, 170, 187–191
  language, 19, 31, 34, 38, 45, 47, 49, 50, 51, 57, 60, 69, 77, 78, 100, 101, 103, 107, 118, 165
Italy, 5, 14, 16, 17, 18, 19, 20, 21, 24, 27, 28, 29, 30, 31, 35, 39, 46, 48, 52, 56, 57, 58, 62, 68, 72, 73, 78, 82, 83, 86, 93, 99, 104, 105, 108, 118, 121, 124, 130, 157, 158, 160, 166, 169, 170
Ixion, 121

James I, King, 14, 15, 120, 141
Janus, 11, 167
Jason, 156
Jerusalem, 109, 121–122
Jesuits, Order of, 14, 17, 18, 19, 116, 117
Jesus, *see* Christ
Jews, 21, 116, 155
Jones, Inigo, 158
Jonson, Ben, 167

The Staple of News, 167
Jove, *see* Jupiter
Junius, Francis, 141
Juno, 53, 58, 62, 71, 149
Jupiter, 47, 50, 71, 95, 96, 108
Juvenal, 65, 89

Kalcovius, Iodocus, 33
Katabasis, 148–153
Keightley, Thomas, 93, 117
Kircher, Athanasius, 80

Lactantius, 116
Laertius, Diogenes, 147
Lamanna, Girolamo, 41
Lamb
  Charles, 113, 117
  Mary, 113
Lancaster, 18
Landor, Walter Savage, 54, 87
Lassels, Richard, 16
Latin (language), 11, 19, 47, 48, 49, 55, 57, 59, 60, 68, 77, 78, 103, 107, 113, 118, 121, 140, 144, 145, 148
Latium, 9, 52, 58, 59, 60
Laureatio, 7, 48–49, 64
Lavinia, 53
Lawes, Henry, 166, 167
Lawrence, Saint, 43
Lazari, Jan Januszowski, 119
Lazzarelli, Lodovico, 119–120
Lazzarini, Luigi, 34
Leghorn, 90
Leiden, 57, 85, 103, 127, 141
  University of, 128
Leipzig, 141, 155
Leonida, Fabio, 36, 76, 103, 121, 124
Lesbos, 57, 60, 63–64, 84, 88
Lescuier, Charles, 61
Lethe, 7, 64, 70, 71, 150
L'Idea della Veglia (1640), 102, 104, 105–106, 115, 124
Ligurian, 84
Limbo, 151
Lingua
  fagiana, 85–86
  ionadattica, 85–86
Lippi, Lorenzo, 85, 86
Lipsius, Iustus, 3
Lithgow, William, 17

Livy, 7, 9, 89, 90, 94
Locus amoenus, 169, 171
Lollino, Luigi, 146
London, 3, 5, 7, 8, 9, 11, 12, 13, 14, 17, 18, 30, 31, 39, 47, 52, 56, 62, 71, 93, 99, 100, 113, 118, 121, 122, 141, 148, 153, 158, 167, 170
  Blackfriars Theater, 167
  British Library, 61, 77
  Royal Society, 39
  St Paul's Cathedral, 141
  St Paul's School, 11, 68
Longo, Giovan Martino, 30, 41, 43, 44, 45, 46, 61, 110,
Lotti, Giovanni, 35–36, 38, 60
Lotus-eaters, 148
Louis XIII, King, 43
Louis XIV, King, 41
Loyola, Ignatius, 117
Lucca, 44
Luchtmans, Samuel, 141
Lucifer, 119
Lucinda, 159, 160, 165
Lucretius, Titus, 36, 75–76, 78, 80, 82, 93–94
Ludlow
  Castle, 168
  town, 158, 168
Luke, Saint, 43
Lunghi, Martino, 30, 41, 43
Lycoris, 2
Lydia, 94
Lyon, 80

Mabillon, Jean, 4
Macerata, 38
Maecenas, Gaius, 35, 64
Maeonides, *see* Homer
Malatesti, Antonio, 18
Malchus, *see* Porphyry, Pomponius
Malvasia, Maestro Fra Bonaventura, 41, 43
Mammarellus, Benedictus, 118
Mancini
  Filippo Maria, 42
  Paolo, 36, 74, 77, 78
Manso, Giovanni Battista, 4–5, 7, 12, 17, 44, 48–49, 52, 56, 84, 89, 100, 109, 121–122, 135, 142
Mantinea, Diotima of, 153

Manto, 51
Mantua, 99, 132
Mantuanus, Baptista, 13
Maratti, Carlo, 79
Marazzoli, Marco, 155
Marenza, Luca, 166
Marescotti, Vincenzo, 115, 122, 136
Marini, Stefano, 41
Marinism, 32, 41
Marino
  Gabriel, 41, 43, 45, 110
  Giambattista, 32, 42, 43, 75, 109
Mars, 24, 41, 69, 93, 94, 124; *see also* Ares
Martin
  Edmund, 4
  Stephanus, 4
Marullus, Michael, 51, 123
Marvell, Andrew, 68–69, 152
Mascardi
  Agostino, 41, 42, 52
  Antonio, 10
  Giacomo, 80, 144
  Vitale, 34, 80, 155
Mascherata, 160
Massa, Pier Francesco, 134
Masson, David, 9, 29, 30, 50, 60, 89, 114, 157
Massucci, Francesco, 41
Materdona, Giovanni Francesco Maia, 41, 43
Maugars, André, 111, 115
Maxwell, David, 118
Mazarin, Jules Raymond, Cardinal, 42
Mazochius, Jacobus, 4
Mazzei, Decio, 41
Mazzocchi, Virgilio, 155, 165
Mazzolari, Giuseppe Maria, 116–117
Meles, 47, 50
Meliboeus, 1, 2
Mellan, Claude, 136
Ménage, Gilles, 149
Mercury, 41, 143, 152
Merlin, 62
Mersenne, Marin, 126, 129
Metaphrase, 68
Meursius, Johannes, 148
Michiele, Pietro, 41
Midas, 166
Milan, 34

Index Nominum et Locorum 225

Milborne, Robert, 62
Milton, John
  Manuscripts
    Biblioteca Apostolica Vaticana
      Barb.lat. 2181, 139, 151, 154, 173
    Trinity College, Cambridge
      MS R. 3.4, 53, 166
    Trinity College, Dublin
      R.dd.39, 142

  poetry
    Ad Leonoram 1, 100, 113–121, 123, 178–179
    Ad Leonoram 2, 100, 101, 114, 121–130, 142, 178–179
    Ad Leonoram 3, 108, 114, 130–137, 142, 178–179
    Ad Patrem, 49, 166
    Ad Salsillum, 19, 27, 29–97, 180–181
    An Epitaph on the Marchioness of Winchester, 19
    Apologus de Rustico et Hero, 13
    Arcades, 157, 168
    At a Solemn Musick, 117, 166
    Comus, see Mask, A
    De Idea Platonica, 118
    Elegia Prima, 12, 167
    Elegia Secunda, 12
    Elegia Tertia, 13
    Elegia Quarta, 12
    Elegia Quinta, 46
    Elegia Sexta, 55
    Elegia Septima, 58
    Epitaphium Damonis, 1–7, 8, 13, 20, 53, 62, 84, 109
    Il Penseroso, 118
    In Inventorem Bombardae, 46
    In Obitum Procancellarii Medici, 12
    In Proditionem Bombardicam 2, 14
    In Proditionem Bombardicam 3, 14, 50
    In Quintum Novembris, 14–15, 50
    Italian sonnets, 49, 134
    L'Allegro, 58
    Latin elegies, 49
    Latin epigrams on the Gunpowder Plot, 14
    Latin epigrams to Leonora Baroni, 19, 27, 45, 99–137, 139, 142, 178–179
    Latin poetry, 3, 11–13, 20, 28, 49, 50, 69, 87, 101
    Mansus, 17, 29, 44, 49, 52, 53, 54, 62, 84, 109, 142
    Mask, A, 27, 58, 116, 131, 133, 157, 168
    Naturam Non Pati Senium, 58
    On Shakespeare, 68, 168
    On the Morning of Christ's Nativity, 46
    Paradise Lost, 13, 14, 22–25, 47, 52, 53, 58, 68, 86, 149, 158, 168, 169
    Paradise Regained, 13, 25, 168, 169
    Poemata (1645), 10, 15, 17, 19, 20, 29, 47, 48, 55, 56
    Poems ... Both English and Latin (1645), 10, 15, 19, 55
    Poems ... Both English and Latin (1673), 176, 178
    Psalm 114 (Greek version), 49
    Samson Agonistes, 168, 169
    Sonnet 13, 166
    Sonnet 15, 50
    Sylvarum Liber, 57
    The Fifth Ode of Horace Liber I, 68

  prose
    Apology for Smectymnuus, 12
    Areopagitica, 13, 151, 153, 170
    Defensio Secunda, 8, 9, 13, 15–16, 17, 18, 89, 109, 125, 142, 188–191
    Doctrine and Discipline of Divorce, 153
    Epistolae Familiares, 14, 15, 19, 20, 28, 39, 62, 84, 94, 139, 142
    Epistola Familiaris 2, 62, 94
    Epistola Familiaris 7, 84
    Epistola Familiaris 8, 20, 142
    Epistola Familiaris 9, 9, 19, 20, 22, 26, 27, 28, 113, 139–173, 182–185
    Epistola Familiaris 10, 15
    Epistola Familiaris 23, 14

History of Britain, 13
Prolusio 6, 83
Reason of Church Government, 14, 19, 46, 53, 54, 60, 108
Milton, John Sr, 13, 49, 166, 167; *see also* Milton, John, *Ad Patrem*
Mincius, 47, 50, 52
Minerva, 38, 153
Mirabilia Urbis Romae, 3
Modena, 31, 32, 42, 99, 156
Moloch, 149
Monesio, Giovanni Pietro, 38
Moneta
  Francesco, 42, 110
  Paolo, 42
Monicus, 2
Montaigne, Michel de, 4
Montecuccoli, Raimondo, 156, 161, 162
Monteverdi, Claudio, 41, 99, 106, 124, 125, 127, 166
Montreglio, Giovanni, 41, 45, 110
Monumentum Romanum Nicolao Claudio Fabricio Perescio (1638), 36, 76, 103–104
Mortier, David, 141
Moryson, Fynes, 17
Moseley, Humphrey, 3, 10
Munday, Anthony, 17
Muses, 23, 25, 35, 55, 57–58, 62, 65, 70, 71, 82, 87, 90, 92, 107, 111, 112, 122–123, 129, 130, 134, 143, 149
Musica Flexanima, 127–130, 142

Naiad, 133
Namur, 39
Naples, 4, 5, 17, 23, 29, 36, 39, 44, 52, 89, 99, 100, 109, 122, 123, 130, 131, 133, 134, 137, 142, 162–163
  Accademia degli Oziosi, 44
  Biblioteca Nazionale, 162–163
  Phlegraean Fields, 23
  Viceroy's Court, 89
Narceate, Dalisto, *see* Casotti, Giovanni Battista
Naudaeus, Gabriel, 144, 170
Neaera, 55
Nebenius, Conradus, 95
Neoplatonism, 118, 153
Neptune, 53

Netherlands, 17
Newcomb, Thomas, 8
Nibby, Antonio, 93
Nicéron, Jean-Pierre, 144
Nicholas V, Pope, 143
Nicippe, 171
Nicolai, Friedrich, 119
Nicomachus, 147
  Enchiridion, 147
Nonacrio, Fidelo, *see* De Totis, Giuseppe
North Wind, *see* Aquilo
Numa, *see* Pompilius
Nymphs, 59, 71, 89, 90, 92, 93, 131, 133, 146, 162, 163, 168, 172

Octavian, *see* Caesar, Augustus
Oedipus, 80
Offenbach, 95
Okes, Nicholas, 18
Oldenburg, Henry, 39
Olympus, Mount, 79, 170, 171
Ondedei, Fabrizio, 33
Orcus, 7
Orient, The, 42
Orion, 171
Orpheus, 123
Orsini
  Lelio, 38
  Paolo Giordano, 112
Orsino
  Ferdinando, 136
  Flavio, 136
  Giovanni Antonio, 136
  Paolo Emilio, 136
Ovid, 7, 12–13, 38, 58, 65, 67, 89, 91, 133, 150, 171
  Amores, 7, 13
  Ars Amatoria, 7, 12, 65
  Fasti, 89
  Heroides, 12, 38, 133
  Ibis, 12
  Metamorphoses, 67, 89, 133, 150
  Remedia Amoris, 58
  Tristia, 12
Oxford, 143, 146, 148
  Bodleian Library, 143, 148

Pace, Antonio, 109
Pacicelli, Giovan Battista, 39

Index Nominum et Locorum

Pacuvius, 126, 128, 133
Paean, 57, 63, 69, 70, 73, 74
Paganism, 11, 116
Pallavicini, Alfonso, 122, 136
Palmerio, Bernardino, 133
Palombara, Oddo Sevelli, 136
Pamphili, Benedetto, Cardinal, 35
Pandaemonium, 22–25
Pandora, 16
Panimolle, Cesare, 41
Pannini, Pietro, 41, 43
Pantheism, 117
Pantheon, *see s.v.* Rome
Paoli, Pierfrancesco, 41
Papacy, 11, 15, 16, 25, 26, 34, 42, 44, 49, 75, 79, 91, 154, 155, 160
Paphos, 49
Parca, 66
Paris, 38, 55
Paris (city), 4, 90, 92, 111, 120, 129, 143, 144, 148, 149, 151
Parma, 32, 41, 42
    Accademia degli Innominati, 32, 41
Parnassus, 49
Paros, 60
Parthenius, Josephus Marianus, *see* Mazzolari, Giuseppe Maria
Parthenope, 131–132, 137, 142
Passion, Feast of the, 33
Pastorale, 160
Patriarchi, Virginio, 41
Patrizi, Francesco, 118
Paul, Saint, 32, 117
Paul V, Pope, 79
Pauli, Pier Francesco, 136
Pavoni, Giuseppe, 52
Peiresc, Nicolas–Claude Fabri de, 36, 76, 92, 103, 153
Pennyboy
    Canter, 167
    Junior, 167
Pentecost, Feast of, 33, 120
Pentheus, 121, 124
Peregrini, Matteo, 85
Permessus, 42
Pesagni, Nicolò, 85
Pesaro, 33
Petrarch
    Francesco, 2, 3, 4, 11, 48, 143, 144, 149, 152
    Gherardo, 2
Pezzana, Nicolò, 41
Philip II, King, 43
Phillips
    Edward Jr, 8, 125, 165–166
    John, 8
Philomusus, 129, 130; *see also* Doni, Giovanni Battista
Phlegraean Fields, *see s.v.* Naples
Phoebus, *see* Apollo
Photius, *see s.v.* Constantinople
Phrontisterion, 80
Piacenza, Giovanni Battista, 41
Piale, Luigi, 93
Piancerreto, 104, 135
Piazza, Bartolomeo, 61
Picarelli, Marco, 41, 43, 44, 96
Piccini, Giuseppe, 38
Piccolomini, Enea Silvio, 4
Picklock, 167
Pieria, 122
Pierides 112, 123
Pindar, 33–34, 38, 40, 57, 60, 63
Pindus, Mount, 42, 64, 103, 111, 112
Pinelli, Antonio, 52
Piranesi
    Francesco, 91
    Giovanni Battista, 91–92
Pisa, 35
Plato, 7, 119, 120, 140, 144, 147, 153
    Symposium, 153
    Theaetetus, 153
Plautus, 87, 151, 167
    Casina, 87
    Manaechmi, 87
    Mostellaria, 87, 151
Pliny the Elder, 75, 96
Plutarch, 89
Po, 156
Poesie de' Signori Accademici Fantastici di Roma (1637), 29–30, 41–46, 47, 49, 50–52, 61, 62–69, 69–74, 96, 110
Poland, 6, 17, 38
Poliphilus, 3
Pollux, 72
Polyhymnia, 63
Polyphemus, 31
Pompilius, Numa, 62, 89–94
Pontanus, Iacobus, 84

Porcio, Gregorio, 123, 131
Porphyry, Pomponius, 145–146, 147, 148, 153, 172
Portumnus, 84, 95
Posillipo, 99, 131, 132–133, 142
  Old Grotto, 133
  Via Antiniana, 133
Prague, 39
Prato, 33
Price, John, 39
Proclus, 144
Prophets, Twelve, see s.v. Bible, Hebrew
Prosperi, Lodovico, 41
Protestantism, 14, 16, 17, 18, 27, 28, 49, 114, 115, 118, 139, 172, 173
Puccinotti, Francesco, 90
Punic Wars, 53
Purgatory, 14, 166
Pymander, 118–120
Pythagoras, 33, 145, 146, 147, 148
Pythagorean, 117, 145, 146, 147, 148, 152

Quevedo, Francisco de, 6
Quintilian, 124
Quirinus, 15, 69, 112, 155; see also Romulus

Raggioli, Giulio Cesare, 136
Raillard, Giacomo, 39
Randolph, Thomas, 83
Rapaccioli, Francesco, 121
Raphael, 25
Rasi, Francesco, 132
Reana (*insula*), see Rhé, Ile de
Remus, 11
Reni, Guido, 137
Rhé, Ile de, 83
Ricci, Napoleone, 41
Richelieu, Cardinal, 41–42
Rigogli, Benedetto, 41
Rivington
  Charles, 170
  John, 17
Robert, King, 48
Rocco, Girolamo, 36, 77, 103
Rodolfini, Angelo, 38–39, 55, 60
Roman
  Catholicism, 8, 9, 14–15, 16, 17, 18, 19, 21, 25, 28, 34, 52, 113–114, 115–117, 121, 135, 139, 172, 173
  comedy, 87
  Empire, 25, 48, 69, 89, 97
  historiography, 14
Rome
  Accademia degli Intrecciati, 33, 34, 40
  Accademia degli Umoristi, 21, 35–40, 42, 46, 49, 54, 74–82, 88, 101–104, 109, 113, 136
  Accademia dei Fantastici, 21, 29–30, 32, 33, 34, 35, 40, 41–46, 49, 54, 61, 62, 69, 110
  Accademia di San Luca, 75
  Accademia Nazionale dei Lincei, 41, 42
  Biblioteca Nazionale Vittorio Emanuele, 32
  Campo de' Fiori, 154
  Carnival Season in, 25–27, 97, 158, 164
  Church of Sant' Urbano alla Caffarella, 90, 91
  Church of SS Nome di Maria al Foro Traiano, 40
  Colosseum, 9
  Convent of the Apostles, 61
  Corso, 74, 78
  English College, 18, 19
  Forum, 40, 49, 63
  Hills of, 9, 14, 62, 88, 94
    Capitoline (Campidoglio), 9, 48
    Quirinal, 155
  Lacus Salutaris, 90
  Palazzo
    della Cancellaria, 154
    Doria Pamphili, 74
    Salviati, 74
  Pantheon, 9, 22, 24, 93
  Piazza San Pietro, 79
  Quattro Fontane, 26, 154
  Ruins of, 3–7, 8, 9, 10
  Tarpeian Rock, 9
  Valle della Caffarella, 90, 93
  Vatican, 28, 34, 139, 143, 149, 154
    Basilica of St Peter, 11, 15, 21–23, 25, 34, 79

Index Nominum et Locorum

Library, 8, 19, 34, 111, 113, 139, 141–142, 143–144, 145, 146, 149, 150, 151, 152, 156, 173
   Press, 153
   Sistine Chapel, 25
Romulus, 11, 15, 108
Ronconi, Francesco, 45, 112, 134, 135
Rospigliosi, Giulio (Pope Clement IX), 26, 75, 100, 113, 131, 136, 155, 160
Rossano, 36
   Accademia degli Spensierati, 36
Rosselli, Hannibal, 118–119
Rossi, Giovanni Vittorio, 33, 140
Rothwell, John, 12, 14
Rouse, John, 148
Rovai, Francesco, 103
Ruccellai, Orazio, 86
Rufus, Jean-Baptiste, 90
Ruggle, George, 167
Russo, Giovanni Battista, 123

Sabioneta, 132
Sale, Anton Giulio Brignole, 84
Sallust, 14
Sallustius, Serenus, 144, 145, 170
Salmasius, Claudius (Claude Saumaise), 87
Salomoni, Generoso, 116
Salting tradition, 83–84
Salus, 69, 74, 79, 84, 86
Salzilli
   Alessandro, 43
   Giovanni, 19, 29–97, 101
Sandys, George, 17
Sannazaro, Iacopo, 13
Santacroce, Scipione, 41
San Vitale, Leonora, 122
Sappho, 57, 60, 63, 67, 68
Sartorius, Adam, 84
Sarzina, Giacomo, 80
Satan, 15, 22, 23–24, 25, 169
Saturnus, 59
Satyrs, 161
Savage, Jane, 19
Savarelli, Vincenzo Maria, 41
Saxon, 103
Scaglia, Giacomo, 52
Scala, Alessandra, 123
Scaliger, Julius Caesar, 87

Scarlatti, Alessandro, 35
Scazons, 57, 71, 86–88
Schenker, Heinrich, 127
Scoppa, Claudio, 41
Scornio, Giovan Battista, 35
Scotland, 17, 157
Sebeto, 47, 51, 131
Secundus, 145, 172
Selvaggio, Matteo, 19–20, 56; *see also* Codner, David
Senarius, 88
Seneca the Younger, 75
Sequanus, Joannes Metellus, 6
Seraphim, 117
Sforza, Mario, 136
Shakespeare, William, 68, 86, 120, 121, 167, 168
Sibyl, 65, 150
Sicily, 5
Sidney, Philip, 113, 117
Siena, 8, 43
Silius Italicus, 53
Silvius, 2
Sinibaldi, Carlo Andrea, 36
Sirens, 105, 110, 112, 124, 130–132, 133, 134, 137, 142
Sixtus IV, Pope, 143
Smectymnuus, 12, 141; *see also s.v.* Milton, John, prose
Smith, Thomas, 141–142
Sobieski, Jan, King, 38
Socrates, 24, 153
Solomon, 22
Solon, 63
Spada, Carlo, 41, 43
Spain, 43, 47–48, 135
Spanish (language), 107
Spenser, Edmund, 89, 120
Sperelli, Alessandro, 80
Spheres, music of the, 109, 115, 117, 118, 166
Spirgatis, Max, 141
Statius, Publius Papinius, 53, 141
   Thebaid, 53, 141
Stigliani, Tommaso, 31–32
Stigliano, Principe di, 132
Stradling, John, 3
Strawberry Hill, 18
Strozzi
   Barbara, 102

Nicolo, 41, 43
Styx, 146, 150
Sunfield, Captain, 167
Swinburne, Algernon, 62
Switzerland, 17, 94
Symmons, Charles, 87
Symonds, Richard, 77–79
Syrtes, 132

Tancredi, 124
Tarpeian Rock, *see s.v.* Rome
Tasso, Torquato, 47, 48–49, 51, 52, 53, 54, 67, 100, 109, 121–124, 126, 142
Tassoni, Alessandro, 75
Taupinart, Adrian, 151
Tempestino, Anton Francesco, 41
Tennyson, Alfred, 61–62
Terence, 87, 143, 144, 152, 167
  Eunuchus, 87
  Heuton Timorumenos, 87
Testi, Fulvio, 41, 42, 43, 44, 99, 114, 115, 131
Teti, Girolamo, 155, 163
Thames, 47, 50, 51, 52, 56
Theaetetus, 153
Thebes, 52, 53, 133, 141
  Cebes of, 52
Theocritus, 2
Thetis, 41
Thoinan, Ernest, 111, 115
Thorin, Ernest, 143
Thracians, 38
Thyrsis, 1–2, 5, 7, 84
Tiber, 9, 56, 57, 59, 69, 84, 95–97, 102, 104, 131, 133, 142, 156, 158
Tinassi, Niccolò Angelo, 38
Tiraboschi, Girolamo, 32, 75
Tityos, 121
Tityrus, 1, 2, 3
Tmolus, Mount, 94
Todd, Henry John, 170
Toland, John, 8–9
Tomis, 12
Torrentino, Lorenzo, 118
Tortoletti, Bartolomeo, 36, 76, 103
Tosi, Clemente, 41
Totti
  Lodovico, 10
  Pompilio, 10–11, 21–22, 42, 74, 91
Trajan, 40

Trevico, 31
Treviso, 118
Trismegistus, Hermes, 118–120
Troise, Carlo, 36
Trojans, 149
Tronsarelli, Ottavio, 61
Troy, 53, 58, 62
Turin, 107
Turkey, 17
Turkish Empire, 17
Turks, 38
Turnus, 51, 53
Tuscan tongue, 33, 47, 49, 52, 69
Tuscany, 21, 24, 47–48, 119, 123, 159
Typhoeus, 57
Tyrrhenian Sea, 132

Ubaldini, Federico, 141
Underworld, 121; *see also* Avernus *and* Orcus
Urania, 13, 25
Urban I, Pope, 91
Urban VIII, Pope, *see* Barberini, Maffeo

Valdarno, 24
Valentini, Giulio Cesare, 41
Vallombrosa, 24
Valuasense, Francesco, 42
Vangelisti, Vincenzio, 97
Vasi, Mariano, 93
Vatican, *see s.v.* Rome
Vecchi, Horatio, 166
Vellori, Viviano, 41
Venice, 5, 7, 26, 41, 42, 49, 52, 75, 80, 99, 102, 109, 110, 125, 164, 165
  Accademia degli Incogniti, 41, 42, 84
  Biblioteca Nazionale Marciana, 75
  Envoy of, 26
Venosa
  Prince of, *see* Gesualdo, Carlo
Venturelli, Vittorio, 41, 43, 44
Venus, 24, 38, 69, 94, 127
Venus (planet), 117
Vergelli, Giuseppe Tiburzio, 22
Verso Sdrucciolo, 88
Vesta, 95, 96
Vida, Marco Girolamo, 13, 25

Index Nominum et Locorum

Vienna, 38, 148
   Österreichische Nationalbibliothek, 148
Viotti
   Erasmo, 41
   Seth, 41
Virgil, 1, 2, 7, 9, 12, 20, 50, 51, 52, 53, 54, 58, 59, 62, 65, 67, 87, 127, 133, 143, 144, 148–152, 171
   Aeneid, 7, 53, 58, 59, 62, 65, 87, 127, 133, 148–152, 171
   Eclogues, 1, 2
   Georgics, 127, 148
Virgo (sign of zodiac), 121
Vitalis, Janus, 5–6
Vittorius, Pierre, 90
Vivaldi, Antonio, 88
Vlacq, Adrian, 16
Von Pflaumern, 143–144, 152
Vossius, Isaac, 141
Vulcan, 58, 87

Wagner, Maximilian, 90
Wales, 168
Wallace, Michael, 15
Webbe, Edward, 17
Winchester, 19
Windebank
   Francis, 157
   Thomas, 157
Witty, Robert, 152
Wolfe, John, 121, 122
Wood, Anthony à, 8, 20

Xanthus, 38

Young
   Patrick, 141, 142, 148
   Thomas, 141

Zanchi, Basilio, 13
Zanni, 165
Zarlino, Gioseffo, 127
Zeno, 147
Zodiac, 121